We are Receiving

THE UNSHAKABLE KINGDOM

And It Shall Stand Forever!

We are Receiving

THE UNSHAKABLE KINGDOM

And It Shall Stand Forever!

"Of the Increase of His Government and Peace
There Shall Be No End"
(Isaiah 9:7 NKJV)

Carl G. Vincent

New Harbor Press

RAPID CITY, SD

Vincent/New Harbor Press
1601 Mt.Rushmore Rd, Ste 3288
Rapid City, SD 57701
www.newharborpress.com

The Unshakable Kingdom / Carl G. Vincent. -- 1st ed.

ISBN 978-1-63357-221-8

This Volume is Dedicated to
Joyce, My Godly Wife and Loving Companion,
and
Our Precious Children:
Carl and Kara Vincent of Tulsa, OK
Paul and Stacey Vincent of Valdosta, GA
Brent and Michelle Cooper of Laurel, DE
Shane and Brenda McCarty of Laurel, DE
and
All Our Grandchildren and Great-Grandchildren.

It is through the abundance of God's unfathomable grace and lovingkindness,
That we as a family have the joy of being citizens in the Kingdom of God.
Redeemed through the work of our Savior, Jesus Christ.
He is the KING of Kings and LORD of Lords,
The King of "the Unshakable Kingdom!"
Hebrews 12:28

CONTENTS

INTRODUCTION

"Therefore, since we are receiving a kingdom which cannot be shaken, let us have grace, by which we may serve God acceptably with reverence and godly fear."
Hebrews 12:28

Among the glories of the kingdom of God is the truth that we did not choose God, but rather it was while we were yet sinners and without hope, He chose us and "delivered us from the power of darkness and conveyed us into the kingdom of the Son of His love."[1] As a consequence of God's lovingkindness manifested through His saving grace, we the redeemed bear witness to the reality of God's love and redemptive purpose, "I will be their God, and they shall be My people."[2] Therefore, we joyfully testify with the Apostle John declaring, "Behold what manner of love the Father has bestowed on us, that we should be called the children of God."[3]

Coming to know Jesus Christ as my personal Savior at a rural Methodist Church revival as a young farm boy, it still fills my heart with gratitude for my Dad and Pastor Jimmy Langrall for leading me into a blessed relationship with Jesus Christ. That relationship has been the focus of my life for over 65 years. After receiving the Baptism of the Holy Spirit in my early thirties, the Lord called me to learn the Bible and how to communicate it. That has influenced every important decision I have made since that call.

---

1. John 15:16
2. 2 Cor. 6:16; Heb. 8:10; Rev. 21:3.
3. 1 John 3:1.

Learning the Scriptures has been a lifetime of transformational experiences from first attending Liberty Bible College in Pensacola, Florida in my mid-thirties, through obtaining a Doctor of Ministry from Beacon University in Columbus, Georgia in my mid-sixties. However, as I tried to understand the word of God and paint the picture of redemption, something always seemed to be missing. It was a few years ago that I began to grasp the missing link by gaining a deeper revelation of the kingdom of God, and I confessed that I felt as though I was born again, again!

It was while under the teaching of Bro. Burl Bagwell and reading "the Gospel of the Kingdom" by George Eldon Ladd, that I first learned about the kingdom of God. The marvelous thing is that the Holy Spirit continues to increase that revelation and transform my understanding of Jesus' teaching on the kingdom. This has created a new paradigm for my life and to the life of the congregations where I minister. Bill Johnson states, "Everything finds its purpose and fulfillment under Jesus' rule, which is called the Kingdom of God."[4]

The kingdom of God is the "pearl of great price."[5] It is the purpose of this book to focus on the glories of the kingdom of God. This will require understanding how the powerful New Testament concepts of the gospel, the church, and the kingdom of God converge in the life of each believer through the anointing of the Holy Spirit. Thus, it empowers him or her to serve the Lord as a citizen of the kingdom of God while living in this world that is dominated by the powers of darkness.

Much emphasis has been placed on personal salvation within the ministry streams where I have fellowshipped. As important as that is, there is more! God is not willing that any should perish, but that every person should be saved and serve in His kingdom through the

---

4. Bill Johnson, "Forward" in *Cosmic Initiative: Restoring the Kingdom, Igniting the Awakening,* by Jack Taylor (New Kensington, PA: Whitaker House, 2017), 13.

5. Matt. 13:45-46.

anointing of the Holy Spirit.[6] The glory of the gospel of the kingdom isn't simply a religious ritual or an empty philosophical tradition, but a personal relationship with the sovereign God of the universe through faith in the Lord Jesus Christ. Our faith, grounded in Jesus Christ and sealed by the Holy Spirit, empowers us to serve others with the heart of a king and rule in life with the heart of a servant. Jack Taylor states: "Basileia or Kingdom is God's end—the goal of Christianity. Ecclesia or Church is God's means—the method of Christianity. Thus, the Kingdom descends in order that the Church may ascend"[7] This will be further elaborated upon in chapter one.

The terms "kingdom of heaven" and "kingdom of God" are synonymous. God's throne is situated in heaven, thus, the term "kingdom of heaven" is meaningful and appropriate, because it is from heaven that God reigns over the entire universe. George Eldon Ladd states "Apart from the reign of God, heaven is meaningless."[8] "Kingdom of God" also conveys the concept of God's reign or rule over the universe. These terms are interchangeable. For example, "where Matthew uses 'kingdom of heaven,' Mark or Luke or both use 'kingdom of God…' Matthew himself uses these two expressions interchangeably in 19:23–24, 'it is hard for a rich man to enter the kingdom of heaven … for a rich man to enter the kingdom of God.'"[9]

Jesus began His ministry by saying, "The time is fulfilled, and the kingdom of God is at hand. Repent and believe the gospel."[10] Near the end of His earthly ministry He said, "And this gospel of the kingdom will be preached in all the world as a witness to all the nations, and then the end will come."[11] The kingdom of God is not simply a matter

---

6. John 3:16; Acts 1:8; 1John 1:20.

7. Jack R. Taylor, *Cosmic Initiative: Restoring the Kingdom, Igniting the Awakening* (New Kensington, PA: Whitaker House, 2017), 108.

8. George Eldon Ladd, *The Gospel of the Kingdom* (Grand Rapids, MI: Wm. B. Eerdmans Publishing Company, 1977), 21.

9. Robert H. Stein, "Kingdom of God," *Evangelical Dictionary of Biblical Theology*, Baker Reference Library (Grand Rapids: Baker Book House, 1996), 451.

10. Mark 1:15.

11. Matt. 24:14.

of good ethics and going to heaven when we die. Jesus' commission to preach the gospel of the kingdom also includes bringing the blessings and dominion of heaven upon our own lives, families, our communities in the here and now.

The Gospel of the Kingdom originated in the heart of God, but its glory is expressed through the life and ministry of Jesus Christ and the lives of those who have received His saving grace, and serve as citizens of the kingdom empowered by the Holy Spirit. Human history is replete with the testimonies of those men and women whose born-again birthright granted them a hope that transcends the limitations of this world and firmly anchors them in the glories of the kingdom of God.

Jesus, the most brilliant man that ever walked upon this earth, commands us "to seek first the kingdom of God and His righteousness." But the reality of the kingdom's presence comes among mankind in stages according to God's redemptive purposes, and His redemptive purposes are spelled out in covenantal terms. In the Old Testament God's relationship with man is expressed through His covenants, with Adam, Noah, Abraham, Moses, and David. Each of these covenants brought a partial and progressive fulfillment of the Everlasting Covenant that was established in the council of the Godhead before the foundation of the world.[12] The Everlasting Covenant is of vital importance because it is to the kingdom of God what the vertebra is to the body; both structure and function depend upon it. The ultimate fulfillment of the Everlasting Covenant comes at the climax of the New Covenant which is established through the blood of the Lord Jesus Christ and sealed in the hearts of believers by the Holy Spirit.[13] It is thought covenantal grace that God makes a name for Himself, a name before which every knee shall bow.[14]

---

12. Gen. 9:16, 17:19; Lev. 24:8; Heb. 13:20; Eph. 1:3-14.
13. Eph. 1:3-14.
14. 2 Sam. 7:23; Phil. 2:6-11.

We must grapple with the mystery of the kingdom that is both "at hand," and "is coming." Mark's Gospel describes the Kingdom as "now in this time" and "in the age to come."[15] As believers we now experience dimensions of kingdom blessings and power, but the fullness of God's kingdom will only be realized according to His redemptive schedule; meaning, the best is yet future. In other words, the Lord has much more available for us than we are presently experiencing! This also will be discussed in chapter one and in greater detail in chapter eight.

The mystery of the kingdom remains because the revelation of its magnitude transcends and surpasses our present understanding and experiences. At best we still "see through a mirror dimly," and have only tasted of the "powers of the age to come."[16] However, we have seen and tasted enough to zealously desire greater revelation and experiences. We are convinced that the best is yet to come! However, we are granted opportunity and privilege as sons of God and citizens of the kingdom to impact this world by bearing testimony to the presence and power of the kingdom!

The concept of "kingdom" expresses the rule, reign, authority, and dominion of a king. The kingdom of God includes God's rule or reign over the church, and far beyond the church, including His dominion over all of creation. "God is the King of all the earth."[17] The concept of "kingdom" places the emphasis on "rule" or "dominion" before it includes a realm or territory. Jesus taught a parable where "A nobleman went into a far country" The question is "Why did the nobleman go there?" Jesus said, "the nobleman went there to receive a kingdom."[18] The nobleman had territory before he left to go into the far country. So, he went to the far country to receive the dominion or kingship to reign over the territory. All authority finds its ultimate source in God,

---

15. Mark 10:30.
16. 1 Cor. 13:12; Heb. 6:4.
17. Psa. 47:7.
18. Luke 19:12.

and He delegates His authority according to the council of His will.[19] Kingdom is God's governing authority over the affairs of men with the intent of bringing liberty and freedom from the present oppressive powers of darkness. In spite of the evil, sin, and oppression God will present His Son, the King of the kingdom, with a beautiful Bride. This powerful reality is discussed in chapter two.

Following Jesus' baptism in the Jordan River, His anointing by the Holy Spirit, and tests by the devil, He returned to Galilee in the power of the Spirit and inaugurated the kingdom by preaching the gospel of the kingdom.[20] Preaching means to proclaim publicly. In other words, Jesus' proclamation of the gospel of the kingdom was a word event whereby His words actually initiated the reality of the presence of the dominion of God on the earth; God confirmed the presence of the kingdom with signs and wonders. Jesus was opposed and rejected by the religious and political authorities of Israel, but it was the appointed time for God's redemptive purposes to be advanced. Therefore, Jesus proclaimed, "The time is fulfilled, and the kingdom of God is at hand. Repent and believe the gospel."[21] Although the kingdom had seemingly small beginnings, it continues to expand until it is proclaimed in every tongue and nation, and the kingdoms of this world will become the kingdom of our God. The Holy Spirit anointing has too often been minimized and even overlooked in much of church history. But the Holy Spirit is God and He has been sent from heaven to empower the Church to overcome the powers of darkness and death with words of light and life, unto the ultimate victory! Chapter three focuses on this reality.

Believers in Jesus Christ are empowered by the Holy Spirit to offer an alternative to the governing systems of this world through the proclamation of the gospel of the kingdom. We are taught to pray and declare "Your kingdom come, and Your will be done on earth as it is

---

19. Rom. 13:1; Eph. 1:11.
20. Matt. 4:23; Luke 4:14.
21. Mark 1:15.

in heaven." We not only preach the gospel but also bear witness to it through our character, lifestyle, and the ministry of the gifts of grace. We are commissioned to "let our light so shine before men, that they may see our good works and glorify our Father which is in heaven."[22] As a royal priesthood we are not to put our light under a bushel, but let it shine.[23] Blessed is the individual and/or community that experiences the reality of the gospel of the kingdom of God. Our ministry as a royal priesthood is emphasized in chapter four.

Kingdoms, governments, and cultures have risen and declined throughout history. But hope for the world remains, because death and all that contributes to it were defeated once and for all by Jesus Christ. The government of God rests upon the shoulders of the resurrected Lord Jesus Christ, and "the increase of His government and peace thereof will be no end."[24] It is within the DNA of the kingdom of God to always increase. As a result, a day is coming when "the kingdoms of this world shall become the kingdoms of our God and His Christ and He shall reign forever and ever." And "All the earth will be filled with the glory of the Lord!"[25] Jesus gave the "keys of the kingdom" to His Church and these keys are illuminated through the parables of Jesus discussed in chapters five and six.

As believers in Jesus Christ and citizens of the kingdom of God, we have a major stake in the fate of the world. The gospel of the kingdom offers hope beyond the present political or economic systems of this world. Chapter seven focuses on prayer as the God given means of grace to bring kingdom of God realities and blessings into our daily experience.

Jesus Christ is the King of the kingdom and His earthly life and ministry is prophesied by types and shadows throughout the Old Testament, especially manifest through the various covenants. This

---

22. Matt. 5:16.
23. 1 Peter 2:9.
24. Isa. 9:7.
25. Rev. 11:15; Num. 14:21.

will be discussed in chapter eight. It will be helpful however to keep the following three things in mind as we move forward:

1. Citizenship in the kingdom of God is presented to us by Jesus as a free gift from God.[26] But it is only offered in response to faith in Jesus Christ and the great price He paid at Calvary for our forgiveness and reconciliation to God the Father.
2. Citizenship in the kingdom of God is freely offered to all who will believe on Jesus, but citizenship is never, ever forced upon anyone.[27] Each person may decide for himself or herself to accept it or reject it.
3. Citizenship in the kingdom of God is a component of every believer's covenantal life in Christ with eternal purpose, privilege, and meaning that makes the frustrations, failures, and sufferings of this present age only a means of preparation for the glories of the age to come.[28]

It would seem quite insufficient to discuss all the above aspects of the kingdom of God if it couldn't be applied to our lives in a practical way. Sometimes life takes us through some difficult and often uncertain places, as the enemy seeks to tempt us to question our citizenship in the kingdom of God as well as the future that God has predestined for us. Trials and troubles are not God's means of destroying our faith but serve as training sessions to strengthen our trust in God, just as physical exercise strengthens our physical bodies.

It was in the early days of my pastoral ministry that a dear friend called for prayer. He and his wife loved the Lord and were faithful participants in our congregation and small group ministry. The wife was near the due date of her pregnancy with their second child when tests indicated she had some serious health problems. When the baby was delivered she learned she had cancer. Enough time was allowed

---

26. Luke 12:32.
27. Rev. 3:20.
28. Phil. 1:29; Rom. 8:18.

for her to recover strength from the birth of their new born daughter before she was admitted back into the hospital for further treatment.

Meanwhile the newborn experienced a fever and they gave her some aspirin. As it turned out the aspirin contributed to the baby contracting Reye's syndrome, which caused severe seizures and convulsions and she almost died. This was followed with months in the hospital suffering from those complications. Meanwhile the husband had to keep working in order to pay the mounting medical bills. So, his mother-in-law came to live with them to help care for the family as his wife was admitted back into the hospital for the growing cancer problems. Through all these problems the baby remained in the hospital because the Reye's syndrome had caused permeant health problems and disabilities. In the midst of all these mounting complications the mother-in-law suddenly died in their home. I sat with the husband as we wept and prayed together affirming our trust in God.

The marvelous thing to me was that they refused to give up on God or throw in the towel in the midst of such overwhelming circumstances. Rather, they continued to put one foot in front of the other and slowly kept moving forward with more tears and prayers trusting God all the way. In the process of time the wife fully recovered, and the baby was placed in a facility that provided special care for children with disabilities. The husband's work required them to move to another city. But, their faith and trust in God through those tragic days has been an inspiration to my faith over all these years. In my heart I can hear God saying, "I will be their God, and they shall be my people."

Our relationship with God is not a matter of a quick fix or instant gratification, as much as we would like that. God is able to immediately perform the miraculous and sometimes He does, and that is wonderful. But at other times the pain, the problems, and the conflict continues as our faith is stretched to where we cry out, "How long oh Lord, how long?" I surely do not have all the answers, but I agree with Graham Cooke's perspective:

> You also realize that some situations cannot be resolved in a few days or weeks. In those circumstances your development is part of a long-termed program of upgrading your identity and cultivating trust, wisdom, and growth necessary to becoming an overcomer.[29]

It wasn't before or during Abram's battle, but following the battle with five kings and the rescue of his nephew Lot, that God appeared to him in a vision and said, "Do not be afraid Abram, I am your shield, your exceedingly great reward."[30] We may not understand why the enemy attacks so unexpectedly and we suddenly experience the traumatic onslaught of a battle; but we do understand, regardless of the circumstances, that we are not orphans. We are the children of God and citizens of the kingdom of God. Every born-again believer has received the Spirit of Adoption and that Holy Spirit arises within our hearts strengthening our confidence and resolve to press forward, trusting God with the knowledge that; "The eyes of the Lord are on the righteous and His ears are open to their prayers."[31] The marvel of our "new birth" takes place in the moment we believe on the Lord Jesus Christ. But our character development and learning how to reign in life as citizens of the kingdom of God is a life-long experience. Derek Prince states, "The ultimate goal of God in this present age is the coming of His kingdom on earth under His chosen king, the Lord Jesus Christ."[32] Through the chapters ahead you will find insights regarding your citizenship in the kingdom of God that will fortify you as an overcomer in this present world and strengthen your faith for life in the glory that will be revealed in the world to come.

---

29. Graham Cooke, *The Nature of Freedom* (Vancouver, WA: Brilliant Book House, 2016), 18.
30. Gen. 15:1.
31. 1 Peter 3:13.
32. Derek Prince, *Rediscovering God's Church* (New Kensington, PA: Whitaker House, 2006), 393.

CHAPTER ONE

THE PRESENCE OF THE KINGDOM

"The time is fulfilled, and the kingdom of God is at hand. Repent, and believe in the gospel."
(Mark 1:15)

Revelation regarding the presence of the kingdom of God has increased over the years, but the kingdom of God is not a recent nor even a New Testament concept. The kingdom has always existed in the eternal and sovereign nature of God. In other words, it is impossible to distinguish between God and His kingdom. God is eternal, and His kingdom is eternal! He did not begin to reign at the beginning of time, rather out of eternity He created time and reigns sovereignly over all creation. He is the Architect and Creator of it. According to Norman Geisler, "Sovereignty (governance) means 'to be in control' or 'to be in charge of'… Since God is before all things, created all things, upholds all things, owns all things, He is the rightful ruler of all things."[33] "A sovereign is etymologically someone who is 'above' others."[34] Our God's authority transcends all governments with the

---

33. Norman Geisler, Systematic Theology, vol. 2, *God, Creation* (Bloomington, MN: Bethany House Publishers, 2003), 536.

34. John Ayto, *Dictionary of Word Origins* (New York, NY: Arcade Publishing Co., 1990). 491.

power to carry out the counsel of His will according to His own purposes. Therefore, God's control or sovereignty over all creation as the Creator affirms His supremacy as "King eternal," and "the increase of His government and peace there shall be no end."[35] Consider the following Scriptures:

> Before the mountains were brought forth, or ever You had formed the earth and the world, even from everlasting to everlasting, you *are* God. (Psalm 90:2)
>
> The earth *is* the LORD'S, and all its fullness, the world and those who dwell therein. (Psalm 24:1).
>
> Yours, O LORD, *is* the greatness, the power and the glory, the victory and the majesty; for all *that is* in heaven and in earth *is Yours;* Yours *is* the kingdom, O LORD, and You are exalted as head over all. Both riches and honor *come* from You, and You reign over all. In Your hand *is* power and might; in Your hand *it is* to make great and to give strength to all. (1 Chronicles 29:11-12)
>
> Whatever the LORD pleases He does, in heaven and in earth, in the seas and in all deep places. (Psalm 135:6)
>
> Now to the King eternal, immortal, invisible, to God who alone is wise, *be* honor and glory forever and ever. Amen. (1 Timothy 1:17)

Michael S. Heiser states:

---

35. 1 Tim. 1:17; Isa. 9:7.

> The kingdom of God is the rule of God. God desires to rule over *all* he has created: the invisible spiritual realm and the visible earthly realm. He will have his way in both domains.... The story of the Bible is about God's will for, and rule of, the realms he has created, visible and invisible, through the imagers he has created, human and nonhuman. This divine agenda is played out in both realms, in deliberate tandem.[36]

God and the Everlasting Covenant:

God is not a man trying to become a god, but the eternal God who is Spirit expressing His sovereignty through the manifestations of His kingdom. As a potter has power and authority over the clay so God has power and authority over all things.[37] He is and always will be sovereign with absolutely no rivals. C. Hassell Bullock makes the following insightful comments about the nature and sovereignty of God: "The Bible makes no attempt to prove that God exists. Rather, the universe is the affidavit of his existence. Moreover, the fact that he is the Creator means that the world belongs to him."[38]

Therefore, whatever God does, He does with sovereign authority and power because with Him nothing is impossible.[39] God in His wisdom has chosen to administer His sovereignty through a covenantal strategy. The everlasting covenant being the initial covenantal framework through which He would accomplish the following kingdom realities: (1) the creation of an environment fitting for mankind, followed by the creation of man in His own image and likeness. (2) The redemption of mankind and all creation through His Son Jesus,

---

36. Michael S. Heiser, *The Unseen Realm: Recovering the Supernatural Worldview of the Bible*, First Edition. (Bellingham, WA: Lexham Press, 2015), 38.

37. Rom. 9:19-24, 13:1.

38. C. Hassell Bullock, "God," in *Evangelical Dictionary of Biblical Theology*, electronic ed., Baker Reference Library (Grand Rapids, MI: Baker Book House, 1996), 289.

39. Gen. 18:14; Matt. 19:26.

the Christ. (3) The anointing of redeemed mankind by the Holy Spirit for service and bearing witness to His reality and grace. And (4), the creation of a new heaven and new earth as an eternal dwelling place for God and His redeemed and glorified royal family. Through these covenantal accomplishments God reveals His nature, His unshakable kingdom, His eternal purposes, and His glory. God will consummate the everlasting covenant by dwelling eternally with the trophies of His grace; that is a family of redeemed sons and daughters who love Him with a love tested by time and proven by fire.[40]

Before time began in eternity past, God the Father, God the Son and God the Holy Spirit bound themselves into an "everlasting covenant." A reason why the Godhead entered the everlasting covenant was because their perfect unity/oneness would be tested by the functions they were to perform by creating and perfecting a royal family. For example, the Word would need to become flesh and bear the sin of mankind and be separated from the Father through death on the cross. You will recall that in the Garden of Gethsemane Jesus sweat drops of blood and asked the Father if it were possible to remove this cup from Him. But He concluded His prayers with, "Not My will but Yours be done."[41] In other words, the persons of the Godhead were and for eternity will continue to be equally divine, and bound by their everlasting covenant to accomplish specific tasks and functions. As a result, they voluntarily subordinated themselves to each other in the everlasting covenant. Millard J. Erickson states:

> The Son did not become less than the Father during His earthly incarnation, but He did subordinate Himself functionally to the will of the Father. Similarly, the Holy Spirit is now subordinated to the ministry of the Son (see John 14-16) as well as to the will of the Father, but this does not imply that He is

40. Rev. 21.3-4.
41. Luke 22:42.

> less than they are.... Each member of the trinity is in His essence identical with the others or with the divine substance itself. They are distinguished in terms of their relationships with the Godhead.... We do not hold the doctrine of the Trinity because it is self-evident or logically cogent. We hold it because God has revealed that this is what He is like.[42]

The Godhead determined to progressively reveal and implement their strategy throughout the history of the world according to the terms of the everlasting covenant. The everlasting covenant extends to and concludes with the unfolding of new heavens and a new earth wherein dwells righteousness.[43] Kevin Conner and Ken Malmin state;

> The Everlasting Covenant is that covenant made in eternity, before time began, in the counsels of the Godhead, between the Father, Son and Holy Spirit. It was made before the creation of man and the entrance of sin into the human race. It embodies, as an all-encompassing Covenant, God's complete plan involving Creation and Redemption. It is the heavenly foundational Covenant in eternity for all Covenants revealed in Time. Man was not a party to it but the object of it.[44]

It is not our purpose here to dwell at length regarding God's covenants. Covenants will be further discussed in the pages ahead especially in chapter eight. However, the Bible is a covenantal book that progressively reveals and defines the terms upon which God relates

---

42. Millard J. Erickson, *Christian Theology,* 3ed. (Grand Rapids, MI; Baker Academic, 2013), 309-313.

43. Heb. 13:20; 2 Peter 3:13; Rev. 21:1.

44. Kevin Conner and Ken Malmin, *The Covenants* (Portland, OR: City Bible Publishing, 1997), 92.

to man. The Holy Spirit has been given to help us interpret the Sacred Covenants and apply them to our lives. It is sufficient to say that according to the terms of God's covenants there is coming a day when "at the name of Jesus every knee will bow… and every tongue should confess that Jesus Christ is Lord, to the glory of God the Father."[45] The word "Lord" indicates high rank, predominance, preeminence, one who has power and authority over others. We may worship God now through the mediation of our Savior, Jesus Christ, or we may refuse to worship Him now. But there is a day coming when everyone will bow in worship of Him!

We have the tendency to focus on our personal circumstances to such a degree that we reduce God to a man with our limitations and problems. But God is not a creature, but the Creator who is all wise, all powerful, present everywhere, eternal, and unchangeable! He is in control and His kingdom is unshakable! It is important to keep in mind that God being sovereign, was under no obligation to create anything. But in keeping with His own nature, He determined to create for Himself a royal family, upon which He would express His unfathomable love. In return His family would love and serve Him with all their heart, soul, and strength. He would place His family in an environment where each one could exercise his or her free will and co-labor with Him in the expansion of His kingdom.

Creation Reveals a Plan of Redemption:

The work of creation, its order, harmony and beauty coming into existence out of darkness and nothingness is not something that happened by chance or without eternal purpose and meaning.[46] Creation was so wisely designed by God so as to reveal His invisible attributes, eternal power, and Godhead.[47] Knowing the end from the beginning, God wove into the fabric of creation the message of redemp-

45. Phil. 2:9-10.
46. Gen. 1:1-2.
47. Rom. 1:20; Psa. 19:1-6.

tion.[48] Creation displays in types and shadows the blueprint of God's intended purpose for His Son to have preeminence over all things. E. Stanley Jones states, "That man and nature and the whole universe were made by Christ and for Christ, that a destiny is therefore written into the structure of new things, and that structure and destiny is Christian unity."[49]

Each day of creation as recorded in Genesis 1:3-2:3 reveals an aspect of God's redemptive design foreshadowing His Son, Jesus, who "is before all things and in Him all things consist."[50] The following chart will illustrate this reality.

Creation Events and Redemption Foreshadowed

Day of Creation	Creation Events	Redemption Foreshadowed
1st Day - 1:3-5	Light, Day/Night	Incarnation-Divine/Human Nature
2nd Day - 1:6-8	Firmament Divided Waters	The Cross Stood between Heaven/Earth
3rd Day - 1:9-13	Dry Land Out of Water	Resurrection of Jesus out of the Grave
4th Day - 1:14-19	Sun, Moon, Stars	Jesus is the Light vs Powers of Darkness
5th Day - 1:20-23	Sea Animals & Birds	Baptism into Christ & Gift of Holy Spirit
6th Day - 1:24-31	The First Adam	Jesus the Last Adam & Inheritance
7th Day - 2:1-3	A Sanctified Day	A Sanctified People & A Sanctified Age

On the sixth day of creation God created man. Mankind was the crowning event of all that was created, because Adam and Eve were

48. Eph. 1:3-12.

49. E. Stanley Jones, *The Unshakable Kingdom and the Unchanging Person* (Bellingham, WA: McNett Press, 1972), 47.

50. Col. 1:17; Rev. 13:8.

created in the very image and likeness of their Creator. Being thus created indicates that the essence of man's nature is like God's nature. When God breathed life into the nostrils of man, He breathed God the Holy Spirit into him just as when Jesus after His resurrection breathed on the Apostles and said, "Receive the Holy Spirit."[51] From the very beginning it was God's intention that man's body would be the dwelling place of God the Holy Spirit. God blessed the man which means that he was empowered to prosper. God delegated to him the dominion over the fish of the sea, birds of the air, all cattle and over all the earth and over every creeping thing that creeps on the earth.[52] In other words, God expressed His sovereignty over creation and the presence of His kingdom through the dominion He delegated to man over the earth realm. It was according to the dictates of God's own nature to create man with a free will. In the beginning the stewardship of man's dominion was to be guided by his conscience. Later after the entrance of sin, God gave the Ten Commandments to affirm His moral boundaries and assist in guiding man's conscience and behavior. Because it was man's moral responsibility to exercise dominion as the delegated administrator of God's kingdom on the earth. However, in the fullness of time when the Day of Pentecost had fully come the Holy Spirit was given to guide man's conscience and stewardship responsibilities as a member of God's royal priesthood. Therefore, man's identity has always been and always will be dependent on his relationship with His Heavenly Father, the Creator. If man were to become separated from his Father Creator, his identity would become distorted and would suffer disorientation regarding the purposes for which he was created and would be unable to maintain dominion over creation. He would also become subject to eternal death unless there would be an intervention by a Savior Redeemer which the Everlasting Covenant provided. The Psalmist asks.

51. John 20:22.
52. Gen. 1:26-28.

> What is man that You are mindful of him, And the son of man that You visit him? For You have made him a little lower than the angels, And You have crowned him with glory and honor. You have made him to have dominion over the works of Your hands; You have put all *things* under his feet, All sheep and oxen-- Even the beasts of the field. The birds of the air, and the fish of the sea that pass through the paths of the seas. O LORD, our Lord, how excellent *is* Your name in all the earth! (Psalm. 8:4-9)

At the conclusion of the sixth day of creation "God saw everything He had made, and indeed it was very good."[53] On the seventh day God rested from all the work He had done and blessed and sanctified that day.[54] God's creation now being in order, He rested and set the seventh day apart from the other six days as a holy day. At this juncture in the creation narrative everything is sacred or holy and man was pure and undefiled. All that had been created during those six days was "very good" or exceedingly beautiful! Man, not only enjoyed dominion over the earth, but also the majesty of daily communion with God in the paradise temple of the Garden of Eden.

The Tree of the Knowledge of Good and Evil:

However, it almost seems out of character with God's nature when we read Genesis 2:9, that He planted a tree in the midst of the Garden of Eden and called it "the tree of the knowledge of good and evil." This is the first mention of "evil" in the Bible. Scripture teaches that sin entered this created realm through Adam's transgression,[55] which did not occur until Genesis 3:6. Therefore, the possibility of evil preceded Adam's sin. The question arises, if "God saw everything that

53. Gen. 1:31.
54. Gen. 2:2-3.
55. Rom. 5:12-14.

He had made, and indeed it was very good,"[56] how and when did evil originate? In seeking the answer to this question, a second question surfaces; "What is evil?" Both questions require an answer for gaining clarity into the reality of the presence of the kingdom of God. Ronald Rhodes provides insights into these tough questions:

> The reality is that it is impossible to distinguish evil from good unless one has an infinite reference point that is absolutely good… The infinite reference point for distinguishing good from evil can be found in the person of God, for God alone can exhaust the definition of 'absolutely good.' If God does not exist, then there are no moral absolutes by which one has the right to judge something (or someone) as being evil.[57]

Isaiah and Ezekiel also provide insights into the origin of evil through the self-will and iniquity that emerged in the life of Lucifer.[58] He is a spiritual being and possibly an archangel that led an angelic host in the worship of God prior to the implementation of God's creation as we know it beginning with Genesis 1:3. Lucifer was "full of wisdom and perfect in beauty" until his heart became prideful because of his beauty; where upon his God given gift of wisdom became corrupted. Five times Lucifer said, "I will,"[59] as opposed to submitting his will to the will of his Creator. Being lifted up in pride and unwilling to submit to God's will, Lucifer became "lawless" and "profane." According to New Testament terms he became an antichrist; that is one who denies and opposes Christ and all for which He stands.[60] As a consequence, the Lord declared to Lucifer, "iniquity was found

56. Gen. 1:31.

57. Ronald Rhodes, "Tough Questions About Evil," in *Who Made God: and Answers to Over 100 Other Tough Questions of Faith,* Ravi Zacharias and Norman Geisler, gen. eds. (Grand Rapids, MI: Zondervan, 2003), 35.

58. Isa. 14:12-17; Eze. 28:11-19.

59. Isa. 14:13-14.

60. 2 Thes. 2:8-9: 1 John 4:3; 2 John 1:7.

in you."[61] Iniquity means; "evil, sin, injustice, dishonesty, fault, i.e., acts, behaviors, or persons which are contrary to a standard, so possibly incurring guilt and punishment."[62] As a result of Lucifer's pride, his created nature and wisdom became corrupted; then evil and foolishness rather than goodness and wisdom characterized his nature. He thereby fell from his status of perfection and became a wicked adversary who opposes God and accuses God and others of wrong.[63] Therefore, Lucifer became the accuser, the devil and is described in God's word as the "evil one."[64] Jesus made the following remarks regarding the devil:

"He was a murderer from the beginning, and *does not* stand in the truth, because there is no truth in him. When he speaks a lie, he speaks from his own *resources,* for he is a liar and the father of it".[65]

We conclude that God did not create evil. God created Lucifer, and Lucifer by the choice of his own free will deliberately rebelled against God. Thus, his nature became corrupt and perverse without the capacity for a remedy. From that juncture forward, he personified evil. Having no remedy, he will always be evil. This contributes to the answer as to how evil originated, but when evil originated is not determined. However, it is reasonable to assume it occurred before or maybe even long before God planted the "tree of the knowledge of good and evil" in the midst of the Garden of Eden.

God is by nature not only sovereign; He is also good and "the goodness of God endures forever."[66] God is also immutable. The Scripture says, "For I am the Lord, I do not change."[67] Therefore, the goodness of God cannot truthfully be called into question even though we experience that which is not good. So, what is the answer to the

61. Eze. 28:15-17.

62. James Swanson, *Dictionary of Biblical Languages with Semantic Domains: Hebrew (Old Testament)* (Oak Harbor: Logos Research Systems, Inc., 1997).

63. Rev. 12:10.

64. John 17:15.

65. John 8:44b

66. Psa. 52:1, 119:68; Luke 18:19.

67. Mal. 3:6a.

question, "What is evil?" Evil is the very antithesis of good. Evil is a parasitic negation that destroys what is good and ends with meaninglessness or nothingness which is the complete and total absence of good. Just as rust eats away metal until all the metal is destroyed, so evil is a destroyer. And like a virus it continues to infect, pervert, and destroy everything it touches if there is no antidote of good to overcome the evil.[68] Evil is parasitic by its nature, therefore can eat away a person's soul until life becomes meaningless. For example, Solomon was given great wisdom and by it accumulated abundant wealth and enjoyed great prosperity.[69] However, he disobeyed the Lord and clung to women in love and married many women from nations which the Lord said not to take wives. Because of Solomon's disobedience and refusal to repent and correct his lifestyle, his wisdom became corrupt; his view of life became twisted and distorted.[70] As a result of his perverted lifestyle and corrupted wisdom he concluded that life was "vanity of vanities, all is vanity."[71] Because of his sustained disobedience he experienced evil as his life and abundance lost their meaning. Oh, how pitiful was Solomon's existence in the end of his life in comparison to such a blessed beginning! This is one of the reasons why we are to pursue holiness, resist the devil and pray, "Father… do not lead us into temptation, but deliver us from the evil one."[72]

The Creator and Free Will:

Looking again at the nature of God we understand that God not only expresses love, He is love.[73] Because God is love, He loves unconditionally. That means that we cannot do anything to make God love us more. Our disobedience and disregard for His will in our

---

68. Rom. 12:21.
69. 1 Kings 10:1-24.
70. 1 Kings 11:1-12.
71. Ecc. 1:2, 12:8.
72. Matt. 6:13.
73. 1 John 4:8.

lives does not negate His unconditional love for us. "God so loved the world that He gave His only begotten Son"[74] to die on the cross for sinners like you and me. Jesus did not die for us because we were good, but because He loved us.[75] The God kind of love is expressed freely without any force, coercion, or manipulation. The God kind of love is risky, because the one who gives love does not control the one who receives it. The receiver has the freedom to turn against the giver just as Lucifer turned against God. Angels and people have been invested with privilege and dignity of free will. But angels have no capacity to repent and no means of forgiveness. Without the shedding of blood there is no remission of sin.[76] They are spirit beings which means that once they turn against God their nature becomes warped, twisted, and reality becomes distorted resulting in making decisions that constantly miss the mark. Thus, they are doomed to eternal judgment. And it is my opinion that is what happened to one third of the angels that were involved in Lucifer's rebellion and lost their heavenly and holy status.[77]

God planted the "tree of the knowledge of good and evil" in the midst of the Garden of Eden in order to give man a choice or opportunity to exercise his free will.[78] Man was given the wonderful privilege of communion with God and dominion over creation, but his privileges came with the responsibility to obey God.

"And the LORD God commanded the man, saying, "Of every tree of the garden you may freely eat; but of the tree of the knowledge of good and evil you shall not eat, for in the day that you eat of it you shall surely die." (Genesis. 2:17).

Man's obedience to God's single prohibition served as a test of his love relationship with God in whose image he was created. Would he obey or disobey? In the course of time man willfully disobeyed

---

74. John 3:16.
75. Rom. 5:8, 8:32.
76. Heb. 9:22.
77. Rev. 12:4-9.
78. Gen. 2:9.

God and suffered the immediate consequence of spiritual death which is separation from God the source of life and eventually succumbed to physical death.[79] Not only was mankind now separated from God, but also forfeited his privilege of reigning over the earth. Through the lure of temptation, the devil usurped man's position of dominion over creation. Therefore, the devil became the "god of this age."[80] God drove man out of the paradise garden temple and placed the earth under a curse from which man would now need to eke out a living by the sweat of his brow. Mankind would now be subjected to the evil oppression of the devil who had earlier not only rebelled against God, but also set himself in opposition to God's purposes for man. Man would now spend his days, not as a privileged son of God, but as an orphan. And live under the deceptive and frustrating dominion of the devil, the prince of the power of the air;[81] until a Savior could redeem him and reconcile him back to His Creator/Heavenly Father.[82] Jim Hodges states, "The Lord never lost His throne despite the Fall of His creation! The Lord God never lost His kingdom! What was lost was the full expression of the Kingdom of God on the earth."[83]

God Is a Trinity:

To gain understanding into the blessed relationship that God granted man and the price He would pay to restore that relationship and dominion to man, it is necessary to again consider the nature of God. God is Spirit and He is a community of three persons in One. God the Father is the source of all love, light, life, and authority.[84] The only begotten Son of God, Jesus, is the Word of God who became flesh. He is God our Savior who paid the ultimate price of redemption by

79. Gen. 3:1-19.

80. 2 Cor. 4:4; 1 John 5:19.

81. Eph. 2:2.

82. Gen. 3:15.

83. Jim Hodges, *What in the World Is the Church to Do?* (Duncanville, TX: Federation of Ministries and Churches International, 2008), 57.

84. John 4:24; 1 John 4:7, 1:5; Rom.6:23, 13:1.

deliberately laying down His life in death as the substitutionary sacrifice for the remission of our sin. Therefore, Jesus as Savior became the means to reconcile man back to God and deliver man from the oppressive powers of the devil.[85] The Holy Spirit was given by the Father through the Son to believers in Jesus Christ, thus restoring the opportunity for the created to again become partakers of the divine nature of the Creator.[86] The Holy Spirit would convict the world of sin, righteousness and judgment,[87] and draw sinners to Jesus Christ as their Savior. Once an individual believes on Jesus Christ as Savior and Lord, the Holy Spirit will come to live in that person's heart, sealing his or her relationship in a covenant with God. This empowers believers to function as the sons and daughters of God with the privileges and responsibilities of His royal family and priesthood.[88]

The administration of God's kingdom is not the exercise of some sort of divine fiat where God speaks His sovereign will, "let there be," and it is accomplished as it was during some of the days of creation. No. The kingdom of God is a relational concept whereby God the Father, God the Son, and God the Holy Spirit are united with redeemed sons and daughters in the process of restoring the rule and reign of God over this earth realm as it is in heaven. The kingdom of God will overcome all demonic powers, principalities, and dominions that oppose His sovereignty and bring those entities to their ultimate and eternal end of existence in this world.

Following Adam's disobedience and exposition from the Garden of Eden, God progressively reveals His strategy to redeem man from the oppression of the devil and restore His dominion over creation through the following interventions:[89] (1) God's kingdom and redemptive purposes were revealed throughout the Old Covenant by the Law, Davidic throne, Messianic prophecies, types and shadows

---

85. 1 John 1:1-3, 3:8.
86. 2 Peter 1:4; Heb. 12:10.
87. John 16:8.
88. Acts 1:8; Heb. 6:4; John 18:10-11.
89. Mark 4:26-32.

in expectation of future fulfillment. (2) The renewed New Testament inauguration of the kingdom among men and a partial fulfillment of Old Testament prophesies came through the life and ministry of the Lord Jesus, the Anointed One. (3) The outpouring of the Holy Spirit on the Day of Pentecost anointed the redeemed with the power to be His witnesses and demonstrate to the world of the presence of His kingship and kingdom. (4) A still future consummation of the kingdom will take place when Jesus returns the second time and "the earth shall be filled with the knowledge of the glory of the Lord as the waters cover the sea," and Jesus "shall reign forever and ever."[90] The reality of God and the presence of God's kingdom is revealed through creation itself.[91] But it is revealed with greater clarity through the gospel of the kingdom and the witness of His redeemed people, and through prophecies yet unfilled regarding the age to come. There are dimensions of the presence of the kingdom of God that may seem mysterious, but Jesus said, "It has been given to you to know the mysteries of the kingdom of heaven."[92]

God and Abraham:

To gain greater insight into the presence of God's kingdom we acknowledge an early but important step in God's redemptive strategy revealed through His relationship with Abram. While Abram was living in Ur of the Chaldeans, God appeared to him and called him to leave his country and go to a country that God would show him. God further said, "I will make you a great nation… and in you all the families of the earth shall be blessed."[93] Abram responded in obedient faith by going out of his native country and not knowing where he was going. He was simply trusting God to fulfill His promises. The name Abram means "exalted father." Myles Munroe states, "Being a

90. Isa. 11:9; Hab. 2:14; Rev. 11:15.
91. Rom. 1:20.
92. Matt.13:11a; Mark 4:11a.
93. Gen. 12:1-3.

'father' is rooted in God's image because God is a Father."[94] God's relationship with Abram developed beyond the boundaries of a call to a life of faith into a covenantal relationship, and His redemptive blessings were extended through Abram to all the families of the earth. When God entered the covenantal relationship with Abram, He changed his name from Abram to Abraham, which means "father of a great multitude" or "father of many nations." The point is that God determined to accomplish His redemptive and kingdom purposes not through a political or military means, but through a covenantal family of faith.

Before Abraham, even before the foundation of the world it was determined in the councils of the Godhead that God the Word would become flesh, dwell among men, die on the cross for the remission of sins, paviing the way for all sinful men to be reconciled to God the Father.[95] According to God's love for all mankind, He Himself would provide a Savior that would come in the flesh through the family of Abraham. This is affirmed in the first chapter of the New Testament, where Matthew traces the genealogy of Jesus the Savior back through David to Abraham.[96]

Our God is a God of order. As a result, His kingdom is ordered and structured to experience increase and the fulfillment of His eternal purposes. God's call and promise to Abraham expresses the intentional priority of God's kingdom in the earth to be ordered and function in the context of loving family relationships. Bill Johnson states, "Once we've left the subject of family, we've left the subject of the kingdom of God."[97] God Himself is a Father and Jesus teaches us to pray by addressing God as "our Father which is in heaven."[98] Our heavenly

94. Myles Munroe, *The Fatherhood Principle: Priority, Position, and the Role of a Male* (New Kensington, PA: Whitaker House, 2008), 27.

95. Eph. 1:3-14.

96. Matt. 1:1-17.

97. Bill Johnson, "Forward" in *Cosmic Initiative: Restoring the Kingdom, Igniting the Awakening,* by Jack Taylor (New Kensington, PA: Whitaker House, 2017), 15.

98. Matt. 6:9.

Father is the source of all life, and every good and perfect gift. God has designated and blessed fathers with the responsibility for providing, protecting, and guiding their families into His kingdom's blessedness. George Boardman states, "God is Father-King, in other words man is made for law as well as love; for loyalty as well as liberty… This is a constituent part of manhood."[99] The family provides the context for relational order and structure to express God the Father's nature and accomplishes His redemptive purposes in heaven and earth. The family structure is God's design for man's defense against chaos and anarchy. Bishop Tudor Bismark states,

"Strong structure is imperative if we are to build anything lasting: and strategy must be utilized if we are to do so. Neither structure nor strategy will exist outside of proper order. God is a God of order—it is a fundamental part of Him and His Kingdom…Problems emerge because of the lack of order. Kingdom increase cannot occur in the midst of disorder."[100]

God Is Love:

The kingdom of God is built on the foundation of God's love and structured in His covenantal terms. God's love is not random or meaningless because there is a great price that only He has the resource to pay in order to secure relationships that will endure throughout eternity. J. Rodman Williams states, "God did not create the world and man in order to have some necessary outlet for expressing His love. God is love—with or without a world."[101] However, God has chosen to express His loving nature to us, not just through the impersonal nature of

---

99. George Dana Boardman, *The Kingdom: The Emerging Rule of Christ Among Men,* compiled by Bob Mumford and Jack Taylor, (Shippensburg, PA: Destiny Image Publishers, 2008), 48.

100. Tudor Bismark, *Increase of the Kingdom* (London, UK: Sozo Publishing Group, 2014), 47.

101. J. Rodman Williams, "Renewal Theology: God, the World, and Redemption" vol. one. *Renewal Theology: Systematic Theology from a Charismatic Perspective,* three vols. in one (Grand Rapids, MI: Zondervan, 1988), 65.

the law, but through the loving and harmonious nature of the Trinity. The law has the propensity to leave us with unfilled expectations for two reasons: (1) because it cannot make us complete or perfect, and (2) we always fail to fulfill its demands. However, "the law *is* holy, and the commandment holy and just and good."[102] The Apostle Paul said, "I would not have known sin except for the law."[103] God's law instructs man's conscience to distinguish between right from wrong and provides the moral boundaries which underwrite godly wisdom and character. Godly wisdom is not some philosophical proposition for someone existing in an academic ivory tower. God's wisdom is an expression of His heart of love. Jesus loves us and "is made unto us wisdom;" and "love is the fulfillment of the law."[104] God's love has already paid the ultimate price to bind individuals into bundles of love with Himself and each other. Jesus said, "If you love Me, keep My commandments.[105]" When we love Him, His commandments are not burdensome.[106] Salvation is not the result of keeping commandments, but by new birth that empowers one to love far beyond his or her previous self-centeredness. The capacity to love God and others unconditionally is initiated by new birth, and it is only through the process of new birth that one enters the kingdom of God.[107] This is one of the reasons why the kingdom of God will fill the whole earth! Social, economic, and political systems rise and fall, but God's covenantal love never fails because it depends on Him to fulfill its demands. "If we are faithless, He remains faithful; He cannot deny Himself."[108] God is expanding His kingdom in such a wise fashion that the powers of the devil cannot prevail against it.

---

102. Rom. 7:12.
103. Rom. 7:7.
104. Rom. 13:10.
105. John 14:15.
106. 1 John 5:3.
107. John 3:3.
108. 2 Tim. 2:13.

Abraham, Isaac, and Jacob were obedient to the Lord and sojourned in the Land of Canaan with the promise from God that one day that land would belong to their children. On one occasion God met with Jacob and changed his name from Jacob to Israel, which means "Prince with God."[109] But in the process of time a severe famine covered the Canaan land and in order for Jacob and his family to survive they moved to the land of Egypt. Over the years the children of Israel grew and multiplied from a family into a nation while in the womb of the land of Egypt. They grew to the point that the Egyptians feared them and therefore placed them under the bondage of slavery. The bondage of slavery became so heavy that the children of Israel cried out to the Lord for deliverance. The Lord heard their cry and sent Moses to deliver them.

God and Moses:

Through the leadership of Moses God sent plagues against the gods of Egypt until the power of Pharaoh was almost exhausted. And then God determined with a final plague to strike the firstborn of the Egyptians with death. However, God instructed the Israelites to take a lamb without a blemish into their houses and on the night of the Passover the children were to kill the lamb and put the blood on the lintel and two doorposts and stay inside their homes. The Lord would see the blood of the Lamb on the doorpost and Passover their homes and not allow the destroyer to enter.[110] But the destroyer would enter the homes without blood on the doorpost and strike the firstborn with death. On the night of the Passover "there was a great cry in Egypt, for there was not a house where there was not one dead."[111] Following the Passover and the death of the firstborn of Egyptians, the power of Pharaoh and the Egyptian gods was broken. Pharaoh told Moses,

---

109. Gen. 32:28.
110. Exod. 12.
111. Exod. 12:30.

"Rise, go from among my people, both you and the children."[112] The Children of Israel also spoiled the Egyptians by asking their Egyptian neighbors for articles of silver and gold and articles of clothing.[113] They gathered their spoil and began their march out of Egypt from under the bondage of slavery. When they reached the Red Sea, Moses stretched forth his rod and God parted the waters and they walked out of Egypt on dry land. Pharaoh's firstborn son was dead, but all the firstborn of Israel were alive because God has purchased them with the price of the blood of the Lamb and called Israel "My son, My firstborn."[114] Upon Israel's deliverance from Egypt God commanded Moses to consecrate the firstborn of Israel to Him and to always keep the Passover as a memorial and a remembrance that "with a strong hand the Lord has brought you out of Egypt."[115]

The Children of Israel continued their journey from the shore of the Red Sea until they came to Mount Sinai in the third month after their departure from Egypt. There at Mount Sinai God met with them and God offered to enter a covenant with them as a nation. God said to Moses,

> "'You have seen what I did to the Egyptians, and *how* I bore you on eagles' wings and brought you to Myself. Now therefore, if you will indeed obey My voice and keep My covenant, then you shall be a special treasure to Me above all people; for all the earth *is* Mine. And you shall be to Me a kingdom of priests and a holy nation.' These *are* the words which you shall speak to the children of Israel.
>
> So, Moses came and called for the elders of the people and said before them all these words which the LORD

112. Exod. 12:31.
113. Exod. 12:35-36.
114. Exod. 4:22.
115. Exod. 13:2-9.

commanded him. Then all the people answered together and said, 'All that the LORD has spoken we will do.' So, Moses brought back the words of the people to the LORD. And the LORD said to Moses, 'Behold, I come to you in the thick cloud, that the people may hear when I speak with you and believe you forever.' So, Moses told the words of the people to the LORD.

Then the LORD said to Moses, 'Go to the people and consecrate them today and tomorrow and let them wash their clothes. And let them be ready for the third day. For on the third day the LORD will come down upon Mount Sinai in the sight of all the people. You shall set bounds for the people all around, saying, take heed to yourselves *that* you do *not* go up to the mountain or touch its base. Whoever touches the mountain shall surely be put to death. Not a hand shall touch him, but he shall surely be stoned or shot *with an arrow;* whether man or beast, he shall not live.' When the trumpet sounds long, they shall come near the mountain.'

So, Moses went down from the mountain to the people and sanctified the people, and they washed their clothes. And he said to the people, 'Be ready for the third day; do not come near *your* wives.' Then it came to pass on the third day, in the morning, that there were thunderings and lightnings, and a thick cloud on the mountain; and the sound of the trumpet was very loud, so that all the people who *were* in the camp trembled.

> And Moses brought the people out of the camp to meet with God, and they stood at the foot of the mountain. Now Mount Sinai *was* completely in smoke, because the LORD descended upon it in fire. Its smoke ascended like the smoke of a furnace, and the whole mountain quaked greatly. And when the blast of the trumpet sounded long and became louder and louder, Moses spoke, and God answered him by voice." (Exodus. 19:4-19).

God had not dwelt among the inhabitants of the earth since the expulsion of Adam from the Garden of Eden. Neither do we have any record where God had ever spoken or manifested His presence in such an awesome fashion. Therefore, the children of Israel were so frightened by God's presence and the sound of His voice that "they trembled and stood afar off. Then they said to Moses, 'You speak with us and we will hear; but let not God speak with us lest we die.'"[116]

God's meeting with Moses and the nation of Israel at Sinai was the occasion for completing the process of establishing a covenant with the children of Israel which had its beginnings with the shed blood of the Passover Lamb in the land of Egypt. As a part of His covenant with the children of Israel God gave them the Ten Commandments, and various laws to guide the civil administration of the nation of Israel.

It was amazing that God said to Moses, "And let them make Me a sanctuary, that I may dwell among them."[117] God-Father-King promised Moses, "I will walk among you and be your God, and you shall be My people."[118] God showed Moses the heavenly Tabernacle of the Testimony that the Children of Israel were to use as a pattern in building His dwelling place among them.[119] He also gave Moses in-

116. Exod. 20:18-19.

117. Exod. 25:8.

118. Lev. 26:12.

119. Exod. 25:9, 40, 38:12.

struction regarding the establishment of the office of High Priest and the priesthood along with laws and guidance for offerings, sacrifices, and holy days. This covenantal relationship with God would make Israel a peculiar nation among all the other nations of the world. In other words, God chose to manifest the presence of His sovereignty or government or kingdom in the earth through His covenantal son, the nation of Israel.[120] It was God's intent that Israel would prosper and be an example of righteousness and prosperity to all the world and thereby attract others to participate in His kingdom. But Israel limited God through their unbelief, and therefore mostly failed to be a shining example of God's goodness and greatness. However, God was determined to fulfill His redemptive purposes even in the face of Israel's unbelief and failures. Therefore, God took an oath saying, "But truly, as I live all the earth shall be filled with My glory."[121]

Because of their unbelief, Israel wandered in the wilderness for forty years before entering the Promised Land.[122] But the day came when Israel finally entered the Promised Land under the leadership of Joshua.[123] Under Joshua's leadership they enjoyed some awesome victories over their enemies followed by seasons of peace and prosperity as they obeyed God. Then, there were cycles of bondage and oppression by the neighboring nations because of their sin and disobedience. When the Children of Israel humbled themselves and cried out for the Lord to deliver them, God would raise up a Judge to lead them in victory over their enemies. Then they enjoyed another cycle of peace and prosperity, followed by rebellion and disobedience, followed by more oppression and bondage, leading to humble cries to God for deliverance. Their situation is summed up in the Book of Judges as follows: "In those days *there was* no king in Israel; everyone did *what was* right in his own eyes."[124]

---

120. Exod. 4:22.
121. Num. 14:21.
122. Num. 14:33; Psa. 78:41.
123. Deut. 31:14-23.
124. Judges 17:6.

The last Judge of Israel was Samuel. It was during the days of Samuel's leadership, that the people of Israel demanded a king like other nations. Therefore, God anointed Saul as king of Israel. However, Saul failed to obey God's commands and God rejected him as king. Samuel told Saul, "The Lord has sought for Himself a man after His own heart."[125] The day came when God sent Samuel to Bethlehem to the house of Jesse and there he anointed Jesse's youngest son, David, the shepherd boy, as king of Israel and "the Spirit of the Lord came upon David from that day forward."[126]

God and David:

It was while Saul was still king of Israel, but after Samuel had anointed David that the Philistines gathered their armies together against Saul and the men of Israel. And a Philistine champion named Goliath came forward each day and challenged Saul and the armies of Israel with these words:

> 'Why have you come out to line up for battle? *Am* I not a Philistine, and you the servants of Saul? Choose a man for yourselves and let him come down to me. If he is able to fight with me and kill me, then we will be your servants. But if I prevail against him and kill him, then you shall be our servants and serve us.' And the Philistine said, 'I defy the armies of Israel this day; give me a man, that we may fight together.' When Saul and all Israel heard these words of the Philistine, they were dismayed and greatly afraid. (1 Samuel. 17:8:11)

---

125. 1 Sam. 13:14; Acts 13:22.
126. 1 Sam. 16:13.

A. W. Pink states, "The terrible giant of Gath continued to menace the army of Israel twice a day for no less than forty days—a period which, in Scripture, is ever associated with probation and testing."[127]

> So David was sent to the camp of Israel by his father with supplies for his brothers. He arrived in the camp of Israel on the fortieth day as "Israel and the Philistines had drawn up in battle array, army against army."[128] This story is so familiar that the details do not need to be elaborated upon here. It is sufficient only to refer to David's comments as he approached Goliath in battle:
>
> 'You come to me with a sword, with a spear, and with a javelin. But I come to you in the name of the LORD of hosts, the God of the armies of Israel, whom you have defied. This day the LORD will deliver you into my hand, and I will strike you and take your head from you. And this day I will give the carcasses of the camp of the Philistines to the birds of the air and the wild beasts of the earth, that all the earth may know that there is a God in Israel.' (1 Samuel 17:45-46)

David killed the giant and Israel chased and plundered the Philistines. The point is that Israel was a nation in a covenant relationship with God and representing His sovereignty in the earth. But that sovereignty was being defied and opposed by the Philistines; but God had anointed a young man to prevail against what appeared as overwhelming odds. David had told the giant that the LORD would deliver him into his hands. Therefore, God's sovereignty and kingdom purposes continued progressing towards fulfilling the terms of

---

127. Arthur Walkington Pink, *The Life of David* (Bellingham, WA: Logos Bible Software, 2005), 1 Sa 17.

128. 1 Sam. 17:16-21.

His Everlasting Covenant. It is of interest to note that "David took off the head of the Philistine and brought it to Jerusalem."[129] Years later Jesus was crucified in "a place called Golgotha, that is to say, Place of a skull."[130] I wonder if there is any relationship between the skull of Goliath and the place where Jesus was crucified?

After the death of Saul, David first reigned as king over Judah from the city of Hebron for seven years.[131] And then He reigned from Jerusalem for thirty-three years. When David became the king of all Israel, he chose Mount Zion in the city of Jerusalem for his home. It was in earlier years that from Jerusalem Melchizedek, the priest of God Most High, had come to Abraham with bread and wine, and to whom Abraham paid tithes. It was from Jerusalem that David's heart panted for God as the deer pants for the water brook.[132] David the "sweet Psalmist of Israel"[133] could not be content until he had brought the ark of God to Mount Zion. He placed it in a tent without a veil and commissioned choirs of singers to sing praises of thanksgiving and worship before the ark of God twenty four hours a day.[134] It was David who sang, "I will praise the name of God with a song and will magnify Him with thanksgiving."[135]

It was while King David was dwelling in his own house that he spoke with the prophet Nathan and declared that he wanted to build a house for God since the ark of God's presence was dwelling in a tent. No one had ever offered to build God a house before. And God responded through Nathan the prophet to David's intentions with these words:

> Go and tell My servant David, thus says the LORD: Would you build a house for Me to dwell in? For I

129. 1 Sam. 17:54.
130. Matt. 27:33; Mark 15:22; John 19:17.
131. 1 Kings 2:11.
132. Psa. 42:1.
133. 2 Sam. 23.
134. 1 Chro. 25.
135. Psa. 69:30.

have not dwelt in a house since the time that I brought the children of Israel up from Egypt, even to this day, but have moved about in a tent and in a tabernacle. Wherever I have moved about with all the children of Israel, have I ever spoken a word to anyone from the tribes of Israel, whom I commanded to shepherd My people Israel, saying, 'Why have you not built Me a house of cedar?' Now therefore, thus shall you say to My servant David, 'Thus says the LORD of hosts: I took you from the sheepfold, from following the sheep, to be ruler over My people, over Israel. And I have been with you wherever you have gone and have cut off all your enemies from before you, and have made you a great name, like the name of the great men who *are* on the earth. Moreover, I will appoint a place for My people Israel, and will plant them, that they may dwell in a place of their own and move no more; nor shall the sons of wickedness oppress them anymore, as previously, since the time that I commanded judges *to be* over My people Israel, and have caused you to rest from all your enemies. Also, the LORD tells you that He will make you a house. When your days are fulfilled, and you rest with your fathers, I will set up your seed after you, who will come from your body, and I will establish his kingdom. He shall build a house for My name, and I will establish the throne of his kingdom forever. I will be his Father, and he shall be My son. If he commits iniquity, I will chasten him with the rod of men and with the blows of the sons of men. But My mercy shall not depart from him, as I took *it* from Saul, whom I removed from before you. And your house and your kingdom

> shall be established forever before you. Your throne shall be established forever. (2 Samuel 7:5-16)

The Lord did not permit David to build Him a house. However, David's heart of worship of the Lord so attracted God's grace that God told David that He was going to make him a house and set up his seed after him. David's son would build a house for God and God would establish the throne of his kingdom forever.[136] Solomon, David's son would build a house for God, but the promise extended beyond Solomon. God was so moved toward David that He considered David's son, His own son. Many scholars see God's covenant with David finding its ultimate fulfillment in the Lord Jesus Christ who was called in the Synoptic Gospels "the Son of David."[137] Conner and Malmin state:

> The Davidic Covenant was made with David after the death of Saul and David's enthronement at Jerusalem. It involved David's Seed, House, Throne and Kingdom both naturally and spiritually. It pointed ultimately to the everlasting Throne and Kingdom of the Lord Jesus Christ, David's greatest Son.[138]

Generations earlier God had entered a covenant with Abraham even before he had a child, stating that He would make Abraham a father of many nations and kings would come from him. The covenant with Abraham was extended into the family of Abraham that had grown into a nation and God at Mount Sinai made a covenant with Moses and the nation of Israel. David, over four hundred years after the Mosaic Covenant, is the Israelite through whom God extended His covenant provisions by establishing the throne of David's kingdom

---

136. 2 Sam. 7:12-13, 16.
137. Matt. 9:27; Mark 10:47; Luke 18:38.
138. Conner and Malmin, *The Covenants.* 59.

forever.[139] The point is that throughout history God was purposefully administrating His kingdom purposes according to the terms of the Everlasting Covenant which was established between the members of the Godhead before the foundation of the world. He was carrying out the progressive administration of His kingdom purposes through the covenants He was making with men created in His image and likeness. These men were redeemed by the blood of the Lamb and anointed to serve God's kingdom purposes and prevail over the powers that opposed His sovereignty.

God and Daniel:

About four hundred years after David, Israel, because of their rebellious disobedience, was taken into captivity by the Babylonians. Even though mankind is created in "the image and likeness of God," with "eternity in his heart," his sinful nature has a propensity toward self-centered pride and arrogance.[140] This is illustrated in the life of Nebuchadnezzar the king of the Babylonian Empire about six hundred years before the birth of Jesus Christ. God granted Nebuchadnezzar the privilege of reigning over the world's largest empire during that period. Then one night he had a dream which his magicians, astrologers, and sorcerers could not interpret, much less recite to him. But God revealed the dream and its interpretation to Daniel. The essence of the dream was that of a "great image" representing four successive world empires. The dream concluded with a stone, cut out of the mountains without hands, striking the great image and completely destroying it; as the stone itself became a great mountain filling the whole earth.[141] This is a prophetic picture of the kingdoms of this world coming to nothing and the kingdom of God filling the whole earth. Daniel prophesied:

---

139. 2 Sam. 7:16.
140. Ecc. 3:11; John 3:19.
141. Dan. 2.

> And in the days of these kings the God of heaven will set up a kingdom which shall never be destroyed; and the kingdom shall not be left to other people; it shall break in pieces and consume all these kingdoms, and it shall stand forever. (Daniel. 2:44)

We know from history that a man reigned over each of the four kingdoms in Nebuchadnezzar's vision. But later, Daniel himself had a night vision and saw not just any man, but the Son of Man coming with the clouds of heaven, and to Him was given dominion by God; and "His dominion is an everlasting dominion, which shall not pass away, and His kingdom *the one* which shall not be destroyed."[142]

Nebuchadnezzar had a second dream. He dreamed of a great tree in the midst of the earth.[143] Its height reached to the heavens and it could be seen to the ends of all the earth. The beasts of the field came under it for shade and food, the birds came in its branches, and all flesh was fed from it. But it was suddenly chopped down with only the stump remaining. Again, the king called on Daniel to interpret the dream because he knew that "The Spirit of the Holy God" was in him. Daniel gave the interpretation which included the humbling of Nebuchadnezzar over a period of seven years and at the end of those years his kingdom would be restored, and he would rule the empire again. Sure enough, one day the king was walking in his royal palace and said, "Is not this great Babylon which I have built for a royal dwelling by my mighty power and for the honor of my majesty."[144] In that moment <u>his kingdom departed</u> from him and he went to live in the field and ate grass like oxen for seven years. At the end of the seven years his sanity and <u>kingdom were restored</u>. After his return to power he said "I, Nebuchadnezzar praise and extol and honored the King of heaven, all of whose works are truth, and His ways justice. And those

---

142. Dan. 7:13-14.
143. Dan.4.
144. Dan. 4:30.

who walk in pride He is able to put down."[145] These illustrations from the Book of Daniel teach us that God's kingdom and redemptive purposes reign supreme over all people and nations both small and great.

Before Israel was taken into Babylonian captivity the Prophet Jeremiah had prophesied, "For thus says the LORD: After seventy years are completed at Babylon, I will visit you and perform My good word toward you and cause you to return to this place."[146] Daniel as a youth had been taken from Jerusalem to Babylon among the first of the captives. Throughout his years in captivity he was used by God as a prophetic voice of wisdom to the leaders of the Babylonian government, and yet remained steadfast in his relationship with the LORD his God. Near the end of Israel's seventy years of captivity the Babylonian Empire was overtaken by the Persians. Daniel immediately found favor with the Persian leader, King Darius.

By this time Daniel was at least eighty-five years old and he read Jeremiah's prophecy regarding God's word to release them from captivity after seventy years and cause them to return to Jerusalem. In response to Jeremiah's prophecy Daniel began to pray and fast and intercede for his nation Israel, because he had himself been in captivity for almost seventy years.[147] It is my belief that it was at this juncture that other government leaders seeking to bring a charge against Daniel persuaded King Darius to make the decree that could not be changed; that "whoever petitions any god or man for thirty days except you O king, shall be cast into the den of lions."[148] Knowing the decree had been signed, Daniel responded as follows:

> Now when Daniel knew that the writing was signed, he went home. And in his upper room, with his windows open toward Jerusalem, he knelt on his knees three times a day, and prayed and gave thanks before

145. Dan. 4:37.
146. Jer. 29:10.
147. Dan. 9.
148. Dan. 6:7-8.

his God, as was his custom since early days. Then these men assembled and found Daniel praying and making supplication before his God. And they went before the king, and spoke concerning the king's decree: 'Have you not signed a decree that every man who petitions any god or man within thirty days, except you, O king, shall be cast into the den of lions?' The king answered and said, 'The thing *is* true, according to the law of the Medes and Persians, which does not alter.'

So, they answered and said before the king, 'That Daniel, who is one of the captives from Judah, does not show due regard for you, O king, or for the decree that you have signed, but makes his petition three times a day.' And the king, when he heard *these* words, was greatly displeased with himself, and set *his* heart on Daniel to deliver him; and he labored till the going down of the sun to deliver him. Then these men approached the king, and said to the king, 'Know, O king, that *it is* the law of the Medes and Persians that no decree or statute which the king establishes may be changed.'

So, the king gave the command, and they brought Daniel and cast *him* into the den of lions. *But* the king spoke, saying to Daniel, 'Your God, whom you serve continually, He will deliver you.' Then a stone was brought and laid on the mouth of the den, and the king sealed it with his own signet ring and with the signets of his lords, that the purpose concerning Daniel might not be changed. Now the king went to his palace and spent the night fasting; and no musicians were

> brought before him. Also, his sleep went from him. (Daniel 6:10-18)
>
> The next morning King Darius went to the lions' den to check on Daniel. When he called out in concern for Daniel's welfare, Daniel responded by saying; "My God sent His angel and shut the lions' mouths, so that they have not hurt me, because I was found innocent before Him; and also, O king, I have done no wrong before you."[149] God had not only shut the mouths of the lions in the protection of Daniel, but it is my summation that just before Daniel's arrest, God had responded to Daniel's prayer recorded in Daniel chapter nine, by sending the archangel Gabriel to inform Daniel and give him "skill to understand."[150] That is the skill to understand God's plan for the continuing presence of His kingdom and His sovereignty over the nations until His redemptive plan was completed by the Messiah.[151] In other words, even though God's covenantal nation of Israel was confined to captivity, the temple and the City of Jerusalem were in ruins, God continued to manifest the presence of His kingdom and dominion through His ambassadors, the Prophets.

Over a hundred and forty years before Israel was taken captive by the Babylonians, Isaiah had prophesied in the name of the LORD: "Who says of Cyrus, '*He is* My shepherd, and he shall perform all My pleasure,' Saying to Jerusalem, 'You shall be built,' And to the

---

149. Dan. 6:22.
150. Dan. 9:22.
151. Dan. 9:24-27.

temple, 'Your foundation shall be laid.'"[152] The Jewish historian Josephus tells us the following:

In the first year of the reign of Cyrus, which was the seventieth from the day that our people were removed out of their own land into Babylon, God commiserated the captivity and calamity of these poor people, according as he had foretold to them by Jeremiah the prophet, before the destruction of the city… For he stirred up the mind of Cyrus, and made him write this throughout all Asia:—"Thus saith Cyrus the King:—Since God Almighty hath appointed me to be king of the habitable earth, I believe that he is that God which the nation of the Israelites worship… This was foretold by Isaiah one hundred and forty years before the temple was demolished. Accordingly, when Cyrus read this, and admired the divine power, an earnest desire and ambition seized upon him to fulfill what was so written; so he called for the most eminent Jews that were in Babylon, and said to them, that he gave them leave to go back to their own country, and to rebuild their city Jerusalem, and the temple of God.[153]

Ezra records Cyrus' decree for the release of the Israelites to return to Jerusalem and authorized everyone to give silver, gold, goods, and livestock for the rebuilding of the temple in Jerusalem.[154] Zerubbabel led those returning to Jerusalem. The building of the temple was delayed but eventually completed within about twenty-five years after the first exiles had returned.[155] Ezra himself returned to Jerusalem in about 456 B.C. Nehemiah returned to rebuild the walls of Jerusalem in the year 445 B.C. The point is that even under the domination of Gentile empires the temple was rebuilt, and formal worship of God was restored. Therefore, God continued to administrate His kingdom and express His voice through His word and His prophets. The walls of Jerusalem were rebuilt under the leadership of Nehemiah and served

---

152. Isa. 44:28.

153. Flavius Josephus and William Whiston, *The Works of Josephus: Complete and Unabridged* (Peabody: Hendrickson, 1987), 286.

154. Ezra 1:1-6.

155. Haggai 2:14-15.

as a defense against marauders, thus giving the Children of Israel the privilege of serving and worshipping God without interference.

The last of the Old Testament Prophets was Malachi. And Malachi concluded his prophecies by saying; "Behold, I will send you Elijah the prophet before the coming of the great and dreadful day of the LORD."[156] Some four hundred years after Malachi, many Jews were looking for Elijah to return, but Jesus said that John the Baptist "is Elijah who is to come."[157] "For all the prophets and the law prophesied until John."[158]

God, John the Baptist, and Jesus:

John the Baptist ministered as the transitional prophetic voice between the Old Testament prophets and the manifestation of the kingdom of God that Jesus was going to demonstrate. John called Israel to repent because the kingdom of God was at hand. He said he was "The voice of one crying in the wilderness: 'Prepare the way of the Lord; Make His paths straight.'"[159] Jesus followed John and began His ministry by calling Israel to "Repent, for the kingdom of God is at hand."[160]

Jesus grew up in the Town of Nazareth and at about age thirty Jesus came to John the Baptist and received water baptism.

> When all the people were baptized, it came to pass that Jesus also was baptized; and while He prayed, the heaven was opened. And the Holy Spirit descended in bodily form like a dove upon Him, and a voice came from heaven which said, 'You are My Beloved Son; in You I am well pleased.' (Luke 3:21-22)

---

156. Mal. 4:5.
157. Matt. 11:14.
158. Matt. 11:13.
159. Isa. 40:3; Matt. 3:1-3.
160. Matt. 3:17.

Following Jesus' water baptism by John the Baptist he was led by the Holy Spirit into the Wilderness to be tested by the devil.[161] The extent of which Adam forfeited his privilege of dominion is informed by a conversation the devil had with Jesus during His tests in the wilderness. In that conversation the devil speaks as if he were God and tempted Jesus by offering to give Him all the kingdoms of this world and their glory if He would fall down and worship him.

Again, the devil took Him up on an exceedingly high mountain and showed Him all the kingdoms of the world and their glory. And he said to Him, 'All these things I will give You if You will fall down and worship me.' Then Jesus said to him, 'Away with you, Satan! For it is written, *'You shall worship the* LORD *your God, and Him only you shall serve.'* (Matthew 4:8-10)

The devil is a liar and could have been deceiving Jesus regarding the extent of his dominion. However, Jesus did not question or refute the devils proposition. Jesus knew who He was and withstood the temptation and refused to bow before the devil. It was in the fullness of time Jesus, the Son of David, the Son of Abraham, the Son of God, Immanuel, came preaching, "The time is fulfilled, and the kingdom of God is at hand."[162] Of all the names given to the Son of God, Immanuel ("God with us") is oh-so-powerful, meaningful and significant precisely because Jesus indeed is "God with us"—not merely as the God-Man who walked the shores of Galilee two millennia ago, rather also as the Ascended Lord and Christ who continues to abide with us forever by His Spirit!

Following Jesus' victory over the devil in the wilderness, He came preaching, "The gospel of the kingdom of God."[163] Early in Jesus' ministry He went as was His custom to the synagogue at Nazareth and publicly declared His anointing by opening the Scroll of Isaiah and reading:

---

161. Matt. 4:1.
162. Mark 1:15; Gal. 4:4-5.
163. Mark 1:14.

> *'The Spirit of the* LORD *is upon Me, Because He has anointed Me To preach the gospel to the poor; He has sent Me to heal the brokenhearted, to proclaim liberty to the captives and recovery of sight to the blind, To set at liberty those who are oppressed; To proclaim the acceptable year of the* LORD.*'* Then He closed the book and gave *it* back to the attendant and sat down. And the eyes of all who were in the synagogue were fixed on Him. And He began to say to them, 'Today this Scripture is fulfilled in your hearing.' (Luke 4:18-21).

The Virgin Mary conceived the Son of God in her womb through the overshadowing of the Holy Spirit[164] Thus, Jesus was conceived by the Holy Spirit, but was not empowered to declare and demonstrate the presence of the kingdom of God until after coming up out of the Jordan River waters of baptism and the Holy Spirit descending upon Him.[165] This indicates the emphasis the Father places upon the value of the anointing by the Holy Spirit. Jesus was definitely the God/man, but during His earthly ministry He functioned only as a man empowered by the anointing of the Holy Spirit.

During His ministry He declared, "But if I cast out demons with the finger of God, surely the kingdom of God has come upon you."[166] When Jesus ministered it wasn't in word only, but with both word and power. His words did not return void but prospered where He sent them, thus fulfilling the prophecy of Isaiah.[167] His gospel had the power within itself to fulfill its claims. Jesus said, "The words I speak to you are spirit and they are life."[168] When He spoke to a corpse it immediately came to life, because His words broke the grip of the

164. Luke 1:35.
165. Luke 3:22.
166. Luke 11:20.
167. Isa. 55:11.
168. John 6:63.

death.[169] George E. Ladd writes it this way; "'The Kingdom exercises its power' and the 'Kingdom is preached' express the same idea: the dynamic presence of the kingdom in deeds and words of Jesus."[170]

Jesus indeed is "God with us" and He calls all people to "Repent and believe in the gospel." The reason He calls for repentance is because all people need to change their minds and understanding regarding the presence of God's kingdom or government. The good news or gospel is that God's kingdom through the leadership of Immanuel is going to replace all the kingdoms of this world with a kingdom of righteousness, peace, and joy. And all who are afar from God, and wild branches by nature receive a gracious invitation to now be grafted into the root and fatness of God's covenant family, through personal faith in the Lord Jesus Christ. Believers in the Lord Jesus Christ are the only people in the world who receive the Spirit of Adoption, whereby we know Almighty God as "Father." No other religion in the world offers sinners the awesome privilege of knowing God in such a loving and intimate relationship.

Jesus surely cast out many demons and healed many sick people besides all the miracles He did such as turning water into wine and feeding thousands with a boy's small lunch. In other words, Jesus came to earth and ministered not as God, but as a man empowered by the Holy Spirit. He never planned to accommodate the devil or the religious powers of His day. He came with the purpose of destroying the devil and swallowing up the power of death with resurrection life.[171] In the Garden of Gethsemane Jesus was severely tested again when faced with becoming sin and laying His life down on the cross. Under the pressure of that test Jesus said, "'Father, if it is Your will, take this cup away from Me; nevertheless, not My will, but Yours, be done'"[172]

---

169. Luke 7:14-15.

170. George Eldon Ladd, *The Presence of the Future: The Eschatology of Biblical Realism* (Grand Rapids, MI: William B. Eerdman's Publishing, 1974), 166.

171. Heb. 2:14.

172. Luke 22:42.

Jesus yielded His will in loving submission to His Father and on the cross, He died for sinners like you and me.

Jesus' Victory Over Sin, Death, and the Grave:

After His death on the cross, He was buried, but on the third day He arose victorious over sin, death, and the powers of darkness.[173] This is His testimony, "I *am* He who lives, and was dead, and behold, I am alive forevermore. Amen. And I have the keys of Hades and of Death."[174] And all the powers of darkness will be destroyed forever. The future holds the promise that a time is coming when there will be no more war, nor suffering, nor tears, nor death.[175] And the redeemed of the Lord will rule and reign with the Lord Jesus Christ forever and ever.

Thus, through Jesus' victory as a Holy Spirit empowered man, He defeated the devil and the power of death and regained man's delegated dominion over the earth. Through His victory Jesus is now empowering by the Holy Spirit an army of believers to rule and reign with Him as a kingdom of priests. God's plan of redemption will conclude when Jesus and His Church have put all enemies under their feet and all things made subject to Jesus. Then Jesus will deliver the kingdom back to the Father that God may be all in all.[176]

Today, believers in Jesus Christ are residents of this world but citizens of the kingdom of heaven.[177] Jesus said, "It is your Father's good pleasure to give you the kingdom."[178] As citizens of the kingdom of God we are experiencing the presence of the future in tangible ways. Even though we have not experienced the consummation of the kingdom, we already possess eternal life and are already seated in

---

173. Col. 2:15.
174. Rev. 1:18.
175. Isa. 2:4, 65:19-25; Rev. 21:3-4.
176. 1 Cor. 15:24-28.
177. Phil. 3:20; Eph. 2:20.
178. Luke 12:32.

heavenly places in Christ. Jesus Christ the source of our authority is already seated on the throne at the right hand of the Father.[179] Now, a believer's perspective on life should not be past/present, but present/future. We are to live by faith! By faith we lay hold of future kingdom realities and bring those blessings into our present experience through prayers of faith. For example, a woman of Canaan came to Jesus and asked Him to have mercy upon her because her daughter was severely demon-possessed. Jesus responded to her cries for help by saying, "It was not good to take the children's bread and throw it to the little dogs."[180] But she refused to give up in defeat. Rather with tenacious faith she gripped that which she as a Gentile could only expect to have access to until after the resurrection of the Messiah. She said, "Yes, Lord, yet even the little dogs eat the crumbs which fall from the master's table."[181] Her faith so impacted Jesus that He said, "Let it be to you as you desire. And her daughter was healed that very hour."[182] Faith requires that believers do not live towards their inheritance, but from their inheritance. It is faith that pleases God. Believers are already "in Christ" and He is the "beginning and the end," the "Alpha and Omega."[183] On the cross Jesus said, "It is finished."[184] Jesus has done all He can do for us and He is not trying to achieve the "end," He is the "End" or the "Future." Derek Morphew states,

> To have an encounter with Jesus is to meet one's ultimate destiny.... There is no period in church history that has not been a time of last days. The last few minutes before the Second Coming will not be some different time, only the climax of the same mysterious dimension Christians have experienced since Jesus

179. Col. 3:1.
180. Matt. 15:26.
181. Matt. 15:27.
182. Matt. 15:28.
183. Rev. 1:8,11, 21:6, 22:13.
184. John 19:30.

> first came.... Understanding the kingdom therefore becomes a worldview, a permanent orientation, a moment-by-moment expectation.[185]

We as believers should live and serve others with an attitude of expectation of kingdom breakthroughs of deliverance, healings, and miracles, just as were experienced in the Book of Acts. Of course, as believers we will make mistakes and even experience failures. But failures are not endings, but steppingstones into our horizon! The best is not behind us in the good old days, but the best is yet to come—it is our destiny![186] E. Stanley Jones states,

> The kingdom of God is God's total order, expressed as a realm and reign, in the individual and in society; and which is to replace the present unworkable world order with God's order in the individual and in society; and while the nature of the kingdom is social the entrance into it is by personal new birth now; the character of that kingdom is seen in the character of Jesus—the Kingdom is Christlikeness universalized; while it comes to earth in the time process it is eternal and is the same rule which is in heaven and because it is Christlikeness this makes it heaven—there and here.... the Kingdom will be consummated when Jesus returns.[187]

When considering the future sometimes Christians have been confused regarding the difference between "last days" and the "great and awesome day of the Lord."[188] "Last days" refer to the period of time

---

185. Derek Morphew, *Breakthrough,* (Cape Town, SA: Vineyard International Publishing, 2006), 80, 84.

186. 1 Cor. 2:9-10.

187. Jones, *The Unshakable Kingdom,* 75.

188. Acts 2:17-20.

between the Day of Pentecost and the Second Coming of Jesus Christ. In other words, the "Last Days" are the Church age in which we are now living, and this age concludes with the Second Coming of Jesus. "The Day of the Lord" is the day of judgment that will come unexpectantly as a thief in the night and conclude with the devil and anyone not found written in the Book of Life being cast into the lake of fire.[189] On the day of judgment, the destroyer and his followers will be destroyed eternally.[190]

As citizens of the kingdom of God believers are already more than conquerors in Christ Jesus, even though we may not feel like it and circumstances may not seem like it. Citizenship in the kingdom of God is a legal standing that is not contingent upon our feelings or surroundings but established and supported through the covenantal shed blood of Jesus and the eternal truth of the new covenant. This is the reality that liberates us from our past, guides our present, and guarantees our future.[191] The vision of our future becomes our present reality through faith in Jesus Christ. Faith is the God given currency that enables us to possess in the here and now kingdom realities, values, and treasures. This is why "unbelief" is such a deadly sin.[192] The Children of Israel wandered in the wilderness for forty years because they were focused on their present circumstances and past experiences rather than their promised future. They failed to perceive the hand of God fulfilling their future in the face of giants. In reality the enemy was their "bread" or strength.[193] God's promises are yes and amen, but we must act upon them in faith knowing that God will fulfill what He has promised. The New Covenant is a conditional covenant: Jesus did His part as our Savior by becoming a propitiation for our sins. Our part is to believe on Jesus Christ as our Savior and Lord and live a lifestyle of faith. If a person refuses to believe in Jesus Christ as their personal

189. 1 Thes. 5:2; 2 Peter 2:9, 3:7-10; Rev. 20:10-14.
190. Exod. 12:23; Rev. 9:11.
191. John 8:32-36.
192. Heb. 3:1-19.
193. Num. 14:9.

Savior, then all that He accomplished on the cross will be of no value to them. A person must believe on Jesus Christ as Savior in order to participate in the privileges of being a citizen of the kingdom of God.

One of the most enlightening illustrations from the New Testament comes from the life of a nameless scribe who asked Jesus this question:

> "Which is the first commandment of all?' Jesus answered him, 'The first of all the commandments *is: 'Hear, O Israel, the* LORD *our God, the* LORD *is one. And you shall love the* LORD *your God with all your heart, with all your soul, with all your mind, and with all your strength.'* This *is* the first commandment. And the second, like *it, is* this: *'You shall love your neighbor as yourself.'* There is no other commandment greater than these.' So, the scribe said to Him, 'Well *said,* Teacher. You have spoken the truth, for there is one God, and there is no other but He. And to love Him with all the heart, with all the understanding, with all the soul, and with all the strength, and to love one's neighbor as oneself, is more than all the whole burnt offerings and sacrifices.' Now when Jesus saw that he answered wisely, He said to him, 'You are not far from the kingdom of God.' (Mark 12:29-34).

Love - A Top Priority of the Kingdom:

In this conversation Jesus expressed the supreme values of life in the kingdom when He told the Scribe that the greatest commandment was to first "love the Lord your God" and the second was to "love your neighbor."[194] The first marvel here is the Scribe's affirmation to Jesus' answer to his question; by saying that the love for

194. Matt. 22:37-39.

God and neighbor was "more than all the whole burnt offerings and sacrifices."[195] Jesus responded with a second marvel by saying to him, "You are not far from the kingdom of God." This teaches us that the priority and supreme value of the kingdom of God is not just loving God! If that were true, life in the kingdom might be easier. But Jesus teaches that life in the kingdom also places the priority and value on loving one's neighbor only secondarily with the priority and value of loving God!

As citizens of the kingdom of God it is our joy to "love God" whole heartily. Likewise, it is also a joy to "love" our neighbor as ourselves, especially if he or she goes to our church and thinks like we do. However, if our neighbor goes to a different kind of church and believes different than we do, then it often seems harder to love them. And further, if they do not go to church at all, and openly oppose our beliefs and moral standards at school board meetings, town hall meetings, there may arise a barrier to love. If they support laws that are contrary to our Biblical standards and if they want to secularize all the public life, can we continue to love them? These circumstances and conditions remind us that life in the kingdom of God is more than a vertical relationship with God; it also includes a horizonal relationship with our fellowman, even when they disagree and openly oppose that which we stand for and believe.

As believers and citizens of the kingdom of God our objective is not simply to go to heaven after death. But we are to pray, "Your kingdom come, and Your will be done on earth as it is in heaven,"[196] and expect to bring the presence, power and blessings of the kingdom into the daily experience of our families, churches, and communities. Because of heresies, extremes, and the powerful political influence upon the church, the Reformation focused on correct doctrine with only limited focus on the kingdom of God and the person and work of the Holy Spirit. Some years later the enlightenment and its emphasis

195. Mark 12:33.

196. Matt. 6:10.

on reason also gave limited attention to the kingdom of God and the Holy Spirit. Without the administration of the Holy Spirit, the church is nothing more than a nice charitable organization. Teaching originating in Germany during the nineteenth and early twentieth centuries contributed to a theology that held that the kingdom of God is futuristic and is only manifested now through the providence of God. The kingdom's manifest or miracle working power would not be experienced until after the second coming of Jesus when the kingdom would finally be consummated. This was the position of the German scholar and theologian Johannes Weiss (1863-1914). Millard J. Erickson states:

> Johannes Weiss theorized that Jesus was thoroughly eschatological, futuristic, and even apocalyptic in His outlook. According to Weiss, Jesus did not look for a gradual spread of the kingdom of God as an ethical rule in the hearts of humans, but for a future kingdom to be introduced by a dramatic action of God.[197]

All of this contributes to the doctrine of cessationism that remains as a spiritual stronghold in churches today. The outpourings of the Holy Spirit during the last century greatly reemphasized the person and ministry of the Holy Spirit as God's very presence among us. Faith that acknowledges God's presence in the here and now will also acknowledge the presence of God's kingdom (manifest authority).

Jon Ruthven states, "The very reason Jesus came was to introduce, model, ratify, vindicate, commission and bestow the New Covenant. The New Covenant itself is the Holy Spirit which enables us to communicate directly with God."[198] Jesus said that we are to be both salt and light amid this world in which we now live. Sometimes we tend to forget that it was while we were still sinners that God loved us and

197. Erickson, *Christian Theology*, 1163-1164.

198. Jon Mark Ruthven, *What Is Wrong with Protestant Theology?* (Tulsa, OK: Word & Spirit Press, 2013), 30.

gave His Son to die on the cross for us. Jesus commands us to "love your enemies, bless those who curse you, do good to those who hate you, and pray for those who spitefully use you and persecute you."[199] In other words, by our lifestyle even in the face of unbelief and opposition we are to demonstrate values and an authority that transcends the powers and authorities that oppose us as citizens of the kingdom of God. Beyond the ethical values we might ask ourselves, "Why would we wait until the second coming of Jesus and the millennium to participate in physical healings, miracles, and casting out demons when all these things were accomplished by believers after the resurrection and ascension of Jesus as recorded in the Book of Acts?" The kingdom of God is at hand and as believers we have a responsibility as God's royal priesthood to take initiative against the darkness, perversions, injustices and suffering that permeates the world around us.

The culture in which we now live is moving more and more away from the kingdom values upon which our nation was founded toward a secularized culture. Our sacred values were first marginalized as our culture moved toward excluding God from our laws, courts, and schools, thus developing a system of government that yields to no authority beyond the vote or consent of the majority. Ravi Zacharias made the following statement in a presentation at the University of Florida:

> Secularization is a great idea over against the dictates of religion. But if secularization does not find a transcend ethic to value every single human life it will lead to human slaughter and to a society that does not have any remorse or any guilt or any shame. You show me a human being who never has any remorse, and I will show you a monster! Secularization takes away the grounds for moral reasoning and absolutes,

199. Matt. 5:44.

> and certainly the grounds to treat your fellow human being with intrinsic worth.[200]

Repent and Believe the Gospel:

Jesus began His public ministry with the words "The time is fulfilled, and the kingdom of God is at hand. Repent, and believe in the gospel."[201] The question must be asked, what were the people thinking when Jesus said, "Repent for the kingdom of heaven is at hand."[202] Much of my preaching used the word "repent" as an imperative to stop some sort of sinning. "The Greek word "repent" is *metanoeo,* signifies 'to change one's mind or purpose,' always, in the NT, involving a change for the better."[203] Therefore, Jesus was calling His audience to change their minds regarding how they perceived God's rule, reign, or government over their lives, the nation, and the world. Because He was introducing a new system of government—the kingdom of God. In other words, there is a wrong-headed way to think about government. And Jesus was calling the people to change their mind and perception regarding how they were as individuals to fit into the flow of the government of God or the kingdom of God that He was proclaiming. Jesus wasn't arbitrarily saying, "do it My way or else." He was trying to persuade His audience to receive a gracious upgrade to replace their failing system with the richest blessings ever offered to mankind.

The Holy Spirit is saying today, "The time is fulfilled, and the kingdom is at hand. Repent and believe the gospel." Secularism excludes

---

200. Ravi Zacharias and Vince Vitale, *Jesus and Secular Gods.* University of Florida Open Forum.

https://www.youtube.com/watch?v=-_vTZVIYdR4. (Accessed 3/5/18).

201. Mark 1:15.

202. Matt. 3:2.

203. W. E. Vine, Merrill F. Unger, and William White Jr., *Vine's Complete Expository Dictionary of Old and New Testament Words* (Nashville, TN: T. Nelson, 1996), 525.

the gospel, the kingdom God, and the Lordship of Jesus Christ. Just as in the days of Jesus so it is today, there is an absolute wrong way to do government. When God is excluded from a culture or personal relationships there remains only weak or insufficient, and often oppressive boundaries to guide human behavior. Who is to determine what is right or wrong? It becomes easier to justify a whole range of ungodly character traits that are self-serving, self-righteous, self-destructive including anger, malice, contempt and unforgiveness. History during the twentieth century clearly demonstrated that human nature without God is capable of atrocities almost beyond comprehension. Today, it is a regular occurrence on both our local and national TV news programs that statements are made and video clips are shown of angry individuals and groups of people. These angry people often use vulgar and hateful language and seem to show no restraint when speaking evil of our government officials. This does not make for peace and prosperity, and Jude warns against this kind of rhetoric.[204] This is not what the kingdom of God is about. These are some of the reasons why I believe that the grace of God is sending the wind of the Holy Spirt to blow conviction and revelation through the message of the presence of the kingdom of God.

Jesus gives great insight into life in the kingdom of God through His teaching recorded in the Sermon on the Mount. In his discussion on that sermon, Dallas Willard asks:

> Would people embrace anger and indulge it? Why would they, as they so often do, bloat their bodies with anger and wear it like a badge of honor while it radiates real and potential harm… Often with deadly effects on their own life health and happiness?[205]

---

204. Jude 1:8-19.

205. Dallas Willard, *The Divine Conspiracy: Rediscovering Our Hidden Life in God.* (New York, NY: HarperCollins Publishers, 1997), 149.

We recognize the challenges of the secularization of our culture and find ourselves in a situation similar to that of the Apostles when they responded to the opposition of their government leaders to their preaching on the kingdom of God by saying;

> "'Lord, You *are* God, who made heaven and earth and the sea, and all that is in them, who by the mouth of Your servant David have said: *'Why did the nations rage, And the people plot vain things? The kings of the earth took their stand, And the rulers were gathered together Against the* LORD *and against His Christ'*" (Acts 4:24b-26).

The Apostles not only addressed the challenges that confronted them, they also prayed and asked God to powerfully intervene.

> "Now, Lord, look on their threats, and grant to Your servants that with all boldness they may speak Your word, by stretching out Your hand to heal, and that signs and wonders may be done through the name of Your holy Servant Jesus.' And when they had prayed, the place where they were assembled together was shaken; and they were all filled with the Holy Spirit, and they spoke the word of God with boldness." (Acts 4:29-31).

The Apostles did not passively yield to the threats and opposition of the Jewish officials, but rather, embraced those challenges through prayer and a commitment to speak the word of God with all boldness. They asked God to boldly speak through them "by stretching out His hand to heal, and that signs and wonders may be done through the name of Your holy Servant Jesus."[206] God responded to their prayers by empowering them to proclaim the gospel of the kingdom, not only

206. Acts 4:29-30.

in Jerusalem, but beyond Jerusalem to the far corners of the earth as He confirmed the gospel with healings, signs and wonders.

When the kingdom of God is marginalized or scrubbed from the consciences and lifestyles of individuals and communities, where can one then go to find life's answers? In the midst of all our differences what can we as individuals or families or communities or as a nation rely upon for the justification for our decisions or actions? Should we accept the consensus of the majority as the standard for guiding our lives? Without the rule of God, evil can become good and our lives and relationships are reduced to everyone doing what is right in his or her own eyes. This manner of life sets us up for the kind of ordeals and oppressions experienced by those living during the days of the Book of Judges. During far too many of those days Israel was not the head, but the tail. They often left God out of the lifestyles and as a result failed to enjoy the bountiful provisions that their covenant with God afforded them. The Scripture says,

> Now all these things happened to them as examples, and they were written for our admonition, upon whom the ends of the ages have come. Therefore, let him who thinks he stands take heed lest he fall. (1 Cor. 10:11-12).

All too often New Testament believers tend to live as though the rule of Jesus Christ and the kingdom of God are almost exclusively future and overlook the privileges and values of seeking the presence of the kingdom and the blessings of heaven that are to be experienced now. Jesus said to the Pharisees, "Neither shall they say, Lo here! Or, lo there! For the kingdom of God is within you."[207] E. Stanley Jones states, "The laws of your being are the laws of the kingdom of God.... Therefore, you break its laws within you and you get broken."[208]

---

207. Luke 17:21.
208. Jones, *The Unshakable Kingdom,* 57.

The New Covenant is in reality a kingdom covenant for two reasons: First, the writer of Hebrews quotes the Prophet Jeremiah,[209] and makes it clear that the New Covenant is not written on stone as the Old Covenant was but written on the heart of man out of which flows "the issues of life."[210] The heart is the center of man's personality where thoughts and words originate that guide one's lifestyle. With God's Law written on the heart, man no longer needs a "guardian"[211] to take him to school to teach him to love God. Because all who believe on the Lord Jesus Christ received the "Spirit of Adoption, whereby we cry, Abba, Father;"[212] the Holy Spirit bearing witness with our spirit that we are no longer orphans but the royal children of God and joint heirs with Jesus Christ. Second, at the point of our "born again" experience and the receiving of the "Spirit of Adoption" the Father delivers us from the power of darkness and transfers us into His kingdom,[213] "where we are no longer strangers and foreigners, but fellow citizens with the saints and members of the household of God."[214]

Therefore, according to the New Covenant we have a twofold relationship with God as both royal sons and citizens of His kingdom resulting from our new birth, adoption and transference from the power of darkness into the kingdom of the Son of His love. Our sonship and citizenship mean that we, in the core of our very being, are partakers of the Father's life and sovereignty. For some of us the confident hope of eternal life is well woven into the fabric of our faith, but it is a little scary to participate in the sovereignty of God. But Jesus said, "All authority has been given to Me in heaven and on earth."[215] When we live in harmony with the presence of the kingdom of God, His blessing will overtake us regardless of our outward circumstances. We cannot

---

209. Heb. 8:10-11, 10:16: Jer. 31:33.
210. Prov. 4:23.
211. Gal. 4:2.
212. Rom. 8:15-16.
213. Col.1:13
214. Eph. 2:19.
215. Matt. 28:18.

live in opposition to the presence of the kingdom of God and expect to be overcomers.

We believe that we are endowed by our Creator with certain inalienable rights, but if we leave the Creator out of our laws, decisions and lifestyles, we expose ourselves to the possibility of people trying to impose godless authority over our lives that would create conflicts with no winners. Even as citizens of the kingdom of God, circumstances become twisted and conflicts arise when we lean on our own understanding. The Scripture says, "There is a way that seems right to man, but its end is the way of death."[216] God is the source of wisdom and our relationship with Him enables us to live in an environment of security and prosperity. That kind of relationship with God is possible because of three factors: (1) While we were still sinners God so loved us that He sent His Son Jesus to die on the cross for the remission of our sins. (2) Jesus was raised from the dead for our justification and offers us the gift of the faith that enables believers to be reconciled to God our Creator. (3) We have also been given the gift of the empowering presence of God the Holy Spirit to guide us into truth and fruitfulness as sons of God and citizens of the kingdom of God.

Sometimes we fail to perceive the presence of the kingdom of God and consider the battle to be between us and other people rather than with the powers of darkness and the spiritual host of wickedness in heavenly places. We as believers, have the responsibility and privilege to co-labor with Jesus Christ in overcoming the forces that oppose God. Remember, the Lord taught us to pray "Your kingdom come, and Your will be done on earth as it is in heaven!"[217] Our responsibility is to align ourselves with the purposes of God and ask Him to empower us to speak boldly and stretch out His hand to heal the sick and do signs and wonders through us for Jesus' sake! This gospel of the kingdom is not in word only, but in the power and demonstration

---

216. Prov. 14:12.
217. Matt. 6:10.

of the Holy Spirit.[218] Our personal strength is limited, but with God nothing is impossible. The Lord has taken an oath saying, “But truly, as I live, all the earth shall be filled with the glory of the LORD”[219] The leaders and governments of this world do not have the final word, God does! Let us therefore, fervently pray for His kingdom to come, and His will be done on earth as it is in heaven! Let us put on the armor of light and confidently and lovingly lift the banner of truth by proclaiming the gospel of the kingdom, because God’s dominion is an undiminished reality. The Psalmist says, “The LORD has established His throne in heaven, And His kingdom rules overall.”[220]

Summary:

In summary, God is an invisible Spirit, eternal Father, and a sovereign King.[221] Before the foundation of the world He purposed in the council of His will to manifest His invisible nature, to create and regenerate a family and to manifest the presence of His kingdom through the following means: (1) God willed to bring forth a royal family of sons and daughters and manifest His kingdom out of the resources of His Fatherhood, His Sovereignty and His Grace. (2) God’s means for administrating His family and kingdom would be through His covenants. (3) The purpose for His administration would be the glory of having a royal family of sons and daughters who would love Him and His Son with a love tested in time and proven by fire, and would joyfully co-labor with Him forever.

The presence of the kingdom of God is at hand, but life in the kingdom of God is like living in a foreign country to all new believers. Therefore, we are instructed by the Lord Jesus to make it a personal priority to “seek first the kingdom of God and His righteousness.”[222]

---

218. John 10:37-38; 1 Cor. 2:4.
219. Num. 14:21.
220. Psa. 103:19.
221. Heb. 12:9.
222. Matt. 6:33.

We must adjust ourselves to the realities of our citizenship in the kingdom of God and face the opposition of the forces of evil operating in the fabric of our culture as we shine as lights in the darkness. The good news is that Jesus the King of kings has gone before us and gained the victory over the devil, sin, death, and hell. Now He is seated in heaven on the throne at the right-hand of the Father and ever lives to make intercession for us. Also, God the Father has sent the Holy Spirit through the Lord Jesus to help us and guide us in paths of righteousness and empower us to live as overcomers. The next chapter will discuss the priorities of the kingdom of God, and how those priorities impact our lives and the world in which we live.

CHAPTER TWO

THE PRIORITY OF THE KINGDOM

"But seek first the kingdom of God and His righteousness, and all these things shall be added to you."
(Matthew 6:33)

Our world is filled with voices and noises many of which are seeking our attention and often our time or money. As we endeavor to live a Christian life we are challenged with how to best steward our time, talent, and resources. Do we focus on personal devotions and discipleship, evangelizing the lost, feeding the poor, educating the young, showing mercy to those suffering injustices and a wide variety of other opportunities needing attention? All of us are surely doing more than just one thing, but none of us can do everything. So, as children of God and citizens of the kingdom of God, what are our priorities? All of us live with the desire of one day hearing our Lord say, "Well done, good and faithful servant; you were faithful over a few things, I will make you a ruler over many things."[223] Wouldn't it be a tragedy to have exhausted our days and to stand before God, only to learn that we had spent our lives on the wrong issues or secondary priorities? I recently heard of a lady who was flying from Los Angeles

223. Matt.25:21, 23.

to Denver with her dog. When she arrived at Denver baggage area she learned that her dog had been mistakenly put on the wrong plane and at that moment was in flight for Japan. This reminds us of the Prophet who was commanded to go to Nineveh but got his priorities reversed and boarded a ship headed for Spain. Thank the Lord for the grace that preserved him from a watery grave as he reordered his agenda and embraced the priorities of the Lord.

Life presents us with many opportunities for spiritual growth and advancement in the kingdom of God. But those same opportunities often present us with seemingly contradictory choices and possibilities that challenge our ability to set the correct priorities. We gain insight regarding kingdom priorities from an example in the early life of Jesus. He so aligned Himself with kingdom priorities that even at the age of twelve His parents found Him after a three-day search in the Temple sitting amid teachers and astonishing them with His understanding. When His anxious parents asked Him why He had not followed them in returning to their home in Nazareth; He responded by asking them, "Did you not know that I must be about My Father's business?"[224] As it was in Jesus' life, so it must be in our lives—the top priority is being "about our Father's business."

Kingdom Priorities Transform Lives:

The Lord Jesus further guides our understanding regarding kingdom priorities by teaching this principle: "Seek first the Kingdom of God and His righteousness."[225] In other words, it is each believer's responsibility to put the first thing first. And our top priority is to align ourselves with God's governmental or kingdom agenda for our life this day, and every day. As Jesus said to His Father, "Not My will, but Yours, be done."[226] This doesn't sound difficult or challenging, except for the fact that we live in a "Me First" culture. As a result, we

224. Luke 2:49.
225. Matt.6:33.
226. Luke 22:42.

are constantly faced with pressures from the world around us seeking to influence how we use our words, and spend our time, money, and energy. Even simple things like starting the day with prayer and Bible reading can be a challenge and may lose its place in the priority of our day. The financial demands of unexpected expenses or unwise purchases can easily overshadow the priority of tithes and offerings that belong to the Lord. Busyness can become a trademark of our schedule that so influences our energies until the end of the day we feel totally spent and exhausted. Then when we reflect over our day, we realize we did not dedicate any portion of it to God in quietness and holy contemplation. And just before we fall into bed we get another call or text that leaves us feeling a bit overwhelmed and we wonder: "Will this ever end?" "Why is this happening to me?" "Where is God?" When it is as the song says, "He was there all the time."[227] We must honestly ask ourselves, "Have I been keeping my agenda in an alignment with God's priorities?" God is gracious, merciful, longsuffering, and forgiving, but each of us has the responsibility of keeping our priorities aligned with God's priorities and guarding ourselves against the possibility of falling into the trap of busyness, negativity, or unbelief.

When we experience weariness of seemingly endless challenges remember to cast our cares upon Him because He cares for each of us.[228] And if we find ourselves trapped between a rock and a wall it will be helpful to ask this question; "Lord what is it that You want me to learn from this situation that You have not been able to teach me from other situations?" Keeping in mind that we are not ultimately seeking simple answers to gain information but seeking to be transformed into the likeness and stature of Jesus Christ as the sons and daughters of our Creator and heavenly Father. Jesus came to earth and died on the cross in order to bring "many sons to glory."[229] That is a fundamental priority of the Father's business. Beyond the priority of

227. He Was There All the Time – Hymn Lyrics. https://www.hymnlyrics.org/newlyrics_h/he_was_there_all_the_time.php (Accessed 5/30/18).

228. 1 Peter 5:7.

229. Heb. 2:10.

a personal relationship with our heavenly Father, there is a work assignment for each one of us in the administration of His kingdom in the here and now. However, a personal relationship with God has a priority over working for God.

To determine our personal priorities, it may require some further understanding regarding the nature of God and what He has chosen as His priorities. Since we are created in His image and likeness, it is insightful to focus on His nature. First, we must always keep in mind that God is not a thing or a force or an impersonal being, but an incomprehensible person. Millard J. Erickson explains:

> The doctrine of God is the central point for much of the rest of theology. One's view of God might even be thought of as supplying the whole framework within which one's theology is constructed, life is lived, and ministry is conducted.... When we speak of the incomprehensibility of God, then, we do not mean that there is an unknown being or essence beyond or behind his attributes. Rather, we mean that we do not know his qualities or his nature completely and exhaustively.... God is spirit; that is, he is not composed of matter and does not possess a physical nature.... He is an individual being, with self-consciousness and will, capable of feeling, choosing, and having a reciprocal relationship with other personal and social beings.[230]

The nature of God is beyond our comprehension to fully or completely grasp. But God has chosen to reveal Himself to us to the extent that we are enabled to draw near Him, love Him, and know Him intimately. God desires communion with us even though His thoughts and ways are higher than our thoughts and ways as far as the heavens

---

230. Erickson, *Christian Theology*, 290-295.

are above the earth.[231] His nature includes His sovereignty and His sovereignty is the essence of His authority.[232] He governs the universe, directing all things, working all things "according to the counsel of His will."[233] Our purpose is to search and carefully consider why God does what He does in order to look beyond His acts and perceive His ways.[234] It is Scripturally clear that we were chosen in Christ before the foundation of the world and the Father predestined us to adoption as sons by Jesus Christ to Himself, according to the good pleasure of His will.[235] This truth provides insight into the reality that God the Father, God the Son, and God the Holy Spirit chose to bind themselves together in the accomplishment of the counsel of their will and purpose through a legal and just commitment to each other that preceded creation. The members of the Godhead bound themselves together in the Everlasting Covenant before the creation of man.[236]

The Kingdom Charter/Covenant:

The Everlasting Covenant is the charter or constitution that guides the administration of the kingdom of God. It was designed by the Godhead to accomplish four divine objectives: (1) creation, (2) redemption, (3) anointings, and (4) the creation of new heavens and new earth wherein dwells righteousness.[237] Through these means God makes known His nature, His eternal purposes, and His glory. He presents you and me with the privileged invitation of participating with Him in the fulfillment of these kingdom objectives. The Bible records these as prophetic objectives, providing both the details of their inauguration and their expected manifestations in time. Conner and Malmin state;

231. Isa. 55:9.
232. Rom. 13:1.
233. Eph. 1:11.
234. Psa. 103:7.
235. Eph. 1:4-5.
236. Heb. 13:20-21.
237. 2 Peter 3:10-13.

> "The 'everlasting covenant' is an eternal covenant because it is not a covenant between God and man, though it involves man. It is a covenant between the persons of the eternal Godhead, the Father, Son and Holy Spirit. Each person in the Godhead would fulfill their part in the contract which involved creation and redemption. The eternal characteristics of the Godhead are thus stamped upon this covenant as well as all other covenants."[238]

God is love and His love never fails,[239] but Scripture does not teach that God loves all things. For example, the Scripture clearly teaches that God hates idols.[240] Therefore, the Everlasting Covenant precedes the creation and fall of man and guides the expressions of God's love as His creation experiences His redemption from evil and sin. Before God created this world including mankind, He determined to set in motion a progressive redemptive process to be expedited through a series of covenants with mankind. Those covenants culminate with the new covenant thus fulfilling the intent of the everlasting covenant. The Adamic, Noahic, Abrahamic, Mosaic, Davidic and New Covenant all express God's redemptive relationships with mankind and flow out of the framework of the everlasting covenant. Consequently, the everlasting covenant guides the administration of the kingdom of God just as the constitution of the United States guides the administration of our government. The everlasting covenant is an everlasting commitment of unconditional love that binds each person in the Godhead to specific obligations to each of the other persons in the Godhead for the purposes of creation, redemption, anointings, and the new heavens and new earth which will be the ultimate expression of the New Covenant.

---

238. Conner and Malmin, *The Covenants,* 93.
239. 1 Cor. 13:8.
240. Deut. 12:29-31.

God willed to create man in His own image and likeness and from the body of the man formed a woman. From that original man and woman, He willed to propagate a family of millions of sons and daughters in His image and likeness. Each of those persons will have the nobility of a free will. That means each person would have the liberty to choose to obey God or choose not to obey God. Therefore, the persons of the Godhead bound themselves to each other in an obligation to complete all that was necessary to have a godly family even if it cost them their life.[241] This reveals some insights about the Trinity and why God does some of the things He does.

Kingdom Objectives:

It is this author's assumption that God had at least four objectives even before Adam was created. (1) Create a family of sons and daughters in His image and likeness that would in response to His grace become partakers of His divine nature, loving Him with all their heart, soul, and mind. (2) And out of the midst of His family raise up a Savior/Redeemer/Messiah, a God/man that would Himself be a propitiation for the sins of the world through the shedding of His own blood on the cross, paying the penalty and judgment for sin and gaining victory over death through His bodily resurrection. And finally, He would cast that serpent of old, called the Devil and Satan, and his followers into the eternal lake of fire, legally and completely cleansing and eliminating the presence of evil from heaven and earth. (3) God will anoint a kingdom of priests to serve as His ambassadors bearing witness to His presence and administer the blessing of His kingdom in the midst of this world until the fullness of time when the kingdoms of this world will become the kingdoms of our God and His Christ.[242] (4) Prepare a bride for His Beloved Son and dissolve the present heavens and earth with a fervent heat and create new heavens and a new earth

241. John 3:16; 1 John 4:8-12.
242. Rev. 11:15.

as a glorious dwelling place for His Son and His bride.[243] Thereafter, God and His redeemed family will dwell together in glory forever, world without end.

But what insights does this reveal regarding God's relationship with the persons He intends to have in His eternal family after the plan of redemption has reached its consummation? To answer this question, we will look at some examples of God relationships with His sons and daughters. First, God created Adam and Eve placed them in the Garden of Eden, which seemed like a perfect environment, yet they willfully disobeyed God. Some have asked, "Why didn't God destroy Adam and Eve and start over right there and then with new persons instead of redeeming them who had become infected with the malignancy of sin and evil?"

For God to destroy Adam and Eve and start again by creating another man and woman would have constituted a violation of the Everlasting Covenant which the Trinity made among themselves before the foundation of the world with its provision for redemption. It is true that Adam and Eve had become infected by sin and evil. But the wisdom of the Everlasting Covenant had made every provision for their redemption which would overcome both sin and evil with righteousness and goodness.

A violation of the Everlasting Covenant would be impossible because God cannot lie and has magnified His word above His name.[244] The Lord has taken an oath saying, "Truly, as I live, all the earth shall be filled with the glory of the Lord."[245] What God says He will do, He does. Man himself, could never accomplish the four objectives listed above, but God the Father, God the Son, and God the Holy Spirit have determined to do it and it will be done. God so loves the world that He predetermined according to the Everlasting Covenant to make the world savable by committing to become man Himself and pay the full

243. 2 Peter 3:10-13.
244. Psa. 138:2; Titus 1:1-3.
245. Num. 14:21.

cost of man's eternal salvation. He would accomplish this grand and righteous plan of salvation "to the praise of the glory of His grace, by which He has made us accepted in the Beloved"[246] and granted us the blessed hope of eternity with Him!!

Consequently, because of Adam's transgression, God according to His covenantal wisdom made an atonement for Adam's sin through the substitutionary sacrifice of an animal that took Adam's place in death. God then took the skin of the animal and covered Adam's nakedness. God's actions expressed His holy, loving, and merciful nature according to the provisions of the Everlasting Covenant. According to that covenant God's only begotten Son, the "last Adam,"[247] would freely give His life as a ransom by shedding His blood as a substitutionary sacrifice on the cross making the salvation of sinners possible.[248] At the cross God condemned sin in the flesh and Jesus gave His life as a ransom for sinners.[249] At the resurrection of Jesus, death was swallowed up in victory.[250]

First Adam and Last Adam:

A further word regarding the "last Adam" may prove helpful in this discussion. "The first man Adam became a living soul"[251] when God breathed His breath into his nostrils. But the key to understanding a great difference between the "first Adam" and the "last Adam" is that the "first Adam" was only a "type of Him who was to come."[252] Look at it this way; suppose you are the owner of a very expensive painting that is requested to be exhibited at an art gallery. You want to protect your exquisite painting, so you have a copy made by a high-quality copier and present the copy for exhibition at the art gallery. To the naked eye the difference between the original and the copy would not

246. Eph. 1:6, 12, 14.
247. 1 Cor. 15:45; Mark 10:45.
248. Heb. 2:17.
249. Rom. 8:3; Mark 10:45.
250. 1 Cor. 15:54.
251. Gen. 2:7, 5:1-27; Rom. 5:18-21.
252. Rom. 5:14.

be distinguishable. At the art gallery exhibition someone viciously damages your painting. However, you as the owner are not ruined because it was only a copy, and you still have the original exquisite painting! The "first Adam" was only a type or copy of Him who was to come, whereas the "last Adam," Jesus the Son of God is the original exquisite "life giving Spirit." When the "first Adam" disobeyed God and marred his life with sin and death, it did not ruin God's plan to have sons and daughters in His image and likeness. God could continue His plan for a family through a new creation accomplished by His Son, Jesus Christ. "For if by the one man's offense death reigned through the one, much more those who receive abundance of grace and of the gift of righteousness will reign in life through the One, Jesus Christ."[253]

As a result of Adam's transgression and the entrance of sin into this world, two major problems were created: First, a legal problem emerged regarding man's offence and injustice against the holiness of God which alienated man from God. Once alienated from God, man became an enemy of God with the need of a Savior to make a propitiation for sin and thus satisfy the wrath of God making reconciliation with God possible. Mankind needed a Savior that would pay the wages of sin and deliver him from eternal separation from God and grant the gift of righteousness. Second, mankind not only needed a Savior to restore his relationship with God but a Savior to provide a solution to the breakdown between man and man. For example, there was a relational breakdown between Cain and Abel that resulted in murder. As a result, a Savior was needed to make forgiveness possible lest mankind destroy each other and the possibility of God having a family of sons and daughters.

During the years between the first Adam's sin and the last Adam's payment for sin by death on the cross, God overlooked sin although the consequences of sin was death and people died.[254] But, "sin was

253. Rom. 5:17.
254. Rom. 5:12-14.

not imputed when there was no law."[255] For example, Noah and Abraham built altars and offered burnt offerings to the Lord, but never sin offerings or trespass offerings.[256] There is no record where they asked for forgiveness. But during the days of Moses, God gave the Law and made expressed provision for the forgiveness of sin through sacrificial animals offered to God through faith in "the Lamb of God" which was to come. Those Old Testament sacrifices could not wash away sin nor cleanse the damaging result of sin. But God accepted those sacrifices offered in faith and forgave those who offered them and asked for forgiveness until the fullness of time when His only begotten Son, Jesus, was born into this world. Jesus' submission to John's baptism is a demonstration of His humility and obedience to the righteous demands of the Law of God as He began His work of redemption.[257] Jesus then received the anointing of the Holy Spirit, followed the leading of the Spirit into the Wilderness to be tempted by the devil just as Adam and every person experiences the temptations.[258] Following His victory over the temptations of the devil, He returned in the power of the Spirit and testified to the reality of God's plan of salvation and the presence of the kingdom of God.[259] He then laid His life down on the cross as our substitute, bearing our judgment and paying the wages of sin as our Savior. Sin separated and alienated man from God, and man from man, but God had already made provision for man's salvation and reconciliation through the Everlasting Covenant. At the heart of God's plan of salvation is the ministry of reconciliation through Jesus Christ.[260]

---

255. Rom. 5:13; Acts 17:30
256. Gen. 8:20, 12:7-8.
257. Matt. 3:15-16.
258. Heb. 4:15.
259. Luke 4:14-19.
260. 2 Cor. 5:18-19.

The Marriage Covenant:

From the creation of Adam and Eve the marriage covenant was instituted by God. The marriage of a man and a woman is not simply two individuals of the opposite sex living together and bearing children. No! Marriage is a sacred covenantal institution ordained by God consisting of three persons—God, one man and one woman for the propagation of humanity in the context of God given blessings and responsibilities. God's redemptive actions toward Adam and Eve provide insights for husbands and wives regarding the pathway of victory over sin and failure while offering hope for the future. This is often true when parents have loved their children and done all they can do to provide an environment for their success, and then a child goes in every direction except the straight and narrow. That is a heart-breaking experience for parents and for God. But God the Father's actions of mercy and forgiveness towards Adam and Eve reveal the powerful bond of love that parents have for their children. As parents we love our children before they are born, and by God's grace we continue to love them even if they rebel and go astray, even as God loves us. God challenges us to a high standard of love and says, "Greater love has no one than this, than to lay down one's life for his friends."[261] Consider the powerful truth in the following verses:

> **<u>But God demonstrates His own love toward us, in that while we were still sinners, Christ died for us</u>**. Much more then, having now been justified by His blood, we shall be saved from wrath through Him. For if **<u>when we were enemies</u>** we were reconciled to God through the death of His Son, much more, having been reconciled, we shall be saved by His life." (Romans. 5:8-10; emphasis is mine).

261. John 15:13.

When we experience the pain and suffering resulting from sin and evil we ourselves may be tempted to ask, "Why didn't God simply destroy Adam and start over building the human race with someone new?" The answer is because God loved His son, Adam, with an everlasting love, just like He loves you and me! It was not because we were good that Jesus died for us. No! Jesus died on the cross for us while we were His enemies and sinners. That is an expression of the God kind of love!

According to God's Father nature and the terms of the Everlasting Covenant it was impossible for God to destroy Adam. To the extent of God's unlimited power and bound by the terms of the Everlasting Covenant the Trinity was committed to redeem Adam and Eve and they did! This was possible because God was viewing sinful mankind through the person and work of Jesus, His only begotten Son. God's priority of creating and redeeming a family of sons and daughters bearing His image and likeness was established in the context of the Everlasting Covenant between the members of the Trinity before the creation of Adam. However, Adam's disobedience introduced sin into this world and it separated man from God. But the terms of the Everlasting Covenant made provision for the gospel of the kingdom to all who would believe on the Lord Jesus as Savior and Lord. However, "the gospel is veiled to those who are perishing whose minds the god of this age has blinded,"[262] But we as believers are commissioned by the Lord Jesus Christ to "go therefore and make disciples of all nations, baptizing them in the name of the Father and the Son and the Holy Spirit, teaching them to observe all things that" Jesus commanded us.[263] As we go proclaiming the gospel of the kingdom and bearing witness to a personal relationship with God through the redemptive love of Jesus Christ, we don't go alone. The Holy Spirit not only goes before us to convict the world of sin, righteousness and judgment;[264]

---

262. 2 Cor. 4:3-4.
263. Matt. 28:19-20.
264. John 16:8.

He also dwells in our hearts and empowers us to bear witness to the presence and power of God that gives us grace and guidance through the challenges of life as we daily seek first the kingdom of God and His righteousness. And as citizens of the kingdom of God we have been given the blessed hope that transcends this world and anchors our soul in a glorious future in the family of God.

Although the Godhead committed themselves to the everlasting covenant it is important to keep in mind that it is the love of God that initiated that covenant and that kind of love "never fails."[265] I have heard Dr. Ronald E. Cottle teach that Jesus Christ gave a new level of meaning to the Greek word "*agape.*" It is a love that is willing to serve rather than be served, a love that extends to your enemies without cursing them but blessing them.[266] The expression of this kind of love is "the more excellent way,"[267] and so powerful that it is commended as the greatest of all virtues. All the Law hangs on loving God and loving your neighbor.[268]

The Spirit of Grace:

Another example of God's relationships with mankind that reveal insights into His nature and kingdom purposes is found in His relationship with mankind in the days of Noah. Probably more than fifteen hundred years had passed since Adam and Eve had been expelled from the Garden of Eden. The presence of sin and evil had reached the point where "the wickedness of man was great on the earth" and "the Lord was sorry that He had made man" as the following Scripture records:

> Then the LORD saw that the wickedness of man *was* great in the earth, and *that* **every intent of the**

265. John 3:16; 1 Cor. 13:8.
266. Matt. 5:44.
267. 1 Cor. 12:31, 13:13.
268. Matt. 22:37-40.

> **thoughts of his heart *was* only evil continually**. And the **LORD was sorry that He had made man** on the earth, and He was grieved in His heart. So, the LORD said, '**I will destroy man whom I have created** from the face of the earth, both man and beast, creeping thing and birds of the air, **for I am sorry that I have made them**.' But **Noah found grace in the eyes of the LORD**. This is the genealogy of Noah. Noah was a just man, perfect in his generations. Noah walked with God. And Noah begot three sons: Shem, Ham, and Japheth. The earth also was corrupt before God, and the earth was filled with violence. So, God looked upon the earth, and indeed it was corrupt; for all flesh had corrupted their way on the earth. And God said to Noah, '**The end of all flesh has come before Me**, for the earth is filled with violence through them; and behold, **I will destroy them with the earth**.' (Gen. 6:5-13; emphasis is mine).

Due to the extent of man's wickedness, corruption and violence God was grieved that He had made man. Now "the LORD said, 'I will destroy man whom I have created from the face of the earth, both man and beast, creeping things and birds of the air, for I am sorry that I have made them.'"[269] In other words man had "been weighed in the balances and found wanting."[270] We ask ourselves, "Why did the people become so wicked and vile that God was sorry that He had made man?" A major factor was the god of this world had blinded their minds to truth and the deceptive and corruptive nature of sin had warped man's understanding with self-centered pride and self-righteousness.

---

269. Gen. 6:7.
270. Dan. 5:27.

There is pleasure in sin for a season, but sin is deceitful and when the season of pleasure is over we are left with emptiness, regrets, disillusioned and feeling foolish. And somehow, we know that there should be more to life than the barrenness and dissatisfaction we are experiencing. That is the exact opposite of what God intends. He has made every provision for man to reign in life through His blessings of godly wisdom, abundant grace, and holiness. That is why Jesus teaches us to "Seek first the kingdom of God and His righteousness, and all these things shall be added to you."[271] However if we allow ourselves to become preoccupied with the practice of sin, we will become hardened by its deceitfulness and held captive by the god of this world to do his will.[272] And in that captivity of godless self-centeredness and bondage to sinful practices, habits, and addictions we will end up with pain, suffering, and meaninglessness. Suffering and meaninglessness are the fruits of sin and evil. And that was the destiny of the generation on the earth in Noah's day; they lost everything. The scary thing for us is found in the following words of Jesus;

> Heaven and earth will pass away, but My words will by no means pass away. But of that day and hour no one knows, not even the angels of heaven, but My Father only. But **as the days of Noah *were*, so also will the coming of the Son of Man be**. For as in the days before the flood, they were eating and drinking, marrying and giving in marriage, until the day that Noah entered the ark, and did not know until the flood came and took them all away, **so also will the coming of the Son of Man be**. (Matthew 24:35-39; emphasis mine).

271. Matt. 6:33.
272. 2 Tim. 2:26.

There are two powerful truths from the Days of Noah that give insight to God's priorities regarding the kingdom of God: (1) In the midst of the wickedness and violence Noah found grace in the eyes of the Lord. (2) Jesus warns us of a generation in the last days that will embrace the same characteristics as the culture of Noah's day. This is the first-time grace is mentioned in the Bible.[273] Later in Scripture the Bible is called "the word of His grace."[274] God's grace is the fountain from which He dispenses His love. The Holy Spirit is called "the Spirit of Grace."[275]

First, in the midst of the wickedness and violence Noah found grace in the eyes of the Lord. The culture of Noah's day had turned their backs on God and had given themselves over to sinful lifestyles. Ravi Zacharias defines sin as, "Redefining God's intended purpose for your life and charting your own course."[276] However, Noah did not go with the flow of the culture around him but followed the priorities of the Lord. He listened to the voice of God's grace and responded in obedient faith as he was "moved with godly fear, prepared an ark for the saving of his household."[277] All the people of his day except for his wife, their three sons and their wives were destroyed by the flood waters. But Noah and his family were saved through the flood waters.[278] Their salvation was because "Noah found grace in the eyes of the Lord!"[279] P. E. Hughes states,

> Grace always means that it is God who takes the initiative and implies the priority of God's action on the behalf of needy sinners. That is the whole point of Grace: it does not start with us it starts with God; it is

273. Gen. 6:8.

274. Acts 20:32.

275. Heb. 10:29.

276. Ravi Zacharias and Vince Vitale, *Why Suffering? Finding Meaning and Comfort When Life Doesn't Make Sense* (New York, NY: FaithWorks, 2014), 42.

277. Heb. 11:7.

278. 1 Peter 3:20.

279. Gen. 6:8.

> not earned or merited by us, it is freely and lovingly given to us who have no resources or deservings of our own.[280]

Noah and his family experiencing the grace of God reveals the operational power of the presence of God that favored them. It is the same God that loves you and me and the world for which Jesus died. The concept of grace includes all that Jesus did for us through His life and His death on the cross. God's grace empowers us to cooperate with truth through which faith is birthed in our hearts. We are powerless to save ourselves but "by grace you have been saved through faith."[281] The Message translation helps us even better understand the power of grace from the Ephesians passage:

> Now God has us where he wants us, with all the time in this world and the next to shower grace and kindness upon us in Christ Jesus. Saving is all his idea, and all his work. All we do is trust him enough to let him do it. It's God's gift from start to finish! We don't play the major role. If we did, we'd probably go around bragging that we'd done the whole thing! No, we neither make nor save ourselves. God does both the making and saving. He creates each of us by Christ Jesus to join him in the work he does, the good work he has gotten ready for us to do, work we had better be doing.[282] (Eph. 2:7-10; The Message)

---

280. P.E. Hughes, "Grace," *Evangelical Dictionary of Bible Theology,* Walter A. Elwell, ed. (Grand Rapids, MI: Baker Book House Company, 2001), 520.

281. Eph. 2:8.

282. Eugene H. Peterson, *The Message: The Bible in Contemporary Language* (Colorado Springs, CO: NavPress, 2005), Eph 2:7–10.

The Spirit of Truth:

Second, Jesus warns us of a generation in the last days that will demonstrate the same characteristics or qualities as the people of Noah's day. We need to take this warning seriously because there always is a tension in our human experience where our Adamic nature demands control. But we intend to harness that created propensity for dominion with the character of the "new man" in Christ-like humility. And at the same time, we exercise our God given authority as His sons and citizens of the kingdom of God as His witnesses in this world as Noah did. Dallas Willard states:

> In creating human beings God made them to rule, to reign, to have dominion in a limited sphere. Only so can they be persons.... He intended to be our constant companion or co-worker in the creative enterprise of life on earth. That is what his love means for us in practical terms.... Apart from God, our nature-imposed objectives go awry.[283]

In Noah's day people were living lives filled with activity but without the knowledge of God's presence. One of the factors contributing to meaninglessness is the absence of truth. Truth has the referent of reality. We are living in a world like Noah's in the sense that there is a diminishing respect for Truth. For example, in 2016 the renowned Oxford Dictionary word of the year was "'post-truth'- an adjective defined as relating to or denoting circumstances in which objective facts are less influential in shaping public opinion than appeals to emotion and personal belief."[284] Life without truth is vanity, emptiness, and self-centered. A priority and objective of our present culture is secularism or government without God. For Believers to be

283. Willard, *The Divine Conspiracy,* 21-23.

284. Oxford Dictionary. https://en.oxforddictionaries.com/word-of-the-year/word-of-the-year-2016 (Accessed 7/7/18).

"overcomers" in our present world they must firmly reject the concept of "post-truth" and whole-heartily embrace "the Spirit of truth."[285] George Eldon Ladd states:

> Jesus demanded violent conduct of those who would be his disciples. "If any one comes to me and does not hate his own father and mother and wife and children and brothers and sisters, yes, and even his own life, he cannot be my disciple" (Luke 14:26). He said that he came not to bring peace but a sword (Matt. 10:34). In his parables, he taught that a man should be willing to surrender everything he possesses to secure the Kingdom of God (Matt. 13:44 ff.). He told a rich man that he must rid himself of all his earthly possessions to enter the Kingdom (Mark 10:21). The presence of the Kingdom demands radical, violent conduct. Men cannot passively await the coming of the eschatological Kingdom as the apocalyptists taught. On the contrary, the Kingdom has come to them, and they are actively, aggressively, forcefully to seize it.[286]

One of the greatest deceivers is the love of money because it will "choke the word of God so that faith becomes unfruitful" in our lives.[287] "For the love of money is a root of all *kinds of* evil, for which some have strayed from the faith in their greediness, and pierced themselves through with many sorrows."[288] When we stray from the faith we forfeit our ability to trust God which leads to an inability to trust other people. This is one cause of failures in marriage in Noah's day and in our day. Our salvation is first a work of the Holy Spirit in one's heart. In other words, faith is first an "inside job." It is in the

285. John 14:17, 15:26, 16:13.
286. Ladd, *The Presence,* 163-164.
287. Mark 4:19.
288. 1 Tim. 6:10.

heart where the incorruptible seed germinates faith out of the implanted word of God and manifests itself in one's actions inspired by "faith working through love."[289] When the word of truth is rejected, one is left without a defense against the deceptions of the devil. The deception of money causes people to trust it to bring success and happiness, but it will not. But one of the things that the love of money will lead to is covetousness which the tenth commandment forbids. Jesus uses the parable of "the rich fool" to teach us that life does not consist in the abundance of things we possess.[290] Ravi Zacharias provides further insights into this principle;

> "Without the cross there is no glory for man.... I am absolutely convinced that meaninglessness does not come from being weary of pain; meaninglessness comes from being weary of pleasure. And that is why we find ourselves emptied of meaning with our pantries still full.... When man lives apart from God, chaos is the norm. When man lives with God, as revealed in the incarnation of Jesus Christ, the hungers of the mind and heart find their fulfillment."[291]

Jesus teaches us to "seek first the kingdom of God and all these things will be added to us."[292] However, being a citizen in the kingdom of God does not eliminate the responsibility of work and good stewardship. Grace positions believers in the sphere of God's blessings or the presence of His operational power that favors them. It is from the fountain of God's grace that all blessings flow. The Apostle Paul said, "But by the grace of God I am what I am, and His grace toward me was not in vain; but I labored more abundantly than they

---

289. Gal. 5:6.

290. Luke 12:

291. Ravi Zacharias, *Can Man Live without God* (Dallas, TX: Word Publishing, 1994), 178-179.

292. Matt. 6:33.

all, yet not I, but the grace of God *which was* with me."[293] So it is in the final analysis that New Testament Believers gain victory over the corruptions and deceptions of this world in the same way that Noah did, by the grace of God. God is gracious to everyone, and His grace can be received or rejected. There is only one way to receive God's grace and that is through faith, and Jesus is the Author and finisher of our faith. In other words, faith is a gift that comes through the word of God, but we are responsible to act in faith and not simply be passive. It is like a football halfback that is designated to catch a short pass from the quarterback. When the quarterback passes the ball, the halfback has the responsibility to catch the ball and run with it. The halfback would soon be off the team if he simply watched the ball come toward him and did not take the proper action to catch it and gain yardage! The receiving of grace is to ignite faith. Noah found grace in the eyes of the Lord and responded in faith. "By faith Noah, being divinely warned of things not yet seen, moved with godly fear, prepared an ark for the saving of his household, by which he condemned the world and became heir of the righteousness which is according to faith."[294] Notice that the grace that Noah received came to him as a word from God; being "divinely warned." He was "moved with godly fear and prepared an ark for the saving of his household." He took the word of warning very seriously, as we should. "We then, *as* workers together *with Him* also plead with *you* not to receive the grace of God in vain."[295] It is the responsibility of every believer in this generation to embrace the grace of God by making it a top priority to "seek first the kingdom of God and His righteousness," and not be entrapped by the violence and ungodliness of the culture around us. It is the believer's responsibility to take the necessary steps of faith to bring his or her household into that place of safety provided for our eternal salvation in the Lord Jesus Christ, the Savior of the world.

293. 1 Cor. 15:10
294. Heb. 11:7.
295. 2 Cor. 6:1.

Remember, "The Lord is not slack concerning *His* promise, as some count slackness, but is longsuffering toward us, not willing that any should perish but that all should come to repentance."[296]

To Obey Is Better than Sacrifice:

A third example of God's relationships with mankind that reveal insights into His nature and kingdom priorities is found in His relationship with Abraham. God called Abraham to leave his native land of Ur of the Chaldeans. God promised to make Abraham into a great nation and in him all the families of the earth would be blessed.[297] "By faith Abraham obeyed when he was called to go out to the place which he would receive as an inheritance. And he went out, not knowing where he was going."[298] Abraham obeyed God's call and "to obey is better than sacrifice."[299] Abraham first traveled from Ur of the Chaldeans to the city of Haran where his father died. At age seventy-five years he left Haran and took his wife Sarah and Lot his nephew with him.[300] Abraham journeyed until he came to the land of Canaan. He went first to Shechem where he built an altar unto the Lord and the Lord appeared to him and promised to give him that land.[301]

The Lord blessed Abraham and he became rich in livestock, in silver and in gold. The blessings of God had increased the size of Abraham's herds to the point that strife developed between his herdsmen and Lot's herdsmen. Abraham did not want the strife to continue because they were family. So, Abraham said, "*Is* not the whole land before you? Please separate from me. If *you take* the left, then I will go to the right; or, if *you go* to the right, then I will go to the left."[302] It doesn't say how long Abraham and Lot had lived in the Canaan land,

296. 2 Peter 3:9.
297. Gen. 12;1-3
298. Heb. 11:8.
299. 1 Sam. 15:22.
300. Gen. 12:1-4.
301. Gen. 12:5-7.
302. Gen. 13:9.

but it is reasonable to assume they had lived there ten to twelve years. So, the Scripture says,

> Lot lifted his eyes and saw all the plain of Jordan, that it *was* well watered everywhere (before the LORD destroyed Sodom and Gomorrah) like the garden of the LORD, like the land of Egypt as you go toward Zoar" (Gen. 13:10-11).

The well-watered plain looked like the kind of place where one could expect to prosper. Therefore, Lot separated from Abraham and dwelt in the city of Sodom. Then, about a year before Isaac was born the Lord and two angels visited Abraham at Mamre. During that visit the Lord told Abraham that Sarah would have a son.[303] Sarah did have a son, Isaac, when Abraham was one hundred years old.[304] That means that Abraham had been in the Canaan land about twenty-five years by the time Isaac was born, and Isaac was probably born about twelve to fifteen years after Abraham and Lot separated from each other.

It was during this same visit with Abraham that the Lord revealed to him the pending judgment upon Sodom and Gomorrah. Upon receiving that revelation Abraham began to intercede for those cities. His intercession began by asking the Lord a question: "Far be it from You to do such a thing as this, to slay the righteous with the wicked, so that the righteous should be as the wicked; far be it from You! Shall not the Judge of all the earth do right?"[305] The Lord responded to Abraham's intercession and promised not to judge those cities if He could find at least ten righteous people. Ten was probably the number of the members of Lot's family. The Lord spent that night in Lot's home in Sodom and made the decision to destroy those wicked cities by the next morning. Lot, his wife, and his two daughters were compelled to leave the city before the Lord destroyed it with fire and

303. Gen. 18:10.
304. Gen. 21:5.
305. Gen. 18:25.

brimstone. In their departure from Sodom Lot's wife looked back and became a pillar of salt.[306]

Jesus admonishes us to "remember Lot's wife."[307] Jesus compares the days of Lot with the days of Noah as a warning to His Church regarding the characteristics of the world culture just before the return of the Son of Man. The point of this chapter centers on the priority of the kingdom of God. It is this authors conviction that Lot disconnected from the priority of the kingdom of God when he departed from God's chosen covenantal leader and father of many nations.[308] Keep in mind that before Lot separated from Abraham his herds were so large that they became a source of strife between his herdsmen and Abraham's herdsmen. It seemed like a good decision to move over the well-watered plain and live in Sodom. When things in life look well-watered we are all faced with the temptation to forget that Lot, you and me, all of us need a Savior every day![309] As it turns out Lot lost everything including his wife, sons-in-laws, and his house. Besides that, Lot had been living in that community for twelve to fifteen years and apparently had absolutely no redemptive impact on it, even though the Scriptures describe him as "righteous Lot."[310] Would Lot have been better off to have given his herds to his Uncle Abraham and worked for him while raising his family under the blessings of those who bless Abraham?[311]

There is a lesson for believers in this story because we all have a propensity for seeking a "well-watered plain" in a quest for self-fulfillment and success. But God doesn't simply look at the outward appearance, He looks at the heart.[312] "There is a way *that seems* right to a man, but its end *is* the way of death."[313] David Kinnaman and

306. Gen. 19:26.
307. Luke 17:28-32.
308. Gen. 17:1-7.
309. 1 Cor. 10:11-13
310. 2 Peter 2:7.
311. Gen. 12:1-3.
312. 1 Sam. 16:7.
313. Prov. 14:12.

Gabe Lyons make comments and quote insights from Dallas Willard that contribute to our understanding regarding the culture in which we live:

> The morality of self-fulfillment has crept into American Christianity.… Large percentages of practicing Christians embrace the principles of the new moral code. Dallas Willard diagnosed this spiritual sickness in his book *Knowing Christ Today,* where he writes: 'The worldview answers people now live by are provided by feelings. Desire, not reality and not what is good, rules our world. That is true for the most part within religion. Most of what Christians do in their religion now is done at the behest of feelings.… The quest for pleasure takes over the house of God. What is good or what is true is no longer the guide.' Too many Christians have substituted comfortable living for a life changed by the gospel.[314]

Abdu Murry agrees by writing, "Willard's indictment is true for some of us all the time. And it is true for all of us at least some of the time."[315] Jesus is the Truth and the one and only way to God, and without Him we can do nothing.[316] Other possibilities may look enticing, but Lot teaches us of the deceitful nature of outward appearances and even our testimony can lose its power of influence in our family and community when our decisions and actions are based on the shallowness of outward appearances and self-fulfillment. Therefore, Jesus

---

314. David Kinnaman and Gabe Lyons, *Good Faith: Being A Christian When Society Thinks You're Irrelevant and Extreme* (Grand Rapids, MI: Baker Publishing Group, 2016), 59.

315. Abdu Murry, *Saving Truth: Finding Meaning and Clarity in a Post-Truth World* (Grand Rapids, MI: Zondervan, 2018), 33.

316. John 14:6, 15:5.

says, "Seek first the kingdom of God and His righteousness and all these other things will be added to you."[317]

A Kingdom of Priests:

A fourth example of God's relationships with mankind revealing insights into His nature and kingdom priorities is found in His relationships with Moses and the Children of Israel. God told Abraham that his descendants would be "as the dust of the earth; so that if a man could number the dust of the earth, then your descendants also could be numbered. Arise and walk in the land through its length and its width, and I give it to you."[318] But God also told Abraham that his "descendants will be strangers in a land that is not theirs, and will serve them, and they will afflict them four hundred years."[319] As a result of a famine in the Canaan land the descendants of Abraham migrated down into Egypt to survive the severity of the drought. They found sustenance there, but eventually became slaves to the Egyptian Pharaoh. "Israel groaned because of the bondage and they cried out; and their cry came up to God because of their bondage. So, God heard their groaning, and God remembered His covenant with Abraham, with Isaac, and Jacob."[320] God called Moses from a burning bush at Horeb, the mountain of God, to deliver the Children of Israel from their Egyptian bondage and lead them into the Promised Land flowing with milk and honey.[321]

Moses, being obedient to God went to Egypt and through powerful signs and wonders led the children of Israel out of the Egyptian bondage, through the Red Sea and down to Mount Sinai where they encountered God. At Sinai God spoke to Moses saying:

---

317. Matt.6:33.
318. Gen.13:16-17.
319. Gen. 15:13.
320. Exo. 2:23-24.
321. Exo. 3:1-32.

> 'Thus, you shall say to the house of Jacob, and tell the children of Israel: You have seen what I did to the Egyptians, and *how* I bore you on eagles' wings and brought you to Myself. Now therefore, if you will indeed obey My voice and keep My covenant, then you shall be a special treasure to Me above all people; for all the earth *is* Mine. And you shall be to Me a kingdom of priests and a holy nation. These *are* the words which you shall speak to the children of Israel.' So, Moses came and called for the elders of the people and laid before them all these words which the LORD commanded him. Then all the people answered together and said, 'All that the LORD has spoken we will do.' So, Moses brought back the words of the people to the LORD. (Exodus 19:3-8)

From that conversation between God and Moses we understand that it was God's intention to move beyond a personal covenant relationship with each of the individuals in the family of Abraham, Isaac and Jacob, and enter a covenantal relationship with them as a kingdom or nation. It was God's purpose that they would be a "Kingdom of priests and a holy nation."[322] He intended to dwell in their midst and be an enemy to their enemies and an adversary to their adversaries on the condition that they would obey Him.[323] However, when God came down on the Mountain and spoke the words of His commandments, it was a terrifying experience for the Children of Israel.

> "All the people witnessed the thunderings, the lightning flashes, the sound of the trumpet, and the mountain smoking; and when the people saw *it,* they trembled and stood afar off. Then they said to Moses,

322. Exo. 19:6.
323. Exo. 23:20-33, 25:8-9.

> 'You speak with us, and we will hear; but let not God speak with us, lest we die.'" (Exo. 20:18-21)

So, Moses drew near the thick darkness where God was, "and so terrible was the sight that Moses said, 'I am exceedingly afraid and trembling.'"[324] God continued speaking various laws and judgments including the Law of Sabbaths and the three annual Feasts of the Lord. God promised to send an Angel before them, to bless them, take sickness away from them and little by little drive out their enemies.[325] Moses wrote all the words of the Lord and built an altar at the foot of the mountain and offered burnt offerings and sacrificed peace offerings to the Lord. The altar Moses built acknowledges Israel's need of a Mediator/Savior. Moses proceeded to lead the Children of Israel into a covenantal relationship with God as follows:

> And Moses took half the blood and put *it* in basins, and half the blood he sprinkled on the altar. Then he took the Book of the Covenant and read in the hearing of the people. And they said, 'All that the LORD has said we will do and be obedient.' And Moses took the blood, sprinkled *it* on the people, and said, 'This is the blood of the covenant which the LORD has made with you according to all these words.' **Then Moses went up, also Aaron, Nadab, and Abihu, and seventy of the elders of Israel, and they saw the God of Israel. And *there was* under His feet as it were a paved work of sapphire stone, and it was like the very heavens in *its* clarity. But on the nobles of the children of Israel He did not lay His hand. So, they saw God, and they ate and drank**. Then the LORD said to Moses, 'Come up to Me on the mountain and

324. Exo. 20:21; Heb. 12:21.
325. Exo. 20:22-23:33.

> be there; and I will give you tablets of stone, and the law and commandments which I have written, that you may teach them.' So, Moses arose with his assistant Joshua, and Moses went up to the mountain of God. And he said to the elders, 'Wait here for us until we come back to you. Indeed, Aaron and Hur *are* with you. If any man has a difficulty, let him go to them.' Then Moses went up into the mountain, and a cloud covered the mountain. Now the glory of the LORD rested on Mount Sinai, and the cloud covered it six days. And on the seventh day He called to Moses out of the midst of the cloud. The sight of the glory of the LORD *was* like a consuming fire on the top of the mountain in the eyes of the children of Israel. So, Moses went into the midst of the cloud and went up into the mountain. And Moses was on the mountain forty days and forty nights. (Exodus 24:6-18; emphasis is mind)

Moses and the elders of Israel saw God and had a meal with Him on the Mountain of God. Following that event God called Moses to come join Him at the top of the Mountain and Moses was there with God for forty days and nights. During that time God instructed him regarding the construction of the Tabernacle and its furniture. He also gave Moses the instructions regarding the consecration of Aaron and his sons as priests and how to make their holy garments. He also included instructions regarding the daily offerings, the holy anointing oil, the incense, the calling of Bezalel the artisan and craftsman, and the Sabbath as a sign of the covenant He was making with the Children of Israel.[326] At the conclusion of the forty days on the Mountain of God, the three primary parts of the covenant between God and the Children of Israel were in place: (1) The words of the covenant had

---

326. Exo. 25:1-31:18.

been spoken by God and Moses had written them in the Book of the Covenant and read them to the Children of Israel, and they said, "All that the Lord has said we will do and be obedient."[327] (2) The blood of the covenant had been shed by the substitutionary sacrifices and the blood had been sprinkled on the altar and the people.[328] (3) The Lord's Sabbaths were to be kept as a sign of the covenant between God and the Children of Israel.[329] All three persons of the Godhead were involved in each Biblical covenant. God the Father is the originator and promise-maker. The shed blood of every animal sacrifice was a shadow of the substance of the atoning blood shed by Jesus on the cross. And every covenant was sealed with a specific sign which foreshadowed the reality of God the Holy Spirit who would come and dwell in the hearts of the people of faith in Jesus Christ as a guarantee of complete redemption of the purchased possession.

Therefore, every covenantal provision was now in place for the activation of the Children of Israel as a "Kingdom of priests and a holy nation."[330] However, while Moses was in the presence of God on Mount Sinai, Aaron and the Children of Israel had misplaced their priorities and had built and were worshipping a golden calf.[331] The ramifications of this misplaced priority brings three powerful realities to our attention regarding God's nature and His purposes.

First, because they rebelled against God and worshipped the golden calf, God's wrath was aroused, and He said to Moses; "Now therefore, let Me alone, that My wrath may burn hot against them and I may consume them. And I will make of you a great nation."[332] Therefore, Moses was given the opportunity of a lifetime and a privilege that few individuals ever receive. God would destroy those rebellious Children of Israel and make a great nation of Moses! But rather than seize

327. Exo. 24:4-7.
328. Exo. 24:6-8.
329. Exo. 31:13-17.
330. Exo. 19:6.
331. Exo. 32:1-24.
332. Exo. 32:10.

the opportunity for personal fame and success, he demonstrated the humility of Jesus,[333] and interceded for the Children of Israel from two powerful positions: first, reminding God that the Egyptians were watching and would say; "'He brought them out to harm them, to kill them in the mountains, and to consume them from the face of the earth? Turn from Your fierce wrath and relent from this harm to Your people."[334] And second, Moses pleaded with God to "remember" His covenant with Abraham, Isaac, and Israel. Moses interceded before God in terms of His covenantal nature. God cannot lie![335] God had made a covenant with Abraham, Isaac, and Israel, promising to give the Land of Canaan to them.[336] As a result of Moses' intercession "the LORD relented from the harm which He said He would do to His people."[337]

Second, Moses went down from the mountain with the two tablets of stone upon which the ten commandments were written. However, when he saw the golden calf and their dancing, his anger burned hot. He broke the tablets containing the writing of God and declared judgment upon the people and three thousand fell that day.[338] Moses then returned to the Lord to make an atonement for their sin. He confessed their great sin and ask the Lord to forgive them. The extra ordinary aspect of his intercession was contained in what he said to God, "Yet now, if You will forgive their sin—but if not, I pray, blot me out of Your book which You have written."[339] Jesus said, "Greater love has no one than this, than to lay down one's life for his friends."[340] God was looking for a man to stand in the gap and make a rock solid defense on the behalf of Israel that He would not destroy them.[341]

333. Num. 12:3.
334. Exo. 32:12.
335. Exo. 32:13; Tit. 1:2.
336. Gen. 15:7, 18; Heb. 6:13.
337. Exo. 32:14.
338. Exo. 32:15-29.
339. Exo. 32:32.
340. John 15:13.
341. Eze. 22:30.

This illustrates the value of placing priority on the things God prioritizes such as "loving not our lives unto death" to overcome evil. The kingdom of God is not empowered by military force but prioritizes love that is committed to the terms of God's everlasting covenant and Moses demonstrated his commitment to God's covenantal purposes. The wages of sin had to be paid, but because of Moses' intercessions God did not destroy the nation, but commanded Moses to lead Israel into the land which He swore to Abraham, Isaac, and Jacob, and God would send His Angel before them.[342]

Third, Moses pitched a tent outside the camp and called it "the tabernacle of meeting."[343] God met with Moses at the tent of meeting in a pillar of a cloud and spoke with him face to face as a man speaks to his friend. In the midst of communing with God, Moses petitioned God in the terms of His grace to not simply send His Angel with them as they traveled, but that God Himself would go with them and consider this nation as His own people. Moses' intercessions were so aligned with God's priorities and nature that the Lord responded to Moses by saying, "'I will also do this thing that you have spoken; for you have found grace in My sight, and I know you by name.'"[344]

God did journey with Israel, dwelling in their midst, leading them forward. Although they provoked God to anger more than once, He did not forsake them. Just after Moses died and before they entered the Promised Land, God spoke to Moses's predecessor, Joshua, saying, "Only be strong and very courageous, that you may observe to do according to all the law which Moses My servant commanded you; do not turn from it to the right hand or to the left, that you may prosper wherever you go."[345] It had been a forty year wilderness journey, but God was faithful!

It was during the life of Moses that the "seed of Abraham" was transformed from individuals in a covenant relationship with God into

342. Exo. 32:34-33:6.

343. Exo. 33:7.

344. Exo. 33:7-23.

345. Josh. 1:7

a "Kingdom of priests and a holy nation." They were purchased by God through the blood of the Passover Lamb and miraculously delivered from Egyptian bondage by God's appointed leadership of Moses. His leadership brought them to Mount Sinai where God Himself met with them and entered a covenant with them as a nation. The giving of the Law, the building of the Tabernacle, and the anointing of the priesthood enabled Israel to align with God's nature and demonstrate the blessings of God's government in the earth. The concept of a "kingdom of priests and a holy nation"[346] clearly indicates that God was entering into a covenant with Israel to set them apart from other nations as a center of His government in the earth. He anointed, empowered, and authorized Israel as a nation to demonstrate the blessings of His sovereignty over all creation.

Anointed to Serve:

It was within the context of establishing Israel as a kingdom of priests that the "anointing" is first mentioned in the Bible.[347] The Lord purchased all the firstborn of Israel with the blood of the Passover Lamb offered on that fateful night when the "destroyer" passed through the Land of Egypt.[348] However, when Israel sinned by worshipping the golden calf while Moses was on the top of Mount Sinai with God; it was the Levites that stood with Moses and executed God's judgment and three thousand died that day. Thereafter, God chose the Levites and exchanged them for the firstborn of Israel to serve Him as priests.[349] After that exchange only the Levites were anointed or authorized to serve God as priests. An example of a violation of extending oneself into an area of administration without the anointing is found in the life of King Uzziah who was anointed as king but not as a priest. King Uzziah and all the kings of Judah were

346. Exo. 19:6.
347. Exo. 25:5, 29:11.
348. Exo. 12:23.
349. Num. 3:1-51

from the lineage of David and the tribe of Judah and not the priestly tribe of Levi. However, King Uzziah "transgressed against the Lord his God by entering the temple of the Lord to burn incense on the altar of incense."[350] Eighty priests of the Lord withstood King Uzziah, but he became furious and insisted on doing the ministry of a priest. Because of his disobedience the Lord struck him with leprosy, and he was cut off from the house of the Lord, and his son reigned as king. The anointing is much more than a religious ritual. It is God's authorization of an individual to access His presence and to serve Him in the administration of His kingdom within a sphere of responsibility undergirded with kingdom power and authority. Without His anointing, man is powerless to do anything in the kingdom of God. The anointing will be discussed in greater detail in the next chapter.

The final examples in this chapter regarding the priority of the kingdom are illustrated in God's relationship with David. After King Saul felt compelled and acted foolishly by offering the burnt offering rather than patiently waiting on the Lord, Samuel told him that his kingdom would not continue. Samuel said, "The Lord has sought for Himself a man after His own heart."[351] God, having rejected Saul as king, sent Samuel to anoint David as king of Israel and "the Spirit of the Lord came upon David from that day forward."[352] David was chosen by God out of an obscure place as a shepherd-boy, but he had a heart for God. The kingdom priority here is the issue of the heart. Jeremiah declares, "I, the Lord, search the heart."[353] Saul's outward appearance made him look like a king because; "*There was* not a more handsome person than he among the Children of Israel. From his shoulders upward, *he was* taller than any of the people."[354] "But

350. 2 Chro. 26:16-21.
351. 1 Samuel 13:12-14.
352. 1 Sam. 16:13.
353. Jer. 17:10a.
354. 1 Sam. 9:2.

the Lord said to Samuel… "man looks on the outward appearance, but God looks on the heart."[355]

Jesus placed the highest priority on the issue of the heart. He said, "You shall love the Lord your God with all your heart, with all of your soul, and with all of your mind."[356] Even in his youth David had a heart for God, was a worshipper and later became known as "the sweet Psalmist of Israel."[357] David expressed his inner yearnings with the words; "As the deer pants for the streams of water, so my soul pants for you, my God."[358] During his lifetime David wrote about half of the Psalms in our Bible. Jack Hayford affirms the priority of our hearts being passionate for God by saying, "God wants our hearts, not just our verbal allegiance, and He desires that our affections be wholly His. Developing the discipline practices that lead to this kind of life must be a high priority."[359] In the Sermon on the Mount Jesus speaks of individuals who thought they were in the kingdom of God, but there will be a day when they will stand before the Lord and say:

> Lord have we not prophesied in Your name, cast out demons in Your name, and done many wonders in Your name? And then I will declare to them, 'I never knew you; depart from Me, you who practice lawlessness.[360]

All of David's brothers by their outward appearances, looked more like kings than he did. But God chose David because He was seeing David's heart. David's heart expressed a love for God that was at least a shadow of the heart of Jesus the Son of David, the Son of God. The

---

355. 1 Sam. 16:7.
356. Matt. 22:37.
357. 2 Sam. 23:1.
358. Psa. 42:1.
359. Jack Hayford, *The Hayford Bible Handbook: The Complete Companion for Spirit-Filled Bible Study* (Nashville, TN: Thomas Nelson, Inc., 1995), 152.
360. Matt. 7:22.

kingdom of God originates in the heart of God and from His heart it is foreshadowed in the earth through the covenant He made with David.

> "'When your days are fulfilled, and you rest with your fathers, I will set up your seed after you, who will come from your body, and I will establish his kingdom. He shall build a house for My name, **and I will establish the throne of his kingdom forever**. I will be his Father, and he shall be My son. If he commits iniquity, I will chasten him with the rod of men and with the blows of the sons of men. But My mercy shall not depart from him, as I took *it* from Saul, whom I removed from before you. And your house and your kingdom shall be established forever before you. **Your throne shall be established forever**.' According to all these words and according to all this vision, so Nathan spoke to David."[361] (2 Sam. 7:12-17; emphasis mine).

The kingdom of God is foreshadowed through God's covenantal relationship with David and inaugurated in the earth through the ministry of Jesus. Jesus began His ministry on the earth by finding His place in the "volume of the book" and preaching the "gospel of the kingdom of God." Then setting His face like flint toward the cross where He said, "Not My will be done, but Yours be done."[362] It was on the cross that He became a propitiation for our sin and our door of access into the kingdom of God through the new birth. Jesus said, "Most assuredly, I say to you, unless one is born again, he cannot see the kingdom of God."[363] When we confess with our mouth the Lord

361. 2 Sam. 23:5; The covenant that God made with David includes David's seed, house, throne, and kingdom while pointing ultimately to David's greatest Son the Lord Jesus and the kingdom of God.

362. Isa. 61;1-2, Like 4:18; Isa. 50:7; Heb. 10:7; Mk. 1:14; Luke 22:42.

363. John 3:3-8.

Jesus and believe in our heart that God raised Him from the dead, we are saved.[364] Believing in our heart is an act of faith whereby we are forgiven and reconciled to God our heavenly Father and declared righteous. At that point the Holy Spirit is united with our spirit and we are regenerated or born again. We are "delivered from the power of darkness and conveyed into the kingdom of the Son of His love."[365]

> But God, who is rich in mercy, because of His great love with which He loved us, even when we were dead in trespasses, made us alive together with Christ (by grace you have been saved), and raised *us* up together, and made *us* sit together in the heavenly *places* in Christ Jesus, that in the ages to come He might show the exceeding riches of His grace in *His* kindness toward us in Christ Jesus. (Ephesians 2:4-7).

Because of the great love with which He loved us we temporarily remain here as residents but permanent citizens of the kingdom of God with our authority and power coming from our position in Jesus Christ who is seated at the right hand of the Father on His throne in heaven. God's kingdom or government rests upon Jesus' shoulders and "the increase of His government and peace there shall be no end."[366] There is coming a day when every knee will bow and "every tongue will confess that Jesus Christ is Lord."[367] And we the Church shall reign with Jesus Christ forever and ever.[368] It is a priority to "seek first the kingdom of God and His righteousness."

---

364. Rom. 10:9.
365. Col.1:13
366. Isa. 9:6-7.
367. Phil. 2:9-11.
368. Rev. 22:5.

A Heart that Pants for God:

Another example of the priority of the kingdom is found in the life of David. In his youth David killed Goliath, thus liberating Israel from the oppression of the Philistines. That event proved to be a turning point in David's life, because, "Saul took him that day, and would not let him go home to his father's house anymore."[369] David proved to be a powerful warrior in Saul's army and it happened when David returned home from victorious battles the women came out of all the cities singing, dancing, and saying "Saul has slain his thousands, and David his ten thousands."[370] As a result Saul was displeased and became very angry and a distressing spirit came upon King Saul and he sought opportunities to kill David. David was probably about seventeen years old when he was anointed by Samuel. Some estimate that it was about three years later or at about age twenty when David slew Goliath.[371] It is estimated that King Saul then pursued David with the intent to kill him for a period of eight or ten years before King Saul was himself killed by the Philistines in the battle that ended on Mount Gilboa. In other words, David was chosen and anointed by God, but his heart motives were surely tested by trial over a period of years before he became a king. There are two occasions that stand out as powerful lessons for us. Saul had tried to kill David on several occasions and David was running and hiding from Saul. Meanwhile a group of those who were in distress, in debt, and discontent had gathered to him.[372] Saul learned that David was in the wilderness of En Gedi. The Scripture says;

---

369. 1 Sam. 18:2.

370. 1 Sam. 18:7.

371. Faithlife Corporation. "Logos Bible Software Timeline." Logos Bible Software, Computer software. Bellingham, WA: Faithlife Corporation, August 22, 2018.

372. 1 Sam.22:1-5.

> Then Saul took three thousand chosen men from all Israel and went to seek David and his men on the Rocks of the Wild Goats. So, he came to the sheep-folds by the road, where there *was* a cave; and Saul went in to attend to his needs. (David and his men were staying in the recesses of the cave.) Then the men of David said to him, "**This is the day of which the** LORD **said to you, 'Behold, I will deliver your enemy into your hand, that you may do to him as it seems good to you**.' " And David arose and secretly cut off a corner of Saul's robe. Now it happened afterward that David's heart troubled him because he had cut Saul's *robe.* And he said to his men, "**The LORD forbid that I should do this thing to my master, the LORD'S anointed, to stretch out my hand against him, seeing he *is* the anointed of the LORD**." So, David restrained his servants with *these* words, and did not allow them to rise against Saul. And Saul got up from the cave and went on *his* way. (1 Samuel. 22:1-5; emphasis mine).

David's men saw this occasion as an opportunity for David to take steps to fulfill God's plan for his life. After all David had been anointed by God to be king, plus he had been treated wrongly for what seemed to be far too long. Some could have said, "This was a clear opportunity for him to function as a real leader and take matters into his own hands." But David restrained himself and his servants from making a grave mistake and a fatal day for King Saul. The kingdom principle is: fulfilling God's purposes, in God's timing, according to God's ways and to seek first the kingdom of God and His righteousness, not seeking to fulfill our personal agenda. David's heart was in the right place. He said to King Saul, "Let the Lord judge between you and me, and see and plead my case, and deliver me out of your hand."[373] Those words reflect the heart of Jesus and true kingdom of God leadership. From this experience we ask ourselves, "Which of these two men would I prefer to serve?" The wisdom of David's restraint and words are clear guidelines as we engage in the day to day trials and challenges that each of us are faced with in our sphere of responsibility.

After a period, David is given another opportunity to take matters into his own hands and again, he demonstrated Christlike restraint. David knew that Saul and three thousand soldiers were pursuing him, and he discovered where Saul had encamped. He determined to go down into Saul's camp while Saul was sleeping and the warrior Abishai agreed to go with David. The Scripture says;

> "So, David and Abishai came to the people by night; and there Saul lay sleeping within the camp, with his spear stuck in the ground by his head. And Abner and the people lay all around him. **Then Abishai said to David, 'God has delivered your enemy into your hand this day. Now therefore, please, let me strike him at once with the spear, right to the earth; and I will not *have to strike* him a second time!' And David said to Abishai, 'Do not destroy him; for who can stretch out his hand against the** LORD'S **anointed, and be guiltless?'** David said furthermore, '*As* the LORD lives, the LORD shall strike him, or his day shall come to die, or he shall go out to battle and perish. The LORD forbid that I should stretch out my hand against the LORD'S anointed. But please, take now the spear and the jug of water that *are* by his head, and let us go.' So, David took the spear and the jug of water *by* Saul's head, and they got away; and no man saw *it* or knew *it* or awoke. For they *were*

373. 1 Sam. 24:15.

> all asleep, because a deep sleep from the LORD had fallen on them. Now David went over to the other side and stood on the top of a hill afar off, a great distance *being* between them. And David called out to the people and to Abner the son of Ner, saying, 'Do you not answer, Abner?' Then Abner answered and said, 'Who *are* you, calling out to the king?' So, David said to Abner, '*Are* you not a man? And who *is* like you in Israel? Why then have you not guarded your lord the king? For one of the people came in to destroy your lord the king. This thing that you have done *is* not good. ***As the* LORD *lives, you deserve to die, because you have not guarded your master, the* LORD'S *anointed. And now see where the king's spear is, and the jug of water that was by his head*.'" (1 Sam. 26:7-16; emphasis mine).[374]

Once again David demonstrates godly wisdom and great restraint. Abishai was ready to take King Saul's head off with just one strike, but David restrained him. There are times in our relationship with God that the kingdom will only advance if we lay our life down. For instance, when the soldiers came to arrest Jesus in the Garden of Gethsemane and Peter cut off a soldier's ear, Jesus said,

> 'Put your sword in its place, for all who take the sword will perish by the sword. Or do you think that I cannot now pray to My Father, and He will provide Me with more than twelve legions of angels?'[375]

Earlier Jesus told His disciples, "No one takes it from Me, but I lay it down of Myself. I have power to lay it down, and I have power to

---

374. The reader will find it worthwhile to read the entire twenty-sixth chapter of First Samuel.

375. Matt. 26:52-53.

take it again."[376] The priority of the kingdom according to the teaching of Jesus is: "If anyone desires to come after Me, let him deny himself, and take up his cross, and follow Me. For whoever desires to save his life will lose it, but whoever loses his life for My sake will find it."[377] Too often we readily defend ourselves because we think we are right and we seek justice. But in the Kingdom of God there are occasions when the only way to victory is to lay our life down, just like Jesus did. God gives grace to the humble, and the grace of God is our sufficiency. In God's timing David was received as the King of Israel. He served God as the King for forty years. David understood the principle, "Do not touch My anointed ones, and do My prophets no harm."[378] Although he was in many battles the sword never took his life and he died of old age.

The final example of the priority of the kingdom of God in the life of David is drawn from his desire for the very presence of God. The ark which symbolized the presence of God had been captured by the Philistines during a battle in the final days of Eli the High Priest. When the wife of Eli's son, who was with child and due to be delivered, heard the news that Eli was dead. Then the news that her husband had been killed in the battle, and the ark of God had been taken captive, she immediately experienced labor pains and gave birth to a child whom she named "Ichabod." She said, "the glory has departed from Israel, for the ark of God has been captured."[379] Throughout the entire reign of King Saul the ark of God remained in an obscure place rather than in the tabernacle of Moses.

---

376. John 10:18.
377. Matt. 16:24-25.
378. Psa. 105:15.
379. 1 Sam. 4:19-22.

Davidic Worship on Mount Zion:

David was thirty years old when he began to reign, and he reigned his first seven years over Judah from the city of Hebron.[380] Then he took the stronghold of Zion which was the southern portion of the City of Jerusalem. David made his home there and brought the ark of God to Mount Zion where he served as king-priest. David placed the ark of God in a tent which became known as David's tabernacle.[381] Unlike Moses' tabernacle it had no courtyard around it to hinder anyone from approaching the tabernacle, nor was there a veil to exclude anyone from the ark of God. Furthermore, David appointed Levitical choirs to offer up the sacrifice of praise unto the Lord twenty-four hours a day.[382] David had such a heart after God that he worshipped with the comprehension that God is "enthroned in the praises of Israel."[383] David understood that God is not delighted in burnt offerings but in the sacrifice of praise and the fruit of our lips, giving thanks unto His name.[384] Kevin Conner writes,

> Zion combines in itself the political and religious unity of the nation and King David exemplifies the ministry of a King (Political or Governmental), and Priest (Religious or Ecclesiastical) unto God…. Zion – The city where the King-Priest dwells…. "The Lord shall send the rod of Thy strength out of Zion: rule Thou in the midst of Thine enemies" (Psa. 110:2). This whole Psalm deals with the Priesthood of Christ after the order of Melchisedek. Read Psalms 110:1-7. It is taken up in detail in the Epistle of Hebrews. The Lord Jesus Christ is the King-Priest, after the Order

---

380. 2 Sam. 5:6-10; 1 Chro. 11:2-9.
381. 2 Sam. 6:12-23.
382. 1 Chro. 16:1-6, 25:1-31; Psa. 134:1-3.
383. Psa. 22:3.
384. Heb. 13:15.

> of Melchisedek. He is King-Priest in Zion, in His Church. Read Hebrews, Chapter 7.[385]

David practiced a style of worship and leadership that transcended the Levitical Law but was so acceptable to God that three hundred years after David's death, Amos prophesied that God would rebuild David's tabernacle.[386] As the Gospel of the Kingdom was being proclaimed by the early church there arose a doctrinal conflict between the Orthodox Jews and the New Testament Believers. Therefore, a council was held in Jerusalem in order to get the mind of the Lord and resolve the conflict. It was during that council meeting that the Apostle James quoted the following prophecy from Amos;

> *"After this I will return and will rebuild the tabernacle of David, which has fallen down; I will rebuild its ruins, And I will set it up; So that the rest of mankind may seek the* LORD, *even all the Gentiles who are called by My name, Says the* LORD *who does all these things."* (Acts 15:16-17; Amos 9:11-12)

The Church Council agreed that no one would be required to be circumcised or keep the ceremonial portions of the Levitical Law in order to have access to God. By the sacrifice of Jesus on Calvary's cross and His resurrection from the dead, the way to God was opened to whosoever would call on the name of the Lord. Jesus is the King of kings and has been appointed by God as our High Priest after the order of Melchisedek. Jesus "has made us kings and priests to His God and Father, to Him *be* glory and dominion forever and ever."[387] All New Testament Believers "*are* a chosen generation, a royal priesthood, a holy nation, His own special people, that you may proclaim

---

385. Kevin J. Conner, *The Tabernacle of David: The Presence of God as Experienced in the Tabernacle* (Portland, OR: City Bible Publishing, 1976), 136-137.

386. Amos 9:11-12.

387. Rev. 1:6.

the praises of Him who called you out of darkness into His marvelous light."[388]

The rebuilding of David's Tabernacle and the restoration of Davidic worship characterizes the season in which we now live. Loving God with all our heart, with all our soul, and with all our mind and loving our neighbor as ourselves is the relational foundation upon which we are enabled to grasp Jesus' imperative to "Seek first the kingdom of God and His righteousness." When David became king of all Israel, he was not content until he brought the presence of God to dwell on Mount Zion and established continual worship with praise and thanksgiving before Him. The ark of God remained in David's tabernacle on Mount Zion for over thirty years, until it was moved into the Temple that Solomon built. Solomon's Temple was eventually destroyed, and the ark disappeared. But the Lord is reviving Davidic worship and rebuilding David's tabernacle for the manifestation of His presence among us in our day. David was a man after God's own heart and lived as a worshipping warrior which exemplifies our priorities as citizens in the kingdom of God and members of God's royal family.

Summary:

This chapter focuses upon the priority of the kingdom of God. Early in Jesus' life He expressed kingdom priorities by asking His parents, "Did you not know that I must be about My Father's business?"[389] So often we make it our business to worry about what to wear or what to eat or drink, but Jesus said, "Your heavenly Father knows you need all of these things. But seek first the kingdom of God and His righteousness, and all these things will be added to you."[390] God loves us so much that He provides for us far beyond what we are capable of providing for ourselves. For example, when Adam sinned and was incapable of paying the wages of sin, God did not destroy him. He

388. 1 Peter 2:9.
389. Luke 2:49.
390. Matt. 6:32-33.

provided a substitutionary sacrifice to die in his place and covered Adam's nakedness and shame. When men's hearts were turned away from truth and hardened by the deceitfulness of sin to the point that judgment was inevitable; "Noah found grace in the eyes of the Lord," which ignited his faith and he built an ark for the saving of his family. When the Children of Israel were under the bondage of Egyptian slavery, God heard their groans and remembered His covenant with Abraham, Isaac, and Jacob. He raised up Moses to deliver them and lead them into a covenant relationship with God as a nation. But when they sinned by worshipping the golden calf, Moses stood in the gap and interceded for them and found grace in the eyes of the Lord to the extent He committed to journey with them and be their God.

Eventually God raised up a king in Israel, David, a man after His own heart. He was a shepherd king, a worshipping warrior that understood fulfilling God's purposes in God's timing. David's heart was not content until he had brought the ark of God up on Mount Zion and appointed choirs to worship Him with praise and thanksgiving twenty-four hours a day. Today God is rebuilding David's tabernacle and manifesting His presence among us as never before in the history of the world. As a result, our priority is to seek first the kingdom of God and His righteousness and worship Him with praise and thanksgiving in celebration of His glorious presence, because He dwells not in temples made with hands but in our hearts. He has given us His precious promises whereby we may be partakers of His divine nature and be anointed with the Holy Spirit and power, enabling us to reign in life.[391] Having discussed these kingdom priorities, we will focus on the anointing of the Holy Spirit in the next chapter.

---

391. Rom. 5:17.

CHAPTER THREE

THE POWER OF THE KINGDOM

"God anointed Jesus of Nazareth with the Holy Spirit and with power, who went about doing good and healing all who were oppressed by the devil, for God was with Him."

(Acts 10:38)

"But you shall receive power when the Holy Spirit has come upon you; and you shall be witnesses to Me in Jerusalem, and in all Judea and Samaria, and to the end of the earth."

(Acts 1:8)

Jesus Christ came from Judea to Galilee preaching the gospel of the kingdom. He ministered under the anointing of the Holy Spirit in a manner that was powerful and miraculous, but never as an end in its self. His ministry always pointed to something greater yet to come. Even His death on the cross was not an end in itself but a doorway into greater kingdom of God possibilities for the Redeemed. Prior to His ascension Jesus commanded His followers not to depart from Jerusalem until they were endued with power or anointed by the Holy Spirit. Gordon Fee provides the following insights into the meaning of the "anointing:"

> "Anointing" came to be associated especially with Jesus and the gift of the Spirit whereby he was appointed/affirmed for his role as Messiah (= Christ). He therefore was the "Anointed One" in a unique sense, so that in time the title became part of the name by which he was known in the early church ("Jesus the Christ" came to be simply "Jesus Christ").[392]

Jesus the Christ:

Even though Jesus was conceived by the Holy Spirit, He did not minister as "the Christ" until after He was anointed by the Holy Spirit following His water baptism. Then He came preaching "the Kingdom of God is at hand."[393] The concept of "kingdom" speaks of the authority and power to rule and reign before it includes territory. This principle is exemplified in the words of the prophet Samuel to King Saul; "The LORD has torn the kingdom of Israel from you today, and has given it to a neighbor of yours, *who is* better than you."[394] The territory of Israel did not change, but the authority and power to rule Israel changed from Saul to David.

Following God's rejection of King Saul, He commanded Samuel to go to Bethlehem and anoint the son of Jesse. Samuel followed the Lord's instructions and "took the horn of oil and anointed David in the midst of his brothers; and the Spirit of the Lord came upon David from that day forward."[395] After David was anointed the "Spirit of the Lord departed from Saul."[396] In other words the power of the Holy Spirit departed from Saul, and now the anointing with Holy Spirit power rested upon David. The authority and power residing in the

---

392. Gordon D. Fee, *God's Empowering Presence: The Holy Spirit in the Letters of Paul* (Grand Rapids, MI: Baker Academic, 2011), 291–292.

393. Mark 1:15.

394. 1 Sam. 15:28.

395. 1 Sam. 16:1-13.

396. 1 Sam. 16:14.

anointing is clearly revealed by the completely different responses given by King Saul and David to Goliath's defiant challenge to the armies of Israel. King Saul was "dismayed and greatly afraid."[397] Whereas David confidently declared to Goliath, "The battle is the Lord's and He will give you into my hands."[398] And sure enough, God empowered David to do what was seemingly impossible and he prevailed over Goliath. David's victory over Goliath foreshadowed Jesus' victory over the devil. Both David and the Lord Jesus were anointed by the same Holy Spirit, and each won the victory over the powers of evil before territory was awarded to their dominion. Each had to take their territory from the dominion of the enemy. David had to fight His way to victory over those who were holding possession of the territory God had promised to Israel. And Jesus also had to overcome the devil and the powers of darkness. He will one day return and bring those powers under submission to His Lordship or exterminate them. And when that final battle is finished "neither shall they learn war anymore."[399]

Both David and Jesus went before others, breaking the power of the enemy, liberating the captives, and establishing a pathway to liberty. One of Jesus' Messianic titles is "The Breaker."[400] David Guzik states regarding Jesus as "The Breaker"; "In this office, He is the captain and leader of His people, advancing in front of His flock."[401] Jesus began His ministry in Nazareth by declaring, "The Spirit of the Lord is upon Me, because He has anointed Me… To proclaim liberty to the captives."[402] And we know that Jesus went forth liberating many, many people from the captivity of the powers of darkness. The point is that the Holy Spirit that anointed David and anointed Jesus

397. 1 Sam. 17:11.

398. 1 Sam. 17:47.

399. Isa. 63:3, 2:4; Micah 4:3.

400. Micah 2:13 KJV.

401. David Guzik, *Micah*, David Guzik's Commentaries on the Bible (Santa Barbara, CA: David Guzik, 2001), Mic 2:12–13.

402. Luke 4:18.

is the same Holy Spirit that anoints New Testament believers today. Consequently, we should live with the expectation of liberating those bound by sickness, addictions, poverty, fear, and breaking every tactic of the devil, because we have been endued with the power of the Holy Spirit. Jesus declared, "Most assuredly, I say to you, he who believes in Me, the works that I do he will do also; and greater *works* than these he will do, because I go to My Father."[403] Therefore, this chapter will focus on the purpose of the anointing and how it is a key component of the Everlasting Covenant and the kingdom of God.

Jesus the way, the truth, and the life inaugurated the kingdom of God in the earth by the power of the Holy Spirit and demonstrated its invisible presence with signs and wonders. Jack Taylor states, "The whole emphasis of Jesus' earthly ministry was the Kingdom of God, which we have defined as His rule both in eternity and in time."[404] Fifty days after His resurrection and ten days after His ascension, when the Day of Pentecost had fully come, the Lord Jesus Christ poured out the Promised Holy Spirit upon the one-hundred and twenty disciples in the Upper Room. For the first time since Adam's sin and expulsion from the Garden of Eden the authority and power to rule and reign on the earth had for the most part been in the hands of the powers of darkness, but now that authority and power was restored to the body of Christ. George Boardman states, "the re-enthronement of God in man" was the "reinstatement of God's dominion in this insurgent world is the grand and blessed fact of human time."[405]

Greater Works than These:

Therefore, the out-pouring of the Holy Spirit on the Day of Pentecost was a world changing event. R. T. Kendall states, "What happened at Pentecost was the inauguration of the supreme manifestation of the

403. John 14:12.
404. Taylor, *Cosmic Initiative,* 103.
405. Broadman, *The Kingdom,* 51.

Spirit now that Jesus had returned to the Father."[406] God, Himself had come to dwell in the hearts of believers and anoint them to bear witness to the presence of His kingdom in the earth realm, even though this world stands in hostile opposition against Him. This further prepares the way for the day when the Lord Jesus Christ will return and literally set up heaven's government upon this earth. At that time the kingdoms of this world will become the kingdoms of our God and His Christ and He shall reign forever with absolute dominion over all things.[407] And "at the name of Jesus every knee should bow, of those in heaven, and of those on earth, and of those under the earth, and *that* every tongue should confess that Jesus Christ *is* Lord, to the glory of God the Father."[408]

Just before Jesus ascended into heaven He commanded the disciples, "not to depart from Jerusalem, but to wait for the Promise of the Father, "which," *He said,* 'you have heard from Me; for John truly baptized with water, but you shall be baptized with the Holy Spirit not many days from now.'"[409] On the Day of Pentecost Jesus' disciples were transformed from being fearful individuals into bold witnesses for the Lord Jesus by the empowering gift of the Holy Spirit. Peter, who only fifty-three days earlier had denied with an oath any knowledge of the Lord, now boldly proclaimed that they were experiencing the fulfillment of Joel's prophecy and God had made Jesus who had been crucified "both Lord and Christ."[410] Peter continued by proclaiming,

> Repent and let every one of you be baptized in the name of Jesus Christ for the remission of sins; and you shall **receive the gift of the Holy Spirit**. **For the**

406. R. T. Kendall, *The Anointing: Yesterday, Today, Tomorrow* (Nashville, TN: Thomas Nelson, Inc., 1999), 10.

407. Rev. 11:15.

408. Phil. 2:10-11.

409. Acts 1:4-5.

410. Acts 2:36.

> **promise is to you and to your children, and to all who are afar off, as many as the Lord our God will call**." And with many other words he testified and exhorted them, saying, 'Be saved from this perverse generation.' Then those who gladly received his word were baptized; and that day about three thousand souls were added *to them.* (Acts 2:38-41; emphasis mine).

John the Baptist declared that Jesus was "the Lamb of God, who takes away the sin of the world."[411] That reality is of great significance to all of us because we all need a Savior to deliver us from sin and the oppression of the devil. The gospel of the kingdom includes the powerful truth that the Father through the crucifixion of Jesus "condemned sin in the flesh, that the righteous requirement of the law might be fulfilled in us who do not walk according to the flesh, but those who live according to the Spirit."[412] Many of the religious leaders of Jesus' day were spiritually blind to the redemptive message of Jesus Christ and the presence of the kingdom He demonstrated. Therefore, Jesus wept over Jerusalem because they did not know the day of their "visitation."[413] Jesus explained "to His disciples that He must go to Jerusalem and suffer many things from the elders and chief priests and scribes, and be killed, and be raised the third day."[414] But their spiritual paradigm was so short-sighted that they were unable to grasp the possibility of their Messiah being sacrificed on a cross. They could only perceive of a Messiah that would overcome the Roman authorities and restore "the kingdom to Israel."[415]

---

411. John 1:29.
412. Rom. 8:3-4.
413. Luke 19:44.
414. Matt. 16:21.
415. Acts 1:6.

Not by Might nor by Power:

It is not difficult from our perspective to see the flaw in their understanding. However, is it possible that we the redeemed have also succumbed to a short-sighted paradigm regarding the kingdom of God? Have we reduced our salvation to being forgiven, reconciled with the Father, and simply going to heaven when we die? What role does the Holy Spirit fulfill in our daily lifestyle? Are we experiencing what it means to be anointed by the Holy Spirit and live as ambassadors of the kingdom of God in the here and now? What do these words mean to us; "the testimony of Jesus is the spirit of prophecy?"[416] Is our faith level adequate to believe the Lord will actually use "Little ole me" to set captives free in this season of harvest? Jack Hayford states,

> The Holy Spirit outpouring in our times is suited to equip the church for our times... The Spirit of prophecy is freshly qualifying multitudes for prophetic ministry; that is, ministry in the Biblical sense of prophecy—proclaiming, unveiling, and renewing... The Church—not as an institutional presence, academically, politically, or ecclesiastically, but as a multitude of millions of Holy-Spirit-filled prophesiers—is being retooled for last-days ministry.... Our best resource for evangelism is not by arguing with the unbelieving world, but by a fresh anointing of the Holy Spirit of prophecy.[417]

Following His water baptism and receiving the anointing of the Holy Spirit, Jesus "the last Adam," spent forty days and nights in the wilderness being tested by the devil. Jesus did not fail His test as the "first Adam" had. Following His victory over the devil, "Jesus

416. Rev. 19:10.

417. Jack Hayford, *The Beauty of Spiritual Language: Unveiling the Mystery of Speaking in Tongues* (Nashville, TN: Thomas Nelson, 1996), 176-177.

returned in the power of the Spirit to Galilee, and news of Him went out through all the surrounding region."[418]

So, He came to Nazareth, where He had been brought up. And as His custom was, He went into the synagogue on the Sabbath day, and stood up to read. And He was handed the book of the prophet Isaiah. And when He had opened the book, He found the place where it was written:

> '***The Spirit of the*** **LORD** ***is upon Me, Because He has anointed Me*** *To preach the gospel to the poor; He has sent Me to heal the brokenhearted, To proclaim liberty to the captives And recovery of sight to the blind, To set at liberty those who are oppressed; To proclaim the acceptable year of the* LORD.' (Luke 4:16-19; Isa. 61:1-2; emphasis mine).

John the Baptist had been preaching in the wilderness of Judea with authority, and the Jewish people were experiencing a world-changing move of God. But this was the first recorded occasion since the days of Malachi that an anointed prophet had spoken with this level of authority. They were so astonished that "the eyes of all who were in the synagogue were fixed on Him. And He began to say to them, 'Today this Scripture is fulfilled in your hearing.'"[419] They "bore witness to Him, and marveled at His gracious words," but their spiritual paradigm was so clouded with religious ritual and unbelief that they could only accept His words as the words of "Joseph's son." To think that Isaiah's prophecy was being fulfilled before their eyes was so unbelievable that they were filled with wrath and attempted to kill Jesus.[420] However, Jesus passed through the midst of them and continued His ministry.

---

418. Luke 4:14.
419. Luke 4:20-21.
420. Luke 4:22-30.

Later Jesus returned to Nazareth and taught in their synagogue, but again they were offended at Him, considering Him to only be "the carpenter's son." Therefore, "He did not do many mighty works there because of their unbelief."[421] The point is that God chooses and anoints ordinary believers like carpenters, teachers, nurses, clerks, farmers, beauticians, and bus drivers, people just like you and me to accomplish His Kingdom purposes. His purposes are accomplished "not by might or by power but by the Spirit of the Lord."[422]

Without the anointing of the Holy Spirit every believer experiences the painful sensations of something missing. An inner unction that says, "There has got to be more than I am experiencing." The inner feeling is like amputees who often experience phantom pains. They experience painful sensations or perceptions of pain relating to a limb or an organ that is not physically part of the body resulting from amputation. So, believers experience the deep desire or intense hunger, and even the sensation of pain in their innermost being as if they have been cut off from who we really are. Thankfully, God has not only made every provision for each of us to be completely whole.[423] He is reconciling us to Himself through the sacrificial blood of Jesus Christ and regenerating our spirit unto eternal life. But beyond that He has clothed us with the Holy Spirit anointing, restoring that dimension of relational dominion that we were originally created to experience. In other words, our heavenly Father has poured out the gift of the Holy Spirit upon His sons and daughters to anoint each of them to become all who they were created to be. And may it be confidently established and graciously experienced in the life of every Spirit-filled believer because "you have an anointing from the Holy One."[424]

---

421. Matt. 13:54-58.
422. Zech. 4:6.
423. Col. 2:9-10.
424. 1 John 2:10.

Be Filled with the Spirit:

All too often the anointing of the Holy Spirit has not been considered as essential to God's plan for our lives on this earth but considered more as an optional addendum to salvation. It is my conviction that the anointing of the Holy Spirit or the baptism of the Holy Spirit is absolutely essential in fulfilling God's purposes in and through each believer. The anointing of the Holy Spirit is the operational power of God which He has granted to the citizens of His kingdom! It is a blessed privilege of every believer to receive the anointing of the Holy Spirit and never to be considered as an option. The Scripture says, "Be filled with the Spirit."[425] Believers are commissioned to serve others in the power of the Holy Spirit and as ambassadors of God's kingdom in this world.

The first mention in the Scriptures of "anointing" is found in Exodus 25:6. God instructed Moses to receive a freewill offering from the children of Israel for the purpose of gathering the materials necessary for the construction of the Tabernacle, oil for the lampstand, spices for the anointing ointment, and for the sweet incense. The first persons in the Scriptures to be "anointed" were Aaron and his four sons to minister to God as priests.[426] In the Old Testament, priests, prophets, and kings were anointed with the holy anointing oil to serve God. Each of the anointed had a special relationship with God whereby they were authorized to access dimensions of God's grace and the responsibility of executing His kingdom purposes. Jack Hayford states,

> In the Old Testament, the anointed person belonged to God in a special sense. The phrases, "the Lord's anointed," "God's anointed," "My anointed," "Your anointed," or "His anointed" are used of Saul (1 Sam.

---

425. Eph. 5:18.
426. Exo. 28:40-43, 30:22-33.

> 26:9-11), David (2 Sam. 22:51), and Solomon (2 Chro. 6:42).[427]

It was the anointing upon the High Priest that authorized him alone access to the ark of the covenant behind the veil and to enter the presence of God one day each year on the Day of Atonement. He went behind the veil with a censor containing hot coals from the golden altar and sweet incense that formed a fragrant cloud when placed upon the hot coals. He also carried in the blood from the sacrifice and sprinkled it seven times upon the mercy seat to make atonement for the sins of Israel. The mercy seat formed the cover or lid of the ark of the covenant which was an earthly type of God's throne in heaven. Kevin J. Conner states, "It was the blood that changed the Throne of Judgment into a Throne of Grace (Heb. 4:14-16)."[428]

The covenant God made with Israel at Sinai included the giving of the Law, the pattern for the Tabernacle, the prescribed Offerings, and the institution of the Aaronic Priesthood, all of which served as types and shadows of the person and work of Jesus Christ. In the New Covenant Jesus Christ is the substance of the Old Covenant types and shadows and the "new and living way" into God's presence.[429] The weakness of the Old Covenant was that it was powerless to make perfect. "For the law, having a shadow of the good things to come, *and* not the very image of the things, can never with these same sacrifices, which they offer continually year by year, make those who approach perfect."[430] It was Jesus, the Anointed One, by the offering of Himself on the cross "has perfected forever those who are being sanctified"[431] and "made us accepted in the Beloved."[432]

---

427. Hayford, *The Hayford Bible Handbook,* 543.

428. Kevin J. Conner, *The Tabernacle of Moses: The Riches of Redemption's Story as Revealed in the Tabernacle* (Portland, OR: City Bible Publishing, 1976), 24.

429. Heb. 10:19-22.

430. Heb. 10:1.

431. Heb. 10:14.

432. Eph. 1:6.

The Holy Anointing Oil:

The anointing oil used in the Old Testament was called "holy anointing oil." It was not to be duplicated or used for any purpose beyond God's specific instructions.[433] The holy anointing oil was a shadow or type representing the person of the Holy Spirit. There were many kinds of ointments, but only one "holy anointing oil." Also, there are many different spirits but only one "Holy Spirit." The holy anointing oil was "an ointment compounded according to the art of a perfumer;"[434] made according to a precise manner with precisely the following five ingredients:

1. Myrrh: 500 shekels – bitter spice - flowed freely from a tree – Christ death
2. Sweet Cinnamon: 250 shekels – sweet and taste agreeable – zeal of Love (jealous)
3. Sweet Calamus: 250 shekels – a cane that had a sweet fragrance when crushed
4. Cassia: 500 shekels - a root signifying to "bow down," as in worship
5. One hin of olive oil = 5 quarts

The holy anointing ointment has emblematic significations or meanings to be derived from the four principal spices and the olive oil. The "myrrh" points to the outpouring of Christ's love in a bitter but fragrant death. The "cinnamon" points to His holy jealousy for the honor and glory of God. The "calamus" to His uprightness and righteousness in a world of sin and wickedness; and the "cassia" to Christ's submission to God the Father. The largest ingredient amount was the olive oil when blended together with the other spices represented the Holy Spirit who anointed Jesus as "the Christ" or "the Anointed One." The Holy Spirit is also titled, "the Spirit of Christ."[435]

433. Exo. 30:22-38
434. Exo. 30:25, 35.
435. Phil. 1:19; 1 Peter 1:11.

In discussing this ointment or "holy anointing oil" Dr. Ron Cottle provides the following insights:

> The word "ointment" is even more insightful as to the meaning of the anointing. It is the word *shemen* from which the word "semen," a man's biological seed, is derived! The *shemen Yahweh* is the life flow of God in the anointing. *Shemen* (semen) is the word used in Exodus 30:22-33 for the Anointing Oil. It is the creative, life giving oil of God. The anointing produces life! birth! productivity![436]

Therefore, to be anointed by God the Holy Spirit, means to have received the life, essence, personality, and nature of God. The most thorough discussion on the Holy Spirit in the teaching of Jesus is recorded in John chapters 14 through 16. John is the only Evangelist that uses the Greek word *"parakletos."* It is used five times by John (John 14:16, 14:26, 15:26,16:7, and 1 John 2:1). Jesus was going to return to the Father, but He was not leaving His followers as orphans. He would be sending the "another" exactly like Himself to abide with them until He returns. R. C. H. Lenski states,

> Jesus calls the Spirit "another Paraclete," implying that he himself was the first Paraclete of the disciples when he walked in their midst. The word is sometimes used in the sense of "advocate" in a court of justice, and John uses the word in this sense in 1 John 2:1, where he speaks of Jesus as our Advocate with the Father when we sin… The Spirit, as the Paraclete, takes the place of Jesus at the side of the disciples; he brings all things to their remembrance which Jesus said to them, 14:26; he testifies to the disciples

---

436. Ronald E. Cottle, *The Crown Prince Anointing: Your Mantle of Anointing in This Time of Transition,* (Columbus, GA: Christian Life Publishers, 1997), 33.

> concerning Jesus, 15:26; Jesus sends him to the disciples (16:7), and he shall glorify Jesus, taking what is his and showing it unto them (16:14). [437]

Jesus uses the word "*parakletos*" to express various functions attributed to the Holy Spirit, for example: Helper, Advocate, Counsellor, Revealer, and Interpreter. All these functions are for the purpose of sanctifying believers and empowering them to fulfill their role as His "witnesses" while prevailing over the powers of the flesh, the world, and the devil. Therefore, the anointed person is empowered to release upon others the life, essence, personality, and nature of God. That is what Jesus Christ did during His earthly ministry. That is why He is entitled "the Christ" or "the Messiah" as the following comments define "Messiah":

> The term "messiah" is the translation of the Hebrew term *māšîaḥ*, which is derived from the verb *māšaḥ*, meaning to smear or anoint. When objects such as wafers and shields were smeared with grease or oil they were said to be anointed; hence the commonly used term was "anoint" when grease or oil was applied to objects by Israelites and non-Israelites. The term "messiah" is not used to refer to "anointed" objects that were designated and consecrated for specific cultic purposes but to persons only. Persons who were anointed had been elected, designated, appointed, given authority, qualified, and equipped for specific offices and tasks related to these.[438]

---

437. R. C. H. Lenski, *The Interpretation of St. John's Gospel* (Minneapolis, MN: Augsburg Publishing House, 1961), 997-998.

438. Gerard Van Groningen, "Messiah," *Evangelical Dictionary of Biblical Theology*, Baker Reference Library (Grand Rapids: Baker Book House, 1996), 523.

> A Hebrew term meaning "anointed one." The OT people of God came to anticipate a person anointed by the Spirit who would function once again as king and priest over Israel. Hence in Jewish (OT and intertestamental) theology, the Messiah was the person, whether supernatural or earthly, endowed with special powers and functions by God, who would appear as the divinely appointed, eschatological deliverer and ruler of Israel. Although Jesus rarely used the title specifically for himself, the NT designation of Messiah (Greek *Christos*) belongs only to Jesus, both as a title and as a personal name. Jesus was the one who was truly anointed by the Holy Spirit, and as the bearer of the Spirit he has the prerogative to pour out the Spirit on his followers.[439]

The birth, life, and ministry of Jesus Christ were not simply occasioning of chance or random acts, but events and actions according to God's will as prerecorded in Scripture.

> Therefore, when He came into the world, He said: *"Sacrifice and offering You did not desire, but a body You have prepared for Me. In burnt offerings and sacrifices for sin You had no pleasure. Then I said, 'Behold, I have come-- In the volume of the book it is written of Me-- To do Your will, O God.'* " Previously saying, *"Sacrifice and offering, burnt offerings, and offerings for sin You did not desire, nor had pleasure in them"* (which are offered according to the law), then He said, *"Behold, I have come to do Your will, O*

439. Stanley Grenz, David Guretzki, and Cherith Fee Nordling, *Pocket Dictionary of Theological Terms* (Downers Grove, IL: InterVarsity Press, 1999), 77.

> *God."* He takes away the first that He may establish the second. (Heb. 10:5-9).

Sealed and Anointed by the Holy Spirit:

The period between the outpouring of the Holy Spirit on the Day of Pentecost and the second coming of the Lord Jesus Christ is designated as the Apostolic Age or Church Age. During this Church Age believers in Jesus Christ are placed by God as citizens of the kingdom of God and granted the privilege of being anointed by the empowering presence of God, the Holy Spirit. "Now He who establishes us with you in Christ and has anointed us *is* God."[440] The anointing is not about a blessing, nor a gift, such as grace, peace, or faith, but a person! The person of the Holy Spirit Himself, with all His holiness, divinity, and power. Something supernatural ought to be expected when a person is anointed by the Holy Spirit. To be sealed by the Holy Spirit is the confirmation of God's ownership, and to be anointed by the Holy Spirit is the affirmation of God's abiding presence upon your life with power.[441]

The Lord has made every provision for our freedom from the bondage of sin. He has given us an abundance of grace for holy living and empowered us by the anointing of the Holy Spirit to serve as citizens in His kingdom as His fruitful witnesses in this world. Therefore, our lives and ministries should not be random acts, but behaviors and actions guided by an alignment with God's will as revealed in Scripture. After Jesus was anointed by the Holy Spirit, He was "led by the Spirit into the wilderness being tempted for forty days by the devil."[442] During those days of temptation Jesus gained victory over the devil through His alignment with the Word of God and firmly declared it as His defense in the face of each temptation, "It is written."[443] It is

---

440. 2 Cor. 1:21.
441. 1 Cor. 6:19-20; 2 Cor. 1:22-23; John 5:30; Acts 1:8; Eph. 1:13, 4:30.
442. Luke 4:1-2.
443. Matt. 4:4, 7, 9.

easy to see how Jesus' response to temptation differed from Adam's response. Jesus relied on the words of truth to guard Him against succumbing to temptation. Adam did not say, "God said, 'of the tree of the knowledge of good and evil you shall not eat, for in the day you eat of it you shall surely die.'"[444] Rather, Adam simply ate the forbidden fruit. As believers we each have the privilege and the responsibility of following Jesus' example by: (1) receiving the anointing of the Holy Spirit. (2) Defining our anointing according to Scripture. And (3) expressing our anointing by a holy lifestyle and power even in the face of temptation, opposition, and persecution.[445]

All believers, no matter how young they are in their relationship with the Lord, will experience some level of communion or fellowship with their heavenly Father. However, intimacy with our heavenly Father and godly character are not Spiritual gifts even though the Holy Spirit helps us develop intimacy and Christlikeness. It takes time and experience to mature and develop godly character and unlearn wrong understandings and habits while coming to a knowledge of the truth. Warren Wiersbe states, "There is a vast difference between age and maturity. Age is a quantity of years, while maturity is a quantity of experience."[446] Jesus never sinned, but learned obedience by the things He suffered.[447] There is little practical difference experienced in the life of a new believer from that of a slave to sin, except the believer's new nature in Christ has capacity to experience transformation with the help of the Holy Spirit. This is one of the reasons why the Apostle Paul instructed Timothy not to appoint a bishop who was a novice.[448] The Scripture says:

---

444. Gen. 2:17.

445. Luke 4:18-19.

446. Warren W. Wiersbe, *The 20 Essential Qualities of an Authentic Christian* (Nashville, TN: Thomas Nelson, Inc., 1996), 136.

447. Heb. 5:8.

448. 1 Tim. 3:6.

> Now I say *that* the heir, as long as he is a child, does not differ at all from a slave, though he is master of all, but is under guardians and stewards until the time appointed by the father. Even so we, when we were children, were in bondage under the elements of the world. (Galatians 4:1-3)

"Newborn babes, desire the pure milk of the word" and that is healthy and good for babies, but it would be unhealthy if the babies did not grow through the discomforting weaning process and develop the need for solid food.[449] All believers have the responsibility to grow-up and "no longer be children tossed to and fro and carried about with every wind of doctrine, by the trickery of men, in the cunning craftiness of deceitful plotting."[450] A maturing person's development should progress to the level of producing and preparing their own food and food for others. That's what responsible people are expected to do. As important as the anointing is, it is not a substitute for mature godly character.

Therefore, making disciples of Jesus is a vitally important aspect of the life of any congregation. Far too often our church services have emphasized a gospel that focused on the atonement or the cross of Christ, the forgiveness of sin, and the new birth. That is powerfully important, and it is never our intention to minimize that powerful aspect of the gospel. But if we limit the gospel of the kingdom to the atonement, we perpetuate Christian infancy. Because the cross is not an end of our journey, but a doorway into a relationship with God that requires the process of growing or maturing "to the measure of the stature of the fullness of Christ.; that we should no longer be children… but grow up in all things into Him who is the head—Christ… "[451] Regarding the atonement and the kingdom of God, Jack Taylor writes;

449. 1 Peter 2:2; Heb. 5:12-14.
450. Eph. 4:14.
451. Eph. 4:13-16.

> There is one gospel with two facets.... The first facet, the gospel of the Kingdom... the other facet is what we call the gospel of the atonement.... The complete gospel embraces both Kingdom and atonement... **The atonement itself is but a means to an end**, and this end is the reestablishment of God's empire in man, the restoration of God's diadem over mankind, the return of Jehovah God to walk again with His children in the garden in the cool of the day. God's re-enthronement means man's salvation, even as man's salvation means God's re-enthronement.... The Kingdom on earth is manifested by the Holy Spirit as He works through the body of Christ, the church, whose members are co-heirs with the King.... The church has also been entrusted with a redeeming narrative called the *gospel* that once proclaimed, enables others to enter the Kingdom, as well, and to understand the eternal Kingdom they have been invited to enter.[452] (Emphasis mine).

Once a person has been convicted of sin, repented of sin, and believed on the Lord Jesus Christ, they received the gift of Hoy Spirit and the gift of righteousness. They are thus regenerated by the indwelling of the Holy Spirit (born again). He or she should then seek to be baptized in the Holy Spirit or filled with the Holy Spirit or endued with the power of the Holy Spirit or anointed by the Holy Spirit. Realistically each of those four expressions generally refer to the same spiritual experience. The anointing of the Holy Spirit is to be experienced by every believer in Jesus Christ. Everyone who has been born again and filled with the Holy Spirit is anointed and endued with power by the Holy Spirit.[453] The Holy Spirit anointing graces

---

452. Taylor, *Cosmic Initiative,* 106-109.
453. Luke 11:13; Acts 19:6; Acts 1:8.

a believer with an alignment to the Father's nature that endues that believer with kingdom power and accesses the grace of the Father's sovereign authority.[454] According to Jack Hayford;

> The Spirit-filled life is the new-dimensional life of worship, witness, and warfare. And the key to its realization is the **anointing** Jesus places on your life—like heavenly oil poured over the heads of the priests, prophets and kings in ancient times. And that **anointing** is the result of being filled with, overflowed by, and baptized in the Holy Spirit.... "The baptism with the Holy Spirit," "being filled with the Holy Spirit," and "becoming Spirit-filled" are generally interchangeable terms, and the fact that a variety of phrases are used for the same spiritual experience shouldn't bother us.... For example, when someone "receives Jesus as Savior," that experience is also frequently described as "being saved," "being born again," or "being converted."[455] (emphasis mine).

A source of misunderstanding regarding "initial evidence" of the baptism of the Holy Spirit originated through the ministry of Charles Parham who began a healing home in Topeka, Kansas where students were invited to study the Scriptures. Frank Bartleman writes;

> In January 1901, one of the students, an eighteen-year-old girl named Agnes Ozman, was baptized in the Holy Spirit and began to speak in other tongues as the Spirit gave utterance. This came as a result of an intense study of the Scriptures concerning the "evidence" of receiving the Holy Spirit. From this

---

454. Eph. 4:7.

455. Jack W. Hayford, *Spirit Filled: The Overflowing Power of the Holy Spirit* (Los Angeles, CA: Foursquare Media, 2007), 10, 82.

> experience, Parham constructed his thesis that glossolalia was the biblical evidence of being baptized in the Holy Spirit.[456]

Parham's misunderstanding regarding the "initial evidence" of the baptism influenced the doctrinal position of the Assemblies of God denomination which became a national organization in 1914. Historian Vinson Synan writes regarding the Assemblies of God, the largest and the best-known Pentecostal fellowship in the world, adopted Charles Parham's position "that speaking in tongues was the "initial evidence" of the baptism of the Holy Spirit, a doctrine that became distinctive of the AG belief concerning the baptism in the Holy Spirit."[457] Vinson Synan also writes of individuals talking in tongues one-hundred years before the Charles Parham's students spoke in tongues. "In the revival that hit the University of Georgia in 1800-1801, students visited nearby campgrounds and were themselves smitten with the "jerks" and "talking in unknown tongues"."[458] Therefore, speaking in tongues was not the new Spiritual experience derived from the student's experience in Topeka, Kansas. The new doctrine was the "initial evidence" of the baptism of the Holy Spirit was that of speaking in tongues.

Jack Hayford references the manifestation of the Holy Spirit throughout church history stating, "There was a loss of focus on the empowering presence of the Spirit of God that was so central to the New Testament experience."[459] Even though there was a loss of focus on the baptism of the Holy Spirit and speaking in tongues through the

---

456. Frank Bartleman, *Azusa Street* (Plainfield, NJ: Logos International, 1980), x.

457. Vinson Synan, *The Century of the Holy Spirit: 100 Years of Pentecostal and Charismatic Renewal* (Nashville, TN: Thomas Nelson, Inc., 2001), 124-125.

458. Vinson Synan, *The Holiness-Pentecostal Movement in the United States* (Grand Rapids, MI: William B. Eerdmans Publishing Company, 1971), 35.

459. Jack W. Hayford and David S. Moore, *The Charismatic Century: The Enduring Impact of the Azusa Street Revival* (New York, NY: Warner Faith, 2006), 24.

centuries following the outpouring on the Day of Pentecost, those experiences did occur throughout church history. Through the years of Church history speaking in tongues was not considered as the "initial evidence" of the baptism of the Holy Spirit. Henry I. Lederle states regarding William Seymour, the leader of the Azusa Street movement, "Seymour was himself later to abandon this theory of "initial evidence," choosing rather to see Christian love as the evidence of Spirit baptism."[460] It is my conviction according to Jesus' words just prior to His ascension, that "power" is the expected evidence of the baptism of the Holy Spirit.[461] I tend to agree with William Seymour in as much as "love" is a powerful virtue that never fails! However, I do not think that love will turn water into wine, but Holy Spirit power will do that.

John the Baptist said regarding Jesus, "I indeed baptize you with water; but One mightier than I is coming, whose sandal strap I am not worthy to unloose. He will baptize you with the Holy Spirit and fire."[462] Just prior to His ascension Jesus said, "You shall receive power when the Holy Spirit has come upon you…"[463] Personally I did not speak in tongues when I received the baptism of the Holy Spirit, but my life was transformed by a burning desire for the Word of God. A few months later I did speak in unknown tongues and continue to exercise that Spiritual gift. When the Holy Spirit descended upon Jesus following His water baptism, there is no record of Him speaking in tongues, but He surely did minister in the power of the Holy Spirit. Therefore, as a result of the general resistance to speaking in tongues and the sometimes confusion regarding the terminology used to describe the baptism of the Holy Spirit, I prefer when possible to use the terms "filled with the Holy Spirit" or "anointed by the Holy Spirit." Jesus described the abiding presence of the Holy Spirit upon Himself as "The Spirit of the Lord is upon Me because He has anoint-

---

460. Henry I. Lederle, *Theology with Spirit* (Tulsa, OK: Word & Spirit Press, 2010), 13.

461. Acts 1:8.

462. Matt. 3:11; Luke 3:16.

463. Acts 1:8.

ed Me…."[464] Remember, Jesus was conceived by the Holy Spirit and at about age thirty experienced the Holy Spirit coming upon Him.[465] The emphasis here is to encourage believers to move beyond their initial salvation experience and receive the empowerment of the Holy Spirit. I affirm that Spirit-filled believers not only have God dwelling in their hearts, and they are going to heaven someday. But they are also clothed upon with His presence to demonstrate the reality and blessings of the kingdom of God in the here and now! Lederle writes,

> The Spirit works *internally,* continually molding our character into conformity with Christ and bringing forth God's image in us relationally. The Spirit also works *externally* intermittently to enable and empower us to operate mightily in word and deed, evincing God's supernatural strength and love.[466]

The anointing by the Holy Spirit intensifies the believer's awareness of God presence and anticipates the manifestation of His operational power in one's work, worship, witness, and warfare. When a person is born again the Holy Spirit comes to dwell in that person's heart, bearing witness to the reality of his or her personal relationship with God as a son or daughter.[467] The Holy Spirit does not come into a believer's heart to visit, but to abide and make His habitation there.[468] When a believer is baptized in the Holy Spirit, the Spirit comes upon the believer just as the Spirit came upon Jesus following His water baptism in the Jordan River. In other words, the Holy Spirit resides in you as a Spirit of Adoption, bearing witness to the reality of your membership in God's royal family. But the Holy Spirit comes upon

---

464. Luke 4:18
465. Matt. 1:20.
466. Lederle, *Theology with Spirit,* 204.
467. Rom. 8:16.
468. 1 Cor. 6:19; Heb. 13:5.

you to anoint or empower you to serve others as a witness of the Lordship of Jesus Christ and the presence of the kingdom of God.

Unveiling a Mystery of the Kingdom:

The anointing or the power of the kingdom of God is wrapped in a mystery.[469] A Biblical mystery isn't something that is absurd or something only available to an elite few, but something that is hidden or veiled from our natural understanding.[470] To unwrap the mysteries of God requires the presence of the Holy Spirit who is our Teacher.[471] He reveals the mysteries of God which are hidden in the Lord Jesus Christ, who is made unto us wisdom. Therefore, it is every believer's privilege and responsibility to respond to Jesus' seven-fold imperative; "He that has an ear let him hear what the Spirit is saying to the churches."[472] Jesus is not commanding believers to simply hear what He has said, but to hear what He is presently saying to the church, that believers may be established in present truth.[473] This does not imply that the Holy Spirit is going to say something beyond Scripture, but He will illuminate or quicken God's written word just as Jesus, after His resurrection took the Old Testament and "opened the Apostles' understanding that they might comprehend the Scriptures."[474]

Jesus Christ is "A stone of stumbling and a rock of offence"[475] to the disobedient of this world, but to us who believe He is precious and the chief cornerstone. It is through God's wisdom revealed by the Holy Spirit that God is in the process of overturning the systems of this world. He is preparing the church for the day when the Lord Jesus Christ shall return and rule and reign on the earth as the King of kings and Lord of lords. It is the Holy Spirit that "searches all

469. Matt. 13:10-11.
470. 1 Cor. 2:6-16.
471. 1 Cor. 2:12-14; Eph. 1:17-21; John 14:26; 1 John 2:20, 27.
472. Rev. 2:7, 11, 17, 29, 3:6, 13, 22.
473. 2 Peter 1:12.
474. Luke 24:45.
475. 1 Peter 2:7-8.

things… that we might know the things that have freely been given to us by God."[476] This at least partially informs us as to why receiving the anointing of the Holy Spirit is very crucial for every disciple of Jesus Christ. John Lake describes the impact that the baptism of the Holy Spirit had on his life and ministry as follows:

> My experience has truly been, as Jesus said: "He shall be within you a well of water springing up into everlasting Life" (John 4:14). That never-ceasing fountain has flowed day and night through my spirit, soul, and body, bringing salvation and healing and the baptism of the Spirit in the power of God to multitudes…. Shortly after my baptism in the Holy Spirit a working of the Spirit commenced in me, which seemed to have for its purpose the revelation of the nature of Christ to me and in me. Through this tutelage and remolding by the Spirit, a great tenderness for mankind awakened in my soul. I saw mankind through new eyes…. The desire to proclaim the message of Christ and to demonstrate His power to save and bless grew in my soul until my life was swayed by this overwhelming passion.[477]

The anointing of the Holy Spirit is not simply a doctrine, but an empowerment to serve as the Lord's ambassadors in this world with the ministry of reconciliation. The Holy Spirit is the Spirit of revelation that truthfully defines our identity in Christ, arms believers against the deceptions of the devil, and empowers us to prevail as overcomers. Roberts Liardon states that John G. Lake, "would also compare the anointing of God's Spirit to the power of electricity. Just as men learned the laws of electricity, Lake had discovered the

476. 1 Cor. 2:10-12; 1 John 2:27.

477. John Lake, *Your Power in the Holy Spirit,* comp. by Roberts Liardon (New Kensington, PA: Whitaker House, 2010), 40.

laws of the Spirit."[478] Under Lake's anointed ministry hundreds of churches were started, thousands were healed of all kinds of diseases and hundreds of thousands were reconciled to Jesus. Today a hundred years later many of the churches Lake pioneered are still flourishing and bringing the blessing of the kingdom of God to bear upon their respective communities especially in South Africa where he served during the early 1900's.

The anointing of the Holy Spirit enhances our perceptions of God, ourselves, and our world. Perception is a spiritual lens that determines how I see what I see. Do I see obstacles or opportunities? Notice how those who had received the baptism of the Holy Spirit on the Day of Pentecost perceived that event far different from those who had not received the baptism of the Holy Spirit. Peter perceived that event as the fulfillment of the prophecy of Joel. But those who had not received the baptism of the Holy Spirit mocked and considered those who spoke in tongues and prophesied as being drunk. They did not perceive what was taking place as the work of God. When the Holy Spirit anoints a believer that individual's creativity or leadership ability isn't diminished or impaired, rather that person suddenly sees from God's perspective and is empowered to be even more creative and effective in his or her work and relationships!

The anointing of the Holy Spirit is the power of God available to be released through every believer. It is also the Holy Spirit or the Spirit of grace that transforms that power into a lifestyle. We as believers must grow beyond the concept that "I am a Christian" or "I am the righteousness of God in Christ."[479] Those things are important and true, but the problem as I see it is that we the church are prone to settle for a powerless Christianity. Biblical ethics and righteousness are essential to our eternal salvation and should never be ignored. However, Jesus specifically commanded His disciples to not depart from Jerusalem, but "tarry in the city of Jerusalem until you are

---

478. Lake, *Your Power,* 295-296.

479. 2 Cor. 5:21.

endued with power from on high."[480] They were enabled to see and perceive with greater insight than ever before because they were perceiving from God's perspective. The key is learning how to adapt to the ways of God and a readiness to contend for the manifestations of God's gracious miracle working power and cooperate with the Holy Spirit. We as members of the body of Christ are to be priests that serve as His representatives that manifest the presence and blessings of the kingdom to this world. In addition, we are to keep the golden rule and live with the expectation of going to heaven when we die. Joshua Mills states;

> The anointing is the manifest power of God that sets us apart.... It is a divine enablement that helps us to accomplish God's supernatural purposes on earth.... The anointing brings a grace to carry out the specific will of God for your life. Without the anointing, your calling could never develop properly.... The hand of the Spirit anoints men and women to fulfill their high calling as ministers of God wherever they find themselves.... In the anointing, we learn how to grow in grace. John the Baptist grew in grace (see Luke 1:80), and Jesus did too (see Luke 2:40).[481]

The anointing of the Holy Spirit empowers every believer to overcome "unbelief", the "mystery of iniquity",[482] and the "spirit of antichrist" that is working so deceptively and insidiously against the kingdom of God and corrupting the world around us. Jesus Christ did not come from heaven to simply teach the wisdom of the kingdom of God, as important as that is. Jesus came to "destroy the works of the devil," "abolish death," and "put all things under His feet," that

---

480. Luke 24:49.

481. Joshua Mills, *Moving in the Glory Realms: Exploring Dimensions of Divine Presence* (New Kensington, PA: Whitaker House, 2018), 51-54

482. 2 Thes. 2:7.

"God may be all in all!."[483] We are called and anointed to be salt and light, influencing the world around us through the power of the Holy Spirit by preaching the gospel of the kingdom of God, interceding with prayers, and by our holy lifestyle. We can do this with a grace and confidence because "greater is He that is in us than He that is in the world."[484]

You Are the Fragrance of Christ:

How do you see yourself? How do you see your spouse or children? How do you think God sees you? Does He see you, as wrong or simply missing something? Every born-again believer is a purified virgin through the cleansing blood of Jesus and betroth to Jesus with that relationship sealed by the Holy Spirit. The Apostle Paul said to the Corinthians, "I am jealous for you with a godly jealousy. For I have betrothed you to one husband, that I may present you as a chaste virgin to Christ."[485] Every born-again believer is engaged to be married to Jesus and sealed by the Spirit of holiness as our engagement ring! "Now He who establishes us with you in Christ and has anointed us *is* God, who also has sealed us and given us the Spirit in our hearts as a guarantee"[486] Believers are not only engaged to be married to Jesus Christ, but also commissioned and anointed to serve as His ambassadors in this world.[487] As the betrothed virgin bride of the Lamb, we are currently serving God in this world by making manifest the knowledge of Christ, as the following Scripture describes:

> Now thanks *be* to God who always leads us in triumph in Christ, and **through us diffuses the fragrance of His knowledge in every place**. For we are to God the

483. 1 John 3:8, 4:3; Heb. 2:14; 2 Tim. 1:10; 1 Cor. 15:27-28.
484. 1 John 4:4.
485. 2 Cor. 11:2.
486. 2 Cor. 1:21-22.
487. 2 Cor. 5:20.

> fragrance of Christ among those who are being saved and among those who are perishing. To the one *we are* the aroma of death *leading* to death, and to the other the aroma of life *leading* to life. And who *is* sufficient for these things? (2 Cor. 2:14-16; emphasis mine).

To receive the anointing means to be clothed upon with the Holy Spirit. Jesus said, "Behold, I send the promise of My Father upon you; but tarry in the city of Jerusalem until you are endued with power from on high."[488] In other words, to receive the anointing of the Holy Spirit is to be clothed upon with the Father's robe of royal power as a citizen of the Kingdom of God. This is the same royal robe that Jesus wore during His earthly ministry that empowered Him to inaugurate the kingdom of God, break the bondage of sin and death, redeem the captives, heal the sick, and destroy the works of the devil. Now that Jesus has gone to be with the Father, He has sent the Holy Spirit to accomplish our sanctification, enable us to become partakers of His divine nature, and empower us to be fruitful witnesses of His invisible presence and kingdom. As we observe the fear, hopelessness, fermenting anger, addictions, and brokenness in our communities we must ask ourselves, "Is there any answer, any hope or peace?" We all know that the answer is an overwhelming yes, because where sin abounds grace does much more abound.[489] We can face these challenges as the Apostle Paul did. He said to the Corinthians;

And my speech and my preaching *were* not with persuasive words of human wisdom, but in demonstration of the Spirit and of power,

---

488. Luke 24:49. "endued" - *endyo = to be clothed upon, to put on* - Galatians 3:27 "For as many of you as were baptized into Christ have put on (*endyo*) Christ." 1 Corinthians 15:53-54 (53) "For this corruptible must put on (*endyo*) incorruption, and this mortal *must* put on (*endyo*) immortality. (54) So when this corruptible has put on (*endyo*) incorruption, and this mortal has put on (*endyo*) immortality, then shall be brought to pass the saying that is written: '*Death is swallowed up in victory.*'"

489. Rom. 5:20.

that your faith should not be in the wisdom of men but in the power of God.[490]

Believers in Jesus Christ are to be an empowered people. Because the Father has also provided an Advocate for us, Jesus Christ, who is seated at His right hand, and ever lives to make intercession for us.[491] On the other hand, He has also sent a second Advocate, the Holy Spirit, into our hearts to help us and guide us through our daily responsibilities and challenges.[492] This affirms the reality that we are no longer orphans, but favored sons, clothed with a royal robe just as Joseph was a favored son with the coat of many colors and made manifest the knowledge of God in a pagan land.

All Spirit-filled children of God are distinguished from orphans in at least four ways. First, all Spirit-filled children of God have been redeemed from sin and death, forgiven and reconciled with the Father, given the gift of righteousness, and conveyed out of the kingdom of darkness into the kingdom of God. Second, all Spirit-filled children of God have received the gift of the Holy Spirit or the Spirit of Adoption that bears witness that he or she is a child of God, thus affirming his or her true identity. Third, all Spirit-filled children of God have been anointed by the Holy Spirit or endued with power from on high or clothed upon by the royal robe of the Father's favor and blessing that sufficiently empowers each of them to reign in life and bring the blessings of the kingdom of God upon others. And fourth, all Spirit-filled children of God have an eternal inheritance, because as members of His royal family they are heirs of God and joint-heirs with Jesus Christ. Orphans exist without a father's gifts or blessings and maintain a survival mentality with no inheritance whatsoever. Furthermore, all Spirit-filled children of God have been commissioned by the Lord Jesus to proclaim the gospel of the kingdom and make disciples of all nations. Because God is not willing that any orphan should perish but

490. 1 Cor. 2:4-5.
491. Heb. 7:25.
492. Rom. 8:14-15, 26-27.

be reconciled with the Father, enjoy the blessings of the royal family, and inherit life eternal.

The Anointing – Heaven's Credit Card:

To better understand the meaningfulness of the anointing of the Holy Spirit, look at it this way: God is sovereign and has created us in His image and likeness. He has equipped the redeemed to serve as His witnesses or ambassadors by affirming His sovereignty in this world, not through a military, political, or economic power, but by the power of anointing of the Holy Spirit. Believers are anointed to demonstrate the presence of God's sovereignty in life's situations today. That demonstration is not an affirmation of the believer's spirituality, but a demonstration of God's sovereignty over the powers of darkness and evil. So, receiving the anointing is something like the privileged authority you experienced after you received your drivers license and your dad entrusted you with the keys to his car. It was more than just transportation. It was a new way of experiencing life and the privilege of freedom! However, to continue experiencing that privilege and freedom you had to drive responsibly. If you were responsible with your dad's car, then in time he would help you get your own car. Just as your dad loved you and trusted you with his car, so God loves you and the world around you. Therefore, He trust you with the power of the anointing and the privilege of serving Him as His personal representative to break the power of the enemy over those that you and the Father love. Remember, privilege and responsibility always go together, and it is the Father's joy to give you the "keys to the kingdom."[493]

To illustrate further, the anointing is something like a credit card. The credit card has no intrinsic value. Your credit card's worth is in the access it gives you to financial resource. The anointing has some personal value, but its true worth is in the access it gives you to

493. Matt. 16:19; Luke 12:32.

Messianic resources of heaven. If you carry your credit card everywhere you go and do not use it, what value is that to you or anyone else? But when you go to Wal-Mart your credit card offers you the opportunity to purchase things that you need or want. So, it is with your anointing. When you go to Wal-Mart and see someone with a need, you may release the power of God upon that person and break their captivity to infirmity, oppression, addiction or fear! The anointing that you have received isn't simply about going to church or Bible study. No! It is about the power of God to set the captives free and bring the blessings of the kingdom of God upon their lives. All this does not happen by chance or accident. Your anointing is activated and released by faith; your faith in action at a given moment will demonstrate the presence of the sovereignty of God over the powers of darkness. That is how Jesus Christ functioned. He is our role model and He has given you access to all the authority and power of heaven.

It is interesting to note that Jesus had sent out His twelve apostles "to preach the kingdom of God and to heal the sick."[494] Later Jesus sent seventy of His disciples out two by two as lambs among wolves to heal the sick and proclaim, "The kingdom of God has come near you." And "the seventy returned with joy, saying, 'Lord, even the demons were subject to Your name.'"[495] In other words Jesus first sent the twelve apostles out and a little later sent the seventy disciples to heal the sick and proclaim the presence of the kingdom of God with His credit card. Hence, they experienced the manifest power of the Messianic anointing. A short time later His disciples could not cast a demon out of a young boy. After Jesus delivered the boy from the demon, He gave His disciples insight regarding the releasing of the anointing. He first focused on their lack of faith and stressed the possibilities with even mustard seed size faith; but faith must be stimulated by prayer and fasting.[496] On the Day of Pentecost the disciples of

494. Luke 9:1-6.
495. Luke 10:1-17.
496. Matt. 17:16-21; Mark 9:17-29.

Jesus received the anointing of the Holy Spirit and thereby were entrusted with a personal credit card to draw on the Messianic resources of heaven as they went preaching the gospel of the kingdom.

Between the third century following the Day of Pentecost and the outpouring of the Holy Spirit in the early days of the twentieth century the person of the Holy Spirit and the power of the anointing received limited recognition. But today we are experiencing a powerful restoration of emphasis on the person of the Holy Spirit and the anointing with power to bear witness to the presence of the kingdom of God and the Lordship of Jesus Christ. The Messianic resources of heaven are being restored to the body of Christ to overcome the demonic onslaught of unbelief, the mystery of iniquity, and the spirit of anti-Christ. "Therefore, gird up the loins of your mind, be sober, and rest *your* hope fully upon the grace that is to be brought to you at the revelation of Jesus Christ."[497]

During the Reformation correct doctrine was a primary issue and remains as an important pillar of Biblical faith. Today God is building upon that doctrinal foundation with an emphasis upon the person and work of the Holy Spirit. That doesn't mean that all so-called Church or Christianity is focused on the Holy Spirit. R. T. Kendall states, "If the Holy Spirit were completely withdrawn from the Church today, 90 percent of the work of the Church would go on as though nothing had happened.[498] However, the anointing of the Holy Spirit isn't for the purpose of making spiritual superstars. There is a brand of excessive confidence to the point of arrogance and supposed superiority that breeds pride and in no way exhibits the character of Christ. That excess is immoral and repulsive to God and must never be tolerated. Having said that, it is important to also understand there is also a brand of false humility that stresses how unworthy we are while placing God in such lofty heights that He can't be reached in our daily experiences. That is also immoral and repulsive and neither extreme

497. 1 Peter 1:13.

498. Kendall, *The Anointing,* 61.

is acceptable within the context of the anointing. Arrogant pride and false humility are both weapons of the enemy to destroy faith and fuel an antichrist spirit. The Apostle Paul instructs us with these words; "For I say, through the grace given to me, to everyone who is among you, not to think *of himself* more highly than he ought to think, but to think soberly, as God has dealt to each one a measure of faith."[499]

The Anointing Breaks the Yoke:

We thank God for the present ministry of the Holy Spirit and we are also grateful for the sacrificial labors of those scholars that have contributed to the availability of correct doctrine. Although correct doctrine is a cornerstone to overcoming faith, it is the person of the Holy Spirit that fires the soul with a zeal that correct doctrine seldom accomplishes.[500] The anointing by the Holy Spirit includes much more than could be included in an academic context. It is a relational treasure that facilitates an intimate relationship within the context of the New Covenant between God and a believer that powerfully enforces the exercise of the kingdom authority granted to the anointed sons of God. The powers of darkness must surrender their strongholds and release their captives to the anointed ones. Thus, "the yoke will be destroyed because of the anointing."[501]

Bill Johnson states, "We reign with the heart of a servant and serve with the heart of a king, all for the benefit of the people around us. Rulers in God's Kingdom never rule for their own sake…always for others.[502] Ministering under the power of the anointing of the Holy Spirit, enables New Testament believers to participate in an ongoing personal communion with God the Holy Spirit. The Holy Spirit ignites a righteous passion and faith that contends for the blessings

---

499. Rom. 12:3.

500. John 2:17; Acts 4:13; Eph. 3:8-12.

501. Isa. 10:27b.

502. Bill Johnson, *The Power that Changes the World: Creating Eternal Impact in the Here and Now* (Minneapolis, MN: Chosen Books, 2015), 63.

of the future Messianic age to be drawn into our present experience. Amos Yong discusses how his view regarding the work of the Holy Spirit includes yet reaches beyond the limits of His work in individuals and extends to the larger world systems. He now "thinks that the work of the Holy Spirit is to redeem and transform our world as a whole along with all of its interconnected parts, systems and structures."[503] However, not everyone desires the manifest presence of the Holy Spirit or the kingdom of God. Therefore, the Lord and His Church will be opposed today just as they have been throughout Church history. The Psalmist ask:

> Why do the nations rage, And the people plot a vain thing? The kings of the earth set themselves, and the rulers take counsel together, against the LORD and against His Anointed, *saying,* "Let us break their bonds in pieces and cast away their cords from us." (Psalm 2:1-3; Acts 4:25-26; emphasis mine).

For this reason, our prayer is for confident faith and boldness to speak His word and demonstrate the presence of the kingdom of God just as the Apostles did even in the face of opposition.[504] It is the anointing that will break the yoke of the oppressor.[505] And "you have an anointing from the Holy One, and you know all things."[506]

The question often arises, "As believers we are privileged to have received the anointing of the Holy Spirit how do I activate or release that anointing; or how do I move beyond a passive belief that I am anointed into a lifestyle of cooperation with the Holy Spirit?" It is helpful to consider how Jesus first released His anointing. His first

---

503. Amos Yong, *Who Is the Holy Spirit? A Walk with the Apostles* (Brewster, MS: Paraclete Press, 2011), x.

504. Acts 3:6, 4:29-31.

505. Isa. 10:27b.

506. 1 John 2:20.

miracle was accomplished while He was attending a wedding feast in Cana of Galilee:

> And they ran out of wine. His mother said to Him, "They have no wine." Jesus said to her, "Woman, what does your concern have to do with Me? My hour has not yet come." His mother said to the servants, "Whatever He says to you, do *it.*" Now there were set there six waterpots of stone, according to the manner of purification of the Jews, containing twenty or thirty gallons apiece. Jesus said to them, "Fill the waterpots with water." And they filled them up to the brim. And He said to them, "Draw *some* out now, and take *it* to the master of the feast." And they took *it.* When the master of the feast had tasted the water that was made wine and did not know where it came from (but the servants who had drawn the water knew), the master of the feast called the bridegroom. And he said to him, "Every man at the beginning sets out the good wine, and when the *guests* have well drunk, then the inferior. You have kept the good wine until now!" This beginning of signs Jesus did in Cana of Galilee and manifested His glory; and His disciples believed in Him.[507]

The question is, "What transpired in Jesus' heart between the time Mary told Him they were out of wine and His command to fill the water pots?" Jesus first responded, "What does that have to do with Me? My hour has not yet come." But within a short time, He commanded them to fill the water pots. What happened? Why the change of mind? First, keep in mind that Jesus functioned during His earthly ministry as a Holy Spirit anointed man, not as God. He was God, but through

507. John 2:3-11.

the incarnation He had emptied Himself of those divine prerogatives or attributes of sovereignty, and "made Himself of no reputation" and came to us "in the likeness of men."[508] Second, the anointing, His anointing and your anointing, includes the Holy Spirit's quickening or the life-giving nature. To quicken means to make alive or give life to. That is how we got saved; we were "made alive by the Spirit."[509] In other words, the Holy Spirit gives life to the "letter" or transforms the "letter" into "life".[510] Third, it is faith that pleases God and Jesus said, "I always do those things that please the Father."[511] Man connects with God through faith and faith comes by hearing the word of God.[512] Therefore, the Holy Spirit following Mary's comments quickened a word of faith in Jesus' heart and He exercised that word of faith by commanding the water pots to be filled. And finally, the Scripture says, "this beginning of signs Jesus did in Cana of Galilee." Signs are not an end in themselves. Rather they point beyond themselves by affirming the presence of the Messiah and/or demonstrating the invisible kingdom of God.

As we are learning how to function under the anointing of the Holy Spirit the question arises, "Who turned the water into wine?" Was it Jesus or the Holy Spirit? Jesus helps us answer this question by stating, "I can of Myself do nothing… for the works which the Father has given Me to finish—the very works that I do—bear witness of Me, that the Father sent Me. And the Father Himself, who sent Me, has testified of Me."[513] Further Jesus said, "I am the vine, you *are* the branches. He who abides in Me, and I in him, bears much fruit; for without Me you can do nothing."[514] Signs and wonders from the kingdom perspective are not for exalting you or me but are designed

---

508. Phil. 2:5-7.
509. Eph. 2:1, 5; Titus 3:5; 1 Peter 3:18.
510. 1 Cor. 3:6.
511. John 8:29.
512. Rom. 10:17.
513. John 5:30a, 36-37.
514. John 15:5.

to magnify the Lord. But the anointing of the Holy Spirit does enable each of us to align with the nature of God, the will of God, and the kingdom of God to the point where "men would see our good works and glorify our Father which is in heaven."[515] After Jesus ascended to the Father's right hand, the Gospel of Mark records, "And they went out and preached everywhere, the Lord working with *them* and confirming the word through the accompanying signs."[516]

The anointing by the Holy Spirit includes much more than is included in this chapter. It is a relational treasure that facilitates an intimate relationship within the context of the New Covenant between God and a believer that powerfully enforces the exercise of the kingdom authority granted to the anointed sons of God. The powers of darkness must surrender their strongholds and release their captives to the anointed ones, and "the yoke will be destroyed because of the anointing."[517]

The anointing of the Holy Spirit upon you and me is an affirmation that we are not alone, and we need not try to build the kingdom by ourselves. The anointing of the Holy Spirit is the presence of God upon each of us providing the privilege and power for co-laboring with Him. Signs and wonders are for the purpose bearing witness or testifying to the invisible presence of the Lord and His kingdom! He is building His kingdom and the increase of His government there shall be no end; and every anointed believer serves as a channel through which He has chosen to manifest Himself to this world. In other words, it is through anointed believers that the Lord manifests the reality of Himself and His invisible kingdom in the here and now. Therefore, if Jesus had not been at the wedding in Cana there would have been no miracle. But Jesus having been anointed by the Holy Spirit and in attendance, thus provided God the opportunity

515. Matt. 5:16.
516. Mark 16:20.
517. Isa. 10:27b.

to manifest the presence of His kingdom and bore witness that He had sent Jesus the Messiah.

The Anointing - Endued with Power:

During the forty days between Jesus' resurrection and His ascension He spoke with His Apostles of the things pertaining to the kingdom of God. It was during His concluding remarks on the Mount of Olives that Jesus told His disciples, "You shall receive power when the Holy Spirit has come upon you; and you shall be witnesses to Me in Jerusalem, and in all Judea and Samaria, and to the end of the earth."[518] During this Church Age the purposes of the Lord are advancing on two fronts. First, Jesus is building His Church and "the gates of Hell shall not prevail against it."[519] And second, The Lord is extending or increasing His kingdom. The Church is a part of the kingdom, but the kingdom extends beyond the boundaries of the church. For example, what the Lord is doing in heaven is a part of His kingdom, but beyond the boundaries of His Church at this juncture in time. During this church-age all born-again and anointed members of Christ's body serve as witnesses or ambassadors of the Lord Jesus Christ in three ways: (1) by a holy lifestyle of service, (2) by proclaiming the gospel of the kingdom, and (3) by signs and wonders.[520]

Jesus said to His Apostles, "But you are those who have continued with Me in My trials. I bestow upon you a kingdom, just as My Father bestowed *one* upon Me."[521] Jesus is conferring His regal or judiciary authority on the Apostles and they would share in His rule and reign on the earth after the Holy Spirit has come upon them with power.[522] There is a distinction between authority and power even though they

518. Acts 1:2-8.

519. Matt. 16:18.

520. Matt. 10:7-8; Luke 10:9; Mark 16:17-18;

521. Luke 22:28-29, 12:32.

522. Acts 1:8.

work closely together in our practical daily experiences. Jonathan Leeman illustrates the difference as follows:

"Power is ability, like the strength to lift a rock. At a young age you might have the power or ability to drive a car, but you do not possess the authority to do so until you have a learner's permit or a license."[523]

A policeman has the authority to stop a criminal with a verbal command or a hand signal. However, if the criminal fails to stop the policeman may be authorized to use the power of a pistol to stop that criminal. Jesus conferred the keys of the kingdom upon His Apostles and keys provide the authority to bind and loose or lock and unlock doors.[524] But the Holy Spirit is the source of a believer's power. That is why Jesus instructed the Apostles to wait in Jerusalem until they were endued with power. There is no record of Jesus performing any miracles until after He was anointed with the Holy Spirit.

The same day we are born-again we could also receive the anointing of the Holy Spirit. Our heavenly Father makes all His gifts available to every believer at the beginning of our journey with Him. But it takes a lifetime to unpack and learn how to walk in the fullness of His incredibly awesome gifts. Jesus was a King from birth but had to fulfill a process of perfection/maturing that included His ministry, crucifixion, resurrection and ascension to be enthroned.[525] The New Testament anointing is experienced as an event similar to David's experience when Samuel anointed him as king of Israel. Just as David had to go through a period of trials and tests before he emerged as King of Israel. So, the Apostles were with Jesus through His trials before they emerged with the authority and power to demonstrate the presence of the kingdom of God. The anointing initiates a more intimate relationship with God, empowering the anointed person to demonstrate the presence of the kingdom of God in the sphere of influence

---

523. Jonathan Leeman, *The Rule of Love: How the Local Church Should Reflect God's Love and Authority* (Wheaton, IL: Crossway, 2018), 135.

524. Matt. 16:19.

525. Luke 1:32-35, 2:11.

that God has granted to that person. God is not anointing a series of lone-rangers but anointing members of the body of Christ who are being knit together to serve Him with power as His witnesses in this world and will rule and reign with Him forever.[526]

A foundational concern to a growing intimacy with God is a clear understanding of our God given personal identity as a new creation in Christ.[527] We know that our old man was crucified with Christ, buried with Him through baptism, and raised with Him to walk in newness of life.[528] The extra-ordinary aspect of our growing in intimacy with God is to resolve that when we are born-again God comes to live from within our very being. For many years my Bible reading and study focused on three things: (1) what does the Bible say, (2) what does that text mean, and (3) how do I apply that text to my life. But I finally arrived at a more intimate relationship with my heavenly Father by asking, "Who is speaking through these words?" In other words, I had read the Bible like reading an e-mail or text message. That is, I was reading the Bible as if God was sending me a love letter from heaven. That depth of reading has value, or we would not send e-mails or text messages. However, the Scriptures took on a deeper level of meaning and value when I came to realize that God was speaking to me from within my own heart. That I was His son and He was speaking His heart to me from within my heart. I came to understand that my internal relationship with God preceded my external relationship with God. That is why Jesus said, "*'You shall love the* LORD *your God with all your heart, with all your soul, and with all your mind.'*"[529] Intimacy with God is an internal issue first and foremost. This is a key to my understanding of intimacy and obtaining the mind of Christ. With this perception we experience the reality of the Apostle John's

---

526. Rev. 1:6, 5:10; 2 Tim. 2:12
527. 2 Cor. 5:17.
528. Gal. 2:20; Rom. 6:4.
529. Matt. 22:37.

words, "You are of God, little children, and have overcome them, because He who is in you is greater than he who is in the world."[530]

Hear What the Spirit Says:

I have no intention of being intimate with Amazon, but I communicate with them often through e-mails. From time to time my wife will send me a text message, but intimacy is carried on at the heart to heart, face to face level. That is why God charged Aaron to bless the people by saying, "The Lord make His face to shine upon you."[531] It is quite possible to communicate responsibilities and directives effectively with servants through e-mails or text messages. However, Jesus intends for our relationship with Him to extend beyond that of being servants. Jesus said, "No longer do I call you servants, for a servant does not know what his master is doing; but I have called you friends, for all things that I heard from My Father I have made known to you."[532] The servant simply obeys orders, but friends maintain a relational trust level whereby they are free to confide with each other and participate in each other's private concerns. Later that same evening while referring to the Holy Spirit, Jesus said:

> However, when He, the Spirit of truth, has come, He will guide you into all truth; for He will not speak on His own *authority,* but whatever He hears He will speak; and **He will tell you things to come**. He will glorify Me, for **He will take of what is Mine and declare *it* to you**. All things that the Father has are Mine. Therefore, I said that **He will take of Mine and declare *it* to you**. (John 16:13-15; emphasis mine).

530. 1 John 4:4.
531. Num. 6:24.
532. John 15:15; Luke 12:4.

It is my experience when Jesus speaks, I mainly hear His voice through one of three sources. First, the Holy Spirit quickens Scripture. I was raised in a Christian home where the Bible was read daily and after marriage my wife and I read the Bible and had daily devotions with our sons before school. After receiving the baptism of the Holy Spirit, we had an unquenchable thirst for the word of God. At that point the Bible seemed like a great forest, but after receiving the baptism of the Holy Spirit (the anointing), the beauty of the individual trees of the forest began to shine forth. The Holy Spirit helped my wife design a memory system whereby she developed pictures on three by five cards that would visually capture the contents of a chapter. That way the Holy Spirit helped us memorize the key message of most of the chapters of the Bible. We started with Genesis and over a period of a couple of years we could by memory walk through the books of the Bible chapter by chapter. This established a Biblical basis in our hearts and minds upon which the Lord could speak through His word to our souls. Many times, He speaks through passages we are familiar with and have read time and again. But suddenly a verse or word within a verse will seemingly jump off the page into our attention. My wife and I attended Liberty Bible College in Pensacola, Florida in our late thirties to study the Bible under the anointed ministry of Brother Ken Sumrall. After graduating from Bible School and twenty-two years of pastoral ministry of which we spent seven years as missionaries in Russia, my wife suffered a cardiac arrest and went home to be with the Lord. Our two sons and their families are Christians and love the word of God. I have remarried to a wonderful godly wife and we continue to cherish the living word of God. We follow a reading schedule whereby we read through the entire Bible every year, and we spend time each day studying the Scriptures because we are still hungry to hear His voice. His word is "A lamp to my feet and a light to my path."[533]

---

533. Psa. 119:105.

Second, the Lord speaks to us through personal prophecy. Prophecy is one of the beautiful gifts of the Holy Spirit restored to the body of Christ and emphasized during the Charismatic Movement. Personal prophecy can be frightening especially if it is spoken through a novice, and we had plenty of that in the seventies and eighties. It was in the mid-seventies when my wife and I were attending an evangelistic meeting, and the Evangelist asked anyone who felt called into full time ministry to come forward for prayer. My wife and I went forward and received prayer for God's guidance and blessings. Then the Evangelist prophesied over us saying, "The Lord has set before you an open door that no man can shut." I remember that we could not withhold the tears. The Lord was intervening on our behalf and there were some major obstacles to overcome before we could leave for Bible School. We were so blessed because we had never received a personal word of prophecy before and it gave us real hope that the Lord would help us on the journey of fulfilling our calling. As we fulfilled God's calling there were obstacles, oppositions, and some set-backs. But we held on to that word from the Lord. We were reminded that the Apostle Paul said, "This charge I commit to you, son Timothy, according to the prophecies previously made concerning you, that by them you may wage the good warfare."[534] The prophetic word we received gave us a stabilizing hope from the Lord that has sustained an overcoming faith time and again in our journey. Since that occasion when we received that word of prophecy, we have heard of a few others who received that same word. May the Lord bless them as He has blessed us because it was our word from the Lord Jesus, communicated by the Holy Spirit through the Evangelist for us and we are not about to forget it! Jesus said, "My sheep hear My voice, and I know them, and they follow Me."[535]

And third, I hear the voice of the Lord through my spirit. It took some time to develop this capacity because I did not understand for

---

534. 1 Tim. 1:18.
535. John 10:27.

many years how my spirit functioned. In other words, I had to learn how to keep the voice of the Holy Spirit from becoming trapped in my reasonings and dismissing it as simply my own thoughts. I have not learned how to distinguish my own thoughts from the voice of the Holy Spirit. Some teach that our spirit consists of our conscience, intuition, and communication. Conscience is the God given capacity to discern right from wrong. Intuition is having a sort of knowing not derived entirely from linguistic definition, evidence, testimony, or sense experience that assists our most basic judgments about the world around us. I more or less accept those definitions for conscience and intuition, but I consider the third aspect of our spirit to be defined beyond communication to include godly desires and imagination. Our God given desires are a powerful platform from which the voice of the Holy Spirit quickens words of faith. In the same manner perverted desire or lust provides a powerful platform from which our flesh conceives sin. Desires must be weighted by Scripture to determine their source. Are they from the Lord or are they the lust of the flesh? Therefore, when I experience a strong desire, I test it to determine if it is in violation or disagreement with Scripture, and if not, I consider it the Holy Spirit speaking to me through that desire. Godly desires are inspired by the Holy Spirit. The Scripture says, "Delight yourself also in the LORD, And He shall give you the desires of your heart."[536] The Holy Spirit reveals God's wisdom to us through our spirit. "But the natural man does not receive the things of the Spirit of God, for they are foolishness to him; nor can he know *them,* because they are spiritually discerned."[537] It is through our spirit that we hear the voice of the Holy Spirit and obtain the mind of Christ. Then "out of the abundance of the heart the mouth speaks."[538]

As anointed believers in Jesus Christ we personally participate in an intimate and transformational relationship with God. "But we all,

---

536. Psa. 37:4.
537. 1 Cor. 2:14.
538. Matt. 12:34.

with unveiled face, beholding as in a mirror the glory of the Lord, are being transformed into the same image from glory to glory, just as by the Spirit of the Lord."[539] The Holy Spirit takes what He hears from Jesus and communicates that to us including telling us things to come. We therefore are stewards of a heavenly relationship that informs us with a measure of inside information regarding God's purposes and plans for the world around us. However, our commission is not simply to be carriers of information, but to be empowered representatives of God as His sons with the capacity to release the blessing of His nature and kingdom as His ambassadors. The Lord Jesus by His words and lifestyle "declared" or "revealed" or "interpreted" His heavenly Father to the world and inaugurated the kingdom of God. For that reason, Jesus is our Teacher and role model instructing each of us how to yield to the guidance of the Holy Spirit, revealing our Father's presence, and releasing the blessings of His kingdom.

Let the Living Waters Flow:

In the Kingdom of God serving others is a primary means whereby believers release the presence of the kingdom of God and Jesus sets the example for us:

> Christ Jesus, who, being in the form of God, did not consider it robbery to be equal with God, **but made Himself of no reputation, taking the form of a bondservant, *and* coming in the likeness of men**. And being found in appearance as a man, He humbled Himself and became obedient to *the point of* death, even the death of the cross. (Phil. 2:5-8; emphasis mine).

The lifestyle of Jesus captures the meaning of "made Himself of no reputation." For example, when He could have called for legions

539. 2 Cor. 3:18.

of angels, but rather He said to His Father, "Not My will, but Yours, be done."[540] That statement guaranteed that He would suffer the agony of becoming sin and die a horribly cruel death on a cross. Serving in the kingdom of God not only cost Jesus His life, but also cost all the Apostles their lives with the possible exception of John. Serving presents every believer with a serious challenge in this "Me first" culture. There is the cultural pressure to climb the ladder of success and not only get ahead yourself, but also compete to get ahead of the others. The admonition "*Let* nothing *be done* through selfish ambition or conceit, but in lowliness of mind let each esteem others better than himself" is easy to overlook.[541] In some congregations the issue of servanthood has been overemphasized to the point that believers are unable to envision themselves as ruling and reigning with Christ. It is a privilege to serve the Lord and the Apostle Paul identified himself on several occasions as a bondservant of Jesus Christ.[542] Jesus taught, "He who is greatest among you shall be your servant.[543]

Giving is another means of releasing the anointing. All three members of the Godhead are givers. Ultimately all of God's gifts are expressions of His grace and are given to us in the context of a loving and growing relationship with Him. Regardless of the gift, the glory always belongs to Him. His gifts to us are not for the purpose of our own personal glory or aggrandizement, but for the purpose of developing His redemptive purposes and the eternal glory of His graciousness. We are always grateful for gracious gifts and the opportunity to serve Him and steward His treasures. Therefore, to better steward what He has given us, I am focusing on the distinction between two gifts we received: the difference between regeneration and the baptism of the Holy Spirit. Again, for my purposes here the following terms; the baptism of the Holy Spirit, filled with the Spirit, and anointed by the Holy Spirit generally mean the same experience. Both

540. Matt. 26:53; Luke 22:42.
541. Phil. 2:3.
542. Rom. 1:1; Titus 1:1.
543. Matt. 23:11.

experiences may occur almost simultaneously because God finishes His purposes in eternity before they are experienced in time. Hence, when we are born again, we are regenerated by the Holy Spirit and may also receive the baptism of the Holy Spirit at that time. But it may take years to unpack the reality of what God initiated in our lives in only a few moments. For example, the Apostle Paul encountered the Lord on the road to Damascus and within a few days received the miracle of his sight being restored, regeneration, and was filled with the Spirit when Ananias laid his hands on him and prayed for him. But years later Paul said;

> Brethren, I do not count myself to have apprehended; but one thing *I do,* forgetting those things which are behind and reaching forward to those things which are ahead, I press toward the goal for the prize of the upward call of God in Christ Jesus." (Phil. 3:13-14).

Paul continued reaching and pressing forward to the prize of the upward call of God in Christ. He did not rest content with what had initiated his relationship with God but continued reaching for more and so should we. Therefore, to assist us in gaining a better grasp of the tremendous work being accomplished in our relationship with God the following statements will focus on the distinction between regeneration and the anointing of the Holy Spirit.

- As the cross of Jesus is central to the redeeming experience of personal regeneration and freedom from the penalty of sin, so the anointing of the Holy Spirit is central to the experience of kingdom power and authority over the power of sin and evil.
- As the shed blood of Jesus cleanses and makes a propitiation for sinners, so the anointing of the Holy Spirit authorizes and empowers believers making the overcoming life possible.
- As redemption delivers sinners out of the realm of darkness and grants him or her citizenship in the kingdom of God with

liberty from the bondage of sin, so the Holy Spirit anoints citizens of the kingdom of God with power to rule over the forces of sin and evil.

- As redemption grants believers the privilege and responsibility of being sons in the royal family of God, so the anointing empowers believers with the privilege and responsibility of being ambassadors in the glorious kingdom of God.

Jesus launched His ministry not by simply preaching the message of the cross, as important as that message is, but by preaching the "gospel of the kingdom."[544] In other words Jesus was proclaiming a message that included but extended beyond a personal salvation. He was proclaiming the present tense reality of God's kingdom, or God's rule or reign on the earth, thus, restoring to mankind the dominion that Adam forfeited by his disobedience. This was a radical message because since the day of Adam's sin the earth had been under the oppressive powers of the devil and wicked rulers of darkness.

Greater Works than These:

However, Jesus was not only inaugurating God's government into the enemy territory of this world, He was also going to be the King of God's kingdom.[545] The day will come when every knee will bow to His Lordship.[546] Further, He was demonstrating the presence and power of God's kingdom with sign and wonders. Jesus even told His followers. "He who believes in Me, the works that I do he will do also; and greater *works* than these he will do, because I go to My Father."[547] The "greater works" would only be possible because the same Holy Spirit that had anointed or empowered Him would anoint and empower those who believed on Jesus and yielded to the leadership of the Holy Spirit. Being an ambassador in the kingdom of God

544. Mark 1:14.
545. John 18:33-37.
546. Phil. 2:10-11.
547. John 14:12.

demands more than good morals, it requires the power of the Holy Spirit.

The Bible records a vision given to the Prophet Ezekiel showing a day in the future when a river originating under the throne of God in the Temple of God in Jerusalem will flow across the land and into the Dead Sea. The river will heal the Dead Sea to the extent that a multitude of fish will be there. Also, trees will grow along the banks of that river yielding fruit every month and their leaves will be for medicine.[548] The Apostle John was shown the following vision over six hundred years later.

> And he showed me a pure river of water of life, clear as crystal, proceeding from the throne of God and of the Lamb. In the middle of its street, and on either side of the river, *was* the tree of life, which bore twelve fruits, each *tree* yielding its fruit every month. The leaves of the tree *were* for the healing of the nations. (Rev. 22:1-2).

Joel also prophesied that a "fountain shall flow from the house of the Lord and water the Valley of Acacias."[549] The Psalmist wrote; "There is a river whose streams shall make glad the city of God."[550] Jesus talked to a Samaritan woman about this water and said;

> Whoever drinks of this water will thirst again, but whoever drinks of the water that I shall give him will never thirst. But the water that I shall give him will become in him a fountain of water springing up into everlasting life. (John:13-14).

548. Ezek. 47:1-12.
549. Joel 3:18b.
550. Psa. 46:4a.

While in Jerusalem at the Feast of Tabernacles Jesus cried out saying:

> If anyone thirsts, let him come unto Me and drink. He who believes in Me, as the Scripture has said, out of his heart will flow rivers of living water. But this He spoke concerning the Spirit, whom those believing in Him would receive; for the Holy Spirit was not yet *given,* because Jesus was not yet glorified. (John 7:37-39).

Jesus makes the point that this "living water" concerns the person of the Holy Spirit that will flow as a river from the heart of believers. Therefore, on this occasion Jesus is not speaking about redemption from sin or righteousness by faith, but He is focused on the on-going ministry of God the Holy Spirit flowing out of those who are already redeemed and standing in the righteousness of God. These are the ones flowing under the anointing of the Holy Spirit and bringing the blessings of the kingdom of God upon this world characterized by sickness, pain, and death. God anointed Jesus "with the oil of gladness" and He has "anointed us" with that same Holy Spirit.[551]

Jesus did not write theological books but proclaimed the gospel of the kingdom with signs and wonders. As a result, the world has never been the same and the kingdom of God continues to expand, breaking the strongholds of darkness and oppression while liberating the captives and oppressed. The Lord is restoring to His church what has been stolen through the ages and is empowering it for the greatest harvest ever known. Isaiah sees our days and says;

> Now it shall come to pass in the latter days *that* the mountain of the LORD'S house Shall be established on the top of the mountains and shall be exalted above

551. Heb. 1:9; 2 Cor. 1:21.

> the hills; And all nations shall flow to it. Many people shall come and say, "Come, and let us go up to the mountain of the LORD, To the house of the God of Jacob; He will teach us His ways, and we shall walk in His paths." For out of Zion shall go forth the law, And the word of the LORD from Jerusalem. (Isa. 2:2-3).

Jesus said, "the fields are already white for harvest."[552] God anoints His son and daughters to serve Him as stewards. We are given the privilege of preaching the gospel of the kingdom and dispensing the blessings of His kingdom. "For the eyes of the LORD run to and fro throughout the whole earth, to show Himself strong on behalf of *those* whose heart *is* loyal to Him."[553] Jesus reveals the mysteries of His kingdom's through His parables which will be discussed in a later chapter.

Summary:

It is my understanding that the anointing by the Holy Spirit is the third of four objectives of the Everlasting Covenant. The anointing is first mentioned in the instructions that God gave Moses while at Mount Sinai. God instructed Moses to anoint Aaron and his four sons as priests with the holy anointing oil. Later, the Prophet Samuel anointed Saul and then David to serve as kings of Israel. E. Gentile states, "Samuel poured the anointing oil over David, giving us a graphic symbol of God's overshadowing power; thus, the word anointed is often used by the Spirit-filled people to describe the action or empowerment of the Holy Spirit."[554]

---

552. John 4:35.

553. 2 Chro. 16:9.

554. Earnest B. Gentile, *Your Sons and Daughters Shall Prophecy: Prophetic Gifts in Ministry Today* (Grand Rapids: Chosen Books, 1999), 165.

The Scripture says, "Do not touch My anointed ones, and do My prophets no harm."[555] This implies that Old Testament prophets were also anointed. This is affirmed by the fact that God took of the Spirit that was upon Moses and placed it upon the seventy elders, and they prophesied.[556] This is further affirmed by the Prophet Joel's words, "I will pour out of My Spirit on all flesh; your sons and daughters will prophesy."[557] In the Old Testament the holy anointing oil was a type or shadow of the reality of the presence of God the Holy Spirit who is experienced in reality in the New Testament.

In the New Testament Jesus having been baptized in the Jordan River by John the Baptist, came up out of the water and was praying and the Holy Spirit came upon Him in the form of a dove.[558] Jesus was "the Messiah," or "the Christ," or "the Anointed One." Jesus began His ministry in the synagogue in Nazareth by reading from Isaiah 61:1-2a and declaring "today this Scripture is fulfilled in your hearing."[559] Another Scripture says, "God anointed Jesus of Nazareth with the Holy Spirit and with power, who went about doing good and healing all who were oppressed by the devil, for God was with Him."[560] Jesus was first conceived or born of the Holy Spirit, and second, He was anointed by the Holy Spirit. Jesus Christ is the role model for all New Testament believers. We are first born again or regenerated by the Holy Spirit who comes to abide in our hearts as children of God. And second, we are baptized in the Holy Spirit or anointed by the Holy Spirit with power.

Jesus promised to send another Helper (*parakletos*) just like Himself.[561] He told his disciples to wait in Jerusalem until they were endued with power.[562] Ten days after His ascension when the day of

555. Psa. 105:15
556. Num. 11:25-29.
557. Joel 2L28.
558. Luke 3:21-22.
559. Luke 4:18-21.
560. Acts 10:38.
561. John 14:16.
562. Luke 24:9.

Pentecost had fully come, they were all in one place in one accord and suddenly the Holy Spirit came upon them. "And they were all filled with the Holy Spirit and began to speak with other tongues, as the Spirit gave them utterance."[563] And Peter said, "This is what was spoken by the prophet Joel."[564] The gift of the Holy Spirit is our birthright as New Testament believers. Therefore, we are commanded as the children of God to move beyond regeneration and be filled with the Holy Spirit.[565] This is not intended to imply that the baptism of the Holy Spirit or the anointing by the Holy Spirit is in any way a substitute for godly Character.

Having been regenerated by the Spirit of Adoption we are no longer orphans but sons. The Holy Spirit helps us by aligning our nature with the nature of God. The baptism of the Holy Spirit or the anointing of the Holy Spirit empowers believers to serve as His ambassadors and bring the blessing of the kingdom of God upon our families, communities and the nations. The heavenly Father wants to first work within you by transforming your character into Christ-likeness. He also wants to do something through you. This is why Jesus taught us to pray, "Your kingdom come, and Your will be done on earth as it is in heaven."[566] Our Father has a plan to take us to heaven one day, but now He wants us to bring heaven to earth and thus cooperate with Him in destroying the strongholds and works of the powers of darkness.

Our anointing facilitates an intimate relationship with the Lord including a friendship whereby we confide in each other. We hear the voice of God through scripture when it is quickened or made alive by the Holy Spirit. The power of that living word is released when we act upon it in faith, just as a plant is released from a seed when that seed is planted in warm moist soil. We also hear the voice of God through prophecy. Further we must train our spirit to discern the voice of God

563. Acts 2:4.
564. Acts 2:16.
565. Eph. 5:18.
566. Matt. 6:10.

and distinguish His voice from our own reasonings. The Holy Spirit will help us hear God and tell us of things to come. Hearing is a key to faith and without faith it is impossible to please God.[567]

We are God's sons and stewards of the anointing. The anointing of the Holy Spirit empowers us to not only confront unbelief, the mystery of iniquity, and the anti-Christ spirit, but to overcome these enemies. The Lord has redeemed us and anointed us with the Messianic resources of heaven in preparation for the great day of harvest that is fast approaching. It is the anointing that empowers us to live as overcomers and bring forth abundant fruit to the glory of God in this world. It is the anointing that breaks the yoke of the oppressor and liberates the captives from the oppression of the devil. In the next chapter the anointing will be discussed regarding how it applies to the priesthood of all believers.

567. Heb. 11:6.

CHAPTER FOUR

THE PRIESTHOOD AND THE KINGDOM

"This hope we have as an anchor of the soul, both sure and steadfast, and which enters the Presence behind the veil, where the forerunner has entered for us, even Jesus, having become High Priest forever according to the order of Melchizedek.

(Hebrews 6:19-20).

"But you are a chosen generation, a royal priesthood, a holy nation, His own special people, that you may proclaim the praises of Him who called you out of darkness into His marvelous light;"

(1 Peter 2:9)

Just as the prophetic ministry was restored to the church during the twentieth century and expresses the continuing and on-going Prophetic ministry of Jesus Christ. So also, the priesthood of the New Testament believer is the ongoing ministry of our High Priest Jesus Christ in the earth today. Every born-again believer is a member of the "royal priesthood" as a birthright into the family of God. David M. Levy states, "When God called the church into being, He granted each believer the stewardship of being a priest unconditionally formed it into a 'kingdom of priests'" (Rev. 1:6).[568] For too long the priesthood of believers has remained simply as a doctrine in many churches. However, through the out-pouring's of the Holy Spirit of the last century there has been an awakening to the practical reality of this great truth. It is the purpose of this chapter to help clarify and emphasize the believer's role and privilege of serving as a priest and a citizen in the kingdom of God.

A Royal Priesthood:

Following your born-again experience which includes being forgiven, declared righteous, and regenerated by the Holy Spirit, you affirm and declare your new life in Christ through water baptism. Water baptism is your public testimony that your old man was crucified with Christ at the cross.[569] Your old man is buried in the baptismal waters, and now you are free from the guilt, shame, and victim mentality of the past and ready to be consecrated unto the Lord and empowered for service. Jesus is our spiritual example. He, being baptized in the Jordan River, coming up out of the water prayed, the heavens opened, and the Holy Spirit descended upon Him in the form of a dove.[570] When He began His ministry, He referred to the Holy Spirit coming upon Him as the "anointing of the Holy Spirit."[571] Just before His ascension He said to His Apostles, "Behold, I send the Promise of My Father upon you; but tarry in the city of Jerusalem until you are endued with power from on high."[572] To be "endued with power from on high" is to be clothed upon by the Holy Spirit and consecrated for service unto the Lord. We generally define "endued" as being

---

568. David M. Levy, *The Tabernacle: Shadows of the Messiah: Its Sacrifices, Services, and Priesthood* (Bellmawr, NJ: Friends of Israel Gospel Ministry, 1993).
569. Gal. 2:20.
570. Luke 3:22.
571. Luke 4:18-19; Isa. 61:1-2a.
572. Luke 24:49.

empowered by the Holy Spirit or baptized in the Holy Spirit and we could also express it as receiving the mantle of Christ. In other words, just as Elijah's mantle conferred the powerful prophet's anointing upon Elisha, so the baptism of the Holy Spirit confers the powerful Messianic mantle upon you. The baptism in the Holy Spirit is His anointing that consecrates and empowers you to serve as a member of God's royal priesthood. "Royal priesthood" means the born-again life is lived as a family member of the King of glory and you are given a personal stewardship as a priest in the kingdom of God.

A priest is considered to be a religious person who functions as a mediator between a god and another person by offering sacrifices and performing religious rituals. The Roman Catholic Church defines a priest as, "One who is ordained or on whom the priesthood has been conferred, who offers sacrifice, and who has the threefold power of teaching, ministering, and governing."[573] In the Old Testament priests were from the Tribe of Levi and served in the Tabernacle and Temple as mediators between God and the Children of Israel.

The first mention of "priest" in the Bible regards an usual person who is mentioned first in the fourteenth chapter of Genesis: "Then Melchizedek king of Salem brought out bread and wine; he *was* the priest of God Most High."[574] The priesthood of Melchizedek will be discussed latter in this chapter. The second mention of "priest" is also found in Genesis, but it is a priest of a different kind. "And Pharaoh called Joseph's name Zaphnath-Paaneah. And he gave him as a wife Asenath, the daughter of Poti-Pherah priest of On."[575] In other words the priest of On was a worshipper of an Egyptian god, but not a worshipper of the God of Abraham, Isaac, and Jacob. David Estes makes the following observations:

---

573. Robert Broderick, *The Catholic Encyclopedia* (Nashville, TN: Thomas Nelson, Inc, 1976), 491.

574. Gen. 14:18.

575. Gen. 41:45.

> In ancient times it was held that men in general could not have direct access to God, that any approach to Him must be mediated by some member of the class of priests, who alone could approach God, and who must accordingly be employed by other men to represent them before Him. This whole conception vanishes in the light of Christianity. By virtue of their relation to Christ all believers have direct approach to God, and consequently, as this right of approach was formerly a priestly privilege, priesthood may now be predicated of every Christian. That none needs another to intervene between his soul and God; that none can thus intervene for another; that every soul may and must stand for itself in personal relation with God—such are the simple elements of the NT doctrine of the priesthood of all believers.[576]

As God unfolded His plan of redemption through His covenantal relationship with Abraham, He extended its promises and provisions through Isaac and Jacob. The day came when He appeared to Moses in the burning bush and commissioned him to go and lead the Children of Israel out of their Egyptian bondage. Through the interventions of plagues, concluding with the Passover, the Children of Israel went out of Egypt by passing through the Red Sea on dry land. In the third month following the children of Israel's release from Egyptian bondage they arrived at Mount Sinai. It was there at Sinai that God entered into a covenant with the nation of Israel. God said;

> Now therefore, if you will indeed obey My voice and keep My covenant, then you shall be a special treasure to Me above all people; for all the earth *is* Mine.

576. David Foster Estes, "Priesthood in the NT," ed. James Orr et al., *The International Standard Bible Encyclopedia* (Chicago, IL: The Howard-Severance Company, 1915), 2446.

> And you shall be to Me a **kingdom of priests** and a holy nation. (Exodus 19:5-6; emphasis is mine).

A Kingdom of Priests:

God had purchased all the firstborn of Israel with the blood of the Passover Lamb. On that night the death angel passed through Egypt killing all the first-born who were not sheltered under the protection of the blood that had been shed and placed on the doorpost of each Israelite house. Therefore, all the firstborn of Israel were to serve the Lord as a kingdom of priests because He had purchased them with the blood of the Passover Lamb. However, it was during the forty days while Moses was up on Mount Sinai receiving the Ten Commandments that Aaron and the children of Israel built and worshipped the golden calf. Their sin angered God and resulted in judgment, whereupon God rejected the first born of all Israel from serving Him as priests and chose the tribe of Levi to be priests and Aaron as high priest.[577]

The responsibilities of the Levitical priesthood are spelled out in the Pentateuch and quite detailed in the Book of Leviticus. The responsibilities of the high priest are also discussed in the Pentateuch with additional insights in the Book of Hebrews. The author of Hebrews states; "For every high priest taken from among men is appointed for men in things *pertaining* to God, that he may offer both gifts and sacrifices for sins."[578] The purpose of the priesthood according to Walter A. Ewell is as follows:

> It is the universal sinfulness of man which makes a sacrificing priesthood a necessity. The sacrifices offered up effect, or symbolize the means of effecting, reconciliation between sinful man and his holy Creator. The function of priesthood, accordingly, is

577. Lev. 8:15-26.
578. Heb. 5:1

> a mediatorial function. The giving of the law through Moses and the institution of the Aaronic or Levitical priesthood belong together.[579]

The marvel of God's love for mankind is graciously expressed through the provisions of the covenant He made with Israel at Sinai. His covenant included the command to build the tabernacle of meeting, the anointing of the priesthood, the offerings, and the annual feasts of the Lord. In other words, through these means God made provision for man to be reconciled to Himself and to enter His presence on the Day of Atonement for the first time since Adam's expulsion from the Garden of Eden. These privileges were of such great value that the Apostle Paul said,

> For I could wish that I myself were accursed from Christ for my brethren, my countrymen according to the flesh, who are Israelites, to whom *pertain* the adoption, the glory, the covenants, the giving of the law, **the service *of God***, and the promises; (Romans. 9:3-4; emphasis mine).

Throughout the Old Testament the ministry of the priesthood was restricted to the tribe of Levi. The royal or kingly line of Israel was from the tribe of Judah. The priesthood and kingship were distinct responsibilities of those tribes for which God had appointed and anointed them. On one occasion in the life of the great king Uzziah, when his heart was lifted up, he transgressed against the Lord by going into the Temple to burn incense on the golden altar of incense. That transgression brought the judgment of God upon him as the following verses describe:

---

579. Walter A. Elwell, *Evangelical Dictionary of Theology: Second Edition* (Grand Rapids, MI: Baker Academic, 2001), 952.

> So Azariah the priest went in after him, and with him were eighty priests of the LORD--valiant men. And they withstood King Uzziah, and said to him, "*It is* not for you, Uzziah, to burn incense to the LORD, but for the priests, the sons of Aaron, who are consecrated to burn incense. Get out of the sanctuary, for you have trespassed! You *shall have* no honor from the LORD God." Then Uzziah became furious; and he *had* a censer in his hand to burn incense. And while he was angry with the priests, leprosy broke out on his forehead, before the priests in the house of the LORD, beside the incense altar. And Azariah the chief priest and all the priests looked at him, and there, on his forehead, he *was* leprous; so, they thrust him out of that place. Indeed, he also hurried to get out, because the LORD had struck him. King Uzziah was a leper until the day of his death. He dwelt in an isolated house, because he was a leper; for he was cut off from the house of the LORD. Then Jotham his son *was* over the king's house, judging the people of the land. (2 Chronicles 26:17-21).

The point I want to make clear is that it is the blood of the Lamb and the anointing of the Lord that authorizes any New Testament believer the privilege of entering God's Holy Presence. But in the Old Testament it was only the tribe of Levi that was anointed by God to serve before Him as priests. The High Priest was the only person in all Israel who had access inside of the holy of holies and that access was only granted once a year on the Day of Atonement. The High Priest entered the holy of holies with the blood of a sacrificial animal and the sweet incense on coals of fire lest he die in God's presence. These realities help New Testament believers better understand the awesome redemptive work that Jesus Christ accomplished through His death on the cross, His resurrection and exaltation. Jesus is the "new and living way" of access to our Father.[580] Now each believer has an invitation to "come boldly to the throne of grace, that we may obtain mercy and find grace to help in time of need."[581]

The interesting thing is that Jesus was from the tribe of Judah and not from the tribe of Levi. Therefore, the question arises, "On what basis does Jesus have the authority to serve as our Great High Priest?" To answer this question, we are required to study Melchizedek, the priest of the God Most High. He is mentioned in only three different places in Scripture: Gen. 14:18; Psa. 110:4; and Heb. 5:6 thru 7:22.

The Order of Melchizedek:

We first meet Melchizedek when Abram returned from the battle with Chedorlaomer and the kings from the East who were with him. They had defeated Sodom and Gomorrah and had taken the people captive and carried away their goods. Abram pursued those armies and overtook them and delivered his nephew Lot and others who had been taken captive. Upon Abram's return to Sodom with the freed captives and their goods he was met by Melchizedek, king of Salem, the priest of God Most High. Melchizedek served Abram with bread and wine and blessed him. Where upon Abraham gave Melchizedek a tithe of all. This is about all we learn of Melchizedek from the fourteenth chapter of Genesis. He is next mentioned briefly by King David in one verse in Psalms: "The LORD has sworn And will not relent, 'You *are* a priest forever According to the order of Melchizedek.'"[582] This is a Messianic Psalm and reflects David's insight or revelation of the coming priestly ministry of Jesus Christ which is expounded upon in the Book of Hebrews.

The writer of Hebrews connects the calling of Jesus the Son of God as High Priest with the order of Melchizedek, by quoting Psalm 110:4,

580. Heb. 10:20.
581. Heb. 4:16.
582. Psa. 110:4.

and declaring Jesus to be "a priest forever according to the order of Melchizedek."[583] Melchizedek is presented in Hebrews chapter seven without genealogy and without reference to His birth or death. He was also the "king of righteousness" and the "king of peace." He is not from the tribe of Levi nor from the tribe of Judah. The conclusion is that Melchizedek did not obtain his priesthood or royal office because of hereditary rights or as citizenship in Israel. Therefore, Christ's priesthood is not through the legal requirement concerning physical descent of Levi according to the Law, but through the power of an indestructible life because His priesthood is forever. D. G. Peterson states, "By means of his ascension and heavenly enthronement, Christ entered into the eternal priesthood of which Psalm 110:4 speaks (see Heb. 8:1–2; 9:11–12).[584] But first we will focus on Hebrews 7:11-17:

> Therefore, if perfection were through the Levitical priesthood (for under it the people received the law), what further need *was there* that another priest should rise according to the order of Melchizedek, and not be called according to the order of Aaron? For the priesthood being changed, of necessity there is also a change of the law. For He of whom these things are spoken belongs to another tribe, from which no man has officiated at the altar. For *it is* evident that our Lord arose from Judah, of which tribe Moses spoke nothing concerning priesthood. And it is yet far more evident if, in the likeness of Melchizedek, there arises another priest who has come, not according to the law of a fleshly commandment, but according to the power of an endless life. For He testifies:

---

583. Heb. 5:5-10.

584. D. G. Peterson, "Melchizedek," ed. T. Desmond Alexander and Brian S. Rosner, *New Dictionary of Biblical Theology* (Downers Grove, IL: InterVarsity Press, 2000), 660.

> *"You are a priest forever According to the order of Melchizedek."* (Heb. 7:11-17).

The High Priestly ministry of Jesus is after the order of Melchizedek and therefore superior to the Levitical Priesthood in the following ways: First, Melchizedek received tithes from Abraham and blessed him while Levi was still in his loins and "beyond all contradiction the lesser is blessed by the better."[585] Second, the order of Melchizedek is not "according to the law of a fleshly commandment, but according to the power of an endless life."[586] Third, the offices of priest and king are combined in the order of Melchizedek, whereas the Levites were priest and the kings of Israel came from the tribe of Judah.[587] The above Scriptures make it clear that Jesus holds His priesthood permanently because of His endless life and it is also superior to the Levitical priesthood because God confirmed His priesthood with an oath.[588]

The above reasons provide the answers to the question regarding the basis of His authority to serve as our Great High Priest. Andrew Murray states, "The priesthood of Christ is the God-devised channel through which the ever-blessed Son could make us partakers of Himself, and with Himself of all the life and glory He has with the Father."[589] Therefore, "now in Christ Jesus you who once were far off have been brought near by the blood of Christ. "[590] We can rejoice and proclaim to the Lord, "You were slain, and have redeemed us to God by Your blood out of every tribe and tongue and people and nation and have made us kings and priests to our God; and we shall reign on the earth."[591] David Levy states;

---

585. Heb. 7:4-8.
586. Heb. 7:16.
587. Heb. 7:1.
588. Heb. 7:20-22.
589. Andrew Murray, *The Holiest of All* (New Kensington, PA: Whitaker House, 1996), 181.
590. Eph. 2:13.
591. Rev. 5:9-10.

> We enjoy a unique privilege that the Israelites were never able to experience. As king-priests, we can come into the throne room of God through Jesus Christ and there feast in fellowship on the blessings He has for us. Child of the King, as a believer-priest, lift up your eyes to the throne of God, and let Him fill your spiritual vision. [592]

The priesthood of all believers was a doctrinal pillar of the Reformation. Jesus Christ died on the cross, was buried and resurrected on the third day. He then ascended to the Father "not with the blood of goats and calves, but with His own blood He entered the Most Holy Place once for all, having obtained eternal redemption."[593] It is through the sacrifice of Jesus on the cross that the propitiation for our sins has been made and through faith in Jesus our sins are forgiven and we are granted the gift of righteousness. The access that Jesus our High Priest established is not limited to a particular class of believers, but regardless of one's position, occupation, gender, race or nationality, all believers are accepted in the Beloved. New Testament believers have no need for a human mediator because Jesus Christ fully performs the mediatorial function. The Apostle Paul writes; "For *there is* one God and one Mediator between God and men, *the* Man Christ Jesus."[594] "Let us therefore come boldly to the throne of grace, that we may obtain mercy and find grace to help in time of need."[595]

The Clergy/Laity Trap:

It is important that we as members of His body, the Church (*ekklesia*), do not become trapped in the false division between clergy and

---

592. Levy, *The Tabernacle,* Chapter 16.
593. Heb. 9:12.
594. 1 Tim. 2:5.
595. Heb. 4:16.

laity that plagued the church for centuries. Michael L. Dusing provides the following insights:

> The Church through the centuries has tended to divide itself into two broad categories: clergy (Gk. *klēros*, "lot," i.e., God's lot or separated ones) and laity (Gk. *laos*, "people"). The New Testament, however, does not make such a marked distinction. Rather, God's "lot," or *klēros*, His own possession, refers to all born-again believers, not just to a selected group (cf. 1 Pet. 2:9).[596]

Every member of the body of Christ has been granted as part of his or her birthright the stewardship of a priestly ministry. Although all believers are "a chosen generation" and included in the New Testament royal priesthood, there are different functions, ministrations, talents, gifts, and unlimited opportunities for service within the church and the kingdom. All believers have the same righteous standing in Christ, but not all have the same ministry. We are all laborers together with the Lord of the harvest; one plants, another waters, but it is the Lord alone who gives the increase.[597] All believers are called to be servants (*diakonos*). Jesus said, "Whoever desires to become great among you shall be your servant. And whoever of you desires to be first shall be slave of all. For even the Son of Man did not come to be served, but to serve, and to give His life a ransom for many."[598] We who are king-priests are made to be sons of His glory and are to dispel the darkness of this world by the light of our lives and testimonies. The darkness cannot understand the light, but the darkness cannot extinguish the light!

---

596. Michael L. Dusing, "The New Testament Church," in *Systematic Theology: Revised Edition*, ed. Stanley M. Horton (Springfield, MO: Logion Press, 2007), 553.
597. 1 Cor. 3:7.
598. Mark 10:43-45.

Every believer in Jesus Christ is urged "by the mercies of God" to present his or her body as a "living sacrifice, holy, acceptable to God which is our reasonable service."[599] A portion of that "reasonable service" includes ministry as a royal priest. The quickening by the Holy Spirit regenerates the believer's spirit and the anointing of the Holy Spirit empowers and authorizes each believer to perform the priestly ministry. Before elaborating on the practical applications of the priestly ministry as a citizen of the kingdom of God it will be beneficial to re-examine how our regenerated spirit functions. All too often believers try to serve in the kingdom of God but ultimately with very limited fruit because they are as unaware of the makeup and nature of their spirit as they are of most of the muscles of their body.

The Spirit Man:

It is generally accepted that our spirit is comprised of our conscience, intuition, and communion. The conscience is the God given capacity to discern right from wrong. Even the unregenerate conscience is capable of discerning that some things are wrong because all people are created in the image and likeness of God. For example, all over the world there are different customs regarding marriage. But there is no place in the world where a man can have any woman he wants anytime he wants her. There are moral boundaries and there are consequences for violating those boundaries. You may have told your small child not to take another cookie. But when he or she thinks it is safe to sneak another one they will reach for it, but just before they grab it, they take a quick glance around to see if you're watching. Why? Because they know it is wrong to take the cookie and if they get caught there will be consequences. Just as when God's moral law is violated there are consequences. However, even when we know something is wrong our flesh may overpower our spirit/conscience to

599. Rom. 12:1.

the point that what we will to do, we do not do, and what we do not want to do, that we do, thus leaving us feeling like a moral failure.[600]

Conscience:

Therefore, a person's conscience must be trained by the word of God in order to be sensitive to the guiding impulses of the Holy Spirit. The Law of Moses was written by the finger of God on tablets of stone and given to Moses on Mount Sinai. Knowing the God given moral boundaries for living in community and right relation with God was indeed a giant step forward for civilization. However, the New Testament believer has an even greater advantage because the Law of God is now written on the tablets of the heart by the Holy Spirit, thus enabling each believer to personally enjoy greater intimacy with God and a personal sensitivity to God's will. Thus, the believer possesses the liberty of walking according to the Spirit and not under condemnation of the law, because Jesus fulfilled the demands of the law on the cross as the following Scripture affirms.

> For what the law could not do in that it was weak through the flesh, God *did* by sending His own Son in the likeness of sinful flesh, on account of sin: He condemned sin in the flesh, that the righteous requirement of the law might be fulfilled in us who do not walk according to the flesh but according to the Spirit. For those who live according to the flesh set their minds on the things of the flesh, but those *who live* according to the Spirit, the things of the Spirit." (Romans 8:3-5).

The conscience functions much like the Urim and Thummim used by the High Priest in the Old Testament. We do not know much about the Urim and Thummim, but it seemed to function when the question

600. Rom. 7:15-25.

was narrowed to a positive or negative response or a simple yes or no answer. Through the Urim and Thummim the High Priest perceived the guiding counsel of God. It seems that this was the method used by Joshua to determine who was guilty of sinning against the Lord at Jericho.[601] David also probably inquired of the Lord by using this method.[602]

Our conscience, when properly trained, is that aspect of our spiritual nature that guides our decisions and actions according to the nature of our heavenly Father. Our conscience checks us when we violate the law and convicts us unto repentance. As a result, we are subject to governmental authorities, speed limits, and pay taxes, not only because we do not want to be fined or go to jail, but also for conscience sake.[603] A law abiding culture is a culture where the Holy Spirit guides consciences of the citizens, and they will enjoy far more personal liberty than citizens living in a police state. When a teenager's conscience is guided by the Holy Spirit parents remain at peace even, when the teenager is away from home, because they know the Holy Spirit will guide their teenager's actions in accord with the nature of God. God does not want to put a bridle on His children and try to control them like a horse. No! He does not want His family to be shackled by the do's and don'ts of the law, but to walk in liberty and obey Him through the Holy Spirit, guiding us by our conscience. "Now the Lord is the Spirit; and where the Spirit of the Lord *is,* there *is* liberty."[604]

If we habitually disobey the Lord and the promptings of the Holy Spirit our consciences will become defiled, seared, and incapable of responding to the guidance of the Holy Spirit. As a result, we will need to humble ourselves before the Lord in repentance and ask for His forgiveness and spiritual cleansing. Our Father is a forgiving God and will give grace to the humble. It is through repentance and

601. Joshua Chapter Seven.

602. 1 Sam. 23:10-13; 2 Sam. 5:9.

603. Rom. 13:5.

604. 2 Cor. 3:17.

forgiveness our conscience is cleansed of defilements and dead works and renewed by the Holy Spirit. However, each believer must personally take the responsibility for his or her disobedience through humble repentance and the acceptance of forgiveness from the Father.

Also, all believers must also be on guard against receiving personal offenses that tend to entrap us in anger and unforgiveness, leaving us with an attitude of wanting to get even with the person that caused the offence. But "this *is* commendable, if because of conscience toward God one endures grief, suffering wrongfully."[605] "Therefore, as *the* elect of God, holy and beloved, put on tender mercies, kindness, humility, meekness, longsuffering; bearing with one another, and forgiving one another."[606] We all make mistakes and violate our conscience by sinning against God and one another. But our heavenly Father loves each of us enough to chasten us and scourge us in order that we "may be partakers of His holiness."[607] Our responsibility is to yield to His disciplines and submit to His chastenings, which may be painful; but if received in the spirit of meekness it will yield the peaceable fruit of righteousness, our conscience will be cleansed, and we can function with fruitful integrity as a member of His royal priesthood.

Intuition:

A second facet of our spirit's nature is our intuition. It is this aspect of our spiritual nature that receives the anointing of the Holy Spirit, thus enabling us to <u>know</u> the truth. "But you have an anointing from the Holy One, and you <u>know</u> all things"[608] (emphasis mine).

---

605. 1 Peter 2:19.
606. Col. 3:12-13.
607. Heb. 12:5-11.
608. 1 John 2:20. Also see 1 John 2:27.

"The term intuition means simply direct knowledge."[609] Watchman Nee provides the following insights:

> We must explain the meaning of "knowing" and "understanding." We usually do not make a distinction between these two words; in spiritual matters, the difference is incalculable: the spirit "knows" while the mind "understands." A believer "knows" the things of God by the intuition of his spirit. Strictly speaking, the mind can merely "understand"; it can never "know" .... The Holy Spirit enables our spirit to know; our spirit instructs our mind to understand.... In spiritual matters it is possible for us to know without understanding it.[610]

Our intuition informs our intellect and aids our powers of reason. We can gain natural or worldly knowledge and facts through our five senses and intellect. However, our five senses and intellect are incapable of grasping an intimate knowledge of God. Because God is a Spirit and our sense-perceptions and powers of reason cannot relate to God beyond what He has revealed of Himself through His creation. It is through our intuition that we know truth which inspires and/or quickens our soul. What we receive and accept through our intuition should never contradict Scripture but may transcend the limits of our intellect and powers of reason, because God's ways and thoughts are higher than our ways and thoughts as far as the heavens are higher that the earth.[611]

There are things that you know in your heart that you did not learn in a classroom or from a textbook. But you know that you know. Each

---

609. Augustus Hopkins Strong, *Systematic Theology* (Philadelphia: American Baptist Publication Society, 1907), 52.

610. Watchman Nee, *The Spiritual Man,* vol. 2 (New York, NY: Christian Fellowship Publishers, Inc., 1968), 73.

611. Isa. 55:9.

of us know things that we haven't yet articulated, but when we hear another person articulate truth, we bear witness to it because we already know it in our spirit. It is through your intuition that you know that "GOD IS!" That's what makes the preaching of the gospel so powerful—It is the truth that convicts and persuades sinners because God has already put eternity in their hearts even though their intellect does not know it.[612] That is why Bible distribution and preaching the gospel are outlawed in many places, because the enemy knows if the people hear the truth they will get saved!

A problem we often face is when a respected authority makes statements that contradict what we know in our hearts; then the enemy uses those authoritative words to cast doubt upon what we know and steal our confidence regarding our knowledge of the truth. This often happens to high school graduates when they go to college. They are Christians but have not yet had the Biblical training nor life experience necessary to sustain the integrity of their intuition when required to take classes that are taught by professors whose presentations are wholly guided by a scientific worldview. As a result, many "Christian" students will dismiss the capabilities and content of their intuition in lieu of the facts and evidence of so called "science." Physical evidence can be very convincing and persuasive to the spiritually untrained and inexperienced student. However, the Apostle Paul said, "Beware lest anyone cheat you through philosophy and empty deceit, according to the tradition of men, according to the basic principles of the world, and not according to Christ."[613]

Many believers struggle with understanding and perceiving the personal ministry of the Holy Spirit. In other words, for many believers the Holy Spirit remains in the category of a doctrine or a creed, but not as a personal friend and counselor. As a result, the intuition is overlooked or underdeveloped and those "Christians" tend to remain uncertain about their spiritual identity and their eternal destiny. Their

---

612. Ecc. 3:11.
613. Col. 2:8.

"Christianity" is then often confined primarily to doing good deeds and ethical conduct as defined by the "golden rule." The Holy Spirit is a "Helper" and He will help believers in their spiritual development if He is called upon and trusted. "The Spirit Himself bears witness with our spirit that we are children of God."[614] Our relationship with God is initiated by the Holy Spirit and developed through the believer's love for God and living by faith in God. Love and faith cannot be observed or measured by any scientific lab or equipment. We cannot relate to God by our five senses or our intellect, although we employ these faculties in the development of our character and our service as the priests of the Lord. It is through our intuition that we receive the knowledge of the truth and truth is the foundation of godly wisdom and personal liberty. Jesus said, "And you shall know the truth, and the truth shall make you free."[615] Truth is more than a proposition, it is a person. The Holy Spirit is the "Spirit of truth."[616] The point is—Truth is to be incarnated in and through each believer's life. As a result, believers are living epistles written by the Holy Spirit and read by those with whom they have contact. Our lives are to be manifestations of Truth that influence our culture just as salt influences the flavor of food.

Communion:

The third facet of our spirit is communion. The Greek word for communion is **κοινωνία:** *fellowship, a close mutual relationship; participation, sharing in; partnership; contribution, gift.*[617] Paul in writing to the Church at Corinth used the word *koinonia* in the following way: "The grace of the Lord Jesus Christ, and the love of God,

---

614. Rom. 8:16.

615. John 8:32.

616. John 14:17, 15:26, 16:13.

617. Barclay M. Newman Jr., *A Concise Greek-English Dictionary of the New Testament.* (Stuttgart, Germany: Deutsche Bibelgesellschaft; United Bible Societies, 1993), 101.

and the **communion** of the Holy Spirit *be* with you all"[618] (emphasis mine). The concept of "communion" means to hold in common as in sharing—what is mine is yours and what is yours is mine. Our heavenly Father wants and expects to enjoy a personal intimate sharing of life with each of His children. Many believers in the body of Christ have at times had a distant or a crisis relationship with the Lord that can basically be described as; "If something comes up that I can't handle, then I will call on God." However, the Lord desires intimate communion with each of us twenty-four hours a day, and not just a distant or crisis solving relationship. Therefore, the Holy Spirit seeks to draw us beyond a fragmented and superficial fellowship into an ongoing sharing of life together through His ways and means of communion.

For the purpose of this discussion we will seek to answer these questions: (1) What are three ways or means the Holy Spirit often utilizes to initiate communion with believers? (2) How do we as members of a royal priesthood sustain communion with the Holy Spirit? And (3) Why should we as citizens of the kingdom of God expect to continually commune with the Holy Spirit? In answer to the first question; communion is initiated by the Holy Spirit through many ways and means but we will confine our discussion to the following three distinct means: (1) godly desires, (2) delight in the Lord, and (3) creative and/or supernatural design.

The first aspect of communion initiated by the Holy Spirit and experienced by every believer is through God given desires. Desire includes the impulses, urges, yearnings, and cravings we all experience. Desires move us towards something that promises enjoyment or satisfaction. However, only some of our desires are initiated by the Holy Spirit and others arise out of our carnal nature. To distinguish between the two sources of desire can be difficult and may require some time and effort. Therefore, our first responsibility is to take the time and make the effort to determine the source and/or the object of a desire. Ask yourself, does this desire I am experiencing reflect the

618. 2 Cor. 13:14.

nature of God and/or will it bring glory to God if I pursue it? Or does this desire originate within my carnal nature? If the desires of my carnal nature are pursued, they will bring forth sin as James explains:

> Let no one say when he is tempted, 'I am tempted by God'; for God cannot be tempted by evil, nor does He Himself tempt anyone. But each one is tempted when he is drawn away by his own **desires** and enticed. Then, when **desire** has conceived, it gives birth to sin; and sin, when it is full-grown, brings forth death (James 1:13-15; emphasis mine).

The Greek word used in the above verses translated "desire" is "*epithymia*" and is often translated "lust." (See: Rom. 6:12; Gal. 5:6; 2 Tim. 3:61 Peter 4:2). Again, a correct understanding of the nature of "desire" is to be determined as positive or negative depending on the source and/or object of that desire. James is not saying that it is sinful or wrong to have desires. But by using the Greek word "*epithymia*" he indicates that desire is a yearning or graving that draws and/or entices us to take action that may be positive or negative. Therefore, we have the personal responsibility to discern if the source and/or the object of a desire is from the Holy Spirit or from our flesh. William D. Mounce helps us understand "*epithymia*" by stating:

> Mostly, however, *epithymia* constitutes wrong sensual and sexual desires that are selfish and result in disobedience to God. Willfully disobedient persons are given up by God to the perverse "*desires* of their hearts" (Rom 1:24). Christians are admonished to change their former sinful behavior, in which (like the heathen) they once followed and performed the lusts of the flesh (Rom 6:12; 7:7; Eph 2:3; 4:22; 1 Thess. 4:5; Tit 3:3; 1 Pet. 1:14; 4:2–3). Salvation

> entails crucifixion of the "flesh with its passions and *desires/lusts*" (Gal 5:24; Col 3:5) and walking in the Spirit (Gal 5:16) so as to "make no provision for the flesh to perform its *lusts*" (Rom 13:14).[619]

Once we determine the source and/or object we have the responsibility to make a personal decision; "Will I fulfill this desire, or will I crucify it?" Just as our conscience needs to be guided by Scripture so the choice and pursuit of our desires need to be guided by Scripture. Many times, we will need to pray for wisdom regarding our decisions and may also need to seek godly counsel in order to choose that which God desires. There is no question that God desires all believers be transformed into the character and likeness of Jesus Christ. However, there are some areas of life where it is difficult to know what God desires. For example, should I marry this person or that person—should I take this job or that one—should I live in this city or that one? For some things the Scriptures are very clear. For example, we know that God desires that if we get married we should be married to a believer in Jesus Christ.[620] But if the choice is between two believers, we will have to make the choice by faith, trusting the Lord to guide us through the unknown road ahead.[621] Following the guidance of Scripture and trusting God through our decision making process are two of the things He desires his children to do.

The Holy Spirit communes with us by breathing the desires of the Father into our spirit. Depending on the level of our faith, those godly desires may simply remain dormant or faith can initiate motivation and passionate zeal for their fulfillment. The key here is to realize that the Holy Spirit communes with each believer through desires. Many times, the Holy Spirit has breathed the desire of God into our spirit, but we just thought it originated within ourselves. And all the while

619. William D. Mounce, *Mounce's Complete Expository Dictionary of Old & New Testament Words* (Grand Rapids, MI: Zondervan, 2006), 173.

620. 2 Cor. 6:14-18.

621. Prov. 3:5-6.

we wondered why the Lord didn't speak to us like He seems to speak to those spiritual people. I served with a dear brother in a nursing home ministry—He was a very faithful person, but he said to me one day, "You know the Lord has never really spoken to me personally." You can be absolutely confident that the Lord over many years tried to commune with that brother, but he was probably never trained to consider that many of his desires were the voice of the Holy Spirit speaking with him. As a result, he passed those desires off with the assumption; "those are just my own thoughts" or "that could never happen to me." The Lord breathes His desires in each believer's heart, because He wants to do wonderful things through each of us! It is each believer's responsibility to choose the correct response to our desires. Communion with God will always demand faith, and faith requires action, because "faith without works is dead."[622] The truth is that God desires to advance His kingdom in the earth through you as a member of His royal priesthood. Therefore, the Holy Spirit breathes godly desires into each believer's heart, and then His eyes go to and fro across the world searching for someone like you, whose heart is ready and willing to agree with Him in faith.[623]

Desires are powerful concepts because they are the seedbed of motivation. In other words, motivation arises out of the desires of our heart. Then when those motivations are inflamed by passion—obstacles, adversaries, and the powers of hell are overcome! The Psalmist said, "Zeal for Your house has eaten Me up."[624] The disciples remembered that Scripture when they saw Jesus over-turning the tables of the money changers and driving them out of the Temple with a whip. The week of Jesus' crucifixion is known as the week of His "Passion." It was so painful that Jesus prayed and asked the Father "if it were possible let this cup pass from Me; nevertheless, not as I will, but as You will."[625] Jesus suffered and died because it was the desire of the

622. James 2:20.
623. 2 Chro. 16:9; Psa. 34:15; 1 Peter 3:12.
624. Psa. 69:9; John 2:17.
625. Matt. 26:29.

Father.[626] The will of God is the expressed desire of God that the Holy Spirit breathes or quickens in our spirit that in turn serves to motivate us into action while influencing the direction of our decisions and choices as a rudder directs a ship. How useful would a ship be without a rudder? How fruitful and rich would the life of a believer be without the Holy Spirit's communion of godly desires?

It seems to me that employers do not motivate employees they only stimulate them by paying them regularly. If the pay were to stop how long do you think the employees would come to work? However, successful employers hire motivated people, which means they hire people who are driven from the heart to do what they do. The employer's responsibility, then, is to keep their employees focused on that which their heart already desires and fan the flames of passion that stir up a zeal to get the job done come hell or high water. Money will usually only purchase stimulation, it seldom purchases any lasting motivation. Therefore, when we observe believers or congregations with no motivation to sacrificially serve others or have no passion to reach the world for Jesus—then it is evident that the reception of Holy Spirit desires is lacking. Serving others and reaching the world for Jesus are a couple of things God desires in the here and now. That is not all that God desires, but it does help us grasp the value of aligning our heart and will in agreement with His desires. Our agreement with His desires brings His presence into our midst and where the Spirit of the Lord is, there is transformation, liberty, and glory! The lack of desire, motivation, and passion can be overcome through prayer, learning, and leadership that models the nature of Jesus Christ and exemplifies being guided by the Holy Spirit. Love is a powerful emotion and Jesus said, "You shall love the LORD your God with all your heart, with all of your soul, and with all of your mind."[627] Our whole-hearted love is our Father's desire and pleasure, and the foundation of our personal communion with the Holy Spirit.

---

626. Isa. 53:10.
627. Matt. 22:37.

The second aspect of our spirit's capacity for communion is "delight." It is "delight" in the sense that someone or something is preferable, pleasurable, pleasing, enjoyable or beautiful, thus initiating our gratitude and rejoicing in the Holy Spirit. Many believers have been working and trying hard to fulfill their "duty" by serving the Lord. But the Holy Spirit wants to so fill us with His nature that we "delight" in those things in which our Lord finds pleasure. For some prayer has been a duty, but the Holy Spirit is now emphasizing Jesus' words; "Until now you have asked nothing in My name. Ask, and you will receive, that your joy may be full."[628] Delight expresses both our attraction and response to the gracious operational power of God's presence which favors and strengthens us as we commune with the Holy Spirit. God has given us His good Spirit to instruct us.[629]

The Greek word that best captures this sense or meaning of delight is "*eudokeo.*" Its usual sense is "to take pleasure or delight in."[630] It also includes the meaning: "to take pleasure or find satisfaction in something, *be well pleased, take delight.* "[631] For example, "*eudokeo*" is translated as "well pleased," "good pleasure," and "pleasure" in the following verses: God said, "This is My beloved Son in whom I am well pleased."[632] Luke writes, "It is the Father's good pleasure to give you the kingdom."[633] And Paul writes. "Therefore, I take pleasure in infirmities, in reproaches, in needs, in persecutions, in distresses, for Christ's sake. For when I am weak, then I am strong."[634]

"The dominant use of *eudokía* shows plainly that the people of good pleasure are the recipients of God's grace by his free and

---

628. John 16:24.

629. Neh. 9:20.

630. Gerhard Kittel, Gerhard Friedrich, and Geoffrey William Bromiley, *Theological Dictionary of the New Testament* (Grand Rapids, MI: W.B. Eerdmans, 1985), 273.

631. William Arndt et al., *A Greek-English Lexicon of the New Testament and Other Early Christian Literature* (Chicago: University of Chicago Press, 2000), 404.

632. Matt. 3:17.

633. Luke 12:32.

634. 2 Cor. 12:10.

unfathomably sovereign choice or counsel."[635] We are created to be attracted to and delighted in the grace of God, because it is preferable, pleasurable, pleasing, enjoyable and beautiful. This is why for generations we have sung the hymn, "Amazing Grace!" Amazing expresses God's nature, which includes His grace, because He is the "Spirit of Grace."[636] After our hopeless existence being separated from our Creator/Father, it is a great delight and joy to be reconciled with Him through the blood of Jesus and worship Him in the beauty of holiness.[637] Our heavenly Father so transcends the five adjectives listed above that our regenerated new nature bows in worship before Him not as a religious duty but out of the delight of our heart. The Psalmist grasps our delight with the words; "In His presence is fullness of joy, at His right hand are pleasures forevermore."[638]

The Psalmist states, "Delight yourself also in the LORD, And He shall give you the desires of your heart."[639] James Montgomery Boice provides the following insights on this passage:

> The promise attached to this verse is that if we delight in God, God will give us the desires of our hearts. This does not mean that God will give us any foolish thing we may long for. It means that if we are delighting in God and longing for God, God will give us himself.[640]

When God gives Himself to us by coming to live in our hearts it completely changes our nature and our future. "We are a new creation, old things are passed away; behold, and all things have become

---

635. Kittel, Friedrich, and Bromiley, *Theological Dictionary,* 274.

636. Heb. 10:29.

637. Col. 1:13-14; Psa. 29:2, 96:9.

638. Psa. 16:11.

639. Psa. 37:4.

640. James Montgomery Boice, *Psalms 1–41: An Expositional Commentary* (Grand Rapids, MI: Baker Books, 2005), 317.

new."[641] It is now a delight to live and have our being in communion with the Holy Spirit who has come not to visit us but to reside in our hearts. Jesus lived daily in delightful communion with the Holy Spirit, demonstrating for us an exemplary lifestyle.[642] Even though the Apostle Paul was buffeted by a messenger from Satan he declared;

> Concerning this thing I pleaded with the Lord three times that it might depart from me. And He said to me, "My grace is sufficient for you, for My strength is made perfect in weakness." therefore most gladly I will rather boast in my infirmities, that the power of Christ may rest upon me. Therefore, I take **pleasure** in infirmities, in reproaches, in needs, in persecutions, in distresses, for Christ's sake. For when I am weak, then I am strong. (2 Cor. 12:8-10 emphasis mine).

Paul learned to delight and boast even in his weaknesses and infirmities because it made way for the operational power of God, the Holy Spirit of grace, to accomplish what Paul could not accomplish in his own strength. Fulfilling our role as the sons of God requires more than knowing what God said in the past. It requires knowing what He is saying now and what pleases Him today; then responding to what He is saying by delighting in fulfilling His pleasure.

So, we need more than knowledge about God, we must commune with God. Jesus said, "He who has ears let him hear what the Spirit says (*verb, present, active = saying*) to the churches."[643] As believers we have the privilege and responsibility to commune with the Holy Spirit and know what He is saying today. Upon hearing His desires, love motivates us to take pleasure or delight in those things that give Him pleasure. The Lord's prayer is not for "our kingdom to come and our will to be done," but "for His kingdom to come and His will to be

641. 2 Cor. 5:17.
642. John 8:29.
643. Rev. 2:11.

done on earth as it is in heaven." Paul prayed for the church at Colosse that they "would walk worthy of the Lord fully pleasing Him."[644] The challenges and trials of life will fade from view in the delight of hearing the following words from the Father, "Well done good and faithful servant."[645] Our fulfillment or daily satisfaction as members of His royal priesthood arises out of our communion with and delight in pleasing our Father.

The third and final aspect of our capacity to commune with the Holy Spirit is "design." It is "design" with the meaning or sense to create, invent, fashion, devise a plan or solution. You are designed by God uniquely different from all of the other billions of people on the earth. No one else can do what you are uniquely designed to do. The challenge is to discover those unique things God has designed and purposed for you to do as only you can do them. Hence, each believer's responsibility is to train his or her spirit to so commune with the Holy Spirit as to inflame our imagination and gain insight into God's design. Thereby we will discover the new innovations and better answers to the challenges and problems that are beyond the ability of our intellect to invent, solve or overcome.

Somewhere in my youth I assumed that imaginations, dreams, and visions were basically fantasy or make-believe and had no part in an educated worldview. Therefore, I dismissed them as having no value in my life. However, I have since discovered that my life revolves around spiritual personalities and realities that cannot be observed even under the world's most powerful microscopes. The Holy Spirit reminded me of men in Scripture that changed the direction of nations by perceiving God's design through dreams and visions. Men like Joseph, Daniel, Isaiah, Zachariah, Peter, and Paul. Consequently, I had to learn to perceive and hear the word of God and receive the quickening of the Holy Spirit in order to grasp the means with which God utilizes to commune with us. I need to hear Him in order to fill in

644. Col. 1:10.
645. Matt. 25:21-23.

the blanks that the natural world, scientific theories, and philosophic propositions leave unanswered.

It is amazing how often dreams and visions are mentioned throughout Scripture. In the first two chapters of Matthew dreams are mentioned five times surrounding the birth of Jesus.[646] On the Day of Pentecost Peter quoted Joel by saying;

> *And it shall come to pass in the last days, says God, That I will pour out of My Spirit on all flesh; Your sons and your daughters shall prophesy, your young men shall see* ***visions****, your old men shall* ***dream dreams****."* (Acts 2:17, emphasis mine).

One of the wonderful things about the New Testament is that it unveils some of the mysteries "which from the beginning of the ages has been hidden in God."[647] Those Holy Spirit revelations have impacted and blessed civilization for the past two thousand years, and I am convinced that the Holy Spirit wants to continue unpacking those texts and illuminating our hearts and minds with God's "design" for discoveries and solutions in this generation. The Apostle Paul wrote;

> But as it is written: *"Eye has not seen, nor ear heard, nor have entered into the heart of man the things which God has prepared for those who love Him."* **But God has revealed *them* to us through His Spirit**. For the Spirit searches all things, yes, the deep things of God. For what man knows the things of a man except the spirit of the man which is in him? Even so no one knows the things of God except the Spirit of God. Now we have received, not the spirit of the world, **but the Spirit who is from God, that we might know the things that have been freely**

646. Matt. 1:20, 2:12, 2:13, 2:29, 2:22.
647. Eph. 3:9.

> **given to us by God**. These things we also speak, not in words which man's wisdom teaches **but which the Holy Spirit teaches, comparing spiritual things with spiritual**. (1 Cor. 2:9-13, emphasis mine).

Our key to living as overcomers in this world will not be accomplished by fantasy or make-believe, but through communion with the Holy Spirit and doing the wonderful works of God. The Holy Spirit is God and has come to live in our hearts "that we might know the things that have been freely given to us by God." We live in the same fallen and broken world where Jesus lived and ministered. God not only had the answers to the poverty, pain, and problems, but Jesus demonstrated God's answers to the poor, hurting, and distressed. Jesus Christ not only grasped God's kingdom design for man, He was moved with compassion to implement the kingdom of heaven on earth. He did what He did not as God, but as a man anointed of the Holy Spirit. He not only came to inaugurate the kingdom of God on earth, He also came to "destroy the works of the devil."[648] He gave us this promise, "Most assuredly, I say to you, he who believes in Me, the works that I do he will do also; and greater *works* than these he will do, because I go to My Father."[649] And further, He has invited us to "come boldly to the throne of grace, that we may obtain mercy and find grace to help in time of need."[650] God could have accomplished all things by Himself alone. However, He willfully and deliberately included you and me in the design of the master plan for His kingdom.

As we commune with the Holy Spirit, He will reveal to each believer his or her part of God's design for their life in His master plan for the manifestation of His kingdom in this world around us. It is my conviction that God has the cure for cancer and birth defects, solutions to overcome hunger and poverty, and holds the keys to inventions that will improve the standard of living for every person on

---

648. 1 John 3:8.
649. John 14:12.
650. Heb. 4:16.

earth. Our responsibility is to commune with the Holy Spirit expecting Him to reveal thoughts, ideas, concepts, and portions of God's design and manifestation of the wonderous presence of His kingdom; just as Jesus Christ made manifest the design and manifestation of the wonderous presence of God's kingdom through His life and ministry.

The Seed Principle:

Having such marvelous possibilities before us generates a mindset of expectation and inspires higher levels of faith. It is well to be reminded that the kingdom of God functions according to the seed principle.[651] For that reason, we as believers need to value small beginnings just as a farmer values his seed. There are preparations that need to be made in the right season, under the right conditions for planting, cultivating, and harvesting a crop. So, there is right timing and conditions in the kingdom of God to expect God given results. Nature itself expresses there is a God given design for how God intends nature to function, because our Creator is a God of order and design. And when Jesus Christ ministered, He faced this world that is fallen, broken, and out of order, and brought all that He ministered to under the blessings of God's design and order. Therefore, we must ask the Holy Spirit to reveal to us God's design for each situation if we are to serve our families and this world as innovators and problem solvers. Jesus said;

> "Go into all the world and preach the gospel to every creature. He who believes and is baptized will be saved; but he who does not believe will be condemned. And these signs will follow those who believe: In My name they will cast out demons; they will speak with new tongues; they will take up serpents; and if they drink anything deadly, it will by no

651. Matt. 13:31.

> means hurt them; they will lay hands on the sick, and they will recover." (Mark 16:15-18).

The devil plans to rob, kill, destroy, and oppose the kingdom of God, just as he opposed Jesus Christ. However, as believers in Jesus we are commissioned to overcome the powers of the devil,[652] proclaim the gospel of the kingdom, and demonstrate the wonderous presence kingdom in the here and now. Therefore, we cannot allow ourselves to become paralyzed by passivity, unbelief or fear. We must continually commune with the Holy Spirit and align with God's design for every situation. Then do what the Holy Spirit says do, so that "men may see our good works and glorify our father in heaven."[653] Hence, no more unbelieving believers or closet Christians, but lovers of God and warriors that set the captives free and bring in the wonderous presence of the kingdom of God upon this world.

The workforce in the kingdom of God on earth includes His Church, His bride, the royal priesthood. In other words, God made things for you to do before He made you.[654] To do what God created you to do and function effectively as members of the priesthood requires that we learn to live and walk in relationship with the Holy Spirit which includes, but transcends the limits of our logic and intellect. The Scripture says, "As many as are led by the Spirit of God, these are the sons of God."[655] So, all believers must learn how to be guided by the Holy Spirit. The starting place is aligning our spirit with the word of God and training our conscience, intuition, and communion to be sensitive to the voice of Holy Spirit.

---

652. Rev. 12:11.
653. Matt. 6:33.
654. Eph. 2:10.
655. Rom. 8:14.

Offer the Sacrifice of Praise:

However, we often fail to hear what the Spirit is saying today because of the tendency to be trapped by complacency in our traditions and familiar interpretations of Scripture, just as the Pharisees quoted Scripture, but were unable or unwilling to hear the voice of God when Jesus was speaking. So, a cornerstone doctrine of the Reformation was the doctrine of the priesthood of believers, but it has not become a practical reality in the experience of most believers. The greatest value of all doctrine or propositional discourse is when it becomes incarnated on our lives and ministry. Biblical wisdom declares, "the path of the just *is* like the shining sun, that shines ever brighter unto the perfect day."[656] Therefore we the church should expect the Holy Spirit to illuminate Scripture and emphasize truths today that have not been focused upon in previous generations. At this present time the Holy Spirit is illuminating realities regarding the kingdom of God and emphasizing the priesthood of believers beyond what the church has experienced since its early days.

As a born-again believer and a member of His royal priesthood you are capable of continual fellowship with God through your spiritual capacities of conscience, intuition, and communion. Born-again believer defines who we are, whereas royal priesthood defines what we do. Among the practical applications of our priestly ministry is to minister first unto the Lord our God. "Therefore, by Him let us continually offer the sacrifice of praise to God, that is, the fruit of *our* lips, giving thanks to His name."[657] Jack Hayford has surely inspired many of us especially in the area of praise and worship. He writes:

> Sacrifice has always been involved at the heart of all worship of the Most High; it is the bite in worship. By bite I mean the cost—and the price is usually blood.

---

656. Prov. 4:18.
657. Heb. 13:15.

> Blood, that is, as in life—the laying down of what we scream to preserve or spare in our own interest.[658]

As members of His royal priesthood our sacrifices of praise and thanksgiving are reasonable offerings unto our Lord, whose gracious generosity transcends our comprehensions. For the Lord says, "A*s* the heavens are higher than the earth, so are My ways higher than your ways, and My thoughts than your thoughts."[659] His lavish love expressed through the sacrifice of Jesus on the cross compels our hearts and voices to join with the heavenly choir and proclaim; "You are worthy, O Lord, to receive glory and honor and power; For You created all things, And by Your will they exist and were created."[660] "We give You thanks, O Lord God Almighty, The One who is and who was and who is to come, Because You have taken Your great power and reigned."[661] Hence, "Blessing and honor and glory and power *Be* to Him who sits on the throne, And to the Lamb, forever and ever!"[662]

The Levitical Priests were charged with the responsibility of teaching the people "the statutes which the Lord had spoken."[663] Jesus, Himself was recognized as the "Teacher."[664] He also commands us to "Go therefore and make disciples of all the nations… teaching them to observe all things that I have commanded you"[665] Consequently, teaching is a responsibility of the New Testament priesthood and obedience to His word promises good success and prosperity.[666] Teaching is necessary because men "love darkness rather than light, because

---

658. Jack W. Hayford, *Worship His Majesty: How Praising the King of Kings Will Change Your Life*, ed. David Webb, Revised and Expanded Edition. (Ventura, CA: Regal, 2000), 25.

659. Isa. 55:9.

660. Rev. 4:11

661. Rev. 11:17.

662. Rev. 5:13

663. Lev. 10:11.

664. John 3:2, 13:13; Acts 1:1-2.

665. Matt. 28:19-20.

666. Joshua 1:7-9.

their deeds are evil."[667] The Apostle Paul writes, "Although they knew God, they did not glorify *Him* as God, nor were thankful, but became futile in their thoughts, and their foolish hearts were darkened.[668] Thus, New Testament teaching must extend beyond doctrinal propositions as important as they are; and must ultimately include personal applications that include the offerings of praise and thanksgiving. R. T. Kendall states, "Gratitude must be taught; we must never assume that it comes automatically… It is encouraging to know how much God loves our gratitude; this should spur us on to be more thankful.[669] Our offerings of praise and thanksgiving are acceptable sacrifices unto the Lord and position the offerer to be edified as well. R. H. Rottschafer makes the following comments:

> When we are truly grateful, we rejoice, and we do so spontaneously from our inner depths. The celebration relieves stress and makes us feel better because we let our guard down and deeply feel the relief or the joy for whatever has pleased us. Part of the happiness usually includes an awareness that we did not achieve our goals by pure chance but by the help of others or the guidance of God.[670]

It is quite difficult to be depressed or angry with an attitude of gratitude. The sacrifices of praise and thanksgiving not only please the Lord;[671] they also take the focus off of ourselves and place our attention on the sufficiency of the Lord. The result is that even greater faith is inspired by our offerings of praise and gratitude. In our culture

---

667. John 3:19

668. Rom. 1:21.

669. R. T. Kendall, *Understanding Theology, Volume Two* (Ross-shire, Great Britain: Christian Focus, 2000), 416.

670. R. H. Rottschafer, "Gratitude," ed. David G. Benner and Peter C. Hill, *Baker Encyclopedia of Psychology & Counseling*, Baker Reference Library (Grand Rapids, MI: Baker Books, 1999), 518.

671. Heb. 13:15-16.

we are blessed with the availability of abundance of the things that make for a pleasant lifestyle. But we have a propensity in the midst of abundance to feel entitled and become lax in our offerings of praise and thanksgiving unto the Lord. There is a French proverb that says, "We never know the worth of water till the well is dry.[672] He is the giver of every good gift and it is so easy to become negligent in our offerings of praise and thanksgiving. Therefore, let us be diligent as His royal priesthood, to daily "Enter into His gates with thanksgiving, *and* into His courts with praise. Be thankful to Him and bless His name."[673]

In fulfilling your priestly ministry of offering the continual sacrifice of praise and thanksgiving it may be necessary to anoint your eyes with eye salve that you may see life in the here and now from God's perspective.[674] Wayne Cordeiro states, "The way in which you define your circumstances will determine, to a large degree, how you will respond… Between each event and your attitude concerning that event lies your definition of that event."[675] We have the propensity to see our circumstances from the natural perspective, thus falling into the category that Jesus described as seeing but not perceiving.[676] From that perspective the world around us looks scary and hopeless. However, we have graciously been granted the capacity to see life through the lens of the Holy Spirit which enables us to interpret life from God's perspective. God always has the best option for any opportunity, the right solution for every problem, and the appropriate weapons to equip us to defend ourselves and/or advance against any enemy. K. Neill Foster with Paul King see praise as a powerful spiritual weapon. They write;

---

672. Mark Water, *The New Encyclopedia of Christian Quotations* (Alresford, Hampshire: John Hunt Publishers Ltd, 2000), 839.

673. Psa. 100:4.

674. Rev. 3:18.

675. Wayne Cordeiro, *Attitudes That Attract Success* (Ventura, CA: Regal Books, 2001), 44-45.

676. Matt. 13:14.

> Praise, then is a weapon, like the Word of God (Heb. 4:12) or similar to the Word of God. Moreover, people are capable by their praise of inflicting vengeance on the nations, punishment on the peoples, binding the kings with fetters, shackling their nobles with iron, carrying out the sentence written against them (Psa. 149:7-9).[677]

Praise as a spiritual weapon seems inconsistent with the way some believers have been taught. Many of us have relied on the double edge sword of the word of God as our offensive and defensive weapon. Of course, the word of God is a powerful weapon, but the following words of the Psalmist teaches us that praise and the word together is also a powerful weapon.

> *Let* the high praises of God *be* in their mouth, and a two-edged sword in their hand, to execute vengeance on the nations, and punishments on the peoples; To bind their kings with chains, and their nobles with fetters of iron; To execute on them the written judgment-- This honor have all His saints. Praise the LORD! (Psa. 149:6-9).

The power of praise as a weapon is illustrated from the experience of Jehoshaphat, a king of Judah. His nation was faced with overwhelming forces coming against them. He responded by praying; "O our God, will You not judge them? For we have no power against this great multitude that is coming against us; nor do we know what to do, but our eyes *are* upon You."[678] The Lord answered his prayer by saying, "The battle is not yours, but the Lord's."[679] Therefore, rather than

---

677. K. Neill Foster with Paul King, *Binding & Loosing: Exercising Authority over the Dark Powers* (Camp Hill, PA: Christian Publishers, Inc., 1998), 78.

678. 2 Chro. 20:12.

679. 2 Chro. 20:15.

the king sending out warriors to fight, he sent out Levitical singers and they "stood up to praise the Lord God of Israel with voices loud and high." As they began to sing the Lord set ambushes and fought against the enemies of Israel, defeating them with such a great victory that it took Israel "three days to gather the spoil because there was so much."[680]

The point is that the priestly offerings of praise and thanksgiving from a heart of humility are not only acceptable sacrifices unto the Lord, they also exalt His majesty and attract His manifest presence even in the face of adversity. Also, seeing life through eyes anointed by the Holy Spirit enables you to see individuals and circumstances from God's perspective. From the clarity of that viewpoint you are enabled to praise Him with thanksgiving, and also teach others the joy of praise and thanksgiving with a grace that inspires them to celebrate the abundance of God's manifold blessings even in the presence of seemingly formidable enemies! Seeing from God's perspective enables us to more effectively fulfill the priestly responsibilities of intercession in alignment with Jesus' High Priestly ministry of intercession, for He "always lives to make intercession" for us.[681]

Intercession:

Jesus in His humanity became acquainted with our frailty and vulnerability, and "being tempted, He is able to aid those who are tempted." [682] His earthly life and sufferings prepared Him to serve as our merciful High Priest because He "can sympathize with our weakness."[683] An example of Jesus' intercession before His ascension is found in His relationship with Peter. The Lord said, "Simon, Simon! Indeed, Satan has asked for you, that he may sift *you* as wheat. But I have prayed for you, that your faith should not fail; and when

---

680. 2 Chro. 20:25b.
681. Heb. 7:25.
682. Heb. 2:18.
683. Heb. 4:15.

you have returned to *Me,* strengthen your brethren."[684] Bruce Barton gives additional insights regarding the High Priestly ministry of Jesus as our intercessor:

> As our High Priest, Christ is our advocate, the mediator between us and God. His purpose is to "intercede" for those who follow God. He looks after our interests, presenting our requests to the Father... Christ makes perpetual intercession before God for us. Christ's continuous presence in heaven as the Priest-King assures us that our sins have been paid for and forgiven (see Romans 8:33, 34; Hebrews 2:17–18; 4:15–16; 9:24).[685]

Prayer, especially intercessory prayer is the divine-human means by which our God includes you and me in on-going expansion of His kingdom over the powers of darkness. As members of His royal priesthood we need to be cautious and avoid the religious trap of asking God to do things for us that He expects us to do for ourselves and others. In other words, if we keep asking our boss to do what he assigned us to do, we probably would not have a job very long. Intercession is not a release from our priestly responsibilities in the expectation that God is going to do what He has given us the responsibility to do. Rather, intercessory prayer is the privilege and responsibility of co-laboring with God and participating with Him in fulfilling His agenda.

It is in the context of intercession that we understand what it means for Jesus to be our "Advocate." An "advocate" "is one who comes forward in behalf of and as the representative of another."[686] Jesus represents you as your advocate before the Father and makes interces-

---

684. Luke 22:22-23.

685. Bruce B. Barton et al., *Hebrews*, Life Application Bible Commentary (Wheaton, IL: Tyndale House Publishers, 1997), 106–107.

686. Spiros Zodhiates, *The Complete Word Study Dictionary: New Testament* (Chattanooga, TN: AMG Publishers, 2000).

sion for each of us. This is extremely important as we realize that we all have an enemy who has an agenda to destroy each of us and our households. The real enemy is not your parents or spouse or family members or neighbors, but the unseen world of the powers of darkness. The Apostle Paul says, "For we do not wrestle against flesh and blood, but against principalities, against powers, against the rulers of the darkness of this age, against spiritual *hosts* of wickedness in the heavenly *places*."[687]

The enemy will try to attack you and bring accusations against you in an effort to bring you under condemnation, guilt, shame, and self-pity for the purpose of crushing your faith. Always remember that Jesus paid for your sin and condemnation through the shedding of His blood on Calvary's cross. Now He is in heaven before the throne of God as your Advocate interceding on your behalf before the Father. He knows that you are under attack because He has also walked in this world. He reminds the Father that He died for you and has not only forgiven you, He has also imparted His righteousness to you. Sin and death no longer have dominion over you.[688] In spite of your sin, your standing before God is as a righteous child and not as a sinner.[689] Your great High Priest not only intercedes for you, but He sends the Holy Spirit to strengthen your faith and confidence. He also sends other members of His royal priesthood to intercede for you and encourage you! Receive these gracious provisions and re-enter the fray and fight the good fight of faith!!

All of us will sin from time to time as we experience life.[690] Sin is not to be taken lightly, and we should never let sin have the last word in our lives. Take responsibility for your sin by confession, repentance, and asking God to forgive you, and He will. However, sometimes we have a sin habit that may take considerable time and effort to overcome. During the meanwhile the powers of darkness will try

687. Eph. 6:12.
688. Rom. 6:6-9.
689. 2 Cor. 5:21.
690. 1 John 1:8-10.

to convince you that you are unworthy and beyond the reach of salvation. On the other hand you may have a child or relative that continues to rebel and resist the way of the Lord. You love them and desperately want them to be saved. Keep in mind that God loves them so much that He sent His Son to die on the cross for each of us. Remember, you are not in this warfare by yourself. You are a member of the body of Jesus, and as such, a member of His royal priesthood with the anointing of the Holy Spirit to bring the blessing and benefits of the kingdom of God upon the sphere in which God has given you responsibility and influence.

Therefore, exercise your privilege as a member of His royal priesthood and intercede for your family standing on the promise; "'Believe on the Lord Jesus Christ, and you will be saved, you and your household.'"[691] Andrew Murray states, "God has made the execution of His will dependent upon the will of man. His promises will be fulfilled as much as our faith allows."[692] Our faith does not rest in our ability but in the promises and power of God who is able to do beyond what we can ask or think. "This is the confidence that we have in Him, if we ask anything according to His will, He hears us. And if we know that He hears us… we know that we have the petitions that we ask of Him."[693] Jesus and you are on the same team. He continually intercedes for you, and if God be for you, who can be against you?[694] Your prayers matter and make a difference for eternity. Jesus taught, "Men always ought to pray and not lose heart.… 'And shall God not avenge His own elect who cry out day and night to Him, though He bears long with them?'"[695] Perseverance then, becomes the key to prevailing as an intercessor and the joy of victorious breakthroughs.

---

691. Acts 16:31.

692. Andrew Murray, *With Christ in the School of Prayer* (Springdale, PA: Whitaker House, 1981), 222.

693. 1 John 5:14-15.

694. Rom. 8:31.

695. Luke 18:1, 7.

Binding and Loosing:

As members of His royal priesthood we not only have the privilege and responsibility of intercession on the behalf of others, but we also have been given the authority to bind and loose. Jesus said, "And I will give you the keys of the kingdom of heaven, and whatever you bind on earth will be bound in heaven, and whatever you loose on earth will be loosed in heaven."[696] It is important to keep in mind that neither intercessory prayer nor binding and loosing are indiscriminate acts, but our co-laboring with the Lord regarding the accomplishment of His will in the here and now. For example, as members of His royal priesthood we cannot of our own volition bind Satan and cast him into the bottomless pit. However, there is coming a day when Satan will be bound and cast into the bottomless pit.[697]

The authority to bind and lose is to be directed by the Holy Spirit just as intercessory prayer is to be so directed. An example of binding and loosing is illustrated by Jesus at the grave of Lazarus. Jesus "cried with a loud voice, 'Lazarus, come forth!' And he who had died came out bound hand and foot with graveclothes, and his face was wrapped with a cloth. Jesus said to them, 'Loose him, and let him go.'"[698] Jesus could have spoken, and the grave clothes would have fallen off of Lazarus, but He included His disciples in the liberating of Lazarus. The Lord has designed His will to include our participation with Him as members of His royal priesthood.

Binding and loosing are especially applicable to several areas of ministry, but for our purposes here we will address four areas. First is the area of church discipline. Paul said, "Some having rejected, concerning the faith have suffered shipwreck, of whom are Hymenaeus and Alexander, whom I delivered to Satan that they may learn not to blaspheme."[699] This may seem heavy handed, but it comports with the

---

696. Matt 16:19, 18:18.
697. Rev. 20:2-3.
698. John 11:43-44.
699. 1 Tim. 1:19-20.

teaching of Jesus regarding a brother who sins against you and refuses to repent when confronted by you, followed by his refusal to hear two or three other witnesses with you, followed by his refusal to hear the entire church. As a disciplinary measure "let him be to you like a heathen or tax collector."[700] In other words if he refuses to repent even after increased witnesses against him, then his liberty to fellowship with the body of Christ is bound in an effort not to destroy him, but awaken him to his error and the need for his repentance. This binding action limits any further sin or offense by this brother against the body of Christ and preserves the possibility of his restoration to fellowship.

The second area is forgiveness. Jesus said, "For if you forgive men their trespasses, your heavenly Father will also forgive you. But if you do not forgive men their trespasses, neither will your Father forgive your trespasses."[701] Forgiveness is not always easy because the offenses against us are painful and we tend to rationalize that the pain we are suffering gives us the right to vengeance.[702] The pain may impair our ability to remember that forgiveness and reconciliation are at the heart of who we are and what we believe. Unforgiveness will bind you in anger and resentment to the point that it will impact your relational capacities, and your health. Everett L. Worthington states:

> You can't hurt the perpetrator by being unforgiving, but you can set yourself free by forgiving... Resentment one of the core elements of unforgiveness, is like carrying around a red-hot rock with the intention of someday throwing it back at someone who hurt you. It tires us and burns us. Harry Emerson Fosdick said, 'Hating people is like burning down your house to get rid of a rat.'[703]

---

700. Matt. 18:15-18.

701. Matt. 6:14-15.

702. Rom. 12:19.

703. Everett L. Worthington, *Forgiving and Reconciling: Bridges to Wholeness and Hope,* rev. ed., (Downers Grove, Il: InterVarsity Press, 2003), 22.

Offenses test our character by giving us an opportunity in a practical way to demonstrate the nature of Jesus who forgives us of our manifold offenses and transgressions. Forgiveness and reconciliation value relationships and that is what the cross of Jesus is all about. Forgiveness is always about relationships between persons, because there is no possibility of forgiving nature, regardless how much hurt or damage the storm causes and neither do we forgive systems. We may vote or labor to change systems, but we do not forgive poverty or slavery. Those systems are not accountable to God, only persons are accountable. The point is that unforgiveness binds an individual to the pain of an offense and forgiveness sets one free from the offense and opens the possibility for reconciliation. And as members of His royal priesthood we have been commissioned with the ministry of reconciliation.

The third area regarding binding and loosing also concerns a person's personal relationship with the Lord. The Greek word for forgive is *aphiemi* and it means: "to dismiss or release someone or something from a place or one's presence, let go, send away."[704] For example, suppose a person has gone through a divorce that was primarily their personal failure. Time has passed and the former spouse has moved on and remarried. But this person is bound by guilt and shame, even though he or she has sincerely repented and adjusted their lifestyle. They know the Scriptures, but they are stuck. They may even be suffering some physical problems as a result of the past sin and guilt, somewhat like the situation with the paralytic that was taken by others and let down through the roof into Jesus' presence. "When Jesus saw their faith, He said to the paralytic, 'Son, your sins are forgiven you.'"[705] This is where your priestly ministry can make a difference in that person's life. Pray with them and affirm their forgiveness by the Lord and their righteous standing before the Lord. The reality is that

---

704. William Arndt et al., *A Greek-English Lexicon of the New Testament and Other Early Christian Literature* (Chicago: University of Chicago Press, 2000), 156.

705. Mark 2:5.

he or she needs for someone in relationship with the Lord to affirm their faith and grant them permission to move forward. Jesus said, "If you forgive the sins of any, they are forgiven them; if you retain the *sins* of any, they are retained."[706] Decree their forgiveness and loose them from their past and grant them permission in the name of Jesus Christ to move forward. Forgiveness is loosing. The principle of loosing a person from their bondage of guilt and shame also applies to other areas beside divorce and includes many areas where people fail and get stuck. Jesus sets people free from their sin and bondages and anoints them as a member of His royal priesthood to do the same. "Where the Spirit of the Lord is there is Liberty."[707]

The fourth and final area of our discussion regarding binding and loosing concerns the area of demonic oppression. For example, Jesus met a woman "who had a spirit of infirmity eighteen years and was bent over and could in no way raise *herself* up. But when Jesus saw her, He called *her* to *Him* and said to her, 'Woman, you are loosed from your infirmity.'"[708] She was immediately set free, made straight, and glorified God. This example, at least in part, demonstrates that we as priests have a ministry responsibility against the demonic powers of darkness. As a policeman has the authority of the state to back up his commands to stop traffic or individuals, so has Jesus Christ given us the authority to bind and loose demonic powers in His name as members of His royal priesthood.

Summary:

Jesus Christ our great High Priest after the order of Melchizedek ever lives to make intercession for us before the throne of God.[709] However, beyond His intercession He administrates the advancement of the kingdom of God on the earth through His royal priesthood.

---

706. John 20:23.
707. 2 Cor. 3:18.
708. Luke 13:11-12.
709. Heb. 7:25.

We, as priests have been anointed by the Holy Spirt and trained to spiritually and continually commune with Him. We who were dead in trespasses and sin, He has "made alive together with Christ and raised us up together and made us sit together in heavenly places in Christ Jesus."[710] Our responsibility as priests is to first offer the sacrifices of praise and thanksgiving unto the Lord. "Great is the Lord, and greatly to be praised; and His greatness is unsearchable."[711] We not only have been granted the privilege of access to the throne of grace where we find mercy and grace to help on a daily basis, but have been afforded the opportunity of participating with the Lord through making intercession on the behalf of our families, churches, communities, and the nations. Jesus taught us to pray "Your kingdom come. Your will be done on earth as it is in heaven."[712] Jesus Christ has given us, His royal priesthood, the keys to the Kingdom. He said, "Whatever you bind on earth will be bound in heaven, and whatever you loose on earth will be loosed in heaven."[713] There is coming a day when each priest will give an account to the Lord for our stewardship as His priests and rewarded accordingly.[714] On that great Day of the Lord the "kingdoms of this world will become the kingdoms of our Lord and of His Christ and He will reign forever and ever."[715] In the next chapter we will discuss the mysteries of the kingdom of God as revealed through the teaching of Jesus using parables.

---

710. Eph. 2:5-6.
711. Psa. 145:3.
712. Matt. 6:10.
713. Matt.16:19.
714. 2 Cor. 5:10.
715. Rev. 11:15.

CHAPTER FIVE

THE PARABLES OF THE KINGDOM

"And the disciples came and said to Him, 'Why do You speak to them in parables?' He answered and said to them, "Because it has been given to you to know the mysteries of the kingdom of heaven, but to them it has not been given."

(Matt. 13:10-11)

Jesus at 12 years of age told his parents that he needed to be about His Fathers business.[716] The question we must answer is, "What was the Father's business from Jesus' perspective?" The Scriptures reveal a number of objectives that Jesus was to accomplish during His earthly ministry including revealing the heavenly Father to mankind, destroying the works of the devil, paying the price for redeeming mankind from sin, and more. But for the purposes of this chapter we will focus on the Father's business as the inaugurating of the kingdom of God among men.

716. Luke 2:48.

Jesus Was Tempted:

Following Jesus' water baptism and the Holy Spirit coming upon Him, He so yielded His humanity to the guidance of the Holy Spirit that He spent the next forty days in the wilderness being tempted by the devil. It makes me wonder how He felt in His humanity and if He experienced any resistance to the leading of the Holy Spirit during those days of testing. It was during the second temptation that the devil took Him up on a high mountain and showed Him all the kingdoms of the world. The devil offered to give Jesus the authority over those kingdoms and their glory if Jesus would simply worship him. "Jesus answered and said to him, "Get behind Me, Satan! For it is written, *'You shall worship the* LORD *your God, and Him only you shall serve.'* "[717]

The temptations that Jesus endured were as real as the temptation that Adam experienced in the Garden of Eden and as authentic as the temptations that you and I experience. It was His humanity that was being tested. Some people have questioned the authenticity of those temptations because they understand that God cannot sin. It is true that God cannot sin nor die. However, Jesus willfully emptied Himself of His divine prerogatives and became a man. He experienced temptations and death, not as God, but as a man filled with the Holy Spirit.[718] Nevertheless, Jesus did not have a sin nature like you and me because He was conceived in His mother's womb, not from the seed of Adam, but from the Holy Spirit.[719] Still, it was absolutely possible that Jesus in His humanity could have sinned just as Adam, who was also created without a sin nature. Yet Adam yielded to temptation and sinned. If Jesus had yielded to any temptation, He would have forfeited the privilege of receiving a name that is above every name. Even in the hour of great trial just prior to the cross, He said to the Father, "Not

717. Luke 4:6-8.
718. Phil. 2:6-7.
719. Luke 1:35.

My will, but Yours, be done."[720] Consequently, "we do not have a High Priest who cannot sympathize with our weaknesses, but was in all *points* tempted as *we are, yet* without sin."[721]

Jesus the Messiah:

Jesus having gained the victory over the devil's temptations, "returned in the power of the Spirit to Galilee, and news of Him went out through all the surrounding region."[722] It was in the area of Galilee in the city of Cana while attending a wedding celebration where Jesus performed His first miracle by turning water into wine. It was during that wedding feast that Jesus' mother told Him "They have no wine." Jesus responded by saying, "'Woman, what does your concern have to do with Me? My hour has not yet come.'"[723] However, it seems that the Holy Spirit in those moments quicken His Messianic awareness and He told the servants to "Fill the waterpots with water." Then "He said to them, "Draw *some* out now, and take *it* to the master of the feast." They did as Jesus instructed and the water was changed to wine and tasted better than the wine that the guest had enjoyed earlier.[724] It was some months later during the Sabbath meeting in the synagogue at Nazareth where Jesus declared the fulfillment of Isaiah 61:1-2 over His life.[725]

The point is that Jesus ministered for only three and a half years, but it took about one-third of that time to fully transition into His Messianic ministry. He knew that He had to be about His Father's business, but the essence of that business was relational, and relationships require process and process requires time. Jesus had to first develop a relationship with the Father as a man filled with the Holy

720. Luke 22:42.
721. Heb. 4:15.
722. Luke 4:14.
723. John 2:3-4.
724. John 2:7-11.
725. Luke 4:18-19.

Spirit just as each of us must do. Then He had to learn how to minister with the mind of the Father just as all believers have to learn to minister with the mind of Christ.[726] It was not His divine nature but the Holy Spirit that enabled Jesus to effectively commune with the Father. It was His human nature that had to learn how to know and express the will of God. Robert F. Capon states:

> The influence of the Spirit alone—acting upon his human nature in no fundamentally different way than it does on ours—is quite sufficient: it covers all the biblical bases; it provides for all the divine "informing" we ever need to speak of; and it does so without turning Jesus into Superman.[727]

It takes time and experience/process to know our true identity in Christ and how to discern and express the mind of the Lord. Most often what we know in our heart by the Holy Spirit needs to be processed and/or experienced in life before it becomes a personal reality or released through ministry. We are all tempted to rush beyond the capacity of our tested and proven relationship with the Holy Spirit into ministry. The Lord wants each of us to minister, but it is the anointing that breaks the yoke not our ability to articulate facts and principles. Jesus was the Son of God, but He also spent much time communing with the Father in the secret place even after He began His Messianic ministry. Accordingly, it is necessary that we develop an incubation system to process what the Holy Spirit is teaching us. That will enable us to minister with confidence and boldness not only in our home and local congregation, but also in the intersections of our culture in the face of opposition and persecution.

---

726. 1 Cor. 2:16.

727. Robert Farrar Capon, *Kingdom, Grace, Judgment: Paradox, Outrage, and Vindication in the Parables of Jesus*, Combined edition. (Grand Rapids, MI; Cambridge, U.K.: William B. Eerdmans Company, 2002), 34.

Jesus and the Gospel of the Kingdom:

The Gospel of Mark opens the ministry of Jesus as follows: "Jesus came to Galilee, preaching the gospel of the kingdom of God saying, 'The time is fulfilled, and the kingdom of God is at hand. Repent, and believe in the gospel.'"[728] Much of what Jesus taught regarding the kingdom is encrypted in parables. The Gospel of Matthew declares; "All these things Jesus spoke to the multitude in parables; and without a parable He did not speak to them."[729] Brian C. Stiller states, "A full third of Jesus' teachings in the Synoptic Gospels were parables, with more than sixty-seven examples of similes and metaphors in the Gospels."[730]

There are powerful reasons why Jesus used parables in teaching about the kingdom of God. First, it is important to grasp that we each have a strong propensity to get to the bottom line of an issue, looking intensely at all the facts. But the kingdom of God is not about a series of facts. The kingdom of God is a relational kingdom. And Jesus uses parables as a literary device to draw each of us into the process of doing life together and governing with Him. His parables functioned to initiate a lifestyle relationship with Him and guide our comprehension of the mysteries of the kingdom. The wheat and tares will grow together but in the end the kingdom of God will overcome the powers of darkness and corruption inculcated within the systems of this world. Keep in mind that Jesus did not come into this world to simply cast out devils and do miracles. No! Surely, He came to do those things, but He also came to inaugurate the kingdom of God, build His church, and destroy the works of the devil.

To better understand why Jesus taught in parables think about the training that Daniel acquired in preparation for influencing the powers of darkness and corruption among the governmental leaders of

---

728. Mark 1:14-15.

729. Matt. 13:34.

730. Brian C. Stiller, *Preaching Parables to Postmoderns* (Minneapolis, MN: Fortress Press, 2005), 9.

Babylon. Daniel was included among the young Hebrew men taken captive in Jerusalem and carried off to Babylon in 606 B.C. They were "good-looking, gifted in all wisdom, possessing knowledge and quick to understand, who *had* ability to serve in the king's palace, and whom they might teach the language and literature of the Chaldeans."[731] These were the guys who had received high SAT scores. In other words, they were already very bright and now they were to be retrained according to the language and literature of the Babylonians. It was early in their re-education experience that they sought and gained permission to not defile themselves of the daily provisions of the king's delicacies and eat only vegetables.[732] The fact is that all of us tend to relish delicacies because that is only natural. However, Daniel and his buddies made a deliberate choice to not let their appetites guide their lifestyle. Most often when we yield in the small issues it weakens our capacity to make the right choices in the bigger issues. As it turned out in their final exam they were "ten times better than all the magicians *and* astrologers who *were* in all his realm."[733]

Following their graduation King Nebuchadnezzar had a dream, "and his spirit was so troubled that his sleep left him."[734] Then the king called all the magicians, astrologers, sorcerers, and wise men before him and commanded them to tell him the dream and its interpretation. If they were unable to do as the king commanded, they were to be executed. Their response was; "*It is* a difficult thing that the king requests, and there is no other who can tell it to the king except the gods, whose dwelling is not with flesh."[735] Now all the wise counselors including Daniel and his three friends found themselves in a death trap if they could not tell the king his dream and the interpretation.

731. Dan. 1:4
732. Dan. 1:8-12.
733. Dan. 1:20.
734. Dan 2:1.
735. Dan. 2:11.

Daniel and his friends sought the mercies of the Lord in prayer in order that they would not perish. And the Lord answered their prayer by revealing the secret to Daniel. Therefore, Daniel requested an audience with the king. This was Daniel's presentation before King Nebuchadnezzar:

> "The secret which the king has demanded, the wise *men,* the astrologers, the magicians, and the soothsayers cannot declare to the king. But there is a God in heaven who reveals secrets, and He has made known to King Nebuchadnezzar what will be in the latter days. Your dream, and the visions of your head upon your bed, were these: As for you, O king, thoughts came *to* your *mind while* on your bed, *about* what would come to pass after this; and He who reveals secrets has made known to you what will be. **But as for me, this secret has not been revealed to me because I have more wisdom than anyone living, but for *our* sakes who make known the interpretation to the king, and that you may know the thoughts of your heart**." (Daniel 2:27-30; emphasis mine).

Daniel continued before the king making known the dream and its interpretation. When Daniel completed the interpretation of the dream the king responded by declaring "'Truly your God *is* the God of gods, the Lord of kings, and a revealer of secrets, since you could reveal this secret.'"[736] The point is that Daniel's impact on the king of Babylon was not the result of his intellect, learning, or literature he had studied. The wisdom to know the dream and its interpretation was given to him from the sovereign God who considers kings and nations as "a drop in a bucket, and are considered as the small dust on the

736. Dan. 2:47.

scales."[737] Daniel's intellect, learning, and studies provided the passport needed to have access to the king and to others in places of power and authority. Therefore, those credentials were very important, but insufficient for the task at hand. What was needed was the wisdom of God and that was granted from God in the process of Daniel's prayer and lifestyle relationship with God Almighty. Earlier Daniel had exercised personal choices that may have seemed small or unimportant but demonstrated the quality of character that could be trusted with larger opportunities and privileges. Jesus expressed this principle as He taught the kingdom parables. He said, "For whoever has, to him more will be given, and he will have abundance; but whoever does not have, even what he has will be taken away from him."[738]

Jesus and Parables:

The second reason why Jesus used parables when teaching about the kingdom of God is illustrated in the life of Solomon. When Solomon was first anointed as the king of Israel he asked God for an "understanding heart."[739] Solomon's father, David, had been a powerful king and had led the nation of Israel in major military victories and the nation had prospered. Solomon suddenly was made king and probably felt overwhelmed by the responsibility to rule and reign over the nation of Israel. He went to the Tabernacle of Moses at Gibeon and offered a thousand burnt offerings on the altar. And it was "At Gibeon the LORD appeared to Solomon in a dream by night; and God said, 'Ask! What shall I give you?'"[740] Solomon first responded to God's offer in the meekness of humility by saying, "I am a child; I do not know how to go out or come in." Then Solomon made his request; "Therefore give to Your servant an understanding heart to judge Your people, that I may discern between good and evil. For who

737. Isa. 40:15.
738. Matt. 13:12.
739. 1 Kings 3:9.
740. 1 Kings 3:5.

is able to judge this great people of Yours?"[741] James Swanson defines "understanding" as follows:

> **9048** שָׁמַע (šā·mă'): v.; Str 8085; **1.** LN 24.52–24.70 (qal) **hear**, i.e., use the perception of hearing with the ears to process information (Ps 44:2[EB 1]); (nif) **be heard** (Ex 23:13); (hif) **cause to hear** (Dt 4:10); [742]

The essence of Solomon's request was for the capacity not just to hear God's voice, but to hear God with understanding and comprehension, enabling him to process and adjudicate difficult matters and govern with divine intelligence. In other words, Solomon wanted to process life as the king of Israel the same way as God processes life. In New Testament kingdom of God terms, it means doing life with "the mind of Christ."[743] The Lord desires doing life together with you and me. This is a key to understanding why Jesus used parables when teaching about the kingdom of God. Jesus' disciples asked Him, "Why do You teach them in parables?" This is how Jesus answered them:

> "Because it has been given to you to know the mysteries of the kingdom of heaven, but to them it has not been given. For whoever has, to him more will be given, and he will have abundance; but whoever does not have, even what he has will be taken away from him. Therefore, I speak to them in parables, because seeing they do not see, and hearing they do not hear, nor do they understand. And in them the prophecy of Isaiah is fulfilled, which says: '*Hearing you will hear and shall not understand and seeing you will see and not perceive; For the hearts of this people have*

741. 1 Kings 3:9.
742. James Swanson, *Dictionary of Biblical Languages.*
743. 1 Cor. 2:9-16.

> *grown dull. Their ears are hard of hearing, and their eyes they have closed, lest they should see with their eyes and hear with their ears, lest they should understand with their hearts and turn, so that I should heal them.'"* (Matthew 13:11-15)

It is often the case that people read the parables and think they understand them because Jesus used examples and terms with which they are familiar. But that may not be what always happens. The parables of Jesus express the mysteries of the kingdom of God,[744] and are in some ways like a riddle. The meaning of the parable is not always on the surface but hidden beneath the words used. For example, when Jesus taught the parable about the Sower and the four different kinds of soils, it seemed simple enough, but the disciples did not understand its meaning until Jesus explained it to them. Dallas Willard states:

> The parable—which, from its origin in the Greek word *paraballein,* literally means to throw one thing down alongside another. Parables are not just pretty stories that are easy to remember; rather, they help us understand something difficult by comparing it to, placing it beside, something with which we are familiar, and always something concrete, specific.[745]

Craig Blomberg wrestles with interpreting parables and states, "The Gospel parables, with or without the alleged additions and interpretations of later tradition, are allegories, and they probably teach several lessons apiece."[746] Consequently, as believers we need to first seek the help of the Holy Spirit and approach the parables of the kingdom with the meekness and humility with which Solomon made his

744. Matt. 13:11.

745. Willard, *The Divine Conspiracy,* 107.

746. Craig Blomberg, *Interpreting the Parables* (Downers Grove, IL: InterVarsity Press, 1990), 69.

request to God. To correctly interpret the parables of the kingdom we need "a wise and understanding heart."[747] Henry Calderwood gives the following insights regarding the hiddenness within the meaning of the parables.

> Their Lord intended to hide the truth so that men should need to search about for it. He meant in a way to bury the truth, so that men should need to dig under the surface for it. He was not making His teaching as clear and simple as He might have done but was even taking pains to wrap it in a covering fitted so far to conceal it.... To those who are seeking light, light is given. To those who do not value and do not seek the light, darkness not only remains, but is deepened. [748]

By using parables Jesus is seeking to draw us beyond mere facts about the kingdom into a governmental relationship with Himself, the Father, the Holy Spirit, and the other members of His body. He is teaching us God's plan for extending the glory of His kingdom across every earthly boundary and overcoming the powers of darkness. This process includes the Lord's desire for us to experience the kingdom of God which moves us beyond hearing and observing into the reality of ruling and reigning with Him. And to enjoy such a rich experience we need to first make the small choices that guide the development of our character so we can be entrusted with heavenly insights that influence nations just as Daniel influenced Babylon. And second, we also need the meekness that grants access to the wisdom of God that enables us to lead the nations in peace and prosperity as Solomon led Israel. As influential as Daniel and Solomon were, it is important to be reminded of Jesus' words, "For I say to you, among those born of women there is not a greater prophet than John the Baptist; but he

747. 1 Kings 3:12.

748. Henry Calderwood, *The Parables of Our Lord: Interpreted in View of Their Relations to Each Other* (London: Macmillan & Co., 1880), 4-5.

who is least in the kingdom of God is greater than he."[749] Therefore, as New Testament born again believers we pray "Your kingdom come and Your will be done on earth as it is in heaven." And as citizens of the kingdom of God we have the opportunity and responsibility to influence the peace and prosperity of the nations to the honor and glory of God. This moves us beyond what was generally possible under the Old Covenant into the reality of New Testament privileges and possibilities whereby the nations will say, "these who have turned the world upside down have come here also!"[750]

Before we launch into the individual parables, it is important to keep in mind that those on the outside were not given the secrets to the mysteries of the kingdom of God. Robert H. Stein states, "The parables are therefore not self-evident illustrations: they were never meant to be!"[751] One reason why Jesus used parables as a literary device was to hide kingdom realities beneath the surface, and that may well have been because of the hardness of the Jewish religious leaders' hearts. They were so protective of their political positions of privilege and power that they hardened themselves against Jesus. They rejected Jesus and the gospel of the kingdom in a manner similar to Pharaoh's rejection of Moses' request for Israel's release from captivity. When one continually hardens his or her heart against the gracious purposes of God, the time will come when God will give that person or nation over to their own stubbornness.[752] Then God will set Himself against that person or nation like He did with the Egyptian Pharaoh. As Jesus was concluding His ministry just prior to the crucifixion, He wept over Jerusalem and said, "How often I wanted to gather your children together, as a hen gathers her chicks under *her* wings, but you were not willing! See! Your house is left to you desolate;"[753] The Jewish

---

749. Luke 7:28.

750. Acts 17:6.

751. Robert H. Stein, *The Method and Message of Jesus' Teachings* (Philadelphia, PA: The Westminster Press, 1978), 41.

752. Rom. 1:21-28.

753. Matt.23:37-38; Luke 19:41-42.

leaders had become so hardened that they were even oblivious to their own forthcoming destruction.

A third reason for using parables may well have been because His teaching regarding the kingdom could have easily been misunderstood by the Roman authorities. Therefore, by using parables it would be quite difficult for the government authorities to bring charges of sedition or rebellion against Jesus. The Parables did such a good job of camouflaging the reality of the kingdom of God that even those within Jesus' inner circle did not understand them until later.[754] Pilate himself believed that the Jews were asking for Jesus to be crucified because of envy,[755] and not because Jesus was a rebel. Pilate's verdict was, "I find no fault in Him at all."[756] Jesus taught regarding the presence of the kingdom of God in the very midst of enemy territory by practicing the same wisdom that He taught His disciples. His instruction to the disciples was, "Behold, I send you out as sheep in the midst of wolves. Therefore, be wise as serpents and harmless as doves."[757] Jesus was the perfect example! He inaugurated the kingdom of God right under the enemy's nose. And the increase of His government continues and thrives all over the world!

Jesus is the Word that became flesh, the Master Communicator. Communication is a two-sided coin that includes both speaking and listing. Jesus spoke with such authority and compassion that after hearing Him speak and experiencing the power of God the crowd said, "A great prophet has risen among us."[758] The Temple officers who were supposed to arrest Jesus returned without Him and reported, "No man ever spoke like this man."[759] After stating the parable of the Sower Jesus said, "He who has an ear, let him hear."[760] Then explaining to

---

754. Luke 24:44-45; Acts 1:3.
755. Matt. 27:18.
756. John 18:38.
757. Matt. 10:16.
758. Luke 7:16.
759. John 7:40-46.
760. Matt. 13:3-9.

His disciples why He spoke in parables, He declared, "But blessed are your eyes for they see, and your ears for they hear."[761]

There are seven parables recorded in Matthew chapter thirteen and four of them will constitute the primary focus of the remainder of this chapter. "Therefore, hear the parable of the Sower."[762] This parable is recorded in all three of the synoptic Gospels. Robert Farrar Capon describes this parable as "the water shed of the parables." Understanding how to interpret this parable is a key to the interpretation of the other parables. From the beginning of Jesus' ministry, He was progressively revealing the nature of the kingdom of God and His personal identity as the Messiah and the Savior of the world. But at this juncture, He chose not to call attention to His identity as He did later when He asked His apostles, "Who do you say that I am?" And Peter received the revelation that He "was the Christ the Son of the living God."[763] But here He conceals Himself in this teaching about the kingdom of God as the "word." It is only later that we come to understand that He is "the Word," the "incorruptible seed" that lives and abides forever.[764]

The Parable of the Four Kinds of Soil:

In this parable there is one kind of seed and four kinds of soil. Each kind of soil responded to the seed differently. However, in each case the seed was the same. The first soil is described as "the wayside." This soil is so hard that the seed cannot penetrate through the crust but lays on the surface and attracts predators. "The birds came and devoured the seed." The "wayside" speaks of the hard-hearted person who refuses to hear because of a closed heart and mind. This describes the situation when Jesus ministered in His home town of Nazareth. "Now He did not do many mighty works there because of

761. Matt. 13:10-17.
762. Matt. 13:3-9, 18-23.
763. Matt. 16:16-20.
764. 1 Peter 1:23.

their unbelief."[765] The residents of Nazareth refused to receive the gospel of the kingdom because they simply considered Jesus as one of the home town family members, a carpenter's son. They probably thought, "Who does He think He is coming here trying to function as a prophet and challenge what we believe?" They were offended at Him and the gospel of the kingdom was not heard. The Word could not take root because of the hardness of their hearts. They had ears but they could not hear the Word of the Lord. They had eyes but they could not see Jesus as the Son of God, but only as Joseph's son.[766]

The people of Nazareth were not the only ones hardened and offended by Jesus. When the teaching of Jesus exposed the hypocrisy of the Pharisees, they were also "offended."[767] The Jewish leaders were so hardened in their legalistic view of God that the powerful words of Jesus fell on hard soil. Having ears, yet they could not hear His words and having eyes, yet they could not see Jesus as the Messiah. Jesus said on one occasion, "They are blind leaders of the blind. And if the blind leads the blind, both will fall in the ditch."[768] Their hardness of heart poised them for utter destruction, yet they were unable to humble themselves in contrition and repentance and openly receive the word of the Lord. Think of Caiaphas the High Priest who charged Jesus with blasphemy because He said He was the "Son of God."[769] The High Priest and the people had become so hardened that they pressured Pilate to crucify Jesus. After thoroughly examining Him, Pilate finally "washed *his* hands before the multitude, saying, 'I am innocent of the blood of this just Person. You see *to it.*' And all the people answered and said, 'His blood *be* on us and on our children.'"[770] The obvious conclusion is that in their hardness of heart they not only rejected the word of God, but that rejection led to a long

765. Matt. 13:58.
766. Luke 4:22.
767. Matt. 15:3-12.
768. Matt. 15:14.
769. Matt 26:63-67.
770. Matt. 27:24-25.

path of pain and hardship. Just think of all the suffering the Jews have had to endure since their rejection of Jesus.

We might be tempted to say, "Hardness of heart will never happen to me." But we each need to guard our heart against being hardened because the writer of Hebrews sends this warning to fellow believers saying, *"Today, if you will hear His voice, Do not harden your hearts."*[771] We must be careful lest the Lord sends a messenger that offends us because he or she may be so familiar that we close our heart to the message of God just as the people in Nazareth did. Or the word of God may expose some errors in our walk with the Lord that need to be repented of and corrected as was the case with the Pharisees. Or the word of the Lord may require dimensions of faith that stretches us beyond our comfort zone. Just as the possibility of entering the Promised Land and facing the giants stretched the faith of the Children of Israel beyond their natural capacity. As a result, they became offended at God and wanted to return to Egypt. The offense hardened their hearts against the promise of God, and they spent the next forty years wandering in the wilderness.

An offense often ignites self-righteousness and the tendency to justify a defensive or get-even attitude. We may fail to remember Jesus' words; "turn the other cheek to him also."[772] Because we tend to remember the offense as someone else's fault, and we charge them with the responsibility to make things right. We may forget that when everyone was wrong and Jesus was the object of their hate and vengeance, He said, "Father forgive them for they do not know what they do." As we point out what we perceive to be the other person's wrongs, we thereby open the door of our heart not only to self-righteousness and personal justification which many times leads to being trapped in darkness as the Pharisees were. We tend to stand firm in our self-righteousness because we are right in our own eyes; it was the

771. Heb. 4:7b.
772. Matt. 5:39, Like 6:29.

other person's fault. Without realizing it we take the bait of Satan and become hardened. John Bevere writes,

> The Greek word for "offend" ... comes from the word *skandalon*. This word originally referred to the part of the trap to which the bait was attached. Hence the word signifies laying a trap in someone's way. In the New Testament it often describes an entrapment used by the enemy. Offense is a tool of the devil to bring people into captivity.[773]

Therefore, we must guard our hearts against the hardness that often results from being offended. We must maintain a tender heart with a confident faith in the promises of God with the willingness to forgive those who would offend us. The key is to "be kind to one another, tenderhearted, forgiving one another, just as God in Christ forgave you."[774] Peter digs beneath the surface and addresses the "heart" and the value of the "word of God" as the "incorruptible seed" by stating;

> Since you have purified your souls in obeying the truth through the Spirit in sincere love of the brethren, love one another fervently with a **pure heart**, having been born again, **not of corruptible seed but incorruptible, through the word of God** which lives and abides forever, because *"All flesh is as grass, And all the glory of man as the flower of the grass. The grass withers, and its flower falls away,* but *the word of the* LORD *endures forever."* Now this is the **word which by the gospel** was preached to you. (1Peter 1:22-25; emphasis mine).

---

773. John Bevere, *The Bait of Satan: Living Free from the Deadly Trap of Offense* (Lake Mary, FL: Charisma House, 2004), 7.

774. Eph. 4:32.

So, the problem of the lack of fruitfulness expressed in the first part of this parable of the Sower isn't with the "seed" that was sown, but with the hardness of the soil. Jesus said, "When anyone hears the word of the kingdom, and does not understand it, then the wicked one comes and snatches away what was sown in his heart."[775] For the person with a hard heart, the gospel of the kingdom has no real value to their life, because they have no comprehension of the eternal treasures being offered to them. Therefore, they out-right personally reject the gospel of the kingdom. The seed is "incorruptible," but it is devoured by the birds rather that taking root and producing new life. James states the value of receiving the "seed" by declaring, "Receive with meekness the implanted word, which is able to save your souls."[776]

Jesus describes the second kind of soil in this parable by stating;

> Some fell on stony places, where they did not have much earth; and they immediately sprang up because they had no depth of earth. But when the sun was up, they were scorched, and because they had no root they withered away.[777]

Again the "seed" was good, but the soil was shallow. The seed germinates, springs up, but endures for only a while before it withers away under the heat of the sun. The plants at first look good and seem to have a promising future, but they are soon "burned out." This is amazing because it takes sunshine for the plants to grow—so sunshine isn't the problem. The issue is with the nature of this soil. It is rocky, and the plants cannot develop sufficient roots. In the Christian life "roots" speak of the development of character and an intimate personal relationship with the Lord. There is more to life in the kingdom than meets the eye. To be born again requires that one believes on the Lord Jesus Christ as the resurrected Son of God and acts on that belief

775. Matt. 13:19.
776. James 1:21.
777. Matt. 13:5-6, 20-21.

by inviting Jesus Christ to be the Lord of his or her life. As powerful and eternally important as that action is, it can happen in a matter of moments!

However, godly character and intimacy with the Lord requires time and often quite a lot of time to develop. It is one thing to learn to speak with a Christian vocabulary or jargon, and act religious like the Pharisees, but much more is required for the development of godly character and intimacy with the Lord. Jesus said, "For I say to you, that unless your righteousness exceeds *the righteousness* of the scribes and Pharisees, you will by no means enter the kingdom of heaven."[778] He described them as those who "draw near to Me with their mouth, and honor Me with their lips, but their heart is far from Me."[779]

It amazes me how often so-called Christians tell me that they intend to read the Bible regularly, but honestly it is not happening with many on any regular basis. As a result, their faith rest on Sunday Morning sermons and maybe hearing a sermon or two during the week on the radio or TV. The lack of Bible reading, and prayer is excused because of all the demands on our time and a daily schedule already packed with activity. As a result, what is our reaction when the hard times hit, like the loss of employment or a sudden sickness, a serious accident or death of a close family member, or the High School son or daughter gets expelled from school because of drugs? Then the question often asked is "Why is this happening to me?" After all, I go to church. I serve on the board of our local civic organization. I give some money to the Red Cross. I don't even own a gun and I would never hurt any-one. I am a good person. Why would God allow something like this to happen to me? Why doesn't God do something about this and get me out of this trouble? What kind of God would treat me like this?

In this parable the "stony places" represent the kind of person that "has no root in himself but endures only for a while. For when tribulation or persecution arises because of the word, immediately he

778. Matt. 5:20.

779. Matt.15:8.

stumbles."[780] The lack of roots or shallowness is reflective of those who never really grapple with Truth and haven't seriously dug deep enough to break through the shallowness of sensual or earthly appetites and values into the golden mines of eternal realities. Therefore, they become distracted by conflict or troubles. When those difficulties occur, they lose their joy, begin to wither, and look for greener pastures. Paul's co-worker Demas was this sort of person. He labored with Paul for a while but then deserted Paul because he loved this present world.[781] The shallowness is often caused by willfully refusing to accept the reality that "We must through many tribulations enter the kingdom of God."[782] Even though most of us possess some stony places in our heart, we can experience transformation and fruitfulness if we will faithfully and prayerfully study and apply the word of God. The Prophet Jeremiah declares that the word of God is "like a hammer that breaks the rock in pieces."[783]

The third type of soil is "he who received seed among the thorns… he who hears the word, and the cares of this world and the deceitfulness of riches choke the word, and he becomes unfruitful."[784] This third type of soil specifically addresses the need to establish and guard the kingdom priorities in our life. Most of us in the process of maintaining a career and raising our family find ourselves running at full speed ahead, but never seeming to have enough time to do all that we would like to do. At this juncture in life we need to be extremely careful in the determining what is really important. The "cares of this world" may pressure us to yield to their demands and incite us to bend the rules just enough to get by one more time. We justify our actions and busyness because we are responsible people and we intend to do our part in our home, church, school, community, and at work. We intend to be a good spouse and parent, a faithful worker, a promise

780. Matt. 13:21.
781. 2 Tim. 4:10.
782. Acts 14:22.
783. Jer. 23:29.
784. Matt. 13:22.

keeper, and a good citizen. The only problem is God probably hasn't heard from us in a while. And that is not good because Jesus is saying in this parable there is a dimension of deceitfulness in all our activity and attitude toward money if we are not careful. And hopefully we will not become so self-righteous that we consider ourselves to be beyond the possibility of being deceived.

Through our own efforts we can choke reality out of our relationship with God and wake up one morning feeling barren and wonder, "What has happened to me?" Keep in mind the big difference between this soil and the two we discussed above is that this soil bears fruit, and then becomes "unfruitful." Just as Jesus had to command the church at Ephesus to "repent," even though they had persevered and labored, they had gotten their priorities wrong and "left their first love." This happens all too often, especially with believers who are task oriented—they can become so focused on getting the job done that personal relationships are neglected. Think of the sisters Mary and Martha. Martha "was distracted with much serving." The question is, what was she distracted from? Martha was serving, so she was not distracted from her work, but she was distracted form spending the time necessary to cultivate a growing relationship with Jesus, her Lord. She really wanted Jesus, their very special guest, to feel welcome in their home and well hosted for dinner. And there was Mary sitting over there doing nothing but talking and listening to the Lord. Finally, Martha had had enough and said to Jesus, "Tell her to help me." Do you ever feel like that? So much work to do and others just sitting around reading their Bible or singing courses or praying in tongues! And you think to yourself, "I wish the Lord would tell somebody to get to work and help out around here!" Jesus responded by saying, "'Martha, Martha, you are worried and troubled about many things. But one thing is needed, and Mary has chosen that good part, which will not be taken away from her.'"[785] WOW! I'm sure those

785. Like 10:38-42.

words grabbed Martha's attention and caused her to really do some reevaluation and adjusting of personal priorities.

In a season when circumstances in Judah were in similar turmoil to our circumstances today. It seemed to the Prophet Habakkuk that the word of the Lord was being choked by the thorns of political and moral corruption and decay. He was so burdened by the violence, iniquity, strife, contention, and injustice that he cried out to the Lord in prayer. But it seemed his prayers were going unanswered. Then the Lord spoke to him and revealed what was about to take place in national and international affairs. That reality even increased his burden until the Lord gave him a vision that enabled him to see the situation through the eyes of faith. The Lord concluded His conversations with Habakkuk by saying, "The Lord is in His holy temple. Let all the earth be silent before Him."[786] Seeing from God's perspective completely transformed Habakkuk's attitude and he concluded his prophecy by saying, "The LORD God is my strength; He will make my feet like deer's *feet,* And He will make me walk on my high hills."[787]

This parable teaches us the need to put down roots and endure the pressures of daily life and the deceitfulness of riches. From my pastoral experience it seems to me that when believer's experience adversity and/or the disillusionment of riches, they often become almost paralyzed with introspection. They ask, "What am I doing wrong?" or "Why is this happening to me?" It is happening because the Lord loves you and me and wants us to grow in grace and mature. As a loving Father, He expects us as His children to endure chastenings "that we may be partakers of His holiness." Because He loves us, He treats us as sons rather than as strangers. The Father knows that "no chastening seems to be joyful for the present, but painful; nevertheless, afterward it yields the peaceable fruit of righteousness to those who have been trained by it."[788] Our Father wants each of us to put down

---

786. Hab. 1:1-2:20
787. Hab. 3:19
788. Heb. 12:11.

deep roots so the word of God is not choked out of our daily walk with Him by the multitude of responsibilities at home and work. He wants us to delight "in the law of the LORD, and in His law… meditate day and night."[789]

The Lord has made every provision for our fruitfulness if we will Biblically prioritize our time and activities. The place to start is by following the teachings of Jesus. First, Jesus said, "No one can serve two masters; for either he will hate the one and love the other, or else he will be loyal to the one and despise the other. You cannot serve God and mammon."[790] Spiros Zodhiates defines "mammon" as the god of materialism; "the comprehensive word for all kinds of possessions, earnings, and gains, a designation of material value, the god of materialism." [791] Riches and material things are for the purpose of meeting our physical needs and enjoyment. They are to serve us; we are not to serve them or make them a top priority. Second, Jesus said, "Seek first the kingdom of God and His righteousness and all these things shall be added to you."[792] From the beginning even before the Ten Commandments and throughout the entire history of the world God is to have first place in all of our lives and priorities. And third, Jesus said, "In the world you will have tribulation, but be of good cheer, I have overcome the world."[793] We can be sure that our lives will intersect with frustrations, troubles, and pain, and there will be difficult seasons of tribulation and even possible persecution. But if we are faithful in our commitment to the Lord, we will by His grace not only endure, but we will overcome and bring forth the fruit of righteousness. The Apostle Peter had to endure more painful and difficult experiences than most of us will have to go through. And he gives the following words of wisdom;

789. Psa. 1:2.

790. Matt. 6:24.

791. Zodhiates, *The Complete Word Study Dictionary.*

792. Matt. 6:33.

793. John 16:33.

> Beloved, do not think it strange concerning the fiery trial which is to try you, as though some strange thing happened to you; but rejoice to the extent that you partake of Christ's sufferings, that when His glory is revealed, you may also be glad with exceeding joy. (1 Peter 4:12-13).

Every citizen of the kingdom of God must be diligent to guard against the illusion of value that arises from the deceitfulness of riches. Every believer must persevere against the ever-present obnoxious thorns that try to choke out the sunlight of God's truth. It is the power of God's word that enables each of us to grow with the increase of God into the fruitful person He has purposed us to be.

This brings us to the fourth and final kind of soil in this parable, "the good ground." Jesus said, "But he who received seed on the good ground is he who hears the word and understands *it,* who indeed bears fruit and produces: some a hundredfold, some sixty, some thirty."[794] According to these words a key issue to fruitfulness in the kingdom of God is the willingness to hear and understand the word of the Lord. Young Samuel expressed the correct attitude by saying, "Speak, for Your servant hears."[795] In this parable the "word of the kingdom" is the "seed" being sown. Jesus on another occasion said, "The words that I speak to you are spirit and they are life."[796] Therefore, the "word" of God is more than "letter", "for the letter kills, but the Spirit gives life."[797] It is not the "letter" nature of the word but the "spirit" nature of the "word" that germinates faith. But "faith by itself, if it does not have works, is dead." "For as the body without the spirit is dead, so faith without works is dead." But "by works, faith is made perfect."[798] The point is that the words of the gospel of the kingdom are spirit

794. Matt. 13:23.
795. 1 Sam. 3:10.
796. John 6:63.
797. 2 Cor. 3:6.
798. James 2:17-26.

and when they are heard, faith is germinated. Hearing the words of the kingdom is the doorway into faith and faith moves through the doorway into understanding and fruitfulness.

There are situations or circumstances when a dimension of understanding is necessary to break-up the rocks of misunderstanding and for faith to germinate and develop roots. However, a personal relationship with God usually does not begin with understanding, but with receiving the word of faith that ignites action. For example, when you received Jesus Christ as your Savior and Lord, you probably did not understand the doctrine of salvation. But you did act on what you did understand by asking Jesus to be your Lord and Savior. Then you told someone about your experience of being saved. At that juncture you probably did not understand or comprehend that the Father had "delivered you from the power of darkness and conveyed you into the kingdom of His Son."[799] But you did realize that you had entered into a wonderful new relationship with the Lord and sensed a desire to move forward and do whatever was necessary to please Him, which means producing fruit.

Jesus quoted Isaiah by stating; "Hearing you will hear and shall not understand."[800] Hardness of heart resists hearing the spirit of what the Lord is saying. So, to "receive" the "word" is a key to faith that leads to understanding or comprehension. Therefore, Jesus warns us "to take heed how you hear."[801] James also stresses the importance of hearing and addresses the relationship between hearing and doing. He states;

> So then, my beloved brethren, let every man be swift to hear, slow to speak, slow to wrath; for the wrath of man does not produce the righteousness of God. Therefore, lay aside all filthiness and overflow of wickedness, and receive with meekness the implanted

799. Col. 1:13.
800. Matt. 13:14.
801. Luke 8:18.

> word, which is able to save your souls. But be doers of the word, and not hearers only, deceiving yourselves. For if anyone is a hearer of the word and not a doer, he is like a man observing his natural face in a mirror; for he observes himself, goes away, and immediately forgets what kind of man he was. But he who looks into the perfect law of liberty and continues *in it and* is not a forgetful hearer but a doer of the word, this one will be blessed in what he does. (James 1:19-25).

Jesus describes Himself as "the true vine" and His disciples as the "branches". He teaches us that "the branch cannot bear fruit of itself, unless it abides in the vine, neither can you unless you abide in Me." He said, "I am the vine, you *are* the branches. He who abides in Me, and I in him, bears much fruit; for without Me you can do nothing."[802] Robert Capon states, "The whole purpose of the coming of the Word into this world is to produce people in whom the power of the kingdom will bear fruit."[803] Fruitfulness was considered to be an evidence of God's blessing upon the Children of Israel, and barrenness was the evidence of a curse. In the New Testament Jesus became a curse on the cross in order to deliver you and me from the curse of barrenness and position us for the blessedness of abundant fruitfulness. "He who received seed on the good ground is he who hears the word and understands *it,* who indeed bears fruit and produces: some a hundredfold, some sixty, some thirty."[804] Jesus said, "By this My Father is glorified, that you bear much fruit; so you will be My disciples."[805]

A final point regarding the "word of the kingdom."[806] It is an obvious fact if we plant corn seed, we expect to reap a corn crop. If we plant watermelon seed, we expect to reap a watermelon crop. So, it

---

802. John 15:1-5.
803. Capon, *Kingdom, Grace, Judgment,* 72.
804. Matt. 13:23.
805. John 15:8.
806. Matt. 13:19.

is with the word of God, when He sows His incorruptible seed in the soil of our hearts, He expects a crop that reveals His likeness or nature. Therefore, having received the "word of the kingdom" we are expected to bring forth the fruit of the Spirit as partakers of His divine nature.[807] The Apostle Peter expresses the truth of the dynamic reality by exhorting us with the following words;

> But also, for this very reason, giving all diligence, add to your faith virtue, to virtue knowledge, to knowledge self-control, to self-control perseverance, to perseverance godliness, to godliness brotherly kindness, and to brotherly kindness love. For if these things are yours and abound, *you will be* neither barren nor unfruitful in the knowledge of our Lord Jesus Christ. (2 Peter 1:5-8)

In this parable (Matthew 13:3-23), Jesus reveals a mystery of the kingdom of God becoming manifest through a sower sowing "seed" in four different types of soil. Jesus said, "Blessed are your eyes for they see, and your ears for they hear."[808] He teaches that the "seed" is the "word of the kingdom" or the manifestation of God's sovereign government among men in the here and now! For the seed to produce it must be sown in the soil of this world as in the midst of humanity. Jesus defines four types of soil. First, the wayside where the word is not understood, and the seed remains exposed and is devoured by the birds. Second, the stony places where the seed is unable to develop roots and is scorched by the sun. Third, is soil infested with weeds that eventually choke the word rendering it incapable of producing fruit. And last, the good soil that receives the word and understands it and produces "some a hundredfold, some sixty, some thirty." This parable is fundamentally about how the kingdom of God is initiated

807. Gal. 5:22-23; 2 Peter 1:2-4.
808. Matt. 13:16.

and how its growth is challenged, but nothing is said in this parable about how the harvest takes place. That will be discussed in the following parable.

The Parable of the Wheat and the Tares:

The second parable recorded in Matthew chapter thirteen is about the wheat and the tares.[809] This parable is similar to the parable of the Sower in that when the disciples are away from the crowd and alone with Jesus, they asked Him for an explanation. This affirms again that even though the language was familiar to His hearers, the meaning remained a mystery. In the previous parable the emphasis focused on the fruitfulness of the soil in which the seed is sown. However, with this parable Jesus discloses another aspect of the mystery of the kingdom of God by revealing a second sower with a different kind of seed. Thus, empowering His hearers with insights to counter the schemes of Satan.

This parable also enforces the reality of the tension that exists in rightly handling the "word of the kingdom." Proper receptivity of the "seed" is one issue in this tension, but also the crucial matter of kingdom timing must be considered. It is important to do the right things, but the right things must also be done at the right time. For example, there were several occasions in the life of Jesus when His enemies sought to end His life, but He evaded their attempts. However, when He knew His hour had come,[810] He refused to defend Himself, which He could have done by calling legions of angels. But knowing that His time had fully come, He willingly laid His life down as He was commanded by the Father.[811] Living in agreement with God's timing requires godly wisdom, plus the grace to endure the powers that oppose the word of the kingdom.

---

809. Matt. 13:24-30, 36-43.
810. John 8:20, 12:27, 13:1.
811. John 10:17-18.

In the parable the "Sower", the "seed" that was sown was the "word of the kingdom." But in this parable the "seeds" that are sown are persons. Jesus reveals that He sows the "good seeds" which are the "sons of the kingdom" and the enemy, whom Jesus identifies as the "devil" sows "sons of the wicked one." Keep in mind that "the field is the world" and not the church. Therefore, in this present age, the world which belongs to God is populated with two different kinds of people. The remarkable thing is that both kinds of people grow together with no distinction until the "crop" or "fruit" is produced. In other words, the wheat and tares look so similar as they are growing that the servants did not realize that tares were among the wheat. In the growth stage the tares look like the real thing. But when the fruit was produced the servants asked the owner two questions: "Sir, did you not sow good seed in your field?" And "How then does it have tares?"

The owner responded by saying, "An enemy has done this." It is amazing that the enemy did his sowing "while men slept." The fact is regardless of how spiritually mature one may become; we all need to sleep sometime. That is a reality of life by which the enemy seeks to take advantage of "the sons of the kingdom." All persons, both good and evil, are created in the image and likeness of God with eternity in our hearts. Many have attended church services for years and even served in various congregational leadership positions, but never accepting Jesus Christ as their personal Savior and Lord. Lloyd Ogilvie states, "Billy Graham is often criticized because so many of his converts are church members."[812] However, without the indwelling of the Holy Spirit, our hearts are darkened because of our inherited sinful nature. And though we mean well and maybe even enjoy a pleasant personality, we were in reality "the sons of the wicked one." We were unaware of being the instruments of the devil and producing fruits

---

812. Lloyd John Ogilvie, *Autobiography of God* (Glendale, CA: Regal Books, 1979), 80.

that God considered as the "filthy rags" of self-righteousness, separated from God and without hope in this world.

But once we were awakened and repented of our sin, rejecting our self-righteousness, and receiving the righteousness of God; we were born again by the regeneration of the Holy Spirit. Thus, by the grace of God and faith in Jesus Christ we became new persons, "delivered from the power of darkness and conveyed into the kingdom of the Son of His love."[813] Now being "the sons of the kingdom" we are empowered to hear and heed the voice of the Lord, the owner of the field, and producing the fruit of the Holy Spirit. The fruit of the Holy Spirit is an altogether different kind of fruit than we had previously produced and clearly distinguishes us from the "sons of the wicked one." We are now sensitive to the difference in the nature between the wheat and the tares and are inclined to ask the Lord the same question as the servants asked; "Do you want us to go and gather them up" and get them out of Your field? However, the Lord does not permit this gathering of tares because they are so numerous among the wheat that gathering them up before harvest time would have a negative impact on the wheat.

Therefore, the owner of the field answered, "Let both grow together until the harvest."[814] We will discuss the harvest shortly, but first it is necessary to define the meaning of the word "let" as used in this parable. "Let" in verse thirty comes from the Greek word "*aphiemi*". It is used over one hundred and fifty times in the New Testament. The NIDNTT defines "**ἀφίημι**" as: "let go, cancel, remit, leave, forgive;... release, pardon, cancellation, forgiveness...; letting pass, passing over."[815] In other words "let" in Matthew 13:30 could also be translated "to allow" or "to pass over ," "to leave behind" or "to

---

813. 2 Cor. 5:17; Col. 1:13.

814. Matt. 13:30.

815. H. Vorländer, "Forgiveness," ed. Lothar Coenen, Erich Beyreuther, and Hans Bietenhard, *New International Dictionary of New Testament Theology* (Grand Rapids, MI: Zondervan Publishing House, 1986), 697.

forgive"".[816] The question at this juncture is "What is it that is "let", "allowed" or "passed over" as we await the harvest at the end of the age?" The answer is found in verse forty-one, "all things that offend and those who practice lawlessness."[817]

First, we will consider "all things that offend." All of us experience offences. Currently offences are a key issue in our families, churches, and communities. Our culture is experiencing a great deal of frustration, pain, and anger resulting from offences. Individuals and whole communities are looking for someone to blame for their injuries and pain. Many women and young people are offended because they have been abused and mistreated. Minorities are offended because they have been discriminated against in schools, colleges and the marketplace. Older white men are offended because they are treated with disrespect and objects of scorn because they are blamed for social problems perceived to be their fault. Some are offended because they have been mistreated and discriminated against because of their sexual orientation. So, what is an offense?

We all know that when our ball team is on the offense it is using tactics to score points against the opposing team. So, it is in the reality of life; an offense is a tactic used by the devil to score points against the Lord and against you and me. It may seem unrealistic to assign credit to the devil for injuries we suffer at the hands of our fellowman. And I am not suggesting that persons involved in the commitment of an offense do not have a personal responsibility to amend for the pain they have caused. However, this parable affirms that the devil is the source of the tares. And "tares" include both "things that offend" and "lawlessness." Further, the Scripture says, "For we do not wrestle against flesh and blood, but against principalities, against powers, against the rulers of the darkness of this age, against spiritual *hosts* of wickedness in the heavenly *places*."[818]

---

816. "*aphiemi*" is twice translated "forgive" in Matthew 6:12 "And forgive us our debts, as we forgive our debtors."

817. Matt. 13:41.

818. Eph. 6:12.

Offenses at their origin are a spiritual reality and are resolved by the spiritual means prescribed by God. For example, Police officers are ministers of God to execute God's wrath on those who practice evil or lawlessness and all of us should be subject to them for-conscience sake.[819] The point is that the devil strategizes to entrap and imprison us through offences. That way we blame persons for our pain and often try to get even with them. But vengeance against the person by whom the devil uses is not to be executed by us, but by God and/or His appointed deputies. "Beloved, do not avenge yourselves, but *rather* give place to wrath; for it is written, '*Vengeance is Mine, I will repay,*' says the Lord."[820] As Believers we can break the entrapment and captivity of an offense through the power of forgiveness. More on this later, but for now we will continue to answer the question, "What is an offense?" Again, we will use John Bevere's insights into the nature of an offense:

> The Greek word for "offend" in Luke 17:1 comes from the word *skandalon.* This word originally referred to the part of the trap to which bait was attached. Hence the word signifies laying a trap in someone's way. In the New Testament it often describes an entrapment used by an enemy. Offense is a tool of the devil to bring people into captivity.[821]

The Greek word *skandalon* is also used in this parable of the wheat and tares.[822] It is used in the New Testament fifteen times. It is translated "offense" or "stumbling block." Spiros Zodhiates, defines ***skandalon*** as;

819. Rom. 13:1-6.
820. Rom. 12:19.
821. Bevere, *The Bait of Satan,* 7.
822. Matt. 13:41.

> The trigger of a trap on which the bait is placed, and which, when touched by the animal, springs and causes it to close causing entrapment… refers to a trap hidden in an ambush…. Always denotes an enticement to conduct that which could ruin the person.[823]

William Arndt, Frederick W. Danker, and Walter Bauer define *skandalon* as:

> (1) a device for catching something alive, *trap* (2) an action or circumstance that leads one to act contrary to a proper course of action or set of beliefs, *temptation to sin, enticement* to apostasy, false belief, (3) that which causes offense or revulsion and results in opposition, disapproval, or hostility, *fault, stain* etc.[824]

Recently I was engaged in a conversation with a university student who had heard a family member use a racial slur that deeply offended him. The slur was painfully offensive without question. But the student's response was to cut off his relationship with that family member and may he go to hell and get what he deserves. Doesn't that sound like the voice of someone suffering from a painful injury? How humanly natural is it for us to be quick and easy to condemn, judge, and remain unforgiving? How would you have responded if you had been in that student's shoes? Does breaking the relationship with the family member resolve that offense? Certainly, there are individuals who have painfully injured us, but does that negate our responsibility before the Lord to forgive and serve as His "ministers of reconciliation?"

---

823. Zodhiates, *The Complete Word Study Dictionary.*

824. William Arndt, Frederick W. Danker, and Walter Bauer, *A Greek-English Lexicon of the New Testament and Other Early Christian Literature* (Chicago: University of Chicago Press, 2000), 926.

> "Now all things *are* of God, who has reconciled us to Himself through Jesus Christ, and **has given us the ministry of reconciliation**, that is, that God was in Christ reconciling the world to Himself, **not imputing their trespasses to them**, and has committed to us the word of reconciliation." (2 Cor. 8:18-19; emphasis mine)

One thing is for sure, all of us were created in the image and likeness of God. Therefore, we are born with a conscience that responds to offences with a demand for balance on the scales of justice. We even hate to see animals mistreated and abused. So, as the disciples of Jesus Christ; "How are we to respond to the offenses we suffer?"

Think of all the offences you and I have perpetrated against the Lord Jesus Christ both before and after we believed on Him as our Savior and Lord. How are we ever going to pay for all the damage we have caused Him by the offences we have committed against His holiness. Jesus, the Son of God "was in all points tempted as we are, yet without sin."[825] As Abel's righteousness was an offense to Cain, so Jesus' righteousness was an offense to the religious leaders of His day. Therefore, they refused to believe Him and stumbled on that "stumbling stone and rock of offense."[826] They demanded His crucifixion saying in the court of justice, "His blood be on us and on our children."[827]

Therefore, Jesus was shamefully and brutally stripped, beaten, and hung on the cross as a condemned criminal. And there in the midst of His shame, agony, and suffering He said, "Father forgive them for they know not what they do."[828] On that day as Jesus suffered the penalty for all our offenses, and broke the power of our sins by bearing our sin in His own body and shedding His blood for the remission

---

825. Heb. 4:15.
826. Rom. 9:32-33.
827. Matt. 27:25.
828. Luke 23:34.

(*aphesis*) of our sin. Thus, He released us from the indebtedness of our offenses and injustices by paying our sin debt in full. He also bore in His body our judgment and forgave our offenses. "God made Him who knew no sin to be sin for us, that we might be made the righteousness of God in Him."[829] The great value of what was accomplished on the cross becomes a reality in our personal life through faith in Jesus as our risen Savior.

The Lord Jesus on the cross sets the example for us as to how to break the power of offenses. That is by maintaining a lifestyle of forgiveness. Earlier He taught us to pray, "And forgive us our debts, as we forgive our debtors…. For if you forgive men their trespasses, your heavenly Father will also forgive you. But if you do not forgive men their trespasses, neither will your Father forgive your trespasses."[830] Sometimes after we have suffered a painful offense it may take a while to bring our emotions under the control of the Holy Spirit. But if we expect our heavenly Father to forgive us, then we have the responsibility of forgiving others of their offences against us. We may be tempted to point our finger and blame someone, but as the "sons of the kingdom" we are planted in the world to serve as representatives of our heavenly Father with the responsibility to do what Jesus would do—not blame or condemn, but forgive. "God did not send His Son into the world to condemn the world, but that the world through Him may be saved."[831] Our salvation includes the indwelling presence of God the Holy Spirit who empowers us to transcend the gripping trap of an offense. The Psalmist says, "Great peace have they who love Your law; nothing shall offend them *or* make them stumble."[832] The word in the Septuagint translated "stumble" is the Greek word *skandalon,* which we have discussed above. So, we as Spirit filled disciples of Jesus are enabled to escape the snare of the devil by resolving an

829. 2 Cor. 5:21.

830. Matt. 6:12-15.

831. John 3:17.

832. *The Amplified Bible* (La Habra, CA: The Lockman Foundation, 1987), Ps 119:165.

offense rather than being held captive by it. In the end to be offended or not to be offended is a choice that we make.

If we do not forgive, we tend to rehearse offenses over and over in our minds until they become a source of anger and eventually a root of bitterness. As we keep rehearsing offenses and continue experiencing the pain, we may even become angry with God. We may think, "If God is a good God why doesn't He do something? I did not do anything to deserve this injury and injustice." Then after months of trying to suppress our anger it turns to depression and we may sink into a pit of hate and despair. Or we may suddenly break out in unrestrained wrath against an unsuspecting person or situation. At which point we may experience a sense of emotional relief, but the offense remains and now we are saddled with the consequences of our outburst. However, if we forgive the offender just as Jesus forgave His offenders, we break the entrapment of the devil that holds us captive to pain, anger, and bitterness. It liberated us to flow in the power of the Holy Spirit and fulfill the ministry of reconciliation rather than building walls of separation. Some may ask is it fair to simply let the offender off the hook by forgiving that person for their offense. After all, the pain I am suffering is their fault. Remember, that's what Jesus did on the cross and that is what He has empowered us to do by giving us the gift of the Holy Spirit. Why would we be unforgiving if we expect Him to forgive us? He has promised that He will in His timing balance the scales of justice.

It is not the blades but the "fruit" that distinguishes the wheat from the tares. Every person suffers from offenses committed against them, but as the disciples of Jesus Christ we are empowered to produce the fruit of the Spirit and forgive offenders. We refuse to be held captive by the tactics of the devil. When tempted to be unforgiving the Holy Spirit will remind us that when Jesus was tempted by the devil He responded with the words, "It is written."[833] The Scriptures are a lamp unto our feet and a light unto our path which the Holy Spirit quickens

833. Matt. 4:4-7.

or makes alive in our hearts to guide our decisions and actions. The Scripture says;

> "Therefore, as *the* elect of God, holy and beloved, put on tender mercies, kindness, humility, meekness, longsuffering; bearing with one another, and **forgiving one another**, if anyone has a complaint against another; **even as Christ forgave you, so you also *must do*.** But above all these things put on love, which is the bond of perfection. And let the peace of God rule in your hearts, to which also you were called in one body; and be thankful." (Colossians 3:12-15, emphasis mine)

Jesus said there is coming a day at the end of this age when "The Son of Man will send out His angels, and they will gather out of His kingdom all things that offend, and those who practice lawlessness, and cast them into the furnace of fire."[834] So, there you have it—those wicked offenders may get away with injustice for a while, but if they do not repent they will burn! WOW! When I am hurting because of the pain of offence, that sentence of judgment lets me know that eventually justice will be served. But that raises another question, "What happens to me if I am the one causing the offense?" Am I doomed to the furnace of fire? I know that I say and do offensive things. How will I ever be able to pay for the damage I am doing? Or am I forced to tip-toe through life on eggshells for fear of committing another offense and risk not only the possibility of being cut off even from family members but also being cast into the fire? As a follower of Jesus are there any solutions for an offender like me?

The reality is, that as a believer in Jesus Christ your past offenses were forgiven when you repented and received Jesus as your Savior and Lord. The Holy Spirit may direct you to go and humble yourself

834. Matt.13:40-42.

before certain persons and confess your faults and ask for their forgiveness. It may also be necessary to make restitution for the damages you caused. But the truth is that you are now a child of God and not a victim to your past sins nor a captive to the tactics of the devil. Now as a child of God and citizen of the kingdom of God, you are empowered by the Holy Spirit to live an overcoming lifestyle. You now have an Advocate with the Father, Jesus Christ the righteous who ever lives to make intercession for you. And when you do sin, "If we confess our sins, He is faithful and just to forgive us *our* sins and to cleanse us from all unrighteousness."[835] Hence, we are to "do all things without complaining and disputing, that you may become blameless and harmless, children of God without fault in the midst of a crooked and perverse generation, among whom you shine as lights in the world."[836] "If we walk in the light as He is in the light, we have fellowship with one another, and the blood of Jesus Christ His Son cleanses us from all sin."[837] Therefore, you do not have to constantly tip-toe on egg-shells for fear of offending God or anyone else. Do not allow yourself to be held in the trap of the devil. When you do commit an offense be responsible for your actions, confess your fault, ask for forgiveness, and walk in the joy and freedom of the Holy Spirit. And "where the Spirit of the Lord is, there is liberty."[838]

Having considered "things that offend" we will now turn our attention to "those who practice lawlessness."[839] "Lawlessness" is acting without regard for the restraints of God's moral law. The restraints of God's moral law are not oppressive as some say, but guard rails that protect us from spiritual, emotional, and physical harm. Many times, we commit mindless and lawless deeds especially in our youth without considering God's law or the consequences of our actions. However, as we mature and assume life's greater responsibilities and

---

835. 1 John 1:9.
836. Phil. 2:14-15.
837. 1 John 1:7.
838. 2 Cor. 3:17.
839. Matt. 13:41.

reap some of the consequences of our actions, we try to become law abiding citizens unless we have given ourselves over to outright rebellion which is lawlessness. It is the God given responsibility of civil government to enforce moral law, because lawlessness is a source of violence and anarchy. No society or culture can exist very long under the destructive nature of anarchy. In the days of Noah, the wickedness was great and "the Lord saw the wickedness of man was great on the earth.... So, the Lord said, 'I will destroy man I have created from the face of the earth, both man and beast.'"[840] Near the end of Jesus' earthly ministry He warns us of lawless conditions that will exist prior to His return. Upon His return and as part of the process of setting up His kingdom on the earth He will command His angels to gather the tares in bundles and cast them into the furnace of fire. Jesus warns us:

> But as the days of Noah *were,* so also will the coming of the Son of Man be. For as in the days before the flood, they were eating and drinking, marrying and giving in marriage, until the day that Noah entered the ark, and did not know until the flood came and took them all away, so also will the coming of the Son of Man be. (Matthew 24:37-39)

We are living in the days like Jesus was referring. When governments all around the world are passing laws that permit abortion on demand, interpret, and enforce laws that affirm homosexuality, and teach school children unbiblical facts regarding sexual orientation. These laws and governmental actions are a disregard for God's law and grant lawlessness. The Apostle John wrote, "Little children, it is the last hour; and as you have heard that the Antichrist is coming, even now many antichrists have come, by which we know that it is the last hour.[841] "Antichrist" means that which is against or stands in

---

840. Gen. 6:5-7.
841. 1 John 2:18.

opposition to Christ and is lawlessness. The Apostle Paul also gives the insights regarding lawlessness:

> "For the **mystery of lawlessness** is already at work; only **He who now restrains** *will do so* until He is taken out of the way. And then the **lawless one** will be revealed, whom the Lord will consume with the breath of His mouth and destroy with the brightness of His coming. **The coming of the *lawless one* is according to the working of Satan**, with all power, signs, and lying wonders, and with all unrighteous deception among those who perish, because they did not receive the love of the truth, that they might be saved" (2 Thessalonians 2:7-10; emphasis mine).

It is my understanding that "He who now restrains" is the person and work of the Holy Spirit. The Holy Spirit was a gift given to the Church of Jesus Christ on the Day of Pentecost. At the close of this age the Church "shall be caught up together with them (*those who have previously died in the Lord*) in the clouds to meet the Lord in the air. And thus, we shall always be with the Lord"[842] (emphasis mine). When the Church is "caught up" or "raptured" the Holy Spirit also will also be "caught up" because He dwells in the hearts of believers. He is a person and doesn't simply exist in open space even though He is a Spirit. Once the Holy Spirit is no longer present on the earth there will be no restraint to the powers of evil. Then a personification of the devil, "the lawlessness one," the antichrist, will emerge as the head of a global governmental system and the stage will be set for the outpouring of God's wrath. The outpouring of God's wrath concludes with the return of Jesus to earth with His bride to set up His kingdom on the earth where they will reign together for a thousand years.

842. 1 Thes. 4:17.

Meanwhile, the Church of Jesus Christ is to be salt and light in this world to preserve moral order until Jesus Christ returns.

Jesus is teaching in this parable that the "tares" include "those who practice lawlessness" and are "the sons of the wicked one." The wheat and tares are to grow together until the end of this age when "the Son of man will send out His angels, and they will gather out of His kingdom all things that offend, and those who practice lawlessness, and will cast them into the furnace of fire. There will be weeping and gnashing of teeth."[843] What a tragic and horrifying conclusion for anyone's life. But that horrifying end is the devil's strategy for every person including you and me. Jesus is unveiling the mystery of the devil's work and strategy to us, His disciples, to empower us to be overcomers in this world as the "sons of the kingdom." That is why Jesus concludes the explanation of this parable with the imperative, "He who has ears, let him hear."[844] It is also translated, "If you're able to understand this, then you'd better respond!"[845] Later Jesus gave another earnest command; "Watch therefore, and pray always that you may be counted worthy to escape all these things that will come to pass, and to stand before the Son of Man."[846]

In this parable[847] there are four primary revelations regarding the kingdom of heaven. The first revelation is that the field is the world where there are two different sowers, sowing two different kinds of seeds. The first sower is Jesus and He sows the "wheat" or "the good seeds" who are "the sons of the kingdom." The second sower is the devil who sows "tares" who are "the sons of the wicked one." The second revelation is that the wheat and tares both grow together and are not distinguishable from each other until fruit is produced. In

843. Matt. 13:41-42.

844. Matt. 13:43.

845. Brian Simmons, tran., *The Passion Translation: New Testament* (BroadStreet Publishing, 2017), Mt 13:43.

846. Luke 21:36.

847. Matt. 13:24-30, 36-43.

other words, "by their fruits you will know them."[848] The third revelation is that the tares are defined as "things that offend and those who practice lawlessness." At the end of this age the Lord will "send out His angels" and they will gather and bundle the tares and "cast them into a furnace of fire" and "there will be wailing and gnashing of teeth." And the fourth revelation is that the "wheat" is defined as "the righteous" and "the righteous will shine forth as the sun in the kingdom of their Father." Considering all that Jesus taught in this parable, He concludes with this command, "He who has ears to hear, let him hear." In this context "hearing" includes heeding with the capacity to process and understand with the mind of Christ. Therefore, as disciples of Jesus our responsibility is to process and resolve offences and live according to the "law of the Spirit of life in Christ."[849] We are to leave vengeance and judgment entirely in the hands of God, because as the owner of the field He knows best how to deal with the devil's tactics and followers. We have the privilege to celebrate in the hope of shining "as the sun in the kingdom of our Father" forever!

The Parable of the Mustard Seed:

The third parable in chapter thirteen of Matthew is the short parable about the "mustard seed" revealing further insights regarding the kingdom of heaven.[850] The "mustard seed" is small in comparison with other seeds. There is no comparison between the size of the mustard seed and the size of the plant into which it grows. Lenski states, "The comparison becomes the more striking when we see that this mustard kernel is Christ himself, for the entire kingdom grows from him as the King."[851]

848. Matt. 7:16 & 20.

849. Rom. 8:2.

850. Matt. 13:31-32.

851. R. C. H. Lenski, *The Interpretation of St. Matthew's Gospel* (Minneapolis, MN: Augsburg Publishing House, 1961), 528.

Was it possible to establish the kingdom of God within the Roman Empire? The emperors thought they were gods and many of their appointed leaders annihilated their supposed competitors. Herod the Great murdered all the male children under two years old trying to abolish the possibility of a king of the Jews being raised up among them.[852] Herod's action was inspired by the devil, the god of this world. The Apostle John was given the revelation of a fiery red dragon standing before the woman "to devour her Child as soon as it was born."[853] But God intervened by warning Joseph in a dream to flee to Egypt with Mary and the Child.[854] The kingdom of God was always present in the sense that God's sovereignty was always present in the earth realm. But Jesus exposed or manifested the reality of the presence of the kingdom of God with power. In the manifestation of the kingdom Jesus' authority offended the Jewish leaders to the point that they accused Jesus of blasphemy and took Him before the Roman leaders demanding His execution. At the trial Pilate asked Jesus, "Are you a king? Jesus answered. 'You say rightly that I am a king. For this cause, I was born, and for this cause, I have come into the world.'"[855] Jesus' beginnings were small, born in a manger in Bethlehem and cared for by poor parents. His kingdom not only started as small as a mustard seed. But against seemingly impossible odds He inaugurated the Kingdom of God, and it has grown to the point that people from all over the world find refuge and sustenance in its branches.

Growth is a powerful and inevitable concept for things that are living. Remember that evil is not a living entity but a parasite that lives off the life of another. God is the source of life and has sent His son to give us eternal life. The Apostle John states regarding Jesus, "In Him was life, and the life was the light of men."[856] Our God is a God

---

852. Matt. 2:16-18.
853. Rev. 12:1-4.
854. Matt. 2:13-15.
855. John 18:37.
856. John 1:4.

of increase: "A little one shall become a thousand, and a small one a strong nation. I, the LORD, will hasten it in its time."[857]

In our culture bigness is often equated with better. Who has the biggest house, or the largest stock portfolio, or attends the biggest church, etc.? We often despise the "day of small things."[858] Smallness is often a source of discouragement. But in the Gospel of Luke Jesus connects "faith" with the "mustard seed." "So the Lord said, 'If you have faith as a mustard seed, you can say to this mulberry tree, Be pulled up by the roots and be planted in the sea,' and it would obey you."[859] How much faith did you have when you began your walk with God? Many of us only had mustard seed size faith, but that was enough to be born again! Even though our talent, resource, or situation may seem small we refused to be discouraged, because "If God be for us who can be against us."[860] Our prayer is, "Your kingdom come, and Your will be done on earth as it is in heaven."[861] The Prophet Daniel saw a stone that was cut out of a mountain without hands and it became a kingdom that overcame every other kingdom and filled the whole earth.[862] There is coming a day when all the towers of Babel will collapse and mighty men will cry out for the rocks to fall on them, but "when Christ who is our life appears, then you also will appear with Him in glory." Therefore, do not despise mustard seed size beginnings or a cloud only the size of a man's hand or a single jar of oil, because in this parable Jesus is revealing that God is a God of increase and "will multiply the seed you have sown and increase the fruits of your righteousness."[863]

---

857. Isa. 60:22.
858. Zech. 4:10.
859. Luke 17:6.
860. Rom. 8:31.
861. Matt. 6:10.
862. Dan. 2:34-35, 44-45.
863. 2 Cor. 2:9.

The Parable of the Leaven:

The fourth parable in Matthew chapter thirteen, and the final one that we will discuss in this chapter is only one sentence long. This parable reveals how the kingdom of heaven is like leaven when mixed into a batch of dough. "Leaven" or yeast as used in several places in Scripture refers to evil or sin as it does in the Feast of Unleavened Bread. But in this parable "leaven" refers to the silent and yet transformational power of the gospel of the kingdom. A key concept regarding leaven is that once it is placed within the dough it cannot be taken out. It continues growing until it permeates the batch.

The gospel of the kingdom so impacts the life of a Believer that the Scripture says, "If anyone is in Christ, he is a new creature; old things are passed away; behold, all thing have become new."[864] The leaven or mystery of the gospel of the kingdom is the person and work of Jesus Christ the King. "God willed to make known what are the riches of this mystery among the Gentiles: which is Christ in you the hope of glory."[865] The kingdom of heaven is not about rules nor works but the invisible and indwelling power of the Spirit of the Lord. We "are being transformed into the same image from glory to glory, just as by the Spirit of the Lord."[866] Then the Lord sends us, His servants, into the world to preach the gospel of the kingdom and thereby influence or leaven a corruptible and dying society with the hope of life eternal through Jesus Christ the King of glory.

To conclude this chapter, it is noted that each of the four parables discussed revealed specific mysteries about the kingdom of God that Jesus was inaugurating. Jesus said, "It is given to you to know the mysteries of the kingdom of heaven.[867] Therefore we will continue our discussion of the parables of Jesus in the next chapter.

---

864. 2 Cor. 5:17.
865. Col. 1:27.
866. 2 Cor. 3:18.
867. Matt. 13:11.

CHAPTER SIX

THE PARABLES OF THE KINGDOM (CONT.)

> *"And the disciples came and said to Him, 'Why do You speak to them in parables?' He answered and said to them, "Because it has been given to you to know the mysteries of the kingdom of heaven, but to them it has not been given."*
>
> *(Matthew 13:10-11)*

The Parable of the Hidden Treasure:

The fifth parable recorded in Mathew thirteen is often entitled, "The Parable of the Hidden Treasure." Jesus said, "Again, the kingdom of heaven is like treasure hidden in a field, which a man found and hid; and for joy over it he goes and sells all that he has and buys that field."[868] This parable is only one sentence in length but by using the word "again" indicates that Jesus is continuing to unveil mysteries regarding the kingdom of heaven. The revelation revealed in this parable is to be found in two places: first, the treasure was hidden in a field and was found. And second, the response of the man who found the hidden treasure.

868. Matt. 13:44.

It was not unusual in the fields of Israel for the farmer to be plowing and hit a rock. The farmer would then dig around the rock and remove it from the field. But on this occasion, something was different! This was not just another rock, but a treasure hidden beneath the surface. It was not uncommon for a man to bury at least a portion of his treasure in a field as a means of protection against unsuspecting raiders or the possibility of foreign soldiers plundering their houses. And besides that, there were no banks for safety deposits. For example, the Dead Sea Scrolls were hidden in a cave in anticipation of a Roman invasion. Jesus does not explain how the treasure came to be hidden in the field, but the man finding it responded by hiding it again until he could purchase the field.

Jesus does not say what the treasure was or how the man discovered it, except that it was "hidden in a field." It was not hidden in heaven or in some far away planet but "in a field" that was accessible to all who passed that way. The "treasure" could have been gold or silver, jewels, or other valuables. One thing is for sure, it was worth more than the field where it was hidden. It makes us wonder how many had walked near this treasure yet remained unaware of its presence and value. Earlier Jesus said, "I thank You, Father, Lord of heaven and earth, that You have hidden these things from *the* wise and prudent and have revealed them to babes."[869] The "things" that Jesus refers to as "hidden" are the precious realities of the kingdom of God and the great principles of life in the kingdom through faith in Jesus Christ. Again, Jesus said:

> I speak to them in parables, **because seeing they do not see, and hearing they do not hear, nor do they understand**. And in them the prophecy of Isaiah is fulfilled, which says: *'Hearing you will hear and shall not understand, and seeing you will see and not perceive; For the hearts of this people have grown*

869. Matt. 11:25.

> *dull. Their ears are hard of hearing, and their eyes they have closed, Lest they should see with their eyes and hear with their ears, Lest they should understand with their hearts and turn, So that I should heal them.'* **But blessed *are* your eyes for they see, and your ears for they hear; for assuredly, I say to you that many prophets and righteous *men* desired to see what you see, and did not see *it*, and to hear what you hear, and did not hear *it***. (Matthew 13:13-17; emphasis mine)

All the treasures of God's wisdom and knowledge are hidden in God the Father and in Jesus Christ. These treasures are eternal, but their value remains a mystery to the rulers of this age. "For had they known they would not have crucified the Lord of glory."[870] However, the discovered treasure in this parable was so valuable in the eyes of the man who found it, that he sold all that he owned and purchased the field. Notice that he sold "all" that he had to purchase the field which included the treasure. Now, the treasure was not just a discovery, but his personal possession. When Jesus said to Peter and Andrew, "Follow Me." "They immediately left their nets and followed Him."[871] This is different from the response of the rich young man who knelt before Jesus and asked "Good Teacher, what good thing shall I do that I may have eternal life?... Jesus said to him, 'If you want to be perfect, go, sell what you have and give it to the poor, and you will have treasure in heaven."[872] But this young man was unable to see the value in the treasure that Jesus was offering him, because "he went away sorrowful, for he had great possessions."[873] He had eyes but he could not see and turned away from an eternal treasure worth more than all the gold and possessions in this world. R. T. France states, "It

---

870. 1 Cor. 2:8.
871. Matt. 4:18-20.
872. Matt. 19:16-21.
873. Matt. 19:21.

is only those who make the kingdom of heaven their top priority who will enjoy its blessings.... To find the kingdom of heaven is to find the one treasure that outweighs all other valuation."[874]

This parable reveals that the kingdom of heaven is a treasure of greater value than all our earthly possessions, yet it is hidden from the natural eye. Jesus said, "The kingdom of God does not come with observation."[875] Neither is the kingdom of heaven discovered in a science laboratory nor entered by self-sufficient arrogant persons. Jesus said, "I thank You, Father, Lord of heaven and earth, that You have hidden these things from *the* wise and prudent and have revealed them to babes."[876] The reality of the kingdom of heaven offers each of us the opportunity for the fulfillment of the greatest purposes for which we were created. The riches of our salvation call for the full commitment of our lives to the King of the kingdom of heaven, the Lord Jesus Christ. "No one can serve two masters; for either he will hate the one and love the other, or else he will be loyal to the one and despise the other. You cannot serve God and mammon."[877] For what profit is it to a man if he gains the whole world, and loses his own soul? Or what will a man give in exchange for his soul?"[878] The reality of the immeasurable value of the kingdom of God inspires us to continually pray for a spirit of wisdom and revelation to clarify our values as we daily serve the King of the Kingdom with steadfast faith and humility.

The Parable of the Pearl of Great Price:

"Again, the kingdom of heaven is like a merchant seeking beautiful pearls, who, when he had found one pearl of great price, went and sold

---

874. R. T. France, *The New International Commentary on the New Testament: The Gospel of Matthew*. Ned B. Stonehouse, F. F. Bruce, and Gordon D. Fee, gen. eds., (Grand Rapids, MI: William B. Eerdmans Publishing, Co., 2007), 539-540.

875. Luke 17:20.

876. Matt. 11:25.

877. Matt. 6:24.

878. Matt. 16:26.

all that he had and bought it."[879] In the previous parable the focus was on the "treasure," but in this parable the focus is on the "merchant." There were many other pearls, but this merchant found the "one pearl" and "sold all that he had and bought it." Robert Farrar Capon states, "His discovery was not a lucky accident, but the logical result of his being already and utterly committed to the pearl business."[880]

To the merchant who had looked with a discriminating eye at many pearls, he discovered "the one pearl" that was supremely valuable above all the others. Notice, that this pearl was not in the bargain basement with a cheap price tag. No, it was a "pearl of great price." This pearl was not hidden but available for all to evaluate and purchase. Some probably said, "this pearl is too expensive" because they did not comprehend its great value. However, this merchant was seeking "beautiful pearls." He was not looking for something inexpensive or cheap. But he was looking among the good for the best, something of rare value.

Upon finding the "one pearl of great price, he went and sold all that he had and bought it." This is a brief parable without much detail. However, it affirms a foundational principle regarding the priorities in the kingdom of God. Jesus said, "Seek first the kingdom of God and His righteousness, and all these other things shall be added to you."[881] Jesus is teaching about a lifestyle that requires making a whole-hearted commitment and alignment with the will of God. Half-hearted commitment makes the Lord nauseated.[882] The merchant sold "all he had" in order to purchase the "one pearl of great price." He did not do like Ananias and Sapphira and keep part of his money just in case something unforeseen happened. No! This merchant was all in and sold everything he had to purchase the "one pearl." The Apostle Paul is an example of this kind of commitment. He testifies:

---

879. Matt. 13:45-46.

880. Capon, *Kingdom, Grace, Judgment,* 120.

881. Matt. 6:33.

882. Rev. 3:16.

> But what things were gain to me, these I have counted loss for Christ. Yet indeed I also count all things loss for the excellence of the knowledge of Christ Jesus my Lord, for whom I have suffered the loss of all things, and count them as rubbish, that I may gain Christ and be found in Him, not having my own righteousness, which *is* from the law, but that which *is* through faith in Christ, the righteousness which is from God by faith; that I may know Him and the power of His resurrection, and the fellowship of His sufferings, being conformed to His death, if, by any means, I may attain to the resurrection from the dead. (Philippians 3:7-11)

I believe the Apostle Paul is saying, "to gain Christ" and "attain to the resurrection from the dead" defines the substance of a "pearl of great price." Life in the kingdom of God is not defined by the shallow proposition of being all about me, the size of my bank account or the position that I have attained on the corporate ladder. Rather, life in the kingdom of God is focused on the eternal values that will endure the testing by fire on the day when every believer will give an account unto God and His eternal rewards are distributed. Comprehending the richness of life in the kingdom of God is foundational to a lifestyle that completely transforms the value system of every follower of Jesus Christ.

The Scriptures recognizes Old Testament Saints who acted in faith by forsaking all in pursuit of "the pearl of great price."

> And truly if they had called to mind that *country* from which they had come out, they would have had opportunity to return. But now **they desire a better**, that is, a heavenly *country*. Therefore, God is not ashamed

> to be called their God, for He has prepared a city for them. (Hebrews 11:15-16; emphasis mine).

When Abraham was called by God to leave the land of his family, he went out not knowing where he was going, but in search of that city "whose builder and maker is God."[883] There were many individuals and leaders who observed Jesus preaching the gospel of the kingdom but could not perceive the value of what He was offering. Even though Jesus Christ was "declared to be the Son of God" and the "chief cornerstone" He was rejected by the builders, but to us who believe "He is precious!"[884] All of us like nice things, but Jesus offers us the opportunity to obtain not just nice things but "the pearl of great price." The gospel of the kingdom is a precious pearl exceeding the temporal and fleeting values of this world.

The Parable of the Dragnet:

The Lord continued revealing the mysteries of the kingdom by giving the "parable of the dragnet."

> Again, the kingdom of heaven is like a dragnet that was cast into the sea and gathered some of every kind, which, when it was full, they drew to shore; and they sat down and gathered the good into vessels, but threw the bad away. So, it will be at the end of the age. The angels will come forth, separate the wicked from among the just, and cast them into the furnace of fire. There will be wailing and gnashing of teeth." (Matthew 13:47-50)

This parable teaches three lessons. First the "dragnet" and its purpose. Watermen use the term "dragnet" to describe a large net

---

883. Heb. 11:10.
884. 1 Peter 2:6-8.

weighted on one side so that when it is pulled through the water it drags along the bottom and gathers everything into it, both fish and trash. Law enforcements use the term "dragnet" to describe a very thorough search. Jesus is using the "dragnet" as a metaphor to illustrate that the reign of God is sovereign, and every person will one day be brought before God for judgment. Some people find it impossible to believe they will be required to stand before God to give an account for their deeds including every word they have spoken.[885] But this is what Jesus is teaching by using the term "dragnet". No one escapes, but everyone will give an account to God for how they used their time and talents on this earth.

This parable further teaches that the wicked will be separated from the righteous. Separating the precious from the vile is the process of making judgments that can at times be a difficult task for all of us, especially parents. As we train and discipline our children there are instances where we misjudge their behavior or fail to accurately evaluate the situation. As a result, we may fail to administer proper discipline, or on the other hand, apply too much discipline. We may only know part of the story or may even see things incorrectly because our minds are biased by other circumstances that are impacting our life at that moment. As a result, we at times make wrong judgments as parents or employees or employers. But as Christians when we judge incorrectly, we must repent and apologize. God is not limited nor bias in His judgments. He doesn't simply observe from the exterior or superficial, "but the Lord looks at the heart."[886] God will never need to apologize because He does "not judge according to appearance, but judges with righteous judgment."[887] "His work *is* perfect; For all His ways *are* justice, A God of truth and without injustice; Righteous and upright *is* He."[888] Hence, He will judge with righteous judgment as He separates the righteous from the wicked.

885. Matt. 12:36.
886. 1 Sam. 16:7.
887. John 7:24.
888. Deut. 32:4.

The dragnet as a metaphor of the kingdom of heaven helps us understand why it is not just certain kinds of people, but every kind of persons will face judgment "at the end of the age." Many things happen in the world around us that are immoral, destructive, and heartbreaking; it makes us wonder why God does not execute His wrath upon those who perpetrate those evil deeds. We may even feel like calling down fire to "consume them just as Elijah did."[889] But Jesus reminds us that He "did not come to destroy men's lives but to save them."[890] Though the dragnet drags in both good and bad, there will be a day when the angels will come and separate the "wicked from among the righteous." That day of separation and judgment will be universal and experienced by all people, even those who have lived in rebellion against God and rejected the Lordship of Jesus Christ. Just as the fisherman separate the good fish from the bad, they also throw the bad away. So, the wicked will be "cast into the furnace of fire. There will be wailing and gnashing of teeth." Jesus on another occasion described the place of eternal separation as the place where "'Their worm does not die, And the fire is not quenched.' "[891]

God hates sin and has made a full provision of every sinner's salvation. Consequently, sinners are not helpless victims of their sins nor of the sins of their fathers. Jesus willfully submitted Himself to the will of God and died on the cross as a substitutionary sacrifice for all sinners. Thus, Jesus provides salvation and the way of escape from "the furnace of fire" for all those who put their trust in Him before it is too late. The reality is that "the furnace of fire" is only for those who reject the gospel of the kingdom and live in rebellion against God. God loves every person and it is not His will that anyone suffer "the furnace of fire." It is His will that all people would repent of their sinful lifestyle and believe on Jesus Christ as their Savior. God loves you so much that He chose you in Christ before the foundation

---

889. Luke 9:54.
890. Luke 9:56.
891. Mark 9:43-44.

of the world.[892] Consequently, when Jesus was crucified you were in Christ and you activate that reality in your life by your profession of faith in Jesus Christ as your Savior. You then follow your profession of faith by submitting to water baptism. In water baptism you are submersed under the surface of the water as buried in a grave. Then you are raised up out of the water to live in the power of the resurrection. Every born again believer in Jesus Christ can confidently say "I have been crucified with Christ; it is no longer I who live, but Christ lives in me; and the *life* which I now live in the flesh I live by faith in the Son of God, who loved me and gave Himself for me."[893] Therefore, your eternal destiny is not determined by the dragnet, but by your relationship with the Lord Jesus Christ your Savior.

Do You Understand Parables of the Kingdom?

Thus far we have been discussing the parables of Jesus recorded in Matthew chapter thirteen. Each of these parables reveal specific realities about the kingdom of God. Then Jesus ask the question, "Have you understood these things?" His disciples responded, "Yes, Lord." What would your response be to the Lord's question? Do you understand or comprehend the mysteries revealed in these parables? Earlier in the thirteenth chapter Jesus said:

> But blessed *are* your eyes for they see, and your ears for they hear; for assuredly, I say to you that many prophets and righteous *men* desired to see what you see, and did not see *it,* and to hear what you hear, and did not hear *it.* (Matthew 13:16-17)

Jesus is impressing upon His disciples that He is not simply rehearsing the same things they have been hearing for generations. Jesus is revealing truths through these parables that have been hidden in the

---

892. Eph. 1:4.
893. Gal. 2:20.

heart of God since before the foundation of the world. And generations of righteous men have desired to see the secrets of the kingdom now being revealed by Jesus. So, Jesus continued by teaching what some scholars consider to be the final parable recorded in Matthew chapter thirteen. "Then He said to them, 'Therefore every scribe instructed concerning the kingdom of heaven is like a householder who brings out of his treasure *things* new and old.'"[894]

Jesus uses the term "scribe" which seems confusing to some scholars, but R. T. France defines the "scribe" as a "discipled writer."[895] One who is "instructed concerning the kingdom of heaven." France continues by stating, "The 'old' is not to be 'abolished', but to be judiciously integrated into the new perspective of the kingdom of heaven."[896] John Nolland states, "It is Matthew's conviction that solid possession and proper uses of the old are tied up with the gaining of the new in the treasure of the kingdom of heaven."[897]

A "householder" was one who had the authority to dispense of the treasures of his storeroom for the benefit of others. Some kingdom valuables are rooted in the Old Testament and some are fresh from the words of Jesus, but all are treasures. The Lord has entrusted His followers with these treasures and given us the authority to dispense them freely. However, we are mindful of the reality that, "We have this treasure in earthen vessels that the excellence of the power may be of God and not of us."[898] The capacity to integrate the old with the new requires the guidance of the Holy Spirit. The Apostle Paul asked the Colossians to pray for him and Timothy; "that God would open to us a door for the word, to speak the mystery of Christ… that I may make it manifest, as I ought to speak."[899] It is humbling to be entrusted

894. Matt. 13:52.

895. France, *The Gospel of Matthew,* 545.

896. Ibid., 546

897. John Nolland, *The Gospel of Matthew: A Commentary on the Greek Text*, New International Greek Testament Commentary (Grand Rapids, MI; Carlisle: W.B. Eerdmans; Paternoster Press, 2005), 571–572.

898. 2 Cor. 4:7.

899. Col. 4:3-4.

with these precious treasures and given the privilege of sharing this wealth with others. However, we are not to "cast our pearls before swine,"[900] but "commit these to faithful men who will be able to teach others also."[901]

Reflecting on the teaching of Jesus throughout the thirteenth chapter of Matthew, Craig Blomberg captures the sense of these parables and summarizes these teachings of Jesus succinctly:

> The central theme uniting all of the lessons of the parables is the kingdom of God. It is both present and future. It includes both a reign and a realm. It involves both personal transformation and social reform. It is not to be equated either with Israel or the church but is the dynamic power of God's personal revelation of himself in creating a human community of those who serve Jesus in every area of their lives.[902]

Not everyone recognizes the presence of the kingdom of God in the here and now because it functions according to spiritual principles. And, "the natural man does not receive the things of the Spirit of God, for they are foolishness to him; nor can he know *them,* because they are spiritually discerned."[903] To comprehend the mysteries of the kingdom of God requires the ministry of the Holy Spirit, and we are blessed to be living in a season of His awesome presence. Ask the Holy Spirit to give you a spirit of wisdom and revelation to help you understand the realities of the kingdom of God as we continue this study of the parables of Jesus.

---

900. Matt. 7:6.
901. 2 Tim. 2:2.
902. Blomberg, *Interpreting the Parables,* 326.
903. 1 Cor. 2:14.

The Parable of the Unforgiving Servant:

The Lord Jesus revealed an essential mystery of the kingdom of God in response to Peter's questions; "Lord, how often shall my brother sin against me, and I forgive him? Up to seven times?" And Jesus answered by giving the parable of the "Unforgiving Servant."

> Therefore, the kingdom of heaven is like a certain king who wanted to settle accounts with his servants. And when he had begun to settle accounts, one was brought to him who owed him ten thousand talents. But as he was not able to pay, his master commanded that he be sold, with his wife and children and all that he had, and that payment be made. The servant therefore fell down before him, saying, 'Master, have patience with me, and I will pay you all.' Then the master of that servant was moved with compassion, released him, and forgave him the debt. But that servant went out and found one of his fellow servants who owed him a hundred denarii; and he laid hands on him and took *him* by the throat, saying, 'Pay me what you owe!' So, his fellow servant fell down at his feet and begged him, saying, 'Have patience with me, and I will pay you all.' And he would not but went and threw him into prison till he should pay the debt. So, when his fellow servants saw what had been done, they were very grieved, and came and told their master all that had been done. Then his master, after he had called him, said to him, 'You wicked servant! I forgave you all that debt because you begged me. Should you not also have had compassion on your fellow servant, just as I had pity on you?' And his master was angry and delivered him to the torturers

> until he should pay all that was due to him. So, My heavenly Father also will do to you if each of you, from his heart, does not forgive his brother his trespasses. (Matthew 18:23-35)

The central truth of this parable concerns forgiveness. Jesus is teaching that every member of His kingdom has a responsibility to forgive others. Jesus is not simply talking about forgiveness, He also practiced forgiveness. It was while the sinless Son of God was suffering the agony of crucifixion that He called out to God on the behalf of those who had falsely accused and condemned Him saying, "Father, forgive them, for they do not know what they do."[904]

During the Sermon on the Mount Jesus taught, "For if you forgive men their trespasses, your heavenly Father will also forgive you. But if you do not forgive men their trespasses, neither will your Father forgive your trespasses."[905] Forgiveness is a relational concept that cancels debt. Forgiveness is your willingness to cancel my debt at your expense. Forgiveness makes reconciliation possible. It is therefore true, that without God's forgiveness we could never be reconciled with Him, because we owed a sin debt far beyond our ability to pay. In other words when we ask Jesus to forgive us—He forgives us of our entire sin debt. He willingly paid our sin debt for us on the cross. "If we confess our sins, He is faithful and just to forgive us *our* sins and to cleanse us from all unrighteousness."[906]

We are indeed grateful that the Lord forgives us rather than giving us what we deserved. Roger L. Hahn states, "Forgiveness is not about what the other deserves; it is about the grace that God would give."[907]

---

904. Luke 23:34.
905. Matt. 6:14-15.
906. 1 John 1:9.
907. Roger L. Hahn, *Matthew: A Commentary for Bible Students* (Indianapolis, IN: Wesleyan Publishing House, 2007), 226.

As the Scripture says, "In Him we have redemption through His blood, the forgiveness of sins, according to the riches of His grace."[908]

In this parable the servant owed his master ten thousand talents which was an enormous debt. It was so large that he would not be able to pay it, even though he told his master he would pay all. Therefore, when he begged his master to be patient with him, his master had compassion on him and forgave him the full amount. There is not anything in this parable indicating the servant deserved forgiveness. However, his master had compassion on him, and compassion is a powerful emotion that arises from the very depths of one's being. Compassion is much more than sympathy or emotional accord. Compassion expresses unbounded mercy. And mercy is the willingness to pay a debt that you do not owe. Jesus was often "moved with compassion"[909] during His earthly ministry. Compassion is to feel the pain of another to such an extent that we are motivated to enter their pain with them; plus having a solution for their suffering with the willingness and ability to pay the full cost of that solution. Apparently, the servant's master had great wealth and had the ability and the willingness to absorb the servant's enormous debt.

After expressing the liberty that was granted through forgiveness; this parable then describes how the forgiven servant apprehended one of his fellow servants that owed him a small amount of money and demanded full payment. The fellow servant could not pay his debt and begged for patience and promised to pay all. But the servant that had been forgiven would not be patient and threw him in prison. Notice that the fellow servant did not deny that he owed the debt or try to wiggle out of his responsibility. Forgiveness always acknowledges the reality of debt. But forgiveness is all about cancelling the debts you are definitely owed. Forgiveness is the grace to rip up the "You owe me." Many times, believers harbor unforgiveness because they can state fully what another person owes them. And they consider it

---

908. Eph. 1:7.

909. Matt. 9:36, 14:14, 18:27; Mk. 1:41, 6:34.

their right to exact full payment from them. But that mindset is not compatible with the nature of the kingdom of God.

In this parable the other servants saw what had been done by the one who had been forgiven so much. They were grieved and reported to the master what had happened. The master called that "wicked servant" and uttered the following severe words to him:

> 'You wicked servant! I forgave you all that debt because you begged me. Should you not also have had compassion on your fellow servant, just as I had pity on you?' And his master was angry and delivered him to the torturers until he should pay all that was due to him. (Matthew 18:32-24)

Jesus had taught, "Blessed are the merciful, for they shall obtain mercy."[910] The "unforgiving servant" had been the recipient of mercy but was unwilling to show mercy. Therefore, his master was angry with him and revoked the debt cancellation and delivered him not simply to prison, but to "the torturers." The idea is that he will be more than confined to prison and servitude, he will also be tortured. He would be confined and tortured "until he should pay all." Because of the size of his debt he will suffer imprisonment and torture for the remaining days of his life. How painful and unnecessary, all because of his self-centered selfishness, and willful refusal to be merciful. He had already been forgiven of his enormous debt but brought this terrible judgment upon himself.

You can imagine how Peter and the others must have felt after hearing this parable. They were probably thinking, "The wicked servant was a complete idiot." That is how this parable made me feel. But Jesus was not through teaching. He probably looked into their faces and continued, "So My heavenly Father also will do to you if each

910. Matt. 5:7.

of you, from his heart, does not forgive his brother his trespasses."[911] That is a sobering statement.

Jesus is not speaking to the Pharisees or some hardhearted evil people, but to you and me. He aims directly at our heart, not at our head. It is one thing to sing "Amazing Grace," but it is a whole other ball game when it is our responsibility to pass out the grace of forgiveness. Sometimes we might ask "I wonder if Jesus really knows how much that person owes me?" Yes, He does, and He is saying to you and me, "Get beyond superficial principles of relationships that says you owe me, and I will not forget it." Jesus is teaching us to function in community with others from a pure and compassionate heart. He has no desire to revoke His forgiveness of our great debt or turn us over to the torturers. It is, however, the testimony of many pastors that physical healing is often hindered by unforgiveness. Jesus intends for each of us to represent His kingdom in our community by a heart of compassion that stands ready to forgive others as He has forgiven us. Forgiveness is such a powerful relational virtue that it clearly separates the nature of those living in the kingdom of God from those not living in the kingdom of God.

The Parable of the Laborers in the Vineyard:

The next parable we will discuss has been entitled by some as "The Laborers in the Vineyard." In this parable Jesus reveals mysteries regarding the sovereignty of God in the dispensing of His grace. This parable follows Jesus's conversation with the "rich young ruler" and His response to the question, "What good thing shall I do that I may have eternal life?" Jesus' response left the disciples greatly astonished regarding the difficulty of rich men entering the kingdom of God. Therefore, they asked Jesus "Who then can be saved?" "Jesus looked at *them* and said, 'With men this is impossible, but with God

---

911. Matt. 18:35.

all things are possible.'"[912] Jesus then assured the disciples of a rewarding future in the Kingdom, but concluded His comments with the words, "But many who are first will be last, and the last first."[913] Then He spoke the following parable:

> For the kingdom of heaven is like a landowner who went out early in the morning to hire laborers for his vineyard. Now when he had agreed with the laborers for a denarius a day, he sent them into his vineyard. And he went out about the third hour and saw others standing idle in the marketplace, and said to them, 'You also go into the vineyard, and whatever is right I will give you.' So, they went. Again, he went out about the sixth and the ninth hour and did likewise. And about the eleventh hour he went out and found others standing idle, and said to them, 'Why have you been standing here idle all day?' They said to him, 'Because no one hired us.' He said to them, 'You also go into the vineyard, and whatever is right you will receive.' So, when evening had come, the owner of the vineyard said to his steward, 'Call the laborers and give them *their* wages, beginning with the last to the first.' And when those came who *were hired* about the eleventh hour, they each received a denarius. But when the first came, they supposed that they would receive more; and they likewise received each a denarius. And when they had received *it,* they complained against the landowner, saying, 'These last *men* have worked *only* one hour, and you made them equal to us who have borne the burden and the heat of the day.' But he answered one of them and

912. Matt. 19:26.
913. Matt. 19:30.

> said, 'Friend, I am doing you no wrong. Did you not agree with me for a denarius? Take *what is* yours and go your way. I wish to give to this last man *the same* as to you. Is it not lawful for me to do what I wish with my own things? Or is your eye evil because I am good?' So, the last will be first, and the first last. For many are called, but few chosen." (Matthew 20:1-16)

This parable is set in the context of a vineyard and it is probably during harvest-time and the landowner needs for workers to gather the harvest. Ripe grapes are perishable and susceptible to serious loss if not gathered in a timely manner. However, the emphasis of this parable does not concern the size of the harvest or the profitability of the harvest but focuses on the discretion and grace of the landowner to compensate the laborers.

"For the kingdom of heaven is like a landowner who went out early in the morning to hire laborers for his vineyard." The landowner made a total of five trips that day to the marketplace to hire laborers. His first trip was early in the morning probably about 6 AM. The landowner returned to the marketplace at 9 o'clock, at noon, at 3 o'clock and again at the eleventh hour which was probably about 5 PM. The workers hired early in the morning had agreed to work all day for a denarius. But the landowner did not offer to pay the others a denarius but told them "whatever is right you will receive."

When the workday was finished the owner called his steward and told him to pay the laborers beginning with those who were hired at the eleventh hour. Those who were hired last were paid a denarius and each group thereafter was also paid a denarius. No one objected to receiving the denarius except those who were first hired in the early morning. After seeing those hired in the later shifts being paid a denarius, those who had worked the full day supposed they would be paid more. But they were likewise paid a denarius. "And when they had received *it,* they complained against the landowner, saying,

'These last *men* have worked *only* one hour, and you made them equal to us who have borne the burden and the heat of the day.'"[914] Of course they had agreed for a denarius for a day's work, but when those who only worked for one hour received a denarius it seemed they were not being treated fairly or contrary to natural justice. So, they expressed their complaint against the landowner. This brings us to the main point in this parable which is the gracious sovereignty of God. The owner responded to their complaint by saying,

> Friend, I am doing you no wrong. Did you not agree with me for a denarius? Take *what is* yours and go your way. I wish to give to this last man *the same* as to you. Is it not lawful for me to do what I wish with my own things? Or is your eye evil because I am good? (Matthew 20:13-15)

Keep in mind as you meditate on this parable that God's grace is a gift of His favor which we cannot earn. Grace is always the Lord's prerogative and never earned nor an entitlement. The Lord told Moses. "I will be gracious to whom I will be gracious, and I will have compassion on whom I will have compassion."[915] God's Grace is the operational power of the kingdom of God that is affirmed by the seal of the Spirit of grace in every believer's heart. "For by grace you have been saved through faith, and that not of yourselves; *it is* the gift of God, not of works, lest anyone should boast."[916] It is God who blesses us with that which we do not deserve, and He is the wise owner of the vineyard. "For *as* the heavens are higher than the earth, so are My ways higher than your ways, And My thoughts than your thoughts.[917]

In this parable as in others, Jesus is revealing mysteries of the kingdom of God. R. C. Lenski states:

---

914. Matt. 20:11-12.
915. Exod. 33:19.
916. Eph. 2:8-9.
917. Isa. 55:9.

> "The kingdom" is the rule and operation of God's grace.... Moreover, the story is purposely molded so as to reflect what occurs in God's rule of grace.[918] There is no law, no principle of right in heaven or on earth to forbid this sovereign exercise of grace.[919]

We are not to think of the kingdom in terms of entitlement, wages, or merit, but in terms of God's grace. God always pays His obligations and in this parable the owner paid the workers exactly the amount they had agreed upon before they went to work in the vineyard. Early in the morning as the workers were standing idol a denarius for a day's work seemed like a good deal. But at the end of the day when they observed the owner's generosity, they "supposed" or "assumed" they deserved or were entitled to receive more than what they had agreed upon. When their expectations were not met, they complained. This should serve as a warning; when we perceive that someone is being blessed beyond what we think they deserve, especially if they are being blessed beyond the level of our personal blessings, we must guard our hearts against envy.

God is not bound by our conception of fairness. Think of Manasseh, the wicked king of Judah; "He acted more wickedly than all the Amorites who were before him and also made Judah sin with is idols."[920] The Amorites were among the nations that God had Joshua to destroy because of their sin. Manasseh's wickedness was so severe that the Lord brought the armies of Assyria against Jerusalem and Manasseh was put in bronze fetters and carried off to prison in Babylon. However, Manasseh humbled himself greatly and God forgave him and brough him back to Jerusalem into his kingdom.[921] Think of all the Jews that suffered because of his wickedness; yet God graciously forgave and restored him. To forgive is to cancel the debt.

---

918. Lenski, *The Interpretation of St. Matthew's Gospel,* 764.
919. Ibid., 779.
920. 2 Kings 21:11.
921. 2 Chro. 33:9-13.

Consider Saul who became the Apostle Paul. He severely persecuted Christians, including holding the coats as Stephen was being stoned to death. Yet God forgave him and appointed him as the Apostle to the Gentiles. If it were not for the grace of God, how would you and I stand before a holy God?

We have every reason to be grateful for the gracious privilege of not only being members of God's royal family, but also His "friend."[922] We may not understand why some things work out as they do, but it is certain that the amount of our wealth accumulated in our bank account will not determine our eternal reward. However, none of us need entertain envy over the blessing of another, but we can always rejoice in the abundance of grace which we have received. Jesus is teaching us to not let our eye be evil because we may feel unfairly treated in comparison with blessings of others or those we may consider underserving of His generosity. In the kingdom of God, "the last will be first and the first shall be last. For many are called but few are chosen."[923] R. C. Trench concludes his commentary on this parable by stating, "Many are called to work in God's vineyard, but few retain that humility, that utter denial of any claim as of a right on their part, which will allow them in the end to be partakers of His reward."[924] The foundation of our faith and expectations rests on the reality that the Lord is gracious and faithful to do what He has promised. Amen.

The Parable of the Two Sons:

This next parable is about a man with two sons. Jesus ask:

> But what do you think? A man had two sons, and he came to the first and said, 'Son, go, work today in my vineyard.' He answered and said, 'I will not,' but

922. Matt. 20:13.

923. Matt. 20:15-16.

924. R. C. Trench, *Notes on the Parables of Our Lord* (Grand Rapids, MI: Baker Book House, 1981), 66.

> afterward he regretted it and went. Then he came to the second and said likewise. And he answered and said, 'I *go,* sir,' but he did not go. Which of the two did the will of *his* father?" They said to Him, "The first." Jesus said to them, "Assuredly, I say to you that tax collectors and harlots enter the kingdom of God before you. For John came to you in the way of righteousness, and you did not believe him; but tax collectors and harlots believed him; and when you saw *it,* you did not afterward relent and believe him. (Matthew 21:28-32)

The setting of this parable is in the Temple area where the chief priests and elders of Israel were questioning Jesus regarding the source of His authority. In response to their questions Jesus asked them, "the baptism of John—where was it from? From heaven or from men?" They reasoned among themselves only to discover that Jesus had them on the horns of a dilemma. So, they responded, "We do not know."[925] Where upon Jesus immediately responded by asking this second question "But what do you think?" It was His segue into this parable about a man with two sons.

In this parable a father came to the first son and said, "Son, go, work today in my vineyard. He answered and said, 'I will not,' but afterward he regretted it and went." The father came to the second son and said the same thing. The second son said. "'I go, sir' but he did not go." Then Jesus asked the third question, "Which of the two did the will of the father?" And the religious leaders answered, "The first."

Jesus was pointing out that both John the Baptist and He Himself had been preaching repentance for the remission of sins. Multitudes including tax collectors and harlots had previously rejected the message of repentance. They had said "No we will not believe," but later

---

925. Matt. 21:24-25.

regretted it and believed and entered the way of righteousness. The religious leaders, including those that were questioning Jesus' authority, were like the first son. They talked a good talk but failed to accept the obligation to obey the gospel call to repentance. There is no obligation to repent when you do not accept the authority of the person calling for repentance. They neither accepted the authority of John nor Jesus. Therefore, Jesus told those religious leaders that "tax collectors and harlots would enter the kingdom before they would."[926] God grants everyone the freedom to reject His gospel or repent and accept it. It is "therefore, by their fruits you will know them."[927]

Do we recognize the authority of the Lord in the gospel call for repentance? If we do, we have an obligation to change the way we think. If we are willing to hear the gospel, faith will be ignited in our heart.[928] And faith is the on-ramp to the way of righteousness, to be followed by obedience that produces the works of righteousness that are "fruits worthy of repentance."[929] The gospel of the kingdom requires a change in the way we think, and that in turn changes the way we behave, to the point that our character is transformed into Christ-likeness. All of us start our journey in life as sinners, but God sends His messengers to proclaim the gospel of the kingdom and call us to repentance. Faith in Jesus Christ is a transformational life-long process, but it begins by accepting the gospel call to repentance. And repentance means that I change my mind from relying on self-righteousness to placing my trust in the righteousness of God that is offered through the gospel of the kingdom of God.

926. Matt. 21:31.
927. Matt. 7:20
928. Rom. 10:17.
929. Matt. 3:8.

The Parable of the Wicked Vinedressers:

It seems that without hesitation Jesus continued speaking another parable to those in Israel who were rejecting the gospel of the kingdom. He said:

> Hear another parable: There was a certain landowner who planted a vineyard and set a hedge around it, dug a winepress in it and built a tower. And he leased it to vinedressers and went into a far country. Now when vintage-time drew near, he sent his servants to the vinedressers, that they might receive its fruit. And the vinedressers took his servants, beat one, killed one, and stoned another. Again, he sent other servants, more than the first, and they did likewise to them. Then last of all he sent his son to them, saying, 'They will respect my son.' But when the vinedressers saw the son, they said among themselves, 'This is the heir. Come, let us kill him and seize his inheritance.' So, they took him and cast *him* out of the vineyard and killed *him.* Therefore, when the owner of the vineyard comes, what will he do to those vinedressers?" They said to Him, "He will destroy those wicked men miserably, and lease *his* vineyard to other vinedressers who will render to him the fruits in their seasons." Jesus said to them, "Have you never read in the Scriptures: *'The stone which the builders rejected Has become the chief cornerstone. This was the LORD'S doing, and it is marvelous in our eyes'?* "Therefore, I say to you, the kingdom of God will be taken from you and given to a nation bearing the fruits of it. And whoever falls on this stone will be

> broken; but on whomever it falls, it will grind him to powder." (Matthew 21:33-44)

The vineyard was familiar to all Israel because it held a practical and functional role in their culture. However, the religious leaders of Israel were not familiar with the mysteries of the kingdom of God that Jesus was unveiling. Jesus wisely engaged those religious antagonists with seemingly non-threating stories that imparted powerful realities regarding the kingdom of God. These realities were often too inflammatory or explosive to present in straight forward narrative. So, Jesus embedded these truths in parables.

The landowner "planted a vineyard and set a hedge around it, dug a winepress in it and built a tower. And he leased it to vinedressers and went into a far country.[930] This describes a customary scene in Israel. Isaiah had said, "For the vineyard of the Lord of host is the house of Israel…."[931] So, the content of this parable addresses issues regarding the privileges and responsibilities granted to Israel. In the days of Moses the Lord had made covenant with Israel saying, "if you diligently obey the voice of the LORD your God, to observe carefully all His commandments which I command you today, that the LORD your God will set you high above all nations of the earth."[932]

However, Israel faltered in their responsibilities to keep the covenant of the Lord and gave themselves over to ungodliness and idolatry. Jesus tells in this parable that the owner of the vineyard sent many servants to receive an income from the fruit of the vineyard—likewise God sent His servants to speak on His behalf to Israel. But they beat some, imprisoned others, and killed some. God sent prophets like Isaiah whom they rejected and killed by sawing his body in half. And Jeremiah, whom they also rejected, was put in a dungeon pit. "Now it happened, when Jeremiah had made an end of speaking all that the LORD had commanded *him* to speak to all the people, the priests and

930. Matt. 21:33.
931. Isa. 5:7.
932. Deut. 28:1.

the prophets and all the people seized him, saying, 'You will surely die!'"[933] In an all-out effort to salvage the relationship with the vinedressers, the owner of the vineyard sent his own son, whom they cast out of the vineyard and killed.

This parable reaches its climax with Jesus asking the question, "Therefore, when the owner of the vineyard comes, what will he do to those vinedressers?"[934] It is amazing how quickly and accurately the listeners responding with a sense of justice. They said, "He will destroy those wicked men miserably, and lease *his* vineyard to other vinedressers who will render to him the fruits in their seasons."[935] Their answer surely vindicates God's judgment on Israel and the establishment of His kingdom with power and blessing through the body of Christ beginning on the Day of Pentecost.

At this point Jesus moves beyond the parable and asked them if they had read the following passage of Scripture: "The stone *which* the builders rejected Has become the chief cornerstone. This was the LORD'S doing; It *is* marvelous in our eyes."[936] Notice that this powerful transition in Jesus' discourse does not come from the tradition of men nor from the wisdom of this world but from their own Scriptures. Also keep in mind that Jesus is speaking to these leaders between Palm Sunday and His crucifixion. Some of His listeners already had plans in their hearts to destroy Jesus before the week was over. Then Jesus rendered His crushing verdict: "Therefore, I say to you, the kingdom of God will be taken from you and given to a nation bearing the fruits of it."[937]

We can only imagine what Jesus' listeners were thinking. But surely some were saying to themselves, "Jesus you are speaking some strong words right now, but we're going to silence you sooner than you think!" Jesus then finished by speaking prophetically; "And whoever

---

933. Jer. 26:8.
934. Matt. 21:40.
935. Matt. 21:41.
936. Psa. 118:22-23.
937. Matt. 21:23.

falls on this stone will be broken; but on whomever it falls, it will grind him to powder."[938] At this point the chief priests and Pharisees perceived that Jesus was speaking to them and they could take no more of this kind of talk and "sought to lay hands on Him."[939] This reminds us of how Joseph's brothers treated him. They said among themselves, "Look, this dreamer is coming! Come therefore, let us now kill him and cast him into some pit; and we shall say, 'Some wild beast has devoured him.' We shall see what will become of his dreams!"[940] However, the chief priests and Pharisees "feared the multitudes," because the multitudes took Jesus to be a prophet. But they poured out their venom on Jesus before the end of the week. They were unable to perceive of the possibility of His resurrection and the day when every knee would bow, and every tongue confess that Jesus Christ is Lord of all!

The Parable of the Wedding Feast:

Jesus, remaining in the Temple area continued to reveal the mysteries of the kingdom of God as He spoke the following parable which others have entitled, "The Marriage Feast." In this parable He describes a king that arranged a marriage for his son and sent his servants to call those who were invited to the wedding celebration.

> And Jesus answered and spoke to them again by parables and said: 'The kingdom of heaven is like a certain king who arranged a marriage for his son, and sent out his servants to call those who were invited to the wedding; and they were not willing to come. Again, he sent out other servants, saying, 'Tell those who are invited, "See, I have prepared my dinner; my oxen and fatted cattle *are* killed, and all things *are*

938. Matt. 21:24.
939. Matt. 21:45-46.
940. Gen. 37:19-20.

> ready. Come to the wedding." ' But they made light of it and went their ways, one to his own farm, another to his business. And the rest seized his servants, treated *them* spitefully, and killed *them.* But when the king heard *about it,* he was furious. And he sent out his armies, destroyed those murderers, and burned up their city. Then he said to his servants, 'The wedding is ready, but those who were invited were not worthy. Therefore, go into the highways, and as many as you find, invite to the wedding.' So those servants went out into the highways and gathered all whom they found, both bad and good. And the wedding *hall* was filled with guests. But when the king came in to see the guests, he saw a man there who did not have on a wedding garment. So, he said to him, 'Friend, how did you come in here without a wedding garment?' And he was speechless. Then the king said to the servants, 'Bind him hand and foot, take him away, and cast *him* into outer darkness; there will be weeping and gnashing of teeth.' For many are called, but few *are* chosen." (Matthew 22:1-14)

On the day that marriage celebration was to be held the king sent his servants first to call the invited guests; and they were not willing to come. Their negative response seems unusual to us. And as a result, the king sent other servants with the message, "Come, for all things are now ready." It is assumed that invitations to the wedding celebration had been sent out earlier and accepted by those who were invited. Did you ever invite guests and spend hours preparing a fine dinner, and at dinner time no one showed up? How do you think that would make you feel? All of us have experienced occasions when we invited guests with an expectation of their presence and at the last minute they had to cancel. We know unforeseen things happen, but when we prepare all things, and the guests are simply preoccupied with personal concerns and make excuses at the last moment, it is so disappointing that we would probably feel offended or upset. In this parable all the invited guests not only made excuses but treated the king's servants disgracefully and even killed them. So, it is not hard to understand why the king became furious.

Can you imagine how the Lord must feel when we become so consumed with our personal agendas that it replaces communion with Him. We pack our schedules to the point that busyness has become a trademark of cool Christianity. Then we wonder, "Why do I feel so stressed and tired all the time?" It is not that we are scheduling unimportant or bad things—it is a matter of priorities. The invited guests to the marriage celebration were probably preoccupied with good things and attending to matters for which they were responsible. However, by their priorities they demonstrated their failure to "seek first the kingdom of God and His righteousness."[941]

Throughout redemptive history people have been tempted to mismanage their priorities and mistreat God's servants. Our God is a jealous God and has commanded us to have no other gods before Him.[942] Later in this same chapter of Matthew, Jesus said to one of the religious lawyers, "*You shall love the* LORD *your God with all your heart, with all your soul, and with all your mind.*"[943] How we spend our time reveals our priorities. This explains why Jesus is speaking a parable like this. For the most part the religious people during His years of ministry had gotten their priorities wrong and rejected the servants of the Lord even Jesus Himself. "He came to His own, and His own did not receive Him."[944] They had excuses for rejecting Him. Why should they fellowship with Him? After all they had watched Him grow up. How could He be their Savior—this was Joseph, the carpenter's son. How could He be their Messiah—He was a friend of

941. Matt. 6:33.
942. Exod. 20:3-5.
943. Matt. 22:37.
944. John 1:11.

sinners. That may be reasonable and logical in their way of thinking, but it is also wrong.

All of us need to prayerfully ask the Holy Spirit to illuminate our hearts and minds with wisdom lest the god of this age blinds us to the reality of God's priorities and they become hidden under the demands of our personal agendas. Divine wisdom is not simply the fruit of our intellect. Godly wisdom is a gift of God's grace,[945] and the capacity to perceive the operational power of His presence. The invited guests were reasonable and logical, but they committed themselves to the wrong priorities. This parable teaches us there are consequences to our actions regardless to how sincere we may feel about the source of our preoccupation. This was a gracious invitation to come and enjoy intimate fellowship with the king and his family.

Jesus further illuminates the fallacy of wrong priorities in the parable of the prodigal son. The older brother demonstrated the foolishness of wrong priorities by his refusal to attend the banquet celebrating his younger brother's return home.[946] The older brother had reasonable and logical excuses, but lacked the wisdom to perceive God's grace and priorities in that situation. It is amazing how easy it is for our self-centeredness to distort God's grace and darken our capacity to see from God's perspective. Most of us have made excuses at some point in our relationship with God, only to later discover our foolish self-centeredness. It is the Holy Spirit who quickens God's priorities to our hearts and grants us the wisdom to perceive His graciousness despite our own arrogance. He calls each of us to repentance while we still have an opportunity to adjust our priorities and to be nourished and strengthened at the supper table of fellowship and communion with our heavenly Father.

In the Sermon on the Mount Jesus distinguished between the wise and foolish house builders. The wise builder built his house upon the solid rock foundation that could endure the storms of life. He was the

---

945. James 1:5; 1 Cor. 12:8.
946. Luke 15:25-32.

one who not only heard the sayings of Jesus, but he also did them.[947] The foolish man built his house on sand and it was destroyed. He heard the word of the Lord but did not apply it to his life. Good intentions are never enough; we must "seek first the kingdom of God and His righteousness." To "seek" is to strive humbly and diligently to follow and obey Him. To "seek" is a present, active, imperative which eliminates passivity and requires our active response to His invitation. The first guests invited foolishly expressed their unwillingness to attend the wedding celebration and when the king sent other servants, they treated them spitefully and killed them. No wonder the king counted them as unworthy guests and "sent out his armies to destroy those murderers and burn their cities."[948]

Then the king sent his servants into the highways to invite whomever they found. Usually these people would not expect an invitation to a king's celebration. However, they were now invited. The master had prepared the oxen and fatted cattle which means that the menu was filet mignon and prime rib! The wedding celebration was now ready! The point is that God has paid the awesome price to have His house filled with redeemed sons and daughters. The invitation to commune and fellowship with Him is now extended even to the least likely including whosoever will come. His invitation is thus fulfilling the prophecy of Isaiah; "Ho! Everyone who thirsts, come to the waters; And you who have no money, Come, buy, and eat. Yes, come, buy wine and milk without money and without price."[949] The Lord is gracious and extends the blessings of His kingdom to whomever is willing, urging them to accept His invitation and come.

Participation in the blessings of the kingdom of God is contingent upon each one's response to His invitation. The Master gives each one the privilege of accepting or rejecting His invitation. However, one cannot ignore His invitation and expect to taste the abundance of

---

947. Matt. 7:24-27.
948. Matt. 22:7-9
949. Isa. 55:1.

good things He has prepared for those who do accept it. The invitation of our Lord takes priority even over our family commitments. Adam "heeded the voice of his wife" and thus disobeyed God.[950] We should love all members of our families and carefully consider their advice. But in the final analysis we each are ultimately answerable to God for all our decisions just as Adam was. Jesus drives this reality home by stating:

> If anyone comes to Me and does not hate his father and mother, wife and children, brothers and sisters, yes, and his own life also, he cannot be My disciple. And whoever does not bear his cross and come after Me cannot be My disciple. (Luke 14:26-27)

Ken Heer states, "The direction and destiny of our lives are not predetermined. We have the freedom to make choices that determine our future."[951] Our life in the kingdom of God is to be governed by God's purposes, priorities, and values. We have the privilege of making choices, but our choices have consequences. God's love is not to be ignored and His grace not to be insulted forever. A primary point of this parable is that we are not to simply live to fulfill our selfish ambitions. Our self-centeredness makes way for hostility against the sovereignty of God and the purposes for which He sends His servants to us. We are to live in a covenant yoke with Jesus. That is the place of ease and rest.[952] Submission to God's will is a means of grace. A positive response to His invitation may not seem joyous at the moment but afterward it yields the peaceful fruits of righteousness.[953] Therefore, any invitation from the Lord is not to be ignored.

---

950. Gen. 3:17

951. Ken Heer, *Luke: A Commentary for Bible Students* (Indianapolis, IN: Wesleyan Publishing House, 2007), 199.

952. Matt. 11:28-30.

953. Heb. 12:11

This parable reaches its climax when the king comes into the banquet hall to visit with the guest and there was a man among the guest without a wedding garment. Many scholars say that Oriental Royalty provided their guest with wedding garments. This may be reflected in Joseph's royal hospitality to his brothers. "He gave to all of them, to each man, changes of garments; but to Benjamin he gave three hundred *pieces* of silver and five changes of garments."[954] Isaiah proclaimed, "For He has clothed me with the garments of salvation, He has covered me with the robe of righteousness."[955] Every believer is looking forward to the great wedding feast at the marriage supper of the Lamb! But all those in attendance will "be granted to be arrayed in fine linen, clean and bright."[956] The believers' robe of righteousness is a gift from God and received through faith in Jesus Christ who became sin that we may be made the righteousness of God in Him.[957] Our personal righteousness is as filthy rags.[958] However, once we believe on the Lord Jesus Christ our filthy rags of self-righteousness are washed away. We then receive God's gift of a robe of righteousness which empowers us to produce the "peaceable fruit of righteousness."[959]

The guest without the wedding garment had responded to the invitation to the celebration but apparently considered his personal garment sufficient for the occasion. However, when the king confronted him and asked; "Friend, how did you come here without a wedding garment? And he was speechless."[960] In other words the guest was struck dumb when suddenly faced with the royal authority of the king and had no words to defend his foolish behavior. Then like a common criminal the man was bound hand and foot and cast "into outer darkness; there will be weeping and gnashing of teeth."[961]

---

954. Gen. 45:22.
955. Isa. 61:10.
956. Rev. 19:8-9.
957. 2 Cor. 5:21.
958. Isa. 64:6.
959. Heb. 12:11.
960. Matt. 22:12.
961. Matt. 22:13.

Jesus concludes this parable with the words, "Many are called, but few are chosen."[962] It is God who does both the calling and the choosing. First, consider the words "many are called." "This can be understood to be a Semitic figure of speech that universalizes the invitation."[963] In other words "many" includes the concept of a multitude. Earlier Jesus said, "The Son of Man did not come to be served, but to give His life for many."[964] In this parable many were invited or called to the wedding celebration, including "both good and bad."

Second, consider the words "few are chosen." The dictionary form or lemma of the Greek word for "chosen" is the noun *ekletos.* The Greek word translated "chosen" is the adjective form of *ekletos* which is *eklektoi.* "The Greek word *eklektoi* can mean "chosen," but it can also be translated "worthy," "pure," "choice," "excellent.""[965] The point is that the context in which the word "chosen" is used is a determining factor in establishing its meaning. In other words, the man in this parable had no wedding garment. Hence, he was "not chosen" or "not worthy" to remain among the other wedding guest at the banquet. The application is that many are called to the wedding feast with Jesus Christ, but only those robed in His righteousness will be "chosen" or "worthy" to participate. Those without a robe of Jesus' righteousness, those unbelievers who are only pretending to be believers will be cast into "outer darkness" or "hell" and "there will be weeping and gnashing of teeth."[966] The Lord is sovereign and the "fear of the Lord is the beginning of wisdom."[967] Therefore, "do not fear those who kill the body but cannot kill the soul. But rather fear Him who is able to destroy both soul and body in hell."[968]

---

962. Matt. 22:14.

963. Brian Simmons, tran., *The Passion Translation: New Testament* (BroadStreet Publishing, 2017).

964. Matt. 20:28

965. Brian Simmons, tran., *The Passion Translation: New Testament* (BroadStreet Publishing, 2017).

966. Matt. 22:13.

967. Psa. 111:10; Prov. 9:10.

968. Matt. 10:28; Heb. 10:31.

In this parable there is no mention of anyone one who was not called to the wedding of the king's son. However, many eliminated themselves from among the "chosen." The first group were invited but "were not willing to come." So, they were not "chosen." The second group invited by the king not only made light of the invitation, but "seized his servants, treated them spitefully, and killed them." As a result, none of them were "chosen." And in the third place a man accepted the invitation and came to the banquet but had no wedding garment. Hence, he was not "chosen." However, the "wedding hall was filled with guest." God has purposed and will have "ten thousand times ten thousand, and thousands of thousands" of guests at the "marriage supper of the Lamb."[969] Therefore, "let us be glad and rejoice and give Him glory!"

The Parable of the Wise and Foolish Virgins:

This next parable has to do with preparedness. Just prior to this parable Jesus taught regarding cultural conditions on earth prior to His second coming. The second coming of the Lord is a pillar of hope and a fundamental belief in the life of every believer. All believers hope for and live in expectation of the day when the trumpet of the Lord shall sound, and we are caught up to meet the Lord in the air. It is the day when grace is turned into glory. And to spend that next period of time at the marriage supper of the Lamb is an experience that none of us want to miss. A key to our participation in that marriage celebration is to be prepared or to be ready to meet the Lord our Bridegroom when He suddenly comes for His bride! In this parable Jesus reveals that His delay in coming is not an excuse for our unpreparedness. He states:

> Then the kingdom of heaven shall be likened to ten virgins who took their lamps and went out to meet

---

969. Rev. 5:11, 19:7.

> the bridegroom. Now five of them were wise, and five *were* foolish. Those who *were* foolish took their lamps and took no oil with them, but the wise took oil in their vessels with their lamps. But while the bridegroom was delayed, they all slumbered and slept. And at midnight a cry was *heard:* 'Behold, the bridegroom is coming; go out to meet him!' Then all those virgins arose and trimmed their lamps. And the foolish said to the wise, 'Give us *some* of your oil, for our lamps are going out.' But the wise answered, saying, '*No,* lest there should not be enough for us and you; but go rather to those who sell, and buy for yourselves.' And while they went to buy, the bridegroom came, and those who were ready went in with him to the wedding; and the door was shut. Afterward the other virgins came also, saying, 'Lord, Lord, open to us!' But he answered and said, 'Assuredly, I say to you, I do not know you.' Watch therefore, for you know neither the day nor the hour in which the Son of Man is coming. (Matt. 25:1-13)

The kingdom of heaven is likened to ten virgins, five were wise and five were foolish. All ten virgins were anticipating the arrival of the bridegroom. The five wise virgins demonstrated personal diligence by bringing enough oil to be prepared for the festivities that followed the bridegroom's arrival. However, the other five virgins were defined by Jesus as foolish because they were not diligent in preparing for the sudden arrival of the bridegroom. They expressed their irresponsibility by asking the others to give them oil from their supply. There are many, many opportunities to share what we have with others, but the time for those opportunities was over. Therefore, the wise virgins had to say “no, lest there should not be for us and you; but go rather to those who sell and buy for yourselves.”[970]

There are three key concepts that unlock the mystery of the parable. The first key concerns each person’s responsibility to be prepared for the coming of the Bridegroom. Jesus is stating this parable just two days prior to His crucifixion and He is trying to prepare His listeners for things they did not yet understand. They still thought that He is going to deliver Israel from Roman bondage. Even His disciples really did not understand what was taking place.[971] But Jesus was impressing upon His listeners the need to be prepared for a future event that would happen suddenly. Jesus had just concluded His teaching about “the end of the age” where He admonished His disciples with these words:

> But know this, that if the master of the house had known what hour the thief would come, he would have watched and not allowed his house to be broken into. Therefore, you also be ready for the Son of Man is coming at an hour you do not expect. (Matthew 24:43-44)

Since the ascension of Jesus, the Church has been looking forward to His return with hopeful expectation. But it has been two thousand years and He still has not returned. And in this parable, it was while the bridegroom was delayed all the virgins “slumbered and slept.”[972] It really does not matter how diligent a person is or how religious one may become, everybody requires sleep. And it was while they slept that “a cry was heard: ‘Behold the bridegroom is coming; go out and meet him!’”[973] And it was only the wise virgins, the ones prepared with enough oil who went with the bridegroom into the wedding cel-

970. Matt. 25:9-10.
971. Luke 24:19-27.
972. Matt. 25:5.
973. Matt. 25:6.

ebration. Are you prepared to meet the Lord? Today is the day of salvation, a day of opportunity to prepare to meet the Lord Jesus. "The night is far spent; the day is at hand."[974] Earlier, Jesus had taught regarding His sudden second coming. He said, "Therefore you also be ready, for the Son of Man is coming at an hour you do not expect."[975] Just as in the days of Noah before the flood, people "were eating and drinking, marrying and giving in marriage, until the day that Noah entered the ark and did not know until the flood came and took them away, so will the coming of the Son of man be."[976] Let's not allow personal carelessness or negligence distract us from being prepared and watchful for the coming of the Lord.

The second mystery revealed in this parable is the tragedy of preparing too late. The five foolish virgins went to buy oil, but when they returned the bridegroom and the five wise virgins had already gone into the wedding celebration and the door was shut. The foolish virgins called out saying, "'Lord, Lord open to us!' But he answered and said, 'Assuredly, I say to you, I do not know you.'"[977] The opportunity to participate in the celebration was now beyond the point of being accomplished—the door was shut and the awful words of rejection "I do not know you" were spoken. They were now prepared, but it was too late! Have you ever gotten to the airline loading gate and it was too late—the gate was already closed? You missed your plane and now faced the consequences of being too late. You feel disappointed and frustrated as you work out the details of trying to arrange another flight. However, when the Lord Jesus returns for His bride there is only one opportunity to be caught-up to meet the Lord in the air.[978] There will be no other flight, no second chance. Today is the day of preparation, not tomorrow. "Behold, now is the accepted time;

974. Rom. 13:12.
975. Matt. 24:44.
976. Matt. 24:37-39.
977. Matt. 25:11b.
978. 1 Thes. 4:16-17.

behold, now is the day of salvation."[979] As the Prophet Amos declared, "Prepare to meet your God!"[980] Prepare now before it is too late! Jesus concluded this parable by saying; "Watch therefore, for you know neither the day nor the hour in which the Son of Man is coming."[981]

The third and final mystery is a question that needs to be answered; "What does the oil represent in this parable?" It was the matter of having or not having enough oil that distinguished between "wise virgins" and the "foolish virgins." The consequences of not having enough oil had the tragic effect of causing the foolish virgins to be unprepared to enter the wedding celebration with the bridegroom and the wise virgins. In the Scripture the anointing of the Holy Spirit is symbolized by the anointing with oil. Aaron and his sons were anointed with the anointing oil.[982] Samuel anointed David with a horn of oil.[983] Isaiah speaks of the "oil of joy."[984] Jesus speaking to the Church of the Laodiceans said, "anoint your eyes with eye salve, that you may see."[985] These examples illustrate that oil is used as a symbol of the person and work of the Holy Spirit.

Most believers agree that the anointing oil symbolizes the Holy Spirit. It was at the River Jordan where Jesus was baptized in the water by John the Baptist, and coming up out of the water Jesus prayed. We do not know what He prayed but it may well have been the prayer of Isaiah; "Oh, that You would rent the heavens and come down."[986] We do know the heavens opened and the Holy Spirit came upon Him.[987] Later, while ministering in the synagogue at Nazareth Jesus testified saying, "the Spirit of the Lord is upon Me because He

---

979. 2 Cor. 6:2b.
980. Amos 4:12.
981. Matt. 25:13.
982. Exod. 29:4-7.
983. 1 Sam. 16:13.
984. Isa. 61:3
985. Rev. 3:18b.
986. Isa. 64:1.
987. Matt. 3:16; Luke 3:21-22.

has anointed Me…"[988] The point is that Jesus was born of the Holy Spirit, but it wasn't until He was anointed by the Holy Spirit that He entered into ministry of proclaiming the gospel of the kingdom and performing miracles.[989]

The Holy Spirit is not a doctrine or faith proposition. He is God and desires a personal relationship with every believer. And "if anyone does not have the Spirit of Christ, he is none of His." For "the Spirit Himself bears witness with our spirit that we are the children of God."[990] Is it a possibility that the foolish virgins lacked a personal relationship with the Holy Spirit? Is it possible that they could have been born again but had never been filled with or baptized in the Holy Spirit? Were they lacking the power to be the witnesses that God had purposed for them to be? One thing is for sure, they were lacking oil. And oil was of such importance that not having it excluded them from the wedding celebration.

It was my experience to be born again at twelve years of age. My life was changed, and the Holy Spirit bore witness that I was saved. But at age thirty-four I received the baptism of the Holy Spirit and my witness radically changed. All of us want to go to heaven when we die. But between now and the time we die the Lord Jesus wants us to proclaim the gospel of the kingdom with power.[991] The Apostle Paul said, "And my speech and my preaching *were* not with persuasive words of human wisdom, but in demonstration of the Spirit and of power, that your faith should not be in the wisdom of men but in the power of God."[992]

I cannot be certain in answering the question, "What did the oil represent in this parable?" But I personally believe the foolish virgins were unprepared to participate in the wedding festivities because they did not have the anointing of the Holy Spirit. The Scripture says, "If

---

988. Luke 4:18.
989. Matt. 1:18; Luke 1:35; John 3:3-8; Acts 1:8.
990. Rom. 8:9, 16.
991. Matt. 24:14.
992. 1 Cor. 2:4-5.

anyone is sick let them call for the elders of the church, and let them pray over him, anointing him with oil in the name of the Lord. And the prayer of faith will save the sick."[993] After His resurrection and before His ascension Jesus "breathed on them [disciples], and said to them, 'Receive the Holy Spirit.'"[994] But just before His ascension He commanded them "not to depart from Jerusalem, but wait for the promise of the Father…. You shall be baptized with the Holy Spirit not many days from now."[995] Then when the Day of Pentecost had fully come, they were "filled with the Holy Spirit." Their lives and ministries were empowered with an anointing to proclaim the gospel with such dramatic power that the small group of Jesus' disciples impacted the entire world with the hope and glory of an unshakable eternal kingdom of righteousness, peace, and joy in the Holy Spirit! If you have not received the anointing of the Holy Spirit are you prepared to meet our Bridegroom?

The Parable of the Talents:

Jesus continued teaching His disciples while at the Mount of Olives. He immediately followed the parable of the Wise and Foolish Virgins by teaching the Parable of the Talents.

> For *the kingdom of heaven is* like a man traveling to a far country, *who* called his own servants and delivered his goods to them. And to one he gave five talents, to another two, and to another one, to each according to his own ability; and immediately he went on a journey. Then he who had received the five talents went and traded with them and made another five talents. And likewise, he who *had received* two gained two more also. But he who had received one

993. James 5:14-15.
994. John 20:22.
995. Acts 1:4-5.

went and dug in the ground and hid his lord's money. After a long time, the lord of those servants came and settled accounts with them. So, he who had received five talents came and brought five other talents, saying, 'Lord, you delivered to me five talents; look, I have gained five more talents besides them.' His lord said to him, 'Well *done,* good and faithful servant; you were faithful over a few things, I will make you ruler over many things. Enter into the joy of your lord.' He also who had received two talents came and said, 'Lord, you delivered to me two talents; look, I have gained two more talents besides them.' His lord said to him, 'Well *done,* good and faithful servant; you have been faithful over a few things, I will make you ruler over many things. Enter into the joy of your lord.' Then he who had received the one talent came and said, 'Lord, I knew you to be a hard man, reaping where you have not sown, and gathering where you have not scattered seed. And I was afraid and went and hid your talent in the ground. Look, *there* you have *what is* yours.' But his lord answered and said to him, 'You wicked and lazy servant, you knew that I reap where I have not sown and gather where I have not scattered seed. So, you ought to have deposited my money with the bankers, and at my coming I would have received back my own with interest. Therefore, take the talent from him, and give *it* to him who has ten talents. For to everyone who has, more will be given, and he will have abundance; but from him who does not have, even what he has will be taken away. And cast the unprofitable servant into the outer darkness. There will be weeping and gnashing of teeth.' (Matthew 25:14-30)

Again, Jesus begins this parable as He had on other occasions with the words, "For the kingdom of heaven is like." Jesus is impressing upon His hearers the reality of what the kingdom of heaven is like and how it functions. He knows that He will be crucified in a couple of days and He is preparing His disciples for what lays ahead. So, Jesus described "a man traveling to a far country, who called his own servants and delivered his goods to them."[996] The Apostles probably did not realize how closely those words paralleled with what they were experiencing. Jesus was in the process of entrusting these apostles with stewarding the precious treasures of the kingdom of God. While He will Himself be ascending to heaven for an undetermined length of time. This parable will help us understand that the stewardship given to us by God is no small nor trivial matter.

The man did not simply distribute his talents indiscriminately to just anyone, but to "his own servants." A talent in this parable is not an ability but a measured weight of gold. He also demonstrated wisdom in that he entrusted his valuables to each servant according to that servant's personal ability. "To one he gave five talents, to another two, and to another one.... And immediately he went on a journey."[997] This parable focuses on the servant's responsibility to be a profitable steward with that with which he was personally entrusted. There will come a day when each servant will be required to give an account for that with which he was entrusted. Jesus had earlier taught, "For everyone to whom much is given, from him much will be required; and to whom much has been committed, of him they will ask the more."[998] All believers in Jesus Christ are entrusted with the treasure of the gospel of the kingdom. "We have this treasure in earthen vessels, that the excellence of the power may be of God and not of us."[999] So, this parable is applicable to every believer.

---

996. Matt. 25:14.
997. Matt. 25:15
998. Luke 12:48.
999. 2 Cor. 4:7.

The first servant took the five talents and entered business transactions that invariably entailed risk. But his faithfulness proved profitable because he gained five more talents. The second servant did likewise and gained two more talents. But the servant having one talent went and "dug in the ground and hid his lord's money."[1000] Hiding valuables in the ground seems strange to us, but some people did that because there were no banks in those days. Hence, people would hide their valuables in the ground to protect them from being stolen by thieves or military raiders. However, these talents were not given to those servants for short term safekeeping, but for long term investment. Just as the gospel of the kingdom is not given to us for safe keeping but to be proclaimed in the world where we invest our lives.

The first servant invested the five talents given to him and through his trading made another five talents. The second servant invested his two talents and gained two more. But the third servant failed to comprehend the purpose for which he was entrusted with the one talent and buried it in the ground. "After a long time, the lord of those servants came and settled accounts with them."[1001] The words "settled accounts" indicates that the servants were given the talents for investment, not for safekeeping.

When the lord came and settled with the first servant who had been given five talents and had gained another five talents he said, "Well *done,* good and faithful servant; you were faithful over a few things, I will make you ruler over many things. Enter into the joy of your lord."[1002] When the lord settled with the second servant who had been given two talents and had gained two more talents he said, "Well *done,* good and faithful servant; you have been faithful over a few things, I will make you ruler over many things. Enter into the joy of your lord."[1003] Even though the lord had been gone "a long time" both servants proved to be faithful in fulfilling their responsibilities.

1000. Matt. 25:18.
1001. Matt. 25:19.
1002. Matt. 25:21.
1003. Matt. 25:23.

Often a delay in settlement is what really tests one's faithfulness. For example, when Moses delayed his return from the meeting with God on Mount Sinai the children of Israel grew restless and said to Aaron, "Come, make us gods that shall go before us; for *as for* this Moses, the man who brought us up out of the land of Egypt, we do not know what has become of him."[1004] Moses proved faithful but Aaron and the children of Israel missed the mark of faithfulness.[1005] As the Lord Jesus has been gone for a seemingly longtime, scoffers will come and saying "Where is the promise of His coming? For since the fathers fell asleep, all things continue as they were from the beginning of creation."[1006] Faithfulness includes persevering, not quitting. Faithfulness is the tenacity to keep on keeping on, even through a long period of time. Earlier this same day Jesus had admonished the Apostles with the words, "He who endures to the end shall be saved."[1007] Jesus is revealing that one of the mysteries of the kingdom of God is "faithfulness." Our God is faithful and when we are faithful, it is evidence of our becoming partakers of His divine nature. The faithfulness of these first two servants was rewarded with an increase of being made rulers "over many things."[1008] Their faithfulness had not been in vain. "Therefore, my beloved brethren, be steadfast, immovable, always abounding in the work of the Lord, knowing that your labor is not in vain in the Lord."[1009]

The lord commended the first two servants as "good and faithful servants." He then gave them this imperative, "enter into the joy of your lord." As their lord, he experienced an increase of wealth because of their faithfulness. Therefore, he rewards them with the increase of authority that empowered them to enter the same joy he is experiencing. Jesus is very intentional in this parable when speaking

1004. Exod. 32:1.
1005. Num. 12:7.
1006. 2 Peter 3:4.
1007. Matt. 24:15.
1008. Matt. 25:21-23.
1009. 1 Cor. 15:58.

about joy. Only a couple of days later Jesus said, "These things I have spoken to you, that My joy may remain in you, and that your joy may be full."[1010] Joy is not an addendum to the kingdom of God, but at the very core of its nature. Keep in mind that the kingdom of God is not about sacrifices and offerings, but "righteousness, peace and joy in the Holy Spirit."[1011] Nehemiah expressed it succinctly when he declared, "The joy of the Lord is our strength."[1012] In other words the privilege of expanded authority is a good thing, but the greater reality is the satisfaction of partaking of the Lord's joy, a reward for our faithfulness. How wonderfully blessed to hear the words, "Well done good and faithful servant; you were faithful over a few things, I will make you a ruler over many things. Enter into the joy of your lord."[1013]

Then the servant who had received one talent came and proclaimed what he knew. He said, "I knew you to be a hard man, reaping where you had not sown, and gathering where you had not scattered seed." The lord did not deny these facts but rather affirmed them. Neither did he accept this servant's lame excuse. It is obvious that this servant had limited ability because his lord entrusted him with only one talent. Yet he projected his limitations onto his lord which in turn paralyzed faith's moral obligation to sow into possibilities for gain; leaving him afraid and eventually robbed of the blessings of faithfulness.

This servant's lord rebuked him, calling him a "wicked and lazy servant."[1014] Wickedness is the exact opposite of faithful and expresses the concept of being untrustworthy or undependable. And lazy expresses the unwillingness to exert the energy required to make a positive decision. He allowed fear to paralyze his faith and crush his ability to simply deposit the talent with the bankers and gain interest. He hid the one talent in the ground. Therefore, his lord said, "take

---

1010. John 15:11.
1011. Rom. 14:17.
1012. Neh. 8:10.
1013. Matt. 25:21.
1014. Matt. 25:26.

the talent from him, and give it to him who has ten talents."[1015] The unprofitable servant wasted his opportunity to be a good and faithful steward, and was cast into the outer darkness where there will be weeping and gnashing of teeth. This is a good place to remind ourselves that we serve in the kingdom of God out of a heart of love for our Lord—not out of fear. Our Lord says what He means and means what He says, but He is not a "hard man."[1016] He is a loving and compassionate Master who expects us to be faithful stewards of all the treasures of the kingdom with which He has entrusted us. There is coming a day when each of us will give an account to the Lord. And all of us look forward to hearing; Well done, good and faithful servant. Enter the joy of your Lord.

Jesus concluded this parable with a powerful kingdom principle; "For to everyone who has, more will be given, and he will have abundance; but from him who does not have, even what he has will be taken from him."[1017] This principle begins with "everyone who has." Abundance begins with first accepting and valuing what God has already given, no matter how small. For example, Jesus took two fish and five loaves and fed over five thousand people. The Apostle Paul started ministry in Ephesus with a group of twelve men, but within three years "all who lived in Asia heard the word of the Lord Jesus Christ."[1018] A mustard seed is very small but will grow large. It is God who increases a small thing into more and increases the more into an abundance. We can plant and water, but it is "God who gives the increase."[1019]

Therefore, we are not to despise the day of small things. This seems counter intuitive to us because we live in a culture that emphasizes bigness. Who has the biggest home, car, boat, TV, bank account, or the biggest congregation, etc.? The servant in this parable was given

1015. Matt. 25:28.
1016. Matt. 25:24.
1017. Matt. 25:29.
1018. Acts 19:7-10.
1019. 1 Cor. 3:7.

just one talent. This may seem like a small portion as compared with the portions given to the other servants, but not too small for God to multiply. However, this man was afraid and unable to trust God to multiply his talent. As a result, his lord took that talent from him and gave it to the servant with ten talents and had the unprofitable servant cast into the outer darkness. When we allow fear to restrict our vision to the level of our personal limited resource and wisdom rather than visualizing our situation from God's unlimited resources, we reduce God to man's capacity. That is idolatry and an abomination to God, whereby we forfeit the little we do have. God will not turn the abundance of His kingdom over to idolaters. We, the servants of the Lord, are here on earth to represent God and His kingdom. And try as we might, the truth is that "without Him we can do nothing."[1020] The wicked and lazy servant was not sent to detention for a couple of days, but cast into eternal darkness where there will be weeping and gnashing of teeth. What a solemn warning as Jesus concludes this parable.

Summary:

In this chapter and the previous one we have discussed fourteen different parables Jesus used to reveal insights regarding the kingdom of God. Of course, there are other parables of Jesus that are not covered in the two chapters. But the parables that we have discussed are sufficient to help us grasp at least a portion of the wisdom that Jesus has revealed about the kingdom. "All these things Jesus spoke to the multitude in parables; and without a parable He did not speak to them."[1021] These parables conceal kingdom mysteries in very ordinary language that hides their wisdom from natural understanding.[1022] They unveil realities of the kingdom of God that the Holy Spirit is helping us apply to our present experience as citizens of the kingdom. In the

---

1020. John 15:1-5.
1021. Matt. 13:34.
1022. 1 Cor. 2:14.

next chapter we will turn our attention to the relationship between prayer and the kingdom of God.

CHAPTER SEVEN

PRAYER AND THE KINGDOM

"Your kingdom come. Your will be done on earth as it is in heaven."

Matthew 6:10

Jesus made an insightful statement regarding prayer saying, "When you pray do not use vain repetitions as the heathen do. For they think they will be heard for their many words. Therefore, do not be like them."[1023] Biblical prayer is man communing with God. By His nature God is a Father and from creation He has desired fellowship with those created in His image and likeness. He loves intimate fellowship and communion with His children. God created Adam and Eve with a DNA to commune with Him and each other. One of the cruelest punishments imposed upon any individual is to seclude that person in solitary confinement. In other words, man has woven into the fabric of his nature a propensity for intimate communion with God. So, the essence of prayer is much more than a religious ritual of memorized words. It is a relational concept of confiding with a loving Father who is willing and able to respond beyond what we may ask or think.

However, after Adam sinned his communion with God was altered, because His sin separated him from God. He was no longer morally pure and full of light, but his heart was darkened and hostile

1023. Matt. 6:7-8.

toward God. Adam passed his sinful nature on to his children and his oldest son, Cain, was a murderer. Of course, not all of Adam's children were murderers, but all mankind experiences the darkness, pain, frustrations, and exasperations of life apart from God. The Scripture says, *"There is none righteous, no, not one; There is none who understands; There is none who seeks after God. They have all turned aside; They have together become unprofitable; There is none who does good, no, not one."*[1024] This passage makes it clear that man in his sinful state is not seeking to commune with God or pray to Him. But sinful man at his best reduces communion with God to a religious experience without God and often accuses or blames God of evil. Mankind in his ungodly condition tends to worship idols that cannot hear nor answer prayer.

The Prayer of Elijah:

Man, in his darken sinful state gropes for God and blindly settles for fellowship with false gods. To commune with and/or please their false gods, man often made long prayers. For example, the following Scripture records a confrontation between Elijah and the prophets of Baal. The Baal worshippers prayed from morning to mid-afternoon trying to get their god to hear them.

> So, they took the bull which was given them, and they prepared *it,* and called on the name of Baal from morning even till noon, saying, "O Baal, hear us!" But *there was* no voice; no one answered. Then they leaped about the altar which they had made. And so, it was, at noon, that Elijah mocked them and said, 'Cry aloud, for he *is* a god; either he is meditating, or he is busy, or he is on a journey, *or* perhaps he is sleeping and must be awakened.' So, they cried aloud, and

---

1024. Rom. 3:10-12.

> cut themselves, as was their custom, with knives and lances, until the blood gushed out on them. And when midday was past, they prophesied until the *time* of the offering of the *evening* sacrifice. But *there was* no voice; no one answered, no one paid attention. (1 Kings 18:26-29)

Unlike the idolaters Elijah prayed the following one sentence prayer: "Hear me, O LORD, hear me, that this people may know that You *are* the LORD God, and *that* You have turned their hearts back *to You* again."[1025] And the Lord immediately answered by fire. James had Elijah in mind when he said, "The effective, fervent prayer of a righteous man avails much."[1026] The prayers of the Old Testament Prophets were much more than "vain repetitions" and the recital of memorized phrases—they were an outpouring from the heart; believing that God was willing and able to deliver them from their troubles.

The Prayer of Solomon:

In the Pentateuch, communion with God was most often initiated by God Himself. Even when Abraham offered his son Isaac on Mount Moriah, he remained silent regarding prayer. But by the time David became King of Israel, prayer was taking a more central role in man's relationship with God. Many, many prayers are recorded in the Psalms and Prophets. One of the longest and most powerful prayers recorded in the Old Testament is the prayer of Solomon at the dedication of the newly completed Temple. It was not a silent prayer, but delivered as Solomon first stood and then knelt "before the altar of the Lord in the presence of all the assembly of Israel and spread out his hands toward heaven" and prayed to the LORD God of Israel.[1027]

1025. 1 Kings 18:37.
1026. James 5:16b.
1027. 1 Kings 8:22-61; 2 Chro. 6:12-42.

A remarkable observation regarding Solomon's prayer is that numerous times throughout his prayer he petitions the Lord to hear the prayers of the people of Israel when they pray "to You toward this temple" or "towards this city."[1028] The Temple in Jerusalem was the dwelling place of God's presence and the place where He communed with Israel through mediatorial ministry of the Levitical Priesthood. It was the place where the Children of Israel expected their sacrifices and offerings to be received, their sins forgiven, petitions, supplications and prayers to be heard. For example, while Daniel was living as a captive in Babylon and facing his hour of crisis, he went home and into his upper room; "with his windows open toward Jerusalem, he knelt down on his knees three times a day and gave thanks before his God, as was his custom."[1029] The Old Testament saints were not yet granted with the privileged access to God's throne in heaven as New Testament Believers enjoy.

Because of the finished redemptive work of Jesus Christ our great and faithful High Priest and the indwelling presence of the Holy Spirit, we as New Testament Believers are already seated in heavenly places where our lives are hidden with Christ in God.[1030] Therefore, we do not pray toward Jerusalem as Solomon, Daniel, and the Old Testament saints. But we are invited by the Lord "to come boldly to the throne of grace, that we may obtain mercy and find grace to help in our time of need."[1031] "Now this is the confidence that we have in Him, that if we ask anything according to His will, He hears us."[1032]

Prayer isn't a religious ritual practiced to merely inform God of our needs and twist His benevolent arm to get what we want. Rather, prayer is an act of humility and faith through which we express our dependence upon the riches of God's grace and abundant provisions for His children. A "father" in Biblical terms is one who provides for

1028. 1 Kings 8:29-30, 33, 35, 38, 42, 44, 48.
1029. Dan. 6:10.
1030. Col. 3:3.
1031. Heb. 4:16.
1032. 1 John 5:14.

His children. Jesus said, "Your Father knows the things you have need of before you ask Him."[1033] Of course we are to make our request known to God, but our prayers are not to be mainly informing God as much as it is expressing our dependence upon Him as our Father. The Palmist said, "I have been young, and *now* am old; Yet I have not seen the righteous forsaken, Nor his descendants begging bread."[1034] God has not paid the high price of reconciling us to Himself to abandon us as beggars. However, under the demands and pressures of the moment, we may be tempted to become anxious by overlooking how deeply God loves us, and yield to unbelief by trying to persuade God to fulfill our grocery list of needs. But always remember that our Father desires to meet all our needs and commune with us through every challenge we face.

God has provided ready access into His presence through Jesus Christ our great and faithful High Priest. The Father so enjoys personal communion with each of His children that Jesus said, "No longer do I call you servants, for a servant does not know what his master is doing; but I have called you friends, for all things that I heard from My Father I have made known to you."[1035] So, New Testament prayer is communion between friends. Yes, we have many needs requiring heaven's help, and yes, we need to pray without ceasing. But prayer is communing with God in the confident expectation of His positive response to our request and the assurance that His purposes will be accomplished. Then "His kingdom will come, and His will be accomplished on earth as it is in heaven."[1036] It is our privilege and responsibility to always pray and not lose heart.[1037] And praying in tongues is speaking to God beyond the limits of our vocabulary and reason about things that are beyond our present comprehension.

1033. Matt. 6:8.
1034. Psa. 37:25.
1035. John 15:15
1036. Paraphrase of Matt. 6:10; Heb. 11:6.
1037. Luke 18:1.

Considering my personal prayer life and years of pastoral ministry it is evident there are many occasions when we desperately need heaven's intervention. However, we often feel helpless and stand perplexed by our lack of understanding and insight regarding the circumstances in which we find ourselves. I can say without reservation, there are many occasions when "we do not know what we should pray as we ought." But God has made provision for us to gain insight into heaven's perspective through the ministry of the Holy Spirit. The Father has given us the gift of the Holy Spirit who makes intercession for us with groanings which cannot be uttered."[1038] Thank the Lord for the gift of the Holy Spirit and thanks to the Holy Spirit for the gift of unknown tongues. "For he who speaks in a tongue does not speak to men but to God, for no one understands *him;* however, in the spirit he speaks mysteries."[1039]

As in The Days of Noah:

Living today in the onslaught of darkness, wickedness, and lawlessness that characterizes our present culture is a challenge for all believers. The deluge of ungodliness distresses and wearies us just as those same conditions vexed Noah and Lot prior to God's intervention with judgment. Jesus said,

> And as it was in the days of Noah, so it will be also in the days of the Son of Man: They ate, they drank, they married wives, they were given in marriage, until the day that Noah entered the ark, and the flood came and destroyed them all. Likewise as it was also in the days of Lot: They ate, they drank, they bought, they sold, they planted, they built; but on the day that Lot went out of Sodom it rained fire and brimstone from heaven and destroyed *them* all. Even so will it

---

1038. Rom. 8:26.
1039. 1 Cor. 14:2.

> be in the day when the Son of Man is revealed. (Luke 17:26-30)

Consider the extent of immorality practiced in our culture today as more and more couples are living together out of wedlock, sexual perversion is being accepted even in many churches. More and more homes are without two parents because too many fathers are absent. Many of our prisons are filled beyond capacity, schools and places of worship have become targets of murder, and numbers of addictions are at all-time high. Some television programs are so vulgar and violent that even adults should not watch them. Yet the economy is roaring at a prosperous rate. There is an overabundance of delicious, nutritious, and affordable food. Just think about how much food gets thrown away every day in school cafeterias, restaurants, and supermarkets throughout our communities! So, how does our culture differ from the culture in the days of Lot or Noah?

Is the solution to the violence, pain, brokenness, and wickedness to be found in the classrooms of academia or the chambers of congress or in our financial institutions? All of us know that each of these institutions fulfill useful roles in our culture, but real solutions to the problems we face will have to come through an intervention of God. The question is, will He intervene through the intercessions of His sons and daughters or will He have to intervene in judgment?

When the City State of Nineveh was within 40 days of judgment, God sent the Prophet Jonah to preach the message of repentance and the nation repented and averted judgment. When the Babylonian Empire was reveling in prideful arrogance God spoke to Nebuchadnezzar in a dream and gave the Prophet Daniel the interpretation which was a warning of judgment. However, Nebuchadnezzar continued in his self-centered glory until God imposed seven years of judgment upon him as Daniel had prophesied. After judgment Nebuchadnezzar returned to power and gave this testimony: "Now I, Nebuchadnezzar, praise and extol and honor the King of heaven, all whose works *are* truth, and His ways justice. And those who walk in pride He is able to put down."[1040]

Praying in The Spirit:

Four hundred years before the birth of Jesus the people of Israel had grown indifferent towards God. They were dishonoring God by half-hearted worship, bringing poor quality offerings and sacrifices to the Temple. They were robbing God of the tithes. They were divorcing their wives and marrying pagan wives. They were involved in witchcraft, idolatry, and lying, thereby provoking God's judgment against them. In the midst of their decadence God raised up the Prophet Malachi to bring the following prophetic message:

> Behold, I will send you Elijah the prophet Before the coming of the great and dreadful day of the LORD. And he will turn the hearts of the fathers to the children, And the hearts of the children to their fathers, Lest I come and strike the earth with a curse." (Malachi 4:5-6)

As we have been experiencing the moral decay taking place in our nation, we have also been experiencing the Holy Spirit raising up Churches empowered by the Holy Spirit across our nation and world. The Spirit of the Lord is raising up a prophetic standard of holiness and righteousness. Joel prophesied and the Apostle Peter affirmed on the Day of Pentecost that in the last days God would "pour out of His Spirit on all flesh; our sons and daughters would prophesy."[1041] Isn't it a reality that God is raising up our sons and daughters to speak prophetically against the humanistic forces of hell that the post-modern world have released among us?

1040. Daniel 4:37.
1041. Joel 2:28; Acts 2:17.

Many of us have memorized the four spiritual laws to better enable us to do the ministry of evangelism. We prepare special events and publicize them to attract those not walking with Jesus. At some point during that event we faithfully call all in attendance to make a decision to follow Jesus Christ. Many times, we lead everyone present in a prayer of repentance and invite Jesus to be our Lord and Savior. Most of our sermons conclude with an altar call. All these things are good and wonderful, and we should keep doing them. Absolutely! But the question being addressed here is what about the person attending our services for thirty years and serves faithfully? Many of them have rededicated their lives to the Lord several times over the years and rejoice exceedingly when others get saved. They embrace the ongoing day to day disciplines of a maturing believer—but they get discouraged and weary and need to be edified. They need to be refreshed and built up in the faith. Are we encouraging them to pray in tongues? The Scripture says, "But you, beloved, building yourselves up on your most holy faith, praying in the Holy Spirit."[1042]

The point I want to emphasize is the ongoing need for the edification among the members of our flock. That is the edification of the believer and building up in the faith by a means that God has so graciously provided. Too often praying in tongues has not been encouraged nor practiced, while the powers of darkness continue to attack and pound believers from every angle. Many hearts become discouraged and vexed by the vulgar and immoral culture around us as well as enduring personal attacks of the enemy. Jesus said, "Because lawlessness will abound, the love of many will grow cold."[1043] Praying and praising God through the gift of tongues is not a cure-all but a positive means of edification that every believer can experience every day.

It's not a matter of encouraging tongues that would be confusing to unbelievers or disruptive in any of our services. It is a concern to

---

1042. Jude 1:20.
1043. Matt. 24:12

encourage our people to keep on practicing the gift of tongues and thereby experiencing the edification that comes through communing with the Holy Spirt in personal devotions and small groups, etc. The Apostle Paul said, "I thank my God I speak with tongues more than you all."[1044]

Another point that needs to be considered is that as we pray in tongues, we should also pray for the interpretation of tongues. Tongues and the interpretation of tongues is equivalent to prophecy. It was while praying in tongues and singing in tongues that I suddenly began to speak and sing in English, with the witness in my heart that the English words were the interpretation of the unknown tongues that I had just spoken. It was and continues to be an edifying experience. The Apostle Paul told the Corinthians "I wish you all spoke with tongues, but even more that you prophesied; for he who prophesies *is* greater than he who speaks with tongues, unless indeed he interprets, that the church may receive edification."[1045]

The Lord throughout the Old Testament powerfully intervened not only in the life of Israel but also in other nations through His prophets. We emphasize the following prophecy of Isaiah during the Christmas season:

> For unto us a Child is born, unto us a Son is given; And the government will be upon His shoulder. And His name will be called Wonderful, Counselor, Mighty God, Everlasting Father, Prince of Peace. Of the increase of *His* government and peace *There will be* no end, Upon the throne of David and over His kingdom, to order it and establish it with judgment and justice from that time forward, even forever. The zeal of the LORD of hosts will perform this. (Isaiah 9:6-7)

1044. 1 Cor. 14:18.
1045. 1 Cor. 14:5

Isaiah's prophecy focuses our attention on the reality that the government is not on the shoulders of the Democrats, Republicans, Socialists, Marxist, or any other political party. They do perform an important function in the purposes of God by maintaining peace and order until the fulness of the Gentiles has come. But God is sovereign over all forms of governments. Our sovereign God has decreed, "I have set My King on My holy hill of Zion."[1046] The Apostle Paul writes,

> God has highly exalted Him and given Him the name, which is above every name, that at the name of Jesus every knee should bow of those in heaven, and those on earth, and those under the earth and *that* every tongue should confess that Jesus Christ *is* Lord, to the glory of God the Father."[1047] (Phil. 2:9-11)

The governments of this world are a temporary provision that God has ordained to constrain anarchy and keep order among the nations until the "fullness of the Gentiles." The Apostle John saw the day when Gentile governments had fulfilled their function: "and there were loud voices in heaven, saying, 'The kingdoms of this world have become *the kingdoms* of our Lord and of His Christ, and He shall reign forever and ever!'"[1048]

There was a day when Malachi's prophecy, as referred to earlier in this chapter, was partially fulfilled with the ministry of John the Baptist. He prepared the way for Jesus Christ. And Jesus inaugurated the presence of the kingdom of God on earth amid this world of spiritual impotency and hostility. He began His ministry by preaching; "The time is fulfilled; the kingdom of God is at hand. Repent, and believe in the gospel."[1049] The picture is that of a king entering enemy

---

1046. Psa. 2:6.
1047. Phil. 2:9-11.
1048. Rev. 11:15.
1049. Mark 1:15.

territory and taking over. Jesus said, "I will build My Church and the gates of hell shall not prevail against it."[1050] The Church of Jesus Christ is man's entry point into the kingdom of God. It is the training ground for the Lord's ambassadors as we infiltrate every aspect of society and bring the blessing of the gospel of kingdom of God upon every person.

Co-laboring With Jesus In Prayer:

Most believers desire to pray and co-labor with Jesus in bringing the blessing of the kingdom of God upon our families, communities, and nation. However, most believers can pray for about ten or fifteen minutes and then seem to run out of things for which to pray. There probably are numerous reasons for this, but one possibility is because the challenges and pressures keep many focused almost entirely on personal and family needs. I am amazed by how often I hear public criticism of government officials, but seldom hear public prayers including intersessions for our President, Governors or Senators, Supreme Court Judges, and other government officials. The Apostle Paul instructed Timothy as follows:

> Therefore, I exhort first of all that supplications, prayers, intercessions, *and* giving of thanks be made for all men, for kings and all who are in authority, that we may lead a quiet and peaceable life in all godliness and reverence. For this *is* good and acceptable in the sight of God our Savior, who desires all men to be saved and to come to the knowledge of the truth." (1 Tim. 2:1-4)

Beyond praying for our own personal needs and challenges there is a second reason to pray in tongues and ask for the interpretation. As we pray in tongues the Holy Spirit has an opportunity to align

1050. Matt. 16:18b.

our prayers with the intercessions of Jesus in heaven. Jesus said, "All things that the Father has are Mine. Therefore, I said that He [the Holy Spirit] will take of Mine and declare *it* to you."[1051] Often when I am praying in tongues, the Holy Spirit will quicken Scriptures that guide my prayers towards needs of pastors, missionaries, state and national officials including our President and Vice President, and also toward the nation of Israel. Occasionally the Holy Spirit will also turn my attention toward other world leaders. The Lord is concerned with our personal and family needs, but He also has concerns far beyond those matters and intends for each believer to co-labor with Him to bring His plans and purposes into a reality.

A third reason for praying in tongues has to do with the quickening power of the Holy Spirit. As I am praying in tongues while facing decisions or challenges, the Holy Spirit will often quicken or make alive God's promises to me which inspires new levels of faith. I remember on an occasion when my wife and I were in deep financial trouble. Our situation seemed beyond hope and we were desperately praying in English and in tongues. The Holy Spirit quickened this promise to us: "Fear not, for I *am* with you; Be not dismayed, for I *am* your God. I will strengthen you, Yes, I will help you, I will uphold you with My righteous right hand."[1052] It was about three years before our situation changed. But that promise sustained our faith, enabling us to endure the hardship and not give up until the breakthrough came.

Think of Daniel, who prayed faithfully every day during his years in Babylon. Then one day after almost seventy years of captivity, the Word of the Lord through the prophecy of Jeremiah was quickened in his heart. According to Jeremiah's prophecy Israel was to be in Babylonian captivity for seventy years, and now those seventy years were almost complete. In response to that quickening of the Word of the Lord, Daniel did not become passive and say, "The will of God be done. What will be will be." No! Daniel committed himself to prayer

---

1051. John 16:15.
1052. Isa. 41:10.

and fasting with such intensity that Gabriel came and gave him the vision of the seventy weeks.[1053] This vision revealed God's plan for Israel until the consummation of the age. The Holy Spirit's quickening or snapping alive of a Scripture is one of the keys to the kingdom of God available to all believers right now. Therefore, we are encouraged to be diligent and fervent in prayer.

Prayer and The Mystery of Lawlessness:

Today all believers anticipate the return of Jesus Christ, but no one knows the day nor the hour. Believers have been anticipating the return of Jesus for two thousand years. The Apostle Peter warns us against becoming passive or slack regarding the promise of the Lord's return and to not be led away with the error of the wicked. He admonishes us to be diligent in our relationship with the Lord, "looking for and hastening the day of God."[1054] There has been and will continue to be scoffers and mockers regarding the return of Jesus. However, Jesus Himself warns us against being passive and commands us to "watch" and live with an expectation of His return. He teaches us to observe the signs and be aware of the season of His coming. Jesus said;

> Now learn this parable from the fig tree: When its branch has already become tender, and puts forth leaves, you know that summer is near. So, you also, when you see these things happening, know that it is near--at the doors! Assuredly, I say to you, this generation will by no means pass away till all these things take place. Heaven and earth will pass away, but My words will by no means pass away. But of that day and hour no one knows, not even the angels in heaven, nor the Son, but only the Father. Take heed, watch and pray; for you do not know when the time

---

1053. Dan. 9:1-27.
1054. 2 Peter 3:1-8.

> is. *It is* like a man going to a far country, who left his house and gave authority to his servants, and to each his work, and commanded the doorkeeper to watch. Watch therefore, for you do not know when the master of the house is coming--in the evening, at midnight, at the crowing of the rooster, or in the morning—lest, coming suddenly, he finds you sleeping. And what I say to you, I say to all: Watch! (Mark 13:28-37)

Jesus commands us to watch and pray thereby maintaining an alertness regarding the season we are in today. Jesus' concern is that we not become preoccupied with the affairs of this life to the extent that we fall asleep regarding His sudden return. My point is that praying in tongues not only builds us up in the faith, but it also is a means whereby the Holy Spirit quickens the Word of God revealing His kingdom agenda. Praying in tongues is God's gift of grace that enables us to commune with Him in prayer beyond our limited understanding of the times and seasons.

Often, we hear an alarm that a certain leader in the world is so corrupt and evil that he must surely be the antichrist and the end of the age is upon us! There are few concepts that frighten Christians more that the concept of "antichrist". Many believe when the antichrist is in control of the world all people will be marked with the dreaded number of 666 or be martyred. Of course, no God-fearing follower of Jesus wants to be forced to take that number of the name of the beast or worship the antichrist.[1055] Neither are we inclined to run to the mountains and hide in a cave or under a rock until Jesus returns. Jesus instructs us as members of His body and citizens of His kingdom, to "occupy" or "do business until He comes."[1056]

It is important to keep in mind that throughout Biblical history there has been numerous antichrists. These rulers opposed the

---

1055. Rev. 13:17-18
1056. Luke 19:12-26

kingdom of God and forcibly promoted lawlessness on large populations. These antichrists include Nimrod, Pharaoh, Sennacherib, Herod the Great, Nero, Hitler, and others. They were all deceivers, haters of God, haters of God's people, and murderers of innocent people. But as these antichrists wreaked chaos and destruction the Lord was not only in control; He was also raising up a standard against their efforts. Therefore, the reign of God has not been extinguished by the lawless deeds of these antichrists. Rather the kingdom of God has continued to grow and expand all over the world until today there are multiplied millions of believers in Jesus Christ as Lord all over the globe.

Writing in the first century the Apostle John says to us; "It is the last hour; and as you have heard that the Antichrist is coming, even now many antichrists have come, by which we know that it is the last hour."[1057] So, the presence of antichrists is not a post Reformation doctrine. The spirit of antichrist has been in operation from the earliest days, as is demonstrated by the presence of the Tempter in the Garden of Eden. What is most relevant and should grip our attention today is found in the following word of the Lord written by the Apostle Paul. He states;

> For **the mystery of lawlessness is already at work; only He who now restrains *will do so* until He is taken out of the way**. And then the lawless one will be revealed, whom the Lord will consume with the breath of His mouth and destroy with the brightness of His coming. **The coming of the *lawless one* is according to the working of Satan**, with all power, signs, and lying wonders, and with all unrighteous deception among those who perish, **because they did not receive the love of the truth**, that they might be saved. And for this reason, **God will send them strong delusion, that they should believe the lie,**

1057. 1 John 2:18.

> **that they all may be condemned who did not believe the truth but had pleasure in unrighteousness**. (2 Thessalonians 2:7-12; emphasis mine).

The above passage affirms what we have been saying—the "spirit of antichrist" or "the mystery of lawlessness" is already at work. Lawlessness or antichrist activities are not simply end of the age realities. Those lawlessness deeds were suffered by Jesus and must also be endured by the people of God. When Jesus intervened in the life of Saul, who later became the Apostle Paul while on the road to Damascus, He asked "Why are you persecuting Me?"[1058] Notice that the question of the Lord was so convicting to Saul that he offered no argument or defense against the charges of persecuting the Lord, but in astonishment asked, "Lord what do you want me to do?" The key here is to understand that as lawless deeds are perpetrated against the people of God, don't think that the Lord is sitting in heaven doing nothing. No! Remember that Jesus told Saul, "It is hard for you to kick against the goads." In other words, as Saul was persecuting Christians, the prayers and cries of the persecuted were initiating the convicting work of the Holy Spirit in the heart of Saul. Suffering persecution is never pleasant, but it is a part of the birthright of every believer. Years later after suffering much persecution because of his relationship with the Lord, Paul said, "For I consider that the sufferings of this present time are not worthy *to be compared* with the glory which shall be revealed in us."[1059] Paul wrote to the saints in Philippi where he had earlier been beaten and imprisoned saying, "For to you it has been granted on behalf of Christ, not only to believe in Him, but also to suffer for His sake, having the same conflict which you saw in me and now hear *is* in me."[1060]

The Apostle Peter who was persecuted and finally executed by lawless hands said:

1058. Acts 9:4-6.
1059. Pom. 8:18.
1060. Phil. 1:29-30.

> Beloved, do not think it strange concerning the fiery trial which is to try you, as though some strange thing happened to you; but rejoice to the extent that you partake of Christ's sufferings, that when His glory is revealed, you may also be glad with exceeding joy. If you are reproached for the name of Christ, blessed *are you,* for the Spirit of glory and of God rests upon you. On their part He is blasphemed, but on your part, He is glorified. (1 Peter 4:12-14)

None of us enjoy looking into a future that includes suffering and persecution. However, God's grace will make us sufficient to wage a good warfare and the Holy Spirit will help us to maintain a good testimony even in the face of pain and tribulations. That is the testimony of those who have gone before us. Remember that we are surrounded by a great cloud of witnesses that endured all kinds of suffering and hardship, yet they kept the faith. We need to pray with our understanding and with the gift of unknown tongues. We do not know all the future holds, but we do know that our God has promised to "never leave us nor forsake us."[1061] Satan desires to weaken our faith through fear and seeks to persuade us to compromise our whole hearted trust in Jesus Christ in an effort to avoid persecution and have all men speak well of us. But Jesus said, "Woe to you when all men speak well of you, for so did their fathers to the false prophets."[1062] "What then shall we say to these things? If God *is* for us, who *can be* against us?"[1063] Our responsibility is to "Love our enemies, do good to those who hate us, bless those who curse us, and pray for those who spitefully use us."[1064]

We are exhorted by Paul to "put on the whole armor of God, that we may be able to withstand in the evil day."[1065] In other words God

1061. Heb. 13:5.
1062. Luke 6:26.
1063. Rom. 8:31.
1064. Luke 6:27-28.
1065. Eph. 6:13.

has made every provision for our victory over the antichrist powers of darkness. The above passage from 2 Thessalonians states clearly that the real source of lawlessness is Satan. Satan wants to be God and as a result he has already been forced out of heaven and cast down to the earth. Being enraged he makes war against those who keep the "commandments of God and have the testimony of Jesus Christ."[1066] Satan hates God and those in the image of God, especially those who represent the kingdom of God on the earth. One of Satan's tactics includes tempting believers to settle for good things rather than trusting God for the best things. Remember the devil tempted Jesus to turn stone into bread. Jesus was hungry and had the power to turn the stone to bread. But Jesus did not yield to the devil's temptation but fulfilled all the Father commanded Him to do. When it pleased the Father, Jesus turned water into wine. Jesus, as our example and Savior, came to defeat the devil on the terms of righteousness, not through a negotiated compromise. The Scripture says;

> Inasmuch then as the children have partaken of flesh and blood, He Himself likewise shared in the same, that through death He might destroy him who had the power of death, that is, the devil, and release those who through fear of death were all their lifetime subject to bondage. For indeed He does not give aid to angels, but He does give aid to the seed of Abraham. Therefore, in all things He had to be made like *His* brethren, that He might be a merciful and faithful High Priest in things *pertaining* to God, to make propitiation for the sins of the people. For in that He Himself has suffered, being tempted, He is able to aid those who are tempted. (Hebrews 2:14-18).

1066. Rev. 12:7-17.

It is important to understand that when God created mankind, He also gave mankind a free will. Man could freely choose to love and obey God or choose to reject and disobey God. However, in giving mankind a free will, God did not relinquish His sovereign will. The "mystery of lawlessness" has been and continues working to disrupt and destroy the people and purposes of God. But the Holy Spirit continues working through the lives and ministries of believers restraining lawlessness "until He is taken out of the way."[1067] The Holy Spirit now tabernacles in the hearts of believers. When the believers are "caught up… to meet the Lord in the air"[1068] the Holy Spirit will no longer be present on the earth to restrain lawlessness. Therefore, lawlessness will abound, and the antichrist will be unrestrained. God will then pour out His wrath according to His sovereign will. The Apostle John describes two different harvests as follows:

> Then I looked, and behold, a white cloud, and on the cloud sat *One* like the Son of Man, having on His head a golden crown, and in His hand a sharp sickle. And another angel came out of the temple, crying with a loud voice to Him who sat on the cloud, 'Thrust in Your sickle and reap, for the time has come for You to reap, for the harvest of the earth is ripe.' So, He who sat on the cloud thrust in His sickle on the earth, and the earth was reaped. (Revelation 14:14-16)

This harvest is yet to be reaped by the Lord, but it is the next major event to be fulfilled in God's plan of redemption. The seven Feasts of the Lord celebrate the redemptive purposes of God through the ages.[1069] Each of the feasts were experienced in the form of shadows in the Old Testament but their fulfillment is accomplished in the reality of the redemptive work of Jesus Christ in the New Testament.

1067. 2 Thes. 2:7.
1068. 1 Thes. 4:17.
1069. Lev. 23:1-44.

The Feasts of Passover, Unleavened Bread, and Firstfruits were each fulfilled through Jesus' crucifixion, resurrection, and the putting away of sin at the cross.[1070] The Feast of Pentecost was fulfilled fifty days after the resurrection of Jesus with the outpouring of the Holy Spirit as recorded in Acts chapter two. The passage from Revelation above reveals the harvest that will take place at the catching up of the church to meet the Lord in the air. A key to understanding the season or timing of this harvest is given by Jesus when He told His Apostles that "Jerusalem will be trampled by the Gentiles until the times of the Gentiles will be fulfilled."[1071] Jerusalem has been trampled under the feet of Gentiles from its destruction by the Roman General Titus in 70 A.D. until it was retaken by Israel during the six day war in 1967.

Pray the Lord of the Harvest for Laborers:

However, most Gentile nations refuse to recognize Jerusalem as the capitol of Israel and maintain their embassies in Tel Aviv. The President of the United States moved the American Embassy from Tel Aviv to Jerusalem in 2017. That is one of the reasons that President Trump is so despised in America and throughout the world. It is a spirit of antichrist that opposes the existence and prosperity of Israel. The devil knows his time is short and he vehemently opposes God and the redemptive purposes of God. But God in His sovereignty will determine when "the fullness of the Gentiles has come."[1072] Meanwhile as the Lord's ambassadors and ministers of reconciliation we are exhorted to pray and intercede for our President and world leaders, "that we may lead a quiet and peaceable life in all godliness and reverence. For this *is* good and acceptable in the sight of God our Savior, who desires all men to be saved and to come to the knowledge of the truth."[1073]

1070. Heb. 9:26.
1071. Luke 21:24b.
1072. Rom. 11:25.
1073. 1 Tim. 2:1-4.

However, as the end of this age draws near we need to give special attention to Jesus' command; "He said to them, 'the harvest truly *is* great, but the laborers *are* few; therefore pray the Lord of the harvest to send out laborers into His harvest.'"[1074] In other words this is not a season to be passive but to be engaged with the Lord in the ministry of reconciliation by praying for laborers to gather a harvest of souls into His kingdom before it is too late. Today is the day of salvation. No one has a guarantee of tomorrow. Jesus said,

> But of that day and hour no one knows, not even the angels of heaven, but My Father only. But as the days of Noah *were,* so also will the coming of the Son of Man be. For as in the days before the flood, they were eating and drinking, marrying and giving in marriage, until the day that Noah entered the ark, and did not know until the flood came and took them all away, so also will the coming of the Son of Man be. (Matthew 24:36-39)

When the fullness of the Gentiles has come God will release the angel with the message to "thrust in the sickle and reap the harvest of the earth." This harvest will be accomplished and celebrated on the exact day of the Feast of Trumpets.

> For the Lord Himself will descend from heaven with a shout, with the voice of an archangel, and with the trumpet of God. And the dead in Christ will rise first. Then we who are alive *and* remain shall be caught up together with them in the clouds to meet the Lord in the air. And thus, we shall always be with the Lord. (1 Thessalonians 4:16-17)

1074. Luke 10:2.

The catching away of the church will remove the restraining power of the Holy Spirit and unrestrained lawlessness will abound. The Church of Christ will not suffer the wrath of God because they believed on Jesus Christ upon whom God poured out His wrath on the cross. We were crucified with Christ and therefore no longer counted among those who are "by nature children of wrath."[1075] When lawlessness is unrestrained it will be a dreadful time on the earth and the second harvest will be gathered and cast into the winepress of God's wrath.

> Then another angel came out of the temple, which is in heaven, he also having a sharp sickle. And another angel came out from the altar, who had power over fire, and he cried with a loud cry to him who had the sharp sickle, saying, 'Thrust in your sharp sickle and gather the clusters of the vine of the earth, for her grapes are fully ripe.' So, the angel thrust his sickle into the earth and gathered the vine of the earth and threw *it* into the great winepress of the wrath of God. And the winepress was trampled outside the city, and blood came out of the winepress, up to the horses' bridles, for one thousand six hundred furlongs. (Revelation 14:14-20)

Jesus warns us by saying, "Watch therefore, and pray always that you may be counted worthy to escape all these things that will come to pass, and to stand before the Son of Man."[1076] We are blessed to live in a season of such presence and operational power of the Holy Spirit. Since Israel has been restored as a nation, there has been tremendous outpourings of the Holy Spirit resulting in a great increase in the revelation and understanding of Scripture. But Satan has also

1075. Eph. 2:3.
1076. Luke 21:36.

been working his works of deception in preparation for the coming of the man of sin, the son of perdition.[1077]

> The coming of the *lawless one* is according to the working of Satan, with all power, signs, and lying wonders, and with all unrighteous deception among those who perish, **because they did not receive the love of the truth, that they might be saved**. And for this reason, **God will send them strong delusion**, that they should believe the lie, that they all may be condemned who did not believe the truth but had pleasure in unrighteousness. (2 Thessalonians 2:9-12; emphasis mine)

Our God is longsuffering, but if a person continually rejects God's love and resists His calling then He will eventually give people over to their own desires and unrighteous deception. And in the final days of this age He will even "send them strong delusion that they should believe the lie, that they might be condemned." Wholehearted love is to be our response to God who has paid such a high price for our salvation. We are admonished to "continue earnestly in prayer, being vigilant in it with thanksgiving."[1078]

Persistence in Prayer:

In preparing His disciples for the end of the age Jesus "spoke a parable to them, that men ought always to pray and not to lose heart, saying;"

> There was in a certain city a judge who did not fear God nor regard man. Now there was a widow in that city; and she came to him, saying, 'Get justice for me

---

1077. 2 Thes 2:3.
1078. Col. 4:2.

> from my adversary.' And he would not for a while; but afterward he said within himself, 'Though I do not fear God nor regard man, yet because this widow troubles me I will avenge her, lest by her continual coming she weary me.' " Then the Lord said, "Hear what the unjust judge said. And shall God not avenge His own elect who cry out day and night to Him, though He bears long with them? I tell you that He will avenge them speedily. Nevertheless, when the Son of Man comes, will He really find faith on the earth? (Luke 18:2-8)

Jesus was aware of the challenging circumstances that we His followers would face in fulfilling our callings while living in the end of the age. Therefore, He exhorts us by saying, "Men ought always to pray and not lose heart." In other words, Jesus is warning us against becoming fainthearted and discouraged in the face of suffering and persecution as we wait for His second coming. He is also teaching us how to overcome hardship and discouragement through persistence in prayer even when circumstances are not changing as quickly as we would like. To make His point He spoke the above parable of the "Unjust Judge."

A central figure in this parable is a judge whom Jesus qualifies as "unjust" and cares nothing about the opinions of others. "He did not fear God nor regard man."[1079] However, he was moved to take action on the behalf of this woman because of her persistence or "continual coming." This woman was experiencing hardship for at least two reasons. First, she had lost her husband and was now a widow, which indicated she possessed limited social or legal standing within her community. And second, she was experiencing injustice from an adversary—someone probably taking advantage of her since she had no husband. Apparently, her case seemed to be of no significance to

---

1079. Matt. 18:4.

this judge. That is why Jesus calls him the "unjust judge." He refused to give her cause any attention at first, but she just kept coming back again and again. She refused to be ignored and kept on bugging that judge because she was determined to have her day in court. Later he said to himself, "I have got to get this woman off my back and vindicate her or she is going to drive me crazy by her continual coming into my court and pleading for my attention." You see this judge decided to avenge this widow, not on the merits of her case, but according to his personal convenience. She was getting under his skin and wearing him out. However, it is important to notice that this widow did not seek revenge against her adversary by taking the law in her own hands but sought the intervention of the judge for justice.

Keep in mind that this parable speaks of imploring a judge to avenge an adversary. Those terms indicate the legal nature of prayer. We are invited "to come boldly to the throne of grace, that we may obtain mercy and find grace to help in time of need."[1080] Again this verse also contains legal terminology. The Law of God spells out the legal framework that defines God's moral nature and the boundaries of man's moral behavior. When Jesus was on the cross and said, "It is finished;"[1081] He was proclaiming that He had completely fulfilled every legal requirement of God's Law. Jesus has therefore broken the devil's legal hold over every believer and restored the dominion Adam lost.[1082] Therefore, as believers in Jesus Christ we have the privilege, responsibility, and authority to come before the sovereign Lord of the universe and in the humility of prayer align ourselves with His plans and purposes. Thus, our prayers set in motion legal action against the powers of evil, breaking demonic strongholds, and shifting the spiritual atmosphere, which releases the blessings of the kingdom of God upon our lives, families, communities, and world.

1080. Heb. 4:16.
1081. John 19:30.
1082. Rom. 5:17.

Jesus informs us that God is nothing like the unjust judge. Jesus said, "I tell you that He [God] will avenge them speedily."[1083] It is the "elect" that God "avenges."[1084] It is comforting to understand that we did not choose God, rather He chooses us; He chose to love us while we were yet sinners.[1085] For some this may be a controversial point, but I have met many people who rejected a relationship with God; but I have never met a person that God did not choose. "The Lord is not slack concerning *His* promise, as some count slackness, but is longsuffering toward us, not willing that any should perish but that all should come to repentance."[1086] Regardless how small or insignificant we may be in the eyes of others; God loves us so much that He has provided for our justice by giving us an Advocate, "Jesus Christ the righteous."[1087] "Therefore He [Jesus] is also able to save to the uttermost those who come to God [the Father] through Him [Jesus], since He [Jesus] always lives to make intercession for them"[1088] (emphasis mine).

Our Savior doesn't come to our assistance out of convenience. Quite the contrary God the Father had to sacrifice His own Son to rescue us from our adversary. And the answers to our prayers may not come as quickly as we would like sometimes, but it isn't because God is preoccupied with His personal needs or leisure. God is always occupied with you and me and our needs. He knows our needs before we pray, but in His wisdom, He has determined to release His gracious provisions through the means of prayer. Sometimes we may perceive things only from our point of view, while the Lord is not only working in our behalf but also far beyond our personal concerns. "*For the eyes of the* LORD *are on the righteous, And His ears are open to their*

1083. Matt. 18:8.
1084. Luke 18:7.
1085. John 15:16; Rom. 5:8.
1086. 2 Peter 3:9.
1087. 1 John 2:1.
1088. Heb. 7:25.

prayers; But the face of the LORD *is against those who do evil.*"[1089] The delay in receiving answers to our prayers is sometimes a test of the "genuineness of your faith, *being* much more precious than gold that perishes, though it is tested by fire, may be found to praise, honor, and glory at the revelation of Jesus Christ."[1090] Always be confident that God is working in your behalf beyond what we may ask or think. We have a High Priest that "is able to aid those who are tempted"[1091] or tested.

In this parable Jesus is teaching us to be persistent in prayer even though God "bears long" with us in arranging circumstances that benefit our redemptive purposes. This is where faith is crucial to our relationship with our Father. Being willing to trust the Lord in the face of circumstances that we do not understand requires steadfast faith. By our human nature we have a strong tendency to want instant everything, instant food, instant sex, instant service, and instant answers to prayer. But the Scripture says, "But let patience have *its* perfect work, that you may be perfect and complete, lacking nothing."[1092] Patience in this passage could just as well be translated "endurance" or "perseverance." Jesus isn't teaching us to simply be passive, but be persistent and persevere in our petitions, trusting that God is working all things together for our good. God is not like the unjust judge who didn't want to be bothered by the widow. No! The Lord invites us to "Come boldly to the throne of grace that we may find mercy and grace to help in our time of need."[1093] The question is will we keep the faith and faithfully trust Him for the answer to our prayers or will we compromise our faith with doubts and unbelief? Will Jesus find faith in my life and your life when He returns?[1094] Yes! I believe He

---

1089. 1 Peter 3:12.
1090. 1 Peter 1:7.
1091. Heb. 2:18.
1092. James 1:2-4.
1093. Heb. 4:16.
1094. Luke 18:8.

will because we continue to pray in faith and trust the Lord to respond faithfully to our request and intercessions with a thankful heart!!

The Tax Collector's Prayer:

In the preceding parable of the Unjust Judge, Jesus was teaching us that faith in God expressed through persistent prayer will prevail in bringing results in the kingdom of God. But in this next parable of the Pharisee and the Tax Collector, Jesus is teaching us that it is faith expressed through humility and prayer that justifies sinners. Jesus "spoke this parable to some who trusted in themselves that they were righteous, and despised others:"

> Two men went up to the temple to pray, one a Pharisee and the other a tax collector. The Pharisee stood and prayed thus with himself, 'God, I thank You that I am not like other men--extortioners, unjust, adulterers, or even as this tax collector. I fast twice a week; I give tithes of all that I possess.' And the tax collector, standing afar off, would not so much as raise *his* eyes to heaven, but beat his breast, saying, 'God, be merciful to me a sinner!' I tell you; this man went down to his house justified *rather* than the other; for everyone who exalts himself will be humbled, and he who humbles himself will be exalted." (Luke 18:9-14) In this parable the Pharisee and the tax collector both prayed, and both expressed some kind of faith. The Pharisee had faith or confidence in his own righteousness. Thus, he went to the appropriate place to pray, the temple. However, when he prayed, he expressed no faith in the God who dwelt in that temple. Rather he expressed his gratitude for the multiple ways that he considered himself superior to other men. It seems

> like he almost was expecting God to be thankful that such an outstandingly moral person as himself had come to bless God by proudly proclaiming his personal righteousness that qualified him as superior to others.

Can you imagine how the arrogant prayers of the self-righteous religious make Jesus feel? Jesus, who "did not consider it robbery to be equal with God, but made Himself of no reputation, taking the form of a bondservant, *and* coming in the likeness of men."[1095] He gave up all of His glory and made Himself of no reputation in order to serve and give His life as a ransom for sinners like you and me. Does it make you wonder if that Pharisee ever read the Bible passage that says, "all our righteousnesses are like filthy rags?"[1096] How do you suppose the Pharisee interpreted the passage that says, "there is none righteous, no not one?"[1097] Lest we also become self-righteous in our views of that Pharisee, we must remember that self-righteousness can so darken our capacity to perceive reality that we can become trapped in the bondage of deception and arrogance. When the Holy Spirit reveals the beauty of holiness manifested through the person of Jesus as He lived on this same earth as we do, it should crush our prideful self-righteousness. One of the reasons the Holy Spirt was given was to "convict the world of sin, and of righteousness, and of judgment."[1098] The convicting power of the Holy Spirit makes manifest the heart felt reality of sin, righteousness, and judgment.

Conviction of sin is what the tax collector was experiencing when "he would not so much as raise his eyes to heaven, but beat on his breast, saying, 'God be merciful to me a sinner!'"[1099] Jesus preached

---

1095. Phil. 2:6-7.
1096. Isa. 64:6.
1097. Psa. 14:3.
1098. John 16:8.
1099. Luke 19:13.

the "gospel of the kingdom,"[1100] and that gospel was the power of God unto salvation. But when that gospel is rejected "the wrath of God is revealed... because what may be known of God is manifest in them, for God has shown it to them."[1101] However, the tax collector embraced the reality that he was a sinner and humbled himself in contrition, asking God for mercy. Therefore, Jesus said, "This man went down to his house justified."[1102] Why? "Because everyone who exalts himself will be humbled [or brought low], and he who humbles himself will be exalted."[1103] "God resists the proud, but gives grace to the humble."[1104] Lucifer lost his exalted place in heaven because of his beauty, he was lifted up in pride.[1105] However Jesus, being the absolute opposite of Lucifer, "humbled Himself and became obedient to the point of death, even the death of the cross. Therefore, God also has highly exalted Him and given Him the name which is above every name."[1106] Jesus didn't simply talk about the kingdom of God, He demonstrated life in the kingdom. He is our role model. "Jesus said to His disciples, 'If anyone desires to come after Me, let him deny himself, and take up his cross, and follow Me.'"[1107] That is why the Apostle Paul says, "Let this mind be in you which was also in Christ Jesus."[1108] In response to Jesus' teaching we are to "humble ourselves under the mighty hand of God, that He may exalt you in due time, casting all your care upon Him, for He cares for you."[1109]

1100. Matt. 4:23; Mark 1:14.
1101. Rom. 1:18-19.
1102. Luke 18:14.
1103. Luke 18:14.
1104. James 4:6; Prov. 3:34.
1105. Eze. 28:17.
1106. Phil. 2:8-9.
1107. Matt. 16:24.
1108. Phil. 2:5.
1109. 1 Peter 5:6-7.

Let the Little Children Come to Jesus:

The parable of the Pharisee and the Tax Collector is followed chronologically in the Gospel of Luke by Jesus having two different encounters and both have to do with receiving or entering the kingdom of God. The first encounter was with little children which is recorded in Matthew, Mark, and Luke. The following is Luke's account:

> Then they also brought infants to Him that He might touch them; but when the disciples saw *it,* they rebuked them. But Jesus called them to *Him* and said, "Let the little children come to Me, and do not forbid them; for of such is the kingdom of God. Assuredly, I say to you, whoever does not receive the kingdom of God as a little child will by no means enter it." (Luke 18:15-17).

Normally little children have not developed a skeptical or unbelieving approach to faith in God. They have the tendency to trust and believe what their parents teach them. These parents wanted their children to be exposed to the person of Jesus and receive His blessing. It was probably with the concern for limitations on Jesus' time and energy that the disciples rebuked these parents. After all, Jesus was drawing crowds of people and taking time with children did not seem like a priority to the disciples. However, Jesus' attitude was different because He "called them to Him and said, 'Let the little children come to Me, and do not forbid them; for such is the kingdom of God.'"

The disciples were probably well intentioned but had not yet grasped a child's tremendous capacity to receive and absorb the love of God. Children do not understand doctrine, but they cherish love and love is the very heart of a relationship with God and the foundation of faith.[1110] It is a cruel injustice to insulate a child from the gospel of

1110. Matt. 22:37-39; Gal. 5:6.

the kingdom. Childlike faith needs to be nurtured and guided as they grow through the years into maturity. A child's faith is a powerful defense against the forces of darkness and the lusts of the flesh as they develop through their teens into adulthood. The Book of Proverbs offers this advice: "Train up a child in the way he should go, and when he is old, he will not depart from it."[1111] This is not a promise but a probable outcome of godly wisdom.

Jesus said, "Assuredly, I say to you, whoever does not receive the kingdom of God as a little child will by no means enter it."[1112] According to Robert H. Stein, "Jesus was not attributing to children an innate goodness. Rather, he appealed to some quality possessed by little children that is essential for entering God's kingdom."[1113] Jesus did not clarify explicitly what childlike quality was needed to enter the kingdom, but considering the previous parable, He was referring to humility. Jesus concluded the previous parable by saying, "For everyone who exalts himself will be humbled, and he who humbles himself will be exalted."[1114] Humility is the quality of heart that attracts God's grace. For "God resists the proud but gives grace to the humble."[1115] From the beginning of His ministry Jesus had proclaimed the gospel of the kingdom but that gospel had basically been rejected. That is why Jesus wept over Jerusalem;[1116] they had missed their day of visitation—they were not receptive to the gospel of the kingdom. The Jews had many reasons for rejecting the Gospel. Their hearts and minds were filled with the wisdom of this age which paralyzed or crushed childlike humility and receptivity. However, Jesus is teaching that the model for entering the kingdom is the child, not the adult.

1111. Prov. 22:6.

1112. Luke 18:17.

1113. Robert H. Stein, *Luke*, vol. 24, The New American Commentary (Nashville, TN: Broadman & Holman Publishers, 1992), 453.

1114. Luke 18:14.

1115. James 4:6.

1116. Luke 19:41-44.

The Rich Young Ruler:

Following His teaching about the receiving of the kingdom of God as a little child, Jesus was approached by a certain rich young ruler saying, "Good teacher, what shall I do to inherit eternal life?"[1117] This encounter is recorded by Matthew, Mark, and Luke. The following is from the Gospel of Luke:

> So, Jesus said to him, "Why do you call Me good? No one *is* good but One, *that is,* God. You know the commandments: *'Do not commit adultery,' 'Do not murder,' 'Do not steal,' 'Do not bear false witness,' 'Honor your father and your mother.'* " And he said, "All these things I have kept from my youth." So, when Jesus heard these things, He said to him, "You still lack one thing. Sell all that you have and distribute to the poor, and you will have treasure in heaven; and come, follow Me." But when he heard this, he became very sorrowful, for he was very rich. And when Jesus saw that he became very sorrowful, He said, "How hard it is for those who have riches to enter the kingdom of God! For it is easier for a camel to go through the eye of a needle than for a rich man to enter the kingdom of God." And those who heard it said, "Who then can be saved?" But He said, "The things which are impossible with men are possible with God." (Luke 18:19-27).

This young man is an achiever. He is rich and a ruler but despite his successes he had not succeeded in securing the one treasure that he is hoping to now obtain. He is respectful, even reverent because Mark says that he came running, and knelt down before Jesus, calling Him

1117. Luke 18:18.

"Good Teacher."[1118] He knelt down, taking the posture of prayer and on the surface seems like the kind of man that any pastor would want to be a member of his congregation. He is young yet reverential with recognizable leadership skills, aggressive, and has money! And he is honest enough to admit there is something he needs and searches out the right person to help him meet that need. He is a mover and shaker at the right place at the right time. On top of these qualities he also asks Jesus the absolute right question; "What shall I do to inherit eternal life?" Notice he is not asking for an immediate takeover because he uses the word "inherit." In other words, he is willing to wait as long as it takes to possess this treasure.

Then Jesus asks an unusual question, "Why do you call Me good?" Suddenly, this young ruler is faced with rethinking his scale of definitions. Jesus continued, "No one is good but One, that is God." Can you imagine what was flashing through the mind of that young ruler? "Oh! If Jesus isn't good where do I fit in on this scale? I thought I understood the meaning of good. Matter of fact I thought I was good! Now just what am I getting myself into with this Teacher?" Then Jesus continued, "You know the commandments: *'Do not commit adultery,' 'Do not murder,' 'Do not steal,' 'Do not bear false witness,' 'Honor your father and your mother.'* "[1119] The young ruler takes a breath of relief; "OK! Great! I got it!" "All these things I have kept from my youth."[1120]

Although the young ruler had expressed his desire for eternal life, he had failed to grasp that the Law could only show him his sin and expose his need for a Savior. Mark records that "Jesus looking at him, loved him."[1121] After all he doesn't seem like one of those sanctimonious arrogant Pharisees. He really seems sincere, forthright, and exemplary. But Jesus perceived his lost condition and knew what eternal life would cost him. Jesus was not simply looking to add members to

1118. Marek 10:17.
1119. Luke 18:20.
1120. Luke 18:21.
1121. Mark 10:21.

His small group but seeking committed disciples. He had taught earlier, "Whoever of you does not forsake all that he has cannot be My disciple."[1122]

So, Jesus said to him, "You still lack one thing. Sell all that you have and distribute to the poor, and you will have treasure in heaven; and come, follow Me."[1123] Just imagine how that felt to the rich young ruler! "What? Can this Teacher be serious? He says that 'I lack one thing' and He wants me to sell everything and then give it all to the poor! WOW! I wasn't expecting something so radical! 'Take up your cross!'[1124] What kind of a deal is this? Oh, Oh! I think I'm going to faint!" The Scripture says, "when he heard this, he became very sorrowful, for he was very rich."[1125]

"And when Jesus saw that he became very sorrowful, He said, 'How hard it is for those who have riches to enter the kingdom of God!'"[1126] The emphasis of Jesus' words is upon the word "hard." It means that the wealthy enter the kingdom "with difficulty" or "it is next to impossible" for them to enter the kingdom. Jesus illustrates how "hard" it is by saying. "For it is easier for a camel to go through the eye of a needle than for a rich man to enter the kingdom of God."[1127] The Passion translation says, "Nothing could be harder! It could be compared to trying to stuff a rope through the eye of a needle." [1128] Why is it hard or difficult? Because Jesus said, "No one can serve two masters; for either he will hate the one and love the other, or else he will be loyal to the one and despise the other. You cannot serve God and mammon."[1129] "In some later Christian sources

---

1122. Luke 14:33.

1123. Luke 18:22.

1124. Mark 10:21.

1125. Luke 18:23.

1126. Luke 18:24.

1127. Luke 18:25.

1128. Brian Simmons, tran., *The Passion Translation: New Testament* (BroadStreet Publishing, 2017), Lk 18:25.

1129. Matt. 6:24.

Mamonas is depicted as a demon, 'wealth' being personified...."[1130] In other words "mammon" is the demon or god of materialism. It is not possible to serve God and money.

When we observe the life of Abraham, we see that he was very wealthy, indicating the blessings of God upon his life. And he is the father of our faith. The point is that God wants to abundantly bless every person. Jesus doesn't ask the rich young ruler to sell all his stuff so he will spend the remainder of his life in poverty. However, riches are deceitful because they appear to offer power and security, but when it comes to eternal treasure, they cannot deliver.[1131] Besides, it is impossible to accumulate enough wealth to purchase salvation. Jesus had taught, "For whoever desires to save his life will lose it, but whoever loses his life for My sake will find it. For what profit is it to a man if he gains the whole world and loses his own soul?"[1132] Therefore, the Apostle Paul instructed Timothy to warn the Ephesians regarding the deceitfulness of riches. "For the love of money is a root of all *kinds of* evil, for which some have strayed from the faith in their greediness, and pierced themselves through with many sorrows."[1133] "Command those who are rich in this present age not to be haughty, nor to trust in uncertain riches but in the living God, who gives us richly all things to enjoy."[1134]

Jesus never condemned the rich young ruler because he was "very rich." What Jesus did was awaken him to the deceitfulness of riches. Eternal life and entrance into the kingdom of God have a price tag that exceeds the value of money. That does not mean that this young ruler was forever doomed. This passage of Scripture does not tell us what eventually happened to him. One thing is for sure, Jesus "loved

---

1130. P. W. van der Horst, "Mammon," ed. Karel van der Toorn and Bob Becking, *Dictionary of Deities and Demons in the Bible* (Leiden; Boston; Köln; Grand Rapids, MI; Cambridge: Brill; Eerdmans, 1999), 543.

1131. Matt. 13:22.

1132. Matt. 16:25-26.

1133. 1 Tim. 6:10.

1134. 1 Tim. 6:17.

him."[1135] When he walked away from his encounter with Jesus you can be certain he was evaluating every word Jesus had spoken to him. Who knows, it could be that one day he again bowed his knees before the Lord and prayed, "God be merciful to me a sinner." And when we get to heaven, may he also be there? But if he is there, it will not be because he kept the Law or because he was rich. It will be because he humbled himself as a little child and repented of trusting in his riches and embraced the grace and mercy of God, trusting the Lord with all his heart and soul.

Those who heard the conversation between Jesus and the rich young ruler now asked, "Who then can be saved?"[1136] It was a soul-searching moment. Apparently, the rich young ruler was such an exemplary person in the community that others were having to reconsider their own value systems; just as each of us need to do from time to time. And Jesus answered, "The things that are impossible with men are possible with God."[1137] The bottom line is that all of us are totally dependent upon God and His gift of grace for salvation. And Jesus "is also able to save to the uttermost those who come to God through Him, since He always lives to make intercession for them."[1138] It doesn't matter how much you think you have had to give up, Jesus concludes by giving His disciples and all believers the following encouragement; "Assuredly, I say to you, there is no one who has left house or parents or brothers or wife or children, for the sake of the kingdom of God, who shall not receive many times more in this present time, and in the age to come eternal life."[1139]

The encounter between Jesus and the rich young ruler may not be considered a prayer, but it addresses the same issue as the previous passage in this eighteenth chapter of Luke. Both passages address the issue of entry into the kingdom of God. In the previous passage Jesus

---

1135. Mark 10:21.
1136. Luke 18:26.
1137. Luke 18:27.
1138. Heb. 7:25.
1139. Luke 18:29-30.

said, "Whoever does not receive the kingdom as a little child will by no means enter it."[1140] And in this passage Jesus said, "How hard it is for those who have riches to enter the kingdom of God."[1141] In both passages the key issue is humility. "Therefore, humble yourselves under the mighty hand of God, that He may exalt you in due time, casting all your care upon Him, for He cares for you."[1142]

Jesus Prayed, "Father Forgive Them:"

Just hours before Jesus' arrest and crucifixion, while at the last supper, Jesus "took the cup, and gave thanks, and gave *it* to them, saying, 'Drink from it, all of you. For this is My blood of the new covenant, which is shed for many for the remission of sins.'"[1143] "And according to the law almost all things are purified with blood, and without shedding of blood there is no remission."[1144] There is a world of difference between Christ "uncrucified" and Christ crucified and risen. The crucified and risen Christ makes our reconciliation with God possible. Jesus is "the propitiation for our sins, and not for ours only but also for the whole world."[1145] His propitiation is the satisfying of the wrath of God and making man's justification possible through the gift of righteousness. The redemptive ministry of Jesus also reveals the gracious character of the God who forgives our sin and establishes the pathway to covenantal union and communion.

One of the greatest prayers ever prayed was the one Jesus prayed while on the cross; "Father forgive them for they know not what they do."[1146] All of us have sinned and fallen short of the glory of God.[1147]

1140. Luke 18:17.
1141. Luke 18:24.
1142. 1 Peter 5:6-7.
1143. Matt. 26:27-28.
1144. Heb. 9:22.
1145. 1 John 2:2.
1146. Luke 23:3 4.
1147. Rom. 3:23.

Therefore, all of us need forgiveness. Forgiveness of sin is necessary for justification to be accomplished. Norman Geisler states:

> The Greek word for *forgiveness* is *aphesis*, which means "to forgive" or "to remit" one's sins.... Forgiveness does not erase the *sin*; history cannot be changed. But forgiveness does erase the *record* of the sin. Like a pardon, the crime of the accused is not expunged from history but is deleted from his account. Hence, it is "in [Christ Jesus that] we have redemption through his blood, the forgiveness of sins, in accordance with the riches of God's grace" (Eph. 1:7; cf. Col. 1:14) ....[1148] Those who are forgiven do not have to pay for their own debt, since Christ's payment has been applied to them. The only incompatibility between forgiveness and substitutionary atonement, then, comes when the Atonement is misconceived as an automatic and unconditional payment applied to everyone's sins. For example, when one buys a bank, he buys all the debts owed to that bank as well. If he decides to cancel (forgive) these debts, the debtor does not have to pay them, but the debt has still been paid for by the one who purchased the bank. Hence, forgiveness and paying the debt are not contradictory.[1149]

Forgiveness is a gracious act and the God given key that unlocks the mercy that pays our sin debt. In New Testament times if a man owed someone, he would write out a debt certificate of all that was owed. When the debt was paid in full, he would nail the certificate up in a public place for everyone to know that he was free from that

---

1148. Norman L. Geisler, *Systematic Theology, vol. 3, Sin, Salvation* (Minneapolis, MN: Bethany House Publishers, 2004), 227.

1149. Ibid., 250.

debt. Our sin debt was nailed to the cross and marked, paid in full.[1150] The goal of forgiveness is to: (1) cancel the debt of sin, transgression, and offense, (2) the absolution of the sinner's guilt, and (3) open the possibility of reconciliation and the restoration of communion with God, with one another, and with the whole Creation. Forgiveness is a powerful expression of God's mercy that demolishes the evil agent that says, "I will pay you back and get even with you," it's called vengeance and revenge. Vengeance belongs only to God. "Beloved, do not avenge yourselves, but *rather* give place to wrath; for it is written, '*Vengeance is Mine, I will repay,*' says the Lord."[1151] But rather than vengeance we have been given the ministry of reconciliation.[1152]

All believers recall the day when they experienced God's forgiveness and the joy of having the burden of sin and guilt lifted. Now that we have experienced forgiveness, the Lord expects us as His followers to be forgiving. Jesus said, "For if you forgive men their trespasses, your heavenly Father will also forgive you. But if you do not forgive men their trespasses, neither will your Father forgive your trespasses."[1153] Everett L. Worthington Jr. states:

> Forgiveness requires both letting go and pulling forward. A forgiver must release the resentment, hatred and bitterness of unforgiveness. A forgiver must release the desire to avoid or seek revenge against the perpetrator.... A forgiver replaces unforgiveness with a sense of agape love. A forgiver wishes the perpetrator well. A forgiver could even enter a relationship with the perpetrator if it were safe, prudent and possible to do so. Forgiveness means giving a gift that enables freedom and love.... It takes courage to grant

1150. Col. 2:13-14.
1151. Rom. 12;19.
1152. 2 Cor. 5:18.
1153. Matt. 6:14-15.

> love that can help both people to feel stronger and better as people.[1154]

It is one thing to forgive an offender, but forgiving a repeated offender stretches our capacity to be forgiving and we find ourselves asking the question that Peter asked; "'Lord, how often shall my brother sin against me, and I forgive him? Up to seven times?' Jesus said to him, 'I do not say to you, up to seven times, but up to seventy times seven.'"[1155] Forgiving repeat offenders requires love, humility, and the power of the Holy Spirit. That is one of the reasons why the Holy Spirit is named by Jesus as the "Helper."[1156] The Holy Spirit helps us by reminding us of Jesus' prayer, "Father forgive them for they know not what they do." That prayer delivers a crushing blow to our self-righteous justification and unforgiveness. The Holy Spirit helps us by reminding us of our need for forgiveness and our responsibility to forgive others. Unforgiveness is one of the greatest hindrances to the ongoing expansion of the kingdom of God among men. Acts of forgiveness genuinely guided by the Holy Spirit enable us to begin the slow, difficult process of unlearning the habits of sin and evil. Those habits tend to be reinforced by our attempts to justify, deceive, or hate ourselves for what we have said or done. But forgiveness is the power to break the strongholds of personal condemnation, guilt, shame, and offences. Plus, forgiveness empowers everyone to release others from the damage they have caused us. Just as Jesus on the cross forgave you and me for all the pain and hurt, we caused Him and our heavenly Father.

1154. Everett L. Worthington Jr., *Forgiving and Reconciliating: Bridges to Wholeness and Hope* (Downers Grove, Il: InterVarsity Press, 2003), 20-21.

1155. Matt. 18:21-22.

1156. John 14:26.

Summary:

The Lord is saying to you and me as New Testament believers and citizens of the kingdom of God, "Call upon Me, and I will answer you, and show you great and mighty things, which you do not know."[1157] Through the ages of redemptive history the purpose of prayer has not simply been a way to inform God about our problems or the affairs of life. Beyond those needs, prayer serves three major functions in the economy of the kingdom of God. First, prayer is not a religious ritual of vain repetitions as Baal worshippers in Elijah's day practiced. But prayer is the means that God has ordained whereby we are continuously welcomed into communion with Him as Solomon desired for the people of Israel. God already knows all things before we pray including all our needs.[1158] Isaiah makes it abundantly clear that God is not taxed by our needs nor reluctant to respond to our prayers. He says, "Behold, the LORD'S hand is not shortened, that it cannot save; nor His ear heavy, that it cannot hear."[1159] But He is always waiting in expectation of the voice of His children expressed in childlike humility and expectation. Our prayers ignite our Father's infinite capacity to express His immeasurable love on His precious children. And on those occasions when we do not know how or what to pray, the Holy Spirit will help us by gracing us to pray mysteries to God through His gift of unknown tongues.[1160] Therefore, Jesus says, "Men always ought to pray and not lose heart."[1161]

Second, prayer is also the means whereby we exercise personal responsibility for our sin through confession and repentance before the Father's throne of grace. The Tax Collector's prayer, "God be merciful to me a sinner," keeps our hearts pure before God and enables us to confess our "trespasses to one another, and pray for one another,

1157. Jer. 33:3.
1158. Matt. 6:8.
1159. Isa. 59:1.
1160. Rom. 8:26; 1 Cor. 14:2.
1161. Luke 18:1.

that we may be healed."[1162] It is humbling to confess our faults to one another, but it breaks the power of arrogance and pride. Thus, it keeps us from being blinded or deceived by lawlessness, as was in Noah's day, plus the deceptive materialism that characterizes our days. God is merciful and compassionate. Therefore, "If we confess our sin, He is faithful and just to forgive us our sins and cleanse us from all unrighteousness."[1163]

Third, the Lord is not willing that anyone should perish. For that reason, He has committed to us the ministry of reconciliation. Prayer is at the heart of the ministry of reconciliation for at least four reasons. First, Jesus admonishes us to "pray the Lord of the harvest to send laborers into His harvest."[1164] Our most powerful ministries do not constitute the position as "Lord of the harvest." "The Lord of the harvest" is the Lord Jesus and our prayer is for Him to send laborers into the harvest field. It is His field, His harvest, and He will send His laborers if we will pray. Second, we must persist in prayer for our government officials and "all who are in authority that we lead a quiet and peaceable life in all godliness and reverence." God "desires all men to be saved and come to a knowledge of the truth."[1165] Third, we must "pray for one another."[1166] In a day when materialism is so prevalent and dominating our culture, we must remain persistent in prayer for personal wisdom and revelation and intercede for each other. We do not want to become so attached to things or money that we walk away from Jesus as the rich young ruler did. Fourth, we experience many things that may be deceitful, harmful, and offensive, but Jesus teaches us to forgive others just as He forgave us. Jesus' model prayer reveals that our most potent spiritual weapon is forgiveness. As God's children and ministers of reconciliation we are to pray for forgiveness and to willingly forgive others.

1162. James 5:16.
1163. 1 John 1:9.
1164. Luke 10:2; Matt. 9:38.
1165. 1 Tim. 2:2.
1166. James 5:16.

Because of the nature of prayer, we as believers can from time to time have a sense of heaviness or burden regarding prayer needs. That may be appropriate for a season, but always keep in mind that the kingdom of God is not heaviness nor a burden, but "righteousness, peace and joy in the Holy Spirit."[1167] Of course we need to take prayer seriously, but always remain thankful and maintain a good supply of joyful praise, because "the joy of the Lord is our strength!"[1168] Joy is an expression of our confident trust in God's response to our prayers. Never forget the words of Jesus, "And whatever you ask in My name, that I will do, that the Father may be glorified in the Son. If you ask anything in My name, I will do *it.*"[1169] Prayer is an essential aspect of our participation in the ever-increasing blessings and manifestations of the kingdom of God. In the next chapter we will focus on Jesus, the King of the kingdom.

1167. Rom. 14:17.
1168. Neh. 8:10.
1169. John 14:13-14.

CHAPTER EIGHT

THE KING OF KINGS AND THE KINGDOM

"And He has on His robe and on His thigh a name written: KING OF KINGS AND LORD OF LORDS."
Revelation 19:16

Following Jesus' water baptism, He spent forty days in the wilderness being tempted of the devil. Then Jesus returned in the power of the Spirit to Galilee. "From that time Jesus began to preach and to say, 'Repent, for the kingdom of heaven is at hand.'"[1170] Throughout His earthly ministry of about three and one half years He proclaimed and demonstrated the presence of the kingdom of God. His preaching inaugurated the presence of kingdom and His miracles confirmed its power. But His message and ministry were both resisted and rejected by the religious leaders of Israel. Their opposition to Jesus culminated when He entered the City of Jerusalem just before Passover on what we traditionally celebrate as Palm Sunday.

1170. Matt. 4:17.

Jesus Was Anointed at Bethany:

Most of Jesus' ministry had not been in the area of Judea and Jerusalem but in the area of Galilee. As the Passover drew near, Jesus steadfastly set His face to go to Jerusalem. He and His disciples came to Bethany upon hearing the news that Lazarus had died.[1171] There Jesus revealed Himself to Martha as "the resurrection and the life."[1172] Lazarus had already been dead for four days, but Jesus commanded that the stone that sealed Lazarus' grave be rolled away and He called Lazarus to "come forth." Jesus then commanded those standing there to "loose" Lazarus from his grave clothes "and let him go."[1173] Following the resurrection of Lazarus, Jesus and His disciples remained in the vicinity of the city of Ephraim for probably three or four months because the religious leaders in Jerusalem were plotting to kill Him.

About a week before Passover Jesus made His way to Jericho where He healed blind Bartimaeus and spent time with Zacchaeus a chief tax collector. Jesus then proceeded toward Jerusalem entering the city of Bethany probably on a Friday afternoon just prior to the beginning of the Sabbath. He spent the Sabbath in Bethany, and after the close of the Sabbath He was invited to supper at the house of Simon the leper.[1174] D. A. Carson states:

> It has been suggested that Simon the Leper (Mk. 14:3) was the father of Lazarus and his sisters, and therefore the real owner of their home, even though for all practical purposes they owned it. This is an attractive hypothesis, but completely without supporting evidence. The actions of Mary and Martha—the latter serving, the former adoring—are consistent

---

1171. John 11:1-16.
1172. John 11:23-27.
1173. John 11:38-44.
1174. Matt. 26:6; Mark 14:3.

> with the picture of the two women presented in Luke 10:38–42.[1175]

It was as they had supper that Mary took a pound of very costly oil of spikenard and anointed the feet of Jesus and wiped His feet with her hair. Judas Iscariot complained and asked why the expensive oil was not sold and the money given to the poor. Jesus replied, "Let her alone; she has kept this for the day of My burial."[1176] In other words Jesus had on several occasions predicted His death would be in Jerusalem. Now He knew that the time had come, and He would be facing the cross during the Passover Celebration that would take place within a week.

On what we celebrate as Palm Sunday morning Jesus departed from Bethany, proceeding toward the Mount of Olives and at Bethphage, "He sent two of His disciples, saying, 'Go into the village opposite *you,* where as you enter you will find a colt tied, on which no one has ever sat. Loose it and bring *it here.* '"[1177] The disciples found the colt, brought it to Jesus, threw their coats on the colt and set Jesus on him. As they proceeded down the Mount of Olives toward Jerusalem many people spread their clothes on the road before Him. As they approached the Kidron Valley a whole multitude was gathering around Jesus as He rode along. The crowd consisted of people gathering for three reasons. (1) Many were coming to Bethany to see Lazarus whom Jesus had raised from the dead.[1178] (2) Many were traveling up to Jerusalem in preparation for the Passover. (3) Many heard that Jesus was coming to Jerusalem and came out of the city to meet

---

1175. D. A. Carson, *The Gospel according to John,* The Pillar New Testament Commentary (Leicester, England; Grand Rapids, MI: Inter-Varsity Press; W.B. Eerdmans, 1991), 428.

1176. Luke 12:1-8.

1177. Luke 19:29-30

1178. John 12:9.

Him.[1179] The point being that a multitude was gathering around Jesus as He crossed the Kidron Valley entering Jerusalem.[1180]

Jesus Wept Over Jerusalem:

The gathering crowd was praising God for the great things they had witnessed and the things they were expecting. They were shouting with loud voices "saying; 'Hosanna to the Son of David! *'Blessed is He who comes in the name of the* LORD*!'* Hosanna in the highest!'"[1181] Many cut palm branches and laid them in the road to honor the coming of Jesus into the city. Many thought that Jesus would become their king and deliver them from the domination of the Roman government. They really did not comprehend what was taking place in the redemptive purposes of God. In the midst of the excitement and the shouting of praises, the Scripture says that "all the city was moved."[1182] This was no small private party but a fulfilling of the redemptive purposes of God who had ordained this occasion before the foundation of the world.

However, the excitement and the praises found no favor with the religious leaders. Some of the religious leaders called out to Jesus commanding Him to rebuke those people that were praising God and celebrating His entry into Jerusalem. Jesus responded by saying, "I tell you that if these should keep silent, the stones would immediately cry out."[1183] They did not realize the eternal significance of what they were witnessing. His entry into Jerusalem had been prophesied by

---

1179. John 12; 12.

1180. D. A. Carson makes the following quote from Josephus. "Josephus (*Bel.* vi. 422–425) describes one Passover, just before the Jewish War (AD 66–70), when 2,700,000 people took part, not counting the defiled and the foreigners who were present in the city. Even if his numbers are inflated, the crowds were undoubtedly immense." D. A. Carson, *The Gospel according to John*, The Pillar New Testament Commentary (Leicester, England; Grand Rapids, MI: Inter-Varsity Press; W.B. Eerdmans, 1991), 431.

1181. Matt. 21:9.

1182. Matt. 21:10-11.

1183. Luke 19:39-40.

Zechariah; "Rejoice greatly, O daughter of Zion! Shout, O daughter of Jerusalem! Behold, your King is coming to you; He *is* just and having salvation, Lowly and riding on a donkey, A colt, the foal of a donkey."[1184] The humble entry of Jesus on that colt of a donkey was a shadow of the great day of the Lord when Jesus shall return riding on a white horse; "And He has on *His* robe and on His thigh a name written: KING OF KINGS AND LORD OF LORDS."[1185]

Meanwhile, Jesus was very much aware of what was about to take place and the future of that city which was hidden from their eyes. As He rode into Jerusalem, "He wept over it."[1186] He said, "O Jerusalem, Jerusalem, the one who kills the prophets and stones those who are sent to her! How often I wanted to gather your children together, as a hen gathers her chicks under *her* wings, but you were not willing!"[1187] Jerusalem was the City of David, the city of Solomon's Temple and the priestly service unto God Almighty, the Holy City, "the perfection of beauty, the joy of the whole earth."[1188] But Jesus wept over Jerusalem because He could see the soon coming day when the city would be surrounded by enemies and completely destroyed because they "did not know the time of their visitation."[1189]

But the people were filled with excitement and praise—they knew that God was doing something in their midst, but they really didn't comprehend the gravity of the occasion. They did not understand Jesus' gospel of the kingdom of God. The religious leaders were blinded by their desire for political authority and were oblivious to the powers of darkness that were influencing their decisions. Their blindness should serve as a wake-up call to you and me. Scripture warns each of us to watch and be alert lest we miss the redemptive purposes of the Lord in our generation. The Apostle Paul says, "See then that

---

1184. Zech. 9:9.
1185. Rev. 19:16.
1186. Luke 19:41.
1187. Matt. 23:37.
1188. Lam. 2:15; Psa. 48:2.
1189. Luke 19:41-44.

you walk circumspectly, not as fools but as wise, redeeming the time, because the days are evil. Therefore, do not be unwise, but understand what the will of the Lord *is*."[1190]

Jesus' Authority Is Questioned:

Once Jesus arrived at the temple, He overturned the tables of the money changers and drove out those who sold doves saying; "It is written, *'My house shall be called a house of prayer,'* but you have made it a *'den of thieves.'*" [1191] Jesus was not a religious person bound by formalism and tradition. No! He was the Son of God and zealous for the redemptive purposes of God.[1192] His zeal and determination to please the Father soon brought Him into a head-on confrontation with the religious and political authorities in Jerusalem. The religious leaders asked Jesus; "Tell us, by what authority are You doing these things? Or who is he who gave You this authority?"[1193] Jesus followed their questions by questioning them, "The baptism of John—was it from heaven or from men?"[1194] The religious leaders could not answer Jesus' question, therefore, He did not answer their questions. Continuing in the temple area Jesus said, "Now is the judgment of this world; now the ruler of this world [the devil] will be cast out"[1195] (emphasis mine).

Later that same week during His trial before Pilate, the Roman political leader, the issue of authority came up again. Jesus was not answering Pilate's questions whereupon Pilate stated, "'Do You not know that I have power [authority] to crucify You, and power [authority] to release You?' Jesus answered, 'You could have no power [authority] at all against Me unless it had been given you from

---

1190. Eph. 5:15-17.
1191. Matt. 21:13.
1192. John 2:17.
1193. Matt. 21:23; Mark 11:28; Luke 20:2
1194. Mark 11:30.
1195. John 12:31.

above'"[1196] (emphasis mine). Jesus understood that His Father was not only His source of authority, but also the authority of the religious leaders, the powers of darkness, and the political leaders, all of which were subject to His Father. The Scripture says, "For there is no authority except from God, and the authorities that exist are appointed by God."[1197]

Therefore, it is helpful at this juncture to reflect on the sovereignty of God, as expressed in creation and take a closer look at how God administers His authority on the earth. This understanding is crucial to our capacity to live as overcomers in this world among the God ordained realms of authority, including family, church, and world governments. It is one thing to know that we have been given authority, but another issue to know how to steward and administer that authority in harmony with the nature and purposes of God. For example, it is one thing to give a teenager the keys to your car but it is another thing for that teenager to know how to drive that car in traffic according to the rules of the road to prevent getting wrecked and possibly injured for life. Authority is powerful and when misused, people suffer abuse and injury. We, as members of the body of Christ, have been given authority to bring the blessing of the kingdom of God upon others and not injure nor destroy them.[1198] Jesus had not only been given all authority; He demonstrated that authority by His lifestyle, understanding how to administer it in accord with the loving purposes of God. The Father said, "This is My beloved Son in whom I am well pleased." Those are the words that all of us want to hear when we stand at the judgement seat of Christ.

God's Sovereignty and His Covenants:

As discussed in previous chapters our God is sovereign and has chosen to administer His sovereignty through the terms of the Everlasting

1196. John 19:10-11.
1197. Rom. 13:1.
1198. Luke 10:19.

Covenant established between the members of the Godhead. It originated in eternity past and includes the present, and eternity future. God is a Father by nature and desired a family of sons and daughters like Himself. Therefore, He used His divine wisdom combined with the pleasure of His will to achieve that desire through the administration of the Everlasting Covenant designed to accomplish at least the following four objectives: (1) The creation of a world to provide an environment suitable for the development and sustaining of a royal family of sons and daughters created by God in His image and likeness. (2) A plan of redemption that guaranteed all the necessary provisions for overcoming any interference or disruption in the relationship between Himself and His sons and daughters. (3) A provision for endowing His sons and daughters with the anointing of the Holy Spirit for the purpose of stewarding creation with kingdom authority and blessings. (4) Concluding the plans and purposes for creation, redemption, and anointing with the creation of a new heaven and new earth as an eternal dwelling place for Himself and His glorified family.

The Everlasting Covenant:

Having established the Everlasting Covenant, God proceeded to accomplish His purposes through a series of subordinating covenants with mankind that would progressively reveal His immutable nature and eternal purposes, concluding by fulfilling the terms of the New Covenant. Peter J. Gentry and Stephen J. Wellum argue "that the Bible presents a plurality of covenants that progressively reveal our triune God's one redemptive plan for His one people, which reaches its fulfillment and terminus in Christ and the new covenant."[1199] In other words, the different covenants that God has made with man in time are aspects or portions of the full overarching plan of God, the Everlasting Covenant, made within the Godhead in eternity before

1199. Peter J. Gentry and Stephen J Wellum, *Kingdom through Covenant: A Biblical – Theological Understanding of the Covenants, 2nd ed.* (Wheaton, Il: Crossway, 2018), 35.

time began. Michael G. Brown and Zach Keele state, "God's purpose in history is to govern His kingdom of creation and bring forth His holy kingdom. His covenants, therefore, are the way that God administers His kingdom."[1200]

The Everlasting Covenant is like the blueprint for a house. The house must be fully designed with every detail written within the blueprint which must then be approved by the county zoning board before the contractors begin the building process. The building process begins with masonry workers putting in the foundation upon which the carpenters frame the house. Then the roofers put on the roof as the electricians wire the house and the plumbers install the plumbing. This is followed by many other facets of construction including putting in the windows and doors, siding on the exterior, installing a heating and cooling system, putting up dry wall and so forth until the house is completely finished. The county building inspector must inspect the building process periodically to verify that every aspect of the construction process complies with the blueprint. The building process will not be finished until a final inspection is made and approved by the building inspector and an occupancy permit is granted by the county zoning board. So, God completely designed the world and all that is in it, including a family of sons and daughters in His image and likeness and wrote all the particulars in a book like a blueprint before He started the process of creation. This world did not simply evolve over thousands of years, but was created according to God's predetermined design and purpose. It was created according to God's specific specifications and nothing is random or by chance. For example, God instructed Moses to build the tabernacle; "According to all that I show you, *that is,* the pattern of the tabernacle and the pattern of all its furnishings, just so you shall make *it.*"[1201] Also, our bodies

---

1200. Michael G. Brown and Zack Keele, *Sacred Bond: Covenant Theology Explored,* (Reformed Fellowship, Inc., 2018), 19.

1201. Exod. 25:9.

are designed according to God's wise design and fashioned in His image and likeness. King David wrote:

> My frame was not hidden from You, when I was made in secret, *and* skillfully wrought in the lowest parts of the earth. Your eyes saw my substance, being yet unformed. And in Your book, they all were written, the days fashioned for me, when *as yet there were* none of them. How precious also are Your thoughts to me, O God! How great is the sum of them! (Psalm 139:15-17).

God not only created all things including mankind according to His unfathomable wisdom,[1202] but He relates to all things according to the gracious provisions of His covenants. A covenant is a mutual and solemn agreement confirmed with oaths or promises that legally binds the parties of the covenant together unto death. There are seven components to a covenant: (1) The words or terms or promises or oath, (2) the blood which signifies that this relationship is unto death. (3) The outward sign which in the case of the New Covenant is the gift of the Holy Spirit, or in the case of the marriage covenant it is the wedding ring. (4) There is a covenantal bond that may be expressed in legal terminology, as Jesus said, all the Law hangs on love—loving God and loving one's neighbor. God is the author or source of love that binds the members of the covenant in a perpetual relationship because "love is the bond of perfection."[1203] (5) Covenant is a commitment to loyalty between the members of the covenant. Always remember that God is for you, not against you even when you are wrong, He is "a friend that sticks closer than a brother."[1204] (6) Revelation is also a key component because one can only know God intimately within the New Covenant. Otherwise one can only know about God from outside of

1202. Prov. 8:22-31.
1203. Matt. 22:37-39; Col. 3:14; 1 Cor. 13:8.
1204. Prov. 18:24.

a covenantal relationship with Him.[1205] (7) Fellowship or communion with God is only possible within a covenantal relationship with Him because "what communion has light with darkness?"[1206] These seven components help us understand how covenantal relationships are far superior to contractional relationships. God expresses His will in covenantal terms which guarantees the fulfillment of His promises which in turn guarantees our eternal inheritance. The Bible is a covenantal book consisting of an Old Covenant and a New Covenant.

The Edenic Covenant:

We do not find the word "covenant" in the first two chapters of Genesis. However, we know that God only relates to this world and mankind in covenantal terms. Kevin Conner and Ken Malmin state, "There is enough covenantal language and covenantal elements in Genesis 1 and 2 as well as subsequent Scripture support to confirm the integrity of the Edenic Covenant (See Jeremiah 31:35-37; 33:19-25)."[1207] The Edenic Covenant was made by God with mankind regarding His purpose for creation before sin entered this world. However, it is not our purpose at this juncture to engage in a full exposition of all the different covenants in Scripture. Nevertheless, it is our intention to follow the progressive revelation made manifest through God's covenants with mankind and give attention to the transitions between the covenants which is often overlooked. This we believe will enlighten our perspective regarding what to anticipate in these final days of this age. Knowing the ways of God and grasping His progressive covenantal revelation through the previous ages better positions us to know how to live and minister in alignment with the

---

1205. Exod. 6:7; Isa. 45:3; 1 Cor. 2:14.

1206. 2 Cor. 6:14.

1207. Conner and Malmin, *The Covenants,* 13. Note: I am deeply indebted to these authors for opening my understanding regarding the significant role of Biblical Covenants in revealing the methods and purposes of God's plan for man throughout the ages..

Holy Spirit today. The Apostle Paul warns us of the suddenness of the coming Day of the Lord and we "are not in darkness, so that this Day should overtake us as a thief."[1208] Jesus said "Behold, I am coming as a thief. Blessed *is* he who watches, and keeps his garments, lest he walk naked and they see his shame."[1209]

Satan entered the Garden of Eden for the purpose of tempting Adam and Eve regarding their obedience to the terms of the Edenic Covenant that God had made with them.[1210] Satan asked the question "Has God indeed said, 'You shall not eat of every tree of the garden'?"[1211] Following Eve's answer the serpent lied to Eve saying, "You shall not surely die."[1212] The serpent's lie deceived Eve and she ate from the tree of the knowledge of good and evil. Adam also ate of the forbidden fruit, but he did so in deliberate disobedience to his complete knowledge of God's command. Immediately their eyes were opened, and they knew they were naked, and their bodies were immediately infected with the malignancy of sin and death. They tried to cover their nakedness with fig leaves. But fig leaves would not resolve their personal predicament nor their now altered relationship with God.

The Adamic Covenant:

We need to now consider what took place between their violation of the terms of the Edenic Covenant and the implementation of the Adamic Covenant. It is insightful to consider the four components that generally constitute the transition between these covenants. First, there were violations of God's sovereign will that are spelled out in the terms of the Adamic Covenant. Second, God made judgments regarding the violations and gave a verdict. Third, the execution of a

---

1208. 1 Thes. 5:4.
1209. Rev. 16:5.
1210. Gen. 1:26, 2:15-18.
1211. Gen. 3:1.
1212. Gen. 3:4.

sentence of punishment was made to commensurate with the judgment verdict. And fourth, a new covenant or at least a new era of kingdom administration was implemented.

First, Adam and Eve eating fruit from the tree of the knowledge of good and evil was a violation of the terms of the Edenic Covenant. Second, God came into the Garden and realized something was wrong. Therefore, He called Adam and Eve who were hiding and clarified what was wrong by asking them three questions: (1) Where are you? (2) Who told you that you were naked? (3) Have you eaten from the tree of which I commanded you that you should not eat? Adam and Eve confessed their sin but also tried to pass the blame for their actions. God did not annihilate Adam and Eve or the serpent but declared a verdict of guilty upon them. To the serpent God pronounced a curse making him go upon his belly and eat dust all his days. God greatly multiplied sorrow and pain upon the woman in conception and childbirth and cursed the ground with thorns and thistles for Adam's sake. Third, God sentenced the serpent with the punishment of enmity between his seed and the seed of the woman. Further, the seed of the woman would bruise the serpent's head and the serpent would bruise His heel. The woman was sentenced with a desire for her husband and he would rule over her. Adam would have to toil and sweat to gain a living from the ground all his days until he returned to the ground from which he was taken. Fourth, because of the terms of the Everlasting Covenant God had already made the necessary provisions in eternity past to resolve the consequences of sin and death. Therefore, He now implemented the first stage of His plan of redemption through the Adamic Covenant. Conner and Malmin state:

> The Adamic Covenant is the Covenant God made with Adam and Eve in the Garden of Eden after the entrance of sin expressing His purpose in redemption.... The Adamic Covenant is a "seed" covenant introducing the other covenants of redemption. The

> covenantal language that is expressed in "seed" form in this covenant is developed in fullness in the covenants that follow, leading up to its ultimate fulfillment in the New Covenant. Jesus Christ as the seed of the woman fulfills this Covenant in redeeming man back to perfect and eternal covenantal relationship with God.[1213]

Consequently, upon facing the reality of their sin, judgement, and sentencing God acted to redeem Adam and Eve from the eternal consequences of their sin through the substitutional sacrifice of an animal that died in their place and furnished a covering for their nakedness. That animal sacrifice was only a shadow of the fullness that was yet to be revealed in the future New Covenant, where Jesus Christ the Lamb of God would take away the sin of the world.[1214] God's redemptive action was not only a benefit to Adam and Eve but also a covenantal blessing to the entire human race for the generations that would follow. "For as by one man's disobedience many were made sinners, so also by one Man's obedience many will be made righteous."[1215] As we were all in Adam when he sinned so we were all in Christ when He bore our sin on the cross and was resurrected from the dead.[1216]

As A. W. Pink argues correctly, Adam was the federal head and representative of all mankind. Pink says, "The whole human race was placed on probation or trial in Eden. Adam acted not for himself alone, but he transacted for all who were to spring from him."[1217] To help us better understand Adam as the federal head or representative of the entire human race Pink offers the following illustration:

1213. Conner and Malmin, *The Covenants,* 21.

1214. John 1:29.

1215. Rom. 5:19.

1216. Gal. 2:20.

1217. Arthur Walkington Pink, *The Divine Covenants* (Grand Rapids: Baker Book House, 1973), 29.

> God did not deal with mankind as with a field of corn, where each stalk stands upon its own individual root; but He dealt with it as with a tree, all the branches of which have one common root and trunk. If you strike with an axe at the root of a tree, the whole tree falls—not only the trunk, but also the branches: all wither and die. So, it was when Adam fell. God permitted Satan to lay the axe at the root of the tree, and when Adam fell, all his posterity fell with him. At one fatal stroke Adam was severed from communion with his maker, and as the result death passed upon all men.... One acting on behalf of others, the one responsible for the many, is a basic principle both of human and divine government.[1218]

Following the implementation of the Adamic Covenant, Adam and Eve were denied access to the tree of life and immortality. Now facing the eventual death of their physical bodies the Lord God sent them out of the Garden of Eden to till the ground from which Adam was taken.[1219] As a consequence of their sin they no longer had unlimited fellowship with God as they had enjoyed under the terms of the Edenic Covenant while dwelling in the Garden of Eden. Now Adam had to work by the sweat of his brow to provide for his family. However, God did not sentence them to this kind of existence without hope.[1220] Their hope was established within the terms of the Adamic Covenant. The Adamic Covenant included the substitutional sacrifice of a lamb whose shed blood temporarily atoned for their sin and whose skin covered their nakedness. That sacrificial lamb was only a shadow of the reality of Jesus, the Lamb of God, who would not be revealed until the implementation of the New Covenant. He would take away the sin

1218. Ibid., 31-32.
1219. Gen 3:23-24.
1220. Rom. 8:20.

of the world, give the gift of righteousness, swallow up death in victory, and give eternal life to all who would believe on Him as Savior.

Adam and Eve now living a different kind of life outside the beautiful Garden of Eden. Because of Adam's disobedience he forfeited mankind's dominion over the earth and came under the bondage of Satan the prince of the power of the air.[1221] Adam also suffered further consequences of sin including a distorted and twisted consciousness of reality. His distorted and twisted consciousness was the result of sin which is captured by the Hebrew word *awon.* Strong's Hebrew Dictionary defines *awon* as number "5771. עָוֹן ʿâvôn, *aw-vone'*; or עָווֹן ʿâvôwn (2 Kings 7:9; Psa. 51:5 [7]), *aw-vone'*; from 5753; *perversity*, i.e. (moral) *evil:*—fault, iniquity, mischief, punishment (of iniquity), sin."[1222] William D. Mounce defines *awon* as follows:

> **Noun:** עָוֹן (ʿāwōn), GK 6411 (S 5771), 233×. ʿāwōn is usually translated "sin, guilt, wickedness, iniquity" and is one of the three primary words for sin in the OT, an offense against God that ranges from willful rebellion to unintentional sins (see sin).[1223]

James Swanson also provides a definition of the Hebrew word *awon;* **"6411** עָוֹן (ʿā·wōn): n.masc.; ≡ Str 5771; TWOT 1577a—**1.** LN 88.289–88.318 **sin**, wickedness, iniquity, i.e., wrongdoing, with a focus of liability or guilt for this wrong incurred (Ex 34:7);"[1224] Notice that all three dictionaries include the words "sin" and "iniquity" in their definitions of *awon.* Iniquity is that aspect of sin that twists, distorts or perverts mankind's perception of reality, and if not corrected it will lead to evil and wicked behavior. In other words, mankind's sinful nature underlies his moral evil and wicked behavior. For ex-

---

1221. Eph. 2:2.

1222. James Strong, *A Concise Dictionary of the Words in the Greek Testament and The Hebrew Bible* (Bellingham, WA: Logos Bible Software, 2009), 86.

1223. Mounce, *Mounce's Complete Expository Dictionary,* 359.

1224. Swanson, *Dictionary of Biblical Languages.*

ample, when Cain's offering was not received by the Lord, he became angry. God intervened by saying to Cain, "If you do well, will you not be accepted? And if you do not do well, sin lies at the door. And its desire *is* for you, but you should rule over it."[1225] Cain refused to rule over or correct his distorted attitude and as a result sin ruled over him to the extent that he killed his brother, Abel.

Adam and Eve were now experiencing pain and frustration resulting from the consequences of their sin infected souls and physical bodies, including an environment now corrupted with decay. However, they remained very much aware of their origin and their Creator because His nature was written into the very fabric of their existence even though it was now marred by sin. Adam and Eve taught their sons and daughters to worship their Creator as evidenced by the fact that Cain and Abel brought offerings to the Lord as recorded in Genesis chapter four.[1226] However, Cain refused to worship God in an acceptable manner and went out from the presence of the Lord. Adam had sons and daughters and lived nine hundred and thirty years and he died.[1227]

From Adam's expulsion from the Garden of Eden until the flood in the days of Noah, all mankind lived under the terms of the Adamic Covenant. Keep in mind that all mankind proceeds from Adam.[1228] In other words, Adam passed his sinful nature to all his offspring including all mankind now being subjugated to the curse of sin and death. The Adamic Covenant provided only a covering for sin. Each offering sacrificed in faith looked forward as a type, shadow, or pattern to the reality of the substance of the Savior, Jesus Christ. Under the terms of the Adamic Covenant, faith was expressed through the sacrifice of animals that were acceptable to God until the fullness of time when His Son Jesus would not simply cover sin, but shed His sinless blood on the cross for the remission of sin. This means that Jesus would wash sin and guilt away as far as the east is from the west to be

1225. Gen. 4:7.
1226. Gen. 4:3.
1227. Gen. 5:5.
1228. Acts 17:26.

remembered no more.[1229] So, throughout the Old Testament starting with the Adamic Covenant and throughout the New Testament "faith" has been and continues to be the key to a right relationship with God.

Since Adam's disobedience mankind was no longer indwelt by the Holy Spirit. Remember that God, Himself, breathed His breath into the nostrils of Adam.[1230] Adam was full of the Spirit of God until he sinned, then his nature changed. There were only a few men in the Old Testament filled with the Holy Spirit. Being filled with the Spirit or anointed by the Spirit was the exception, not the ordinary experience, even for the Children of Israel. As a result, men were not guided by the Holy Spirit nor had they received the Law of Moses to define the boundaries of moral conduct. Hence, as mankind began to multiply on the earth, their sinful conduct increased. They were further perverted and corrupted by rebellious angelic beings that co-habited with the daughters of men and produced an offspring of giants.[1231]

> Now it came to pass, when men began to multiply on the face of the earth, and daughters were born to them, that the sons of God saw the daughters of men, that they *were* beautiful; and they took wives for themselves of all whom they chose. And the LORD said, 'My Spirit shall not strive with man forever, for he *is* indeed flesh; yet his days shall be one hundred and twenty years.' There were giants on the earth in those days, and also afterward, when the sons of God came into the daughters of men and they bore *children* to them. Those *were* the mighty men who *were* of old, men of renown. "Then the LORD saw that the wickedness of man *was* great in the earth, and *that* every intent of the thoughts of his heart *was* only evil continually. And the LORD was sorry that He had

1229. Psa. 103:12.
1230. Gen. 2:7.
1231. Gen. 6:1-4.

> made man on the earth, and He was grieved in His heart. So the LORD said, 'I will destroy man whom I have created from the face of the earth, both man and beast, creeping thing and birds of the air, for I am sorry that I have made them.'" (Genesis 6:1-7).

Having seen the great wickedness and the evil intent of mankind, God was sorry that He had made man. Man had violated God's moral order to such an extent that God now entered judgment with mankind and sentenced all mankind to destruction including the destruction of beast, creeping things and birds of the air. It had been about sixteen hundred and fifty years since the inception of the Adamic Covenant. But now the execution of God's sentence against mankind was going to be a great flood and all mankind would be destroyed. "But Noah found grace in the eyes of the Lord."[1232]

The Noahic Covenant:

The transition between the Adamic Covenant and God's further covenantal revelations would be the final period of one hundred and twenty years of God's longsuffering in view of man's wickedness and may also refer to the length of time it took Noah to build an ark.[1233] "By faith Noah, being divinely warned of things not yet seen, moved with godly fear, prepared an ark for the saving of his household, by which he condemned the world and became heir of the righteousness which is according to faith."[1234] The Apostle Peter provides additional insight regarding God's judgment by stating;

> For if God did not spare the angels who sinned, but cast *them* down to hell and delivered *them* into chains of darkness, to be reserved for judgment; and did not

1232. Gen. 6:8.
1233. Gen. 6:3.
1234. Gen. 6:3; Heb 11:7.

> spare the ancient world, but saved Noah, *one of* eight *people,* a preacher of righteousness, bringing in the flood on the world of the ungodly..." (2 Peter 2:4-5).

God was longsuffering but the day came when Noah was commanded to enter the ark and the flood waters came upon the earth. "So, He destroyed all living things which were on the face of the ground: both man and cattle, creeping thing and bird of the air. Only Noah and those who *were* with him in the ark remained *alive."*[1235] Noah and his three sons and their wives with the animals were on the ark a total of 371 days.[1236] The execution of God's judgment now passed, Noah and his family disembarked from the ark. Noah then built an altar to the Lord and offered burnt offerings on the altar. God then entered a covenant with Noah as He had promised.[1237] Conner and Malmin state:

> The Noahic Covenant contains a reaffirmation of the creative purposes stated in the Edenic Covenant. It is also an extension of "the seed" promises of redemption as in the Adamic Covenant. Though it arises out of a time of great judgment, it establishes a hope that God's purposes of creation in creation will be fulfilled through redemption. The hope of the Noahic Covenant finds its complete fulfillment in the New Covenant.[1238]

The Noahic Covenant was established between God and Noah and Noah's descendants after him.[1239] In other words this covenant would

---

1235. Gen. 7:23.

1236. John C. Whitcomb, Jr. and Henry M. Morris, *The Genesis Flood: The Biblical Record and Its Scientific Implications,* (Grand Rapids, MI: Baker Book House, 1974), 3.

1237. Gen. 6:18, 8:2-9:17.

1238. Conner and Malmin, *The Covenants,* 26.

1239. Gen. 9:11.

be with all mankind and the source of what many consider as common grace upon all people for the ages to come. The sign of the covenant was the rainbow. God said, "The rainbow shall be in the cloud, and I will look on it to remember the everlasting covenant between God and every living creature of all flesh that *is* on the earth."[1240] All believers know the sense of assurance we experience when we see the rainbow after a storm.

As Noah and His descendants began to repopulate the earth, they had one language and one speech.[1241] And again mankind began to rebel against the Lord and this time in an organized manner by building a tower whose top would reach into heaven.[1242] Therefore, two powerful events took place: (1) God confused their language and they were scattered over the face of the earth.[1243] (2) For the first time since creation of the world "nations" are mentioned.[1244] In other words it was after the flood and the inception of the Noahic Covenant that God inaugurated nations as a new system of government to restrain evil and maintain moral order among men until the fullness of time when He could send the Messiah into the world.

Principalities and Powers:

It seems at this juncture that God placed principalities and angelic rulers over the nations as His delegated authorities to influence their governments toward His redemptive purposes. We will consider why God delegated principalities and angelic powers over nations, but first we need to address the fact that out of all the nations God called one man, Abram.

1240. Gen. 9:16.
1241. Gen. 11:1.
1242. Gen. 11:4.
1243. Gen. 11:6-9.
1244. Gen. 10:5

> Now the LORD had said to Abram: 'Get out of your country, from your family and from your father's house, to a land that I will show you. I will make you a great nation; I will bless you and make your name great; And you shall be a blessing. I will bless those who bless you, And I will curse him who curses you; And in you all the families of the earth shall be blessed.' (Genesis 12:1-3).

God specifically chose Abram out the midst of the nations and promised to bless all the families of the earth through him. So, how or why would God delegate principalities and angelic powers to administrate His kingdom authority over the nations without violating the free will of mankind? A consideration of the following Scriptures may shed light on the role or function of principalities and angelic powers and offer the possibility that they failed in their responsibilities. First, the Apostle Paul informs us that by Jesus "all things were created that are in heaven and that are on earth, visible and invisible, whether thrones or dominions or principalities or powers. All things were created through Him and for Him."[1245] Hence, principalities and powers were created by Jesus for a specific purpose. That purpose seems to be for serving God as His administrative assistants over the governments of the nations. Second, it was while Daniel was praying that he had a great vision and Gabriel said to him, "I have come because of your words. But the prince of the kingdom of Persia withstood me twenty-one days; and behold Michael, one of the chief princes, came to help me, for I had been left alone there with the kings of Persia."[1246]

Therefore, it seems between the days of their delegated authority over nations and the day of Daniel's vision at least some principalities and angelic rulers had turned from God's purposes and positioned themselves in opposition to God. This is demonstrated by the prince

---

1245. Col. 1:16.
1246. Dan. 10:12-13.

of the kingdom of Persia who withstood Gabriel and the purposes of God in response to Daniel's prayers. Third, the Apostle Paul informs us that Jesus has "disarmed principalities and powers, He made a public spectacle of them, triumphing over them in it."[1247] Consequently, it seems they had armed themselves with the power of the Law against mankind, using the Law as a means of accusation against all mankind. Satan means "Accuser".[1248] The Law made nothing perfect, it could only define what is wrong, thus giving Satan and his cohorts plenty of fodder with which to accuse man before God since we all fall short to the standards of the Law.[1249] However, when Jesus died on the cross He fulfilled the demands of the Law and principalities and powers were disarmed. As a result, "we do not wrestle against flesh and blood, but against principalities, against powers, against the rulers of the darkness of this age, against spiritual *hosts* of wickedness in the heavenly *places.*"[1250] In other words, people cannot hinder us from receiving answers to our prayers but principalities and angelic powers will try to hinder us as they hindered Daniel's answers to his prayer for twenty-one days. But Jesus has disarmed them, and we are empowered by the Holy Spirit to live in the victory Jesus gained for us. So, we are to wrestle in prayer against their influence in our lives and government today.

We may ask ourselves, "Why would God delegate authority to principalities and powers over nations if they themselves might possibly turn and oppose God?" To answer this question, it will be helpful to consider God's response to Israel's sin in the days of Moses. Moses was with God on Mount Sinai receiving the Ten Commandments. Meanwhile the Children of Israel under the leadership of Aaron were worshipping a golden calf. God in His anger said to Moses:

1247. Col. 2:15.
1248. Rev. 12:10.
1249. Heb. 7:19.
1250. Eph

> 'I have seen this people, and indeed it *is* a stiff-necked people! Now therefore, let Me alone, that My wrath may burn hot against them and I may consume them. And I will make of you a great nation.' Then Moses pleaded with the LORD his God, and said: 'LORD, why does Your wrath burn hot against Your people whom You have brought out of the land of Egypt with great power and with a mighty hand? Why should the Egyptians speak, and say, 'He brought them out to harm them, to kill them in the mountains, and to consume them from the face of the earth'? 'Turn from Your fierce wrath and relent from this harm to Your people. Remember Abraham, Isaac, and Israel, Your servants, to whom You swore by Your own self, and said to them, 'I will multiply your descendants as the stars of heaven; and all this land that I have spoken of I give to your descendants, and they shall inherit *it* forever.' So, the LORD relented from the harm which He said He would do to His people. (Exodus 32:9-14).

A key to understanding the dynamic of this passage is found in the intercession of Moses before God. Also consider God's willingness to relent from the harm which He would do to the Children of Israel because of the terms of His covenant with their fathers, Abraham, Isaac and Jacob. Following his intercession Moses proceeded down Mt. Sinai to the camp of Israel. Seeing the Children of Israel worshipping the golden calf, Moses himself became very angry and threw the tablets of the Ten Commandments down and broke them in pieces. This was followed by judgment upon the Children of Israel, whereby three thousand were executed for their sin. Moses then scolded the people and said he would go up to the Lord and perhaps make an atonement for their sin.[1251]

1251. Exod. 32:30.

Moses went before the Lord and confessed the sin of the people and concluded his intercession by saying; "Yet now, if You will forgive their sin--but if not, I pray, blot me out of Your book which You have written."[1252] The Lord responded to Moses' intercession by saying; "Now therefore, go, lead the people to *the place* of which I have spoken to you. Behold, My Angel shall go before you. Nevertheless, in the day when I visit for punishment, I will visit punishment upon them for their sin."[1253] The Lord then commanded Moses to lead the Children of Israel to the land He had promised to Abraham, Isaac, and Jacob. Then the Lord spoke these extremely important words to Moses:

> And I will send *My* Angel before you, and I will drive out the Canaanite and the Amorite and the Hittite and the Perizzite and the Hivite and the Jebusite. *Go up* to a land flowing with milk and honey; **for I will not go up in your midst, lest I consume you on the way**, for you *are* a stiff-necked people." (Exodus 33:2-3; emphasis mine).

God's words to Moses give valuable insight into His nature and one possible reason why He uses delegated authority in place of His personal presence in many governmental related circumstances. He is a holy God with "purer eyes than to behold evil and cannot look on wickedness."[1254] Therefore, rather than God personally going with Moses and Israel to the Promised Land and risking the possibility of destroying the very people He had made covenant to bless—God promised to send His Angel with them. God was not withholding His presence because He was trying to punish them, rather He was trying to keep from destroying them—that is an expression of His amazing grace. They were a stiff-necked people and prone to rebellion, God

1252. Exod. 32:32.
1253. Exod. 32:34.
1254. Hab. 1:13.

did not want to run the risk of destroying them while trying to achieve a short term goal that could totally disrupt His long term goal of blessing all the families of the earth by bringing a Messiah into the world through them. The zeal of the Lord is a powerful force. It is like fire, it can warm you and help you, but it can also consume you. Even Jesus overturned the tables of the money changers and drove them out of the temple and "His disciples remembered that it was written, '*Zeal for Your house has eaten Me up.*'"[1255] This is possibly a reason why God placed principalities and angelic authorities over nations. God is gracious and did not want to destroy the nations until He could clearly demonstrate for all to see how much He loved them by sending His own Son to die on the cross for them. This is the heart of the gospel of the kingdom!!

Free will is a principle of God written into the core of His relationship with mankind and angels. For love to be God's kind of love it cannot be coerced. It can only be love when it flows from a free will. God is love. Therefore, He does not love the world because He is forced to love it. No! God does not do love; He is love and He wants a family of sons and daughters that freely choose to love Him with all their heart, soul, strength, and mind. So, God has granted men and angels free will. However, when God's creatures freely, willfully, deliberately, and habitually rebel against His moral boundaries to the point where they are destroying themselves and/or others—then God will override their free will with His sovereign will. Even though God is gracious, merciful, and longsuffering He will always have the final word.

Before we leave the context of Moses interceding before God, it is insightful to look at one further passage.

> And it came to pass, when Moses entered the tabernacle, that the pillar of cloud descended and stood *at* the door of the tabernacle, and *the Lord* talked with

1255. John 2:17.

> Moses. All the people saw the pillar of cloud standing *at* the tabernacle door, and all the people rose and worshiped, each man *in* his tent door. So, the LORD spoke to Moses face to face, as a man speaks to his friend. And he would return to the camp, but his servant Joshua the son of Nun, a young man, did not depart from the tabernacle. Then Moses said to the LORD, "See, You say to me, 'Bring up this people.' But You have not let me know whom You will send with me. Yet You have said, 'I know you by name, and you have also found grace in My sight.' Now therefore, I pray, if I have found grace in Your sight, show me now Your way, that I may know You and that I may find grace in Your sight. And consider that this nation *is* Your people." And He said, "**My Presence will go *with you*, and I will give you rest**." Then he said to Him, "If Your Presence does not go *with us,* do not bring us up from here. For how then will it be known that Your people and I have found grace in Your sight, except You go with us? So we shall be separate, Your people and I, from all the people who *are* upon the face of the earth." So, the LORD said to Moses, "**I will also do this thing that you have spoken; for you have found grace in My sight, and I know you by name**." (Exodus 33:9-17; Emphasis mine).

Moses proved his metal before the Lord earlier when he said, "If You will forgive their sin--but if not, I pray, blot me out of Your book which You have written."[1256] For God to accomplish His redemptive purposes He needed a man to stand in the gap between Himself and other men. A mediator that was willing to love sinners the way He

1256. Exod. 32:32.

loved sinners. "Greater love has no one than this, than to lay down one's life for his friends."[1257] In the days of Ezekiel God said, "So I sought for a man among them who would make a wall, and stand in the gap before Me on behalf of the land, that I should not destroy it; but I found no one."[1258] Moses' intercession before the Lord made an enormous difference in God's ongoing relationship with the nation of Israel. Following Moses' intercession God promised to travel with the Children of Israel and His presence would distinguish them from other nations. Moses proved to be a powerful intercessor but the Book of Hebrews explains that Jesus is even better since He willingly laid down His life for us and yet He ever lives to continually make intercession for us.[1259]

The Abrahamic Covenant

Now that we have addressed the issue as to why God possibly delegated principalities and angelic rulers with spiritual authority and influence over the governments of nations. We will now move forward by addressing why God called Abram alone out of the midst of the nations. Remember, it was while God was speaking to the serpent in the Garden of Eden that God said that the seed of the woman would bruise the head of the serpent.[1260] Even though that was about two thousand years before Abram's call, God was deliberately and progressively fulfilling His word. To further accomplish His redemptive purposes God called Abram to a life of faith and in the process of time God entered a covenant with him. Regarding the Abrahamic Covenant, Conner and Malmin make the following comments:

> The Abrahamic Covenant is a Covenant God made with Abraham, Isaac and Jacob. It was made after the

1257. John 15:13.
1258. Eze. 22:30.
1259. Heb. 3:3-6, 7:25
1260. Gen. 3:15.

> Tower of Babel and the scattering of the descendants of Noah. It involves National Israel, the Seed Messiah, and all believers of all nations. It is the most comprehensive of all the Old Testament Covenants.[1261]

As part of making a covenant with Abram God changed his name from Abram to Abraham, and promised to give him and heir, and gave circumcision as the sign of the Abrahamic Covenant.[1262] God also told Abraham that his descendants would be strangers in a land that is not theirs, and will serve them, and they will afflict them four hundred years.[1263] Even though Abraham and Sarah had no children God promised them a son in their old age.[1264] So it was when Abraham was one hundred and Sarah at age ninety, they had the promised son Isaac. Then the day came when God tested Abraham's faith by asking him to go to the Mountains of Moriah and sacrifice Isaac to the Lord. Abraham was obedient to God's command but as he stretched out his hand and took the knife to slay his son, the Angel of the Lord called to him from heaven and said,

> 'Abraham, Abraham! So, he said, 'Here I am.' And He said, 'Do not lay your hand on the lad, or do anything to him; for now I know that you fear God, since you have not withheld your son, your only *son,* from Me.' Then Abraham lifted his eyes and looked, and there behind *him was* a ram caught in a thicket by its horns. So, Abraham went and took the ram, and offered it up for a burnt offering instead of his son. And Abraham called the name of the place, The-LORD-Will-Provide; as it is said *to* this day, "In the Mount of The LORD it shall be provided." Then the Angel

1261. Conner and Malmin, *The Covenants,* 27.
1262. Gen. 17:1-11.
1263. Gen. 15:13.
1264. Gen. 17:16-17.

> of the LORD called to Abraham a second time out of heaven, and said: "By Myself I have sworn, says the LORD, because you have done this thing, and have not withheld your son, your only *son*--blessing I will bless you, and multiplying I will multiply your descendants as the stars of the heaven and as the sand which *is* on the seashore; and your descendants shall possess the gate of their enemies. In your seed all the nations of the earth shall be blessed, because you have obeyed My voice. (Genesis 22:11-18).

God was testing the strength of the covenant bond He had with Abraham, because God knew that one day, He would have to sacrifice His only begotten Son. Abraham proved faithful in his covenant bond with God. And in the process of time God established His covenant with Isaac and also with his son Jacob.[1265] In the days of Jacob there was a famine in the land and it became so severe that Jacob moved his entire household of seventy persons to the land of Egypt for survival.[1266] Jacob and his family were shepherds and shepherds were an abomination to the Egyptians.[1267] As a result, the Children of Israel remained separate from the Egyptians and multiplied, becoming the size of a nation. However, because of their growing numbers, the Pharaoh of Egypt became afraid that the Children of Israel would become a military or political enemy. Therefore, he made a decree to kill all the male children as soon as they were born and burdened the Children of Israel with the heavy bondage of slavery. The cry and pain of their bondage came up before the Lord and He called and charged Moses with the responsibility of leading the Children of Israel out of their Egyptian bondage.[1268]

1265. Exod. 2:24.
1266. Gen. 46:27.
1267. Gen. 46:34.
1268. Exod. 2:23-3:22.

The Mosaic Covenant:

As Moses obeyed and God powerfully intervened against Pharaoh with a series of plagues concluding with the death of the firstborn of all Egyptians during the Passover.[1269] Consequently, Pharaoh released the Children of Israel; "And the LORD went before them by day in a pillar of cloud to lead the way, and by night in a pillar of fire to give them light, so as to go by day and night."[1270] They followed the pillar of cloud until they came to the Red Sea. There, Moses stretched out his rod over the water and the waters parted just as a mother's birth canal opens, the water breaks and a child is born. So, the newly birthed nation of Israel walked out of Egypt through the Red Sea on dry land. But when the Egyptians tried to pass through the Red Sea on dry land in pursuit of the Children of Israel the waters came over them and their horses and riders were destroyed in the sea.[1271]

From the shore of the Red Sea the Lord led the Children of Israel to Mount Sinai. There under the leadership of Moses the Lord entered a covenant with them as a nation. As a part of the Mosaic Covenant God gave the Ten Commandments, appointed and consecrated the priesthood under Aaron the High Priest, and gave the pattern for the building of the Tabernacle so He could dwell in their midst. God would dwell in the Holy of Holies of the Tabernacle, and the High Priest could enter before the presence of God once a year on the Day of Atonement. But the marvelous reality was that for the first time since the Garden of Eden, God would dwell among men. Regarding the Mosaic Covenant, Conner and Malmin make the following comments:

> The Mosaic Covenant is the most complicated and most difficult of all the covenants to interpret. The elaborate wording of the covenant, the prolific and intricate details of the sacrifices, priesthood and

---

1269. Exod. 12:1-51.
1270. Exod. 13:21.
1271. Exod. 14:22-31.

> sanctuary and the complete governing of the national life of Israel by sabbaths and religious festivals makes it the fullest expression of a covenant in Scripture.... The Abrahamic Covenant, which was an everlasting and irrevocable, was not annulled by the Mosaic Covenant, which was temporarily imposed upon Israel until the time when the New Covenant would fulfill the Abrahamic Covenant and abolish the Mosaic Covenant.[1272]

The point we are seeking to emphasize is that despite man's sinful condition God has always loved all people and offered eternal hope of glory. The hope He offers is established in His sovereignty and personal nature of lovingkindness and made manifest through the terms of His covenants. Covenant terms include the unfolding revelation of redemption, the coming of a Redeemer, the establishment of His kingdom in the here and now, and a future glory. All this happened despite mankind's propensity to sin and rebel against God. First, God reveals in the Adamic Covenant His plan to overcome the consequences of sin and death through His substitutionary sacrifice and promises that the seed of the woman will bruise the head of the serpent. Second, even when man's wickedness and rebellion against God was so great that He determined to destroy the world with a flood, yet Noah found grace in the eyes of the Lord. Following the flood God made a covenant with Noah and the terms of that covenant applies to all men. God will never again destroy the world with a flood and placed the rainbow in the sky as a sign of the Noahic Covenant.

Following the flood in the days of Noah God instituted "nations" to govern mankind and restrain evil until the fullness of time when His Messiah could be revealed. Then out of the nations God called a single individual, Abraham, and made a covenant with him promising to give him an heir, make of him into a great nation, give his

---

1272. Conner and Malmin, *The Covenants,* 40-43.

descendants the Canaan Land as an inheritance, and make him a blessing to all nations. Abraham's family grew from seventy individuals into a nation while in the womb of Egypt. God led them by the hand of Moses out of Egypt to Mt. Sinai where he entered into the Mosaic Covenant with them. Israel was to be a holy nation, a shining example of God's righteousness and blessings to attract other nations to the God of Israel. However, Israel failed in that endeavor because of their unbelief and desire to be like other nations. They rebelled against God, violated His law, and succumbed to idolatry, to the point that God had to severely discipline them and eventually bring judgment upon them as a nation.

The Davidic Covenant:

It is not our intention to review all the twist and turns in Israel's relationship with God from the time of the Mosaic Covenant until the inception of the New Covenant. However, it is essential to our understanding of the kingdom to briefly address God's Covenant with David made about five-hundred years after the inception of the Mosaic Covenant. God sent the Prophet Samuel to anoint the young man David as King of Israel to replace King Saul. After King David had made Jerusalem his capitol city, he was not content until he had brought the Ark of the Covenant into Mt. Zion and placed it in a tent and organized priestly choirs to sing and offer praises to God twenty-four hours a day.[1273] Because the Ark of God was in a tent, it came into David's heart to build God a house of cedar, a temple. But when David proposed to do that the Lord spoke to Nathan the prophet to tell King David that he was not to build the temple. But God further spoke through the prophet Nathan, expressing His love for David by entering a covenant with him saying; "'And your house and your kingdom shall be established forever before you. Your throne shall

---

1273. 1 Chro. 25:1-31; Psa. 134:1-3.

be established forever.'"[1274] The Davidic Covenant includes the terms "throne" and "kingdom" which indicates that its ultimate fulfillment will not be complete in David's lifetime, but will find its ultimate fulfillment in the life and ministry of Jesus Christ, the son of David. A thousand years after the life of David, the angel Gabriel came to the virgin Mary and said:

> And behold, you will conceive in your womb and bring forth a Son and shall call His name JESUS. He will be great and will be called the Son of the Highest; and the Lord God will give Him the throne of His father David. And He will reign over the house of Jacob forever, and of His kingdom there will be no end. (Luke 1:31-33).

Gabriel's message also includes the words "throne" and "kingdom". John the Baptist prepared the way for the ministry of Jesus by proclaiming, "Repent for the kingdom of heaven is at hand."[1275] Following Jesus' water baptism He received the anointing of the Holy Spirit. Then Jesus was led by the Spirit into the wilderness to be tempted of the devil for forty days and nights. After the wilderness testings Jesus went in the power of the Spirit to the area of Galilee and began to preach saying, "Repent, for the kingdom of heaven is at hand."[1276] With this gospel Jesus was inaugurating a new phase of God's government among men in the very territory (*this world*) where the devil had illegitimately ruled since Adam's sin in the Garden of Eden. What a liberating gospel this was, because it offered victory over the bondage of sin and the powers of evil. "For this purpose, the Son of God was manifested, that He might destroy the works of the devil."[1277] After three years of ministry proclaiming the gospel of the kingdom

1274. 2 Sam. 7:16.
1275. Matt. 3:2.
1276. Matt. 4:17.
1277. 1 John 3:8.

Jesus entered Jerusalem on Palm Sunday. There, most people were excited and expecting Him to bring about Israel's independence from the Roman government. However, Jesus was not entering Jerusalem for political purposes but redemptive purposes. He came to deliver mankind from the bondage of sin and death and "destroy him who had the power of death, that is, the devil."[1278] Jesus was in Jerusalem to fulfill the purposes of the New Covenant by offering Himself as "the Lamb of God who takes away the sin of the world."[1279]

The New Covenant:

God had been planning this Passover since before the foundation of the world and had this day in mind when He told the serpent that the seed of the woman would bruise his head. The Adamic, Noahic, Abrahamic, Mosaic, and Davidic Covenants all culminate in and through the person and work of Jesus Christ, Immanuel, who shares our flesh and blood nature. "He has obtained a more excellent ministry, inasmuch as He is also Mediator of a better covenant, which was established on better promises."[1280] At the Passover meal, the Last Supper, Jesus "took the cup after supper, saying, 'This cup is the New Covenant in My blood.'"[1281] The New Covenant which Jesus was inaugurating fulfilled all the terms of the prior Covenants. Conner and Malmin state:

> The New Covenant was made by the Lord Jesus Christ immediately prior to His death at Jerusalem.... It became the fulfillment of all previous Covenants, fulfilling and abolishing in itself their temporal elements and making possible their everlasting elements. The New Covenant makes possible and brings

1278. Heb. 2:4b.
1279. John 1:29.
1280. Heb. 8:6.
1281. 1 Cor. 11:25.

> the believer into the Everlasting Covenant, thus completing the cycle of Covenantal revelation.[1282]

Jesus lived among us without sin, but on the cross God "made Him who knew no sin *to be* sin for us, that we might become the righteousness of God in Him."[1283] "What the law could not do in that it was weak through the flesh, God *did* by sending His own Son in the likeness of sinful flesh, on account of sin: He condemned sin in the flesh."[1284] "And you *He made alive,* who were dead in trespasses and sins, in which you once walked according to the course of this world, according to the prince of the power of the air"[1285] The devil is an "accuser" and a "destroyer."[1286] His accusations are a warfare tactic against God and mankind for the purpose of inciting God against us or inciting us against God or inciting us against each other.[1287] "The wages of sin is death,"[1288] and when Jesus was crucified you and I were in Christ; when He died we died, when He was raised from the dead, we were raised from the dead.[1289] As a result, sin and death no longer have dominion over you and me because the Law has been fulfilled.[1290] Jesus died once and for all making a "propitiation for our sins, and not for ours only but also for the whole world."[1291] Upon His resurrection Jesus entered heaven "Not with the blood of goats and calves, but with His own blood He entered the Most Holy Place once for all, having obtained eternal redemption."[1292] Jesus, our crucified and resurrected Savior fulfilled the demands of the law and sprinkled His own blood on the mercy-seat, thus purify-

1282. Conner and Malmin, *The Covenants,* 69.
1283. 2 Cor. 5:21.
1284. Rom. 8:3.
1285. Eph. 2:1-2.
1286. Rev. 12:10.
1287. Job 2:3; Acts 24:13; Gal. 5:15.
1288. Rom. 6:23.
1289. Gal. 2:20; Rom. 8:11.
1290. Rom. 6:9-14.
1291. 1 John 2:2.
1292. Heb. 9:12.

ing heaven. As a result, the devil no longer has access to God's throne nor any legal grounds to accuse us before the presence of God. His illegitimate position as the "ruler of this world" was revoked by the death and resurrection of Jesus Christ who is the "King of Kings and Lord of Lords." God's judgment against the devil has been made and the verdict has been decided. There was war in heaven and Satan was cast down no longer having access to the throne of God.[1293] Now we are waiting for the return of Jesus and the sentence against the devil to be executed by binding him and casting him into the bottomless pit for a thousand years.[1294] Then it will come to pass, "The kingdoms of this world have become *the kingdoms* of our Lord and of His Christ, and He shall reign forever and ever!"[1295] That is what Jesus meant by His words, "Now is the judgment of this world; now the ruler of this world will be cast out."[1296]

About seven hundred years before Jesus was born the Prophet Isaiah received the following revelation regarding the government of God:

> For unto us a Child is born, unto us a Son is given; And the government will be upon His shoulder. And His name will be called Wonderful, Counselor, Mighty God, Everlasting Father, Prince of Peace. Of the increase of *His* government and peace *There will be* no end, Upon the throne of David and over His kingdom, to order it and establish it with judgment and justice from that time forward, even forever. The zeal of the LORD of hosts will perform this. (Isaiah 9:6-7).

The government or the kingdom is upon the shoulders of Jesus. And Jesus taught that the kingdom of heaven is like a mustard seed,

1293. Rev. 12:7-9.
1294. Rev. 20:1-3.
1295. Rev. 11:15
1296. John 12:31.

"which indeed is the least of all seeds; but when it is grown it is greater than all herbs and becomes a tree."[1297] That parable affirms Isaiah's prophecy, "The increase of His government and peace there shall be no end." Isaiah also prophesied, "For the earth shall be full of the knowledge of the Lord as the waters cover the sea."[1298] Therefore, believers must keep in mind that the kingdom of God has come, it is increasing, but not yet fully arrived. We, as citizens of the kingdom of God, are presently living through a transition period. The kingdom is present, but there is more to come when Jesus returns and sets His kingdom in order on the earth. As citizens of the kingdom of God we expect and contend for kingdom realities, including peace that passes our understanding, healing of our physical bodies, financial prosperity over poverty, and harmony in relationships, etc. As we now contend for those kingdom blessings we will also continue being tempted by the devil. Therefore, we must continue exercising vigilance in prayer, wrestling against principalities and rulers of darkness, because the devil continues to "walk about like a roaring lion, seeking whom he will devour."[1299] So, our walk with God is a walk of faith, "and this is the victory that has overcome the world—our faith."[1300]

As members of the body of Christ, the Church, it may be helpful to think of the kingdom of God in this world from this perspective. As the Apostle John says, "We know that we are of God, and the whole world lies *under the sway of* the wicked one."[1301] Jesus entered this world which the devil was controlling to inaugurate the government or kingdom of God. In other words, Jesus left the glories of heaven and entered hostile enemy territory, not to pick a fight, but to take back control for this world He had created. To accomplish His mission He said, "I will build My church, and the gates of Hades shall

---

1297. Matt. 13:31-32.
1298. Isa. 11:9.
1299. 1 Peter 5:8.
1300. 1 John 5:4.
1301. 1 John 5:19.

not prevail against it."[1302] Jesus started with a few disciples and after teaching them for about three years He commissioned them to make disciples of all nations. In other words, Jesus entered the devil's territory and started building His church (*ekklesia*).

The Church of Jesus Christ:

All that was accomplished through God's Covenantal arrangements throughout the history of mankind culminates in the New Covenant. The New Covenant is not concerned with ritual or land, but with the heart of man. "*For this is the covenant that I will make with the house of Israel after those days, says the LORD: I will put My laws in their mind and write them on their hearts; and I will be their God, and they shall be My people.*"[1303] The kingdom of God does not consist of rules and regulations, buildings or real estate, but consist of the sovereign authority and love of God that is enthroned in the hearts of men. Jesus said. "the kingdom of God is within you."[1304] All New Covenant Believers in Jesus Christ can testify without reservations, "Greater is He who is in me than he who is in the world."[1305] Ron Cottle states,

> The local church stands as an embassy of Kingdom activity. Its facilities are on sovereign soil, dedicated to the purposes of the kingdom. Its congregants are citizens of God's Kingdom, separate from the world around them while living within the world. In other words, the local expression of the Body of Christ is alive and well and standing on the sovereign soil of God's good ground in a world gone awry.[1306]

1302. Matt. 16:18.

1303. Heb. 8:10.

1304. Luke 17:21.

1305. 1 John 1:4.

1306. Dr. Ron Cottle, *The Kingdom Embassy: The Foundational Role of the Local Church in the World* (Columbus, GA: REC Ministries, 2015).

Jesus at this present time sits at the right hand of God on the Father's throne in heaven.[1307] Jesus is the King of the kingdom and He is also the head of the Church.[1308] The Holy Spirit is the chief administrator on the earth for both the kingdom of God and the church.[1309] We affirm that when the church age is completed and Jesus has put all enemies under His feet, He will subject Himself to the Father and the Father will be "all and in all."[1310] But for our purposes in the present time there is a distinction between kingdom of God and the Church of Jesus Christ. Jack Taylor defines this distinction as follows, "The kingdom is the whole into which everything else fits."[1311] The Church fits within the kingdom of God and the church members are also citizens of the kingdom. The kingdom of God extends across all government authority and functions. For example, the kingdom of God includes the state and local police officers. They function in the rule and reign of God or the kingdom of God as His ministers keeping moral order and peace even though they may not be members of the Church of Jesus Christ.[1312]

Church members serve as ambassadors of the kingdom representing its King and His kingdom values through their lifestyle lived within the context of this present world system. Thus, the church is the embassy for the kingdom, administrating its nature and values, not in a formal sense, but through the lifestyle of the members of the church. In every nation of the world there exists cultural constructs or customs that contribute to abusive and sinful practices, for which the Holy Spirit, working through Spirit filled believers, raises up a standard of restraint.[1313] Many times, these cultural practices contribute to violence, drunkenness, and immorality. For example, in our culture

---

1307. Col. 3:1.

1308. Psa. 2:6; Eph. 5:23; Col. 1:18.

1309. John 16:13-15,

1310. 1 Cor. 15:28.

1311. Taylor, *Cosmic Initiative,* 100.

1312. Rom. 13:3-5.

1313. Isa. 59:19.

large sports events like the Superbowl, draws huge crowds together and tensions among fans often arise to high levels that spill over into the community after the game. Restaurant owners, motel managers, and convenience store operators in the area of the event often report excessive vulgar language, broken furniture, trash everywhere, and pilferage.

One convenience store owner whose store is located at an interstate exit about one hundred miles from the city where the Superbowl was held, told me that many fans traveling to and from the Superbowl came in his store. But many were so rude and destructive that he actually feared for his personal safety, and so much was stolen that he lost money. He said if another Superbowl were held in that city he would close his store for a period of about ten days to avoid the abuse and troubles. The point is that kingdom culture is to be lived out in this world under those kinds of circumstances. The training ground for life in the kingdom of God is the church with its disciplines and accountability structures informed by the example and teaching of Jesus:

> But I say to you, love your enemies, bless those who curse you, do good to those who hate you, and pray for those who spitefully use you and persecute you, that you may be sons of your Father in heaven; for He makes His sun rise on the evil and on the good, and sends rain on the just and on the unjust.[1314]

The local church consists of men and women in a covenant relationship with God through faith in Jesus Christ, the resurrected Savior. When the citizens of the kingdom of God gather in an assembly, Jesus is in the midst and that constitutes a local church.[1315] All the members of the church are empowered by the Holy Spirit to serve as ambassadors of the kingdom of God. The local church serves as a

1314. Matt. 5:44-45.
1315. Matt. 18:20.

strategic base of operations through which the kingdom of God will continually expand until it infiltrates every nation and people group on the face of the earth. Under the Mosaic Covenant God was working His redemptive agenda in and through the one nation of Israel. In order to participate in the blessings of that Covenant, one had to become an Israelite. From the inception of God's Covenant with Abraham until the Day of Pentecost, it was God's strategy to release His gracious blessings through the family structure. And the family structure remains a powerful institution in the purposes of God. However, under the terms of the New Covenant, when a person places their faith in Jesus Christ, that person is granted the gift of God's righteousness; then he or she is justified and regenerated by the Holy Spirit—that is born again—born into the family of God. As a result, that person is no longer a spiritual orphan, but a member of the family of God, heir and joint heir with Jesus Christ.[1316]

> Therefore, from now on, we regard no one according to the flesh. Even though we have known Christ according to the flesh, yet now we know *Him thus* no longer. Therefore, if anyone *is* in Christ, *he is* a new creation; old things have passed away; behold, all things have become new. Now all things are of God, who has reconciled us to Himself through Jesus Christ, and has given us the ministry of reconciliation, (2 Corinthians 5:16-18)

Hence the church of Jesus Christ is not confined to one nation or ethnic group. Jesus commissioned His disciples to go and make disciples of all nations.[1317] God is not willing that any should perish, but all should come to repentance.[1318] So how is God's redemptive purposes going to be accomplished? The simple answer is that the redemptive

1316. Rom. 8:17.
1317. Matt. 28:19-20.
1318. 2 Peter 3:9.

purposes of God will be accomplished by the Holy Spirit empowered church, living and ministering all around the world. The Church both, local and worldwide, is called by the Lord to be salt and light and has been given the ministry of reconciliation. First, that means that Christians are to so live in this world in such a manner that others will see our good works and glorify our Father which is in heaven.[1319] For example, there was a sudden death of a small child in our community. The parents of that child seldom attended church. However, during that time of grief and pain, the ladies of a local church carried food to that family, loved and cried with them and prayed for them. That grieving family having experienced the blessings of the kingdom of God in a tangible and meaningful way, now attends church. Likewise, Apostle Peter says, "Wives, likewise, *be* submissive to your own husbands, that even if some do not obey the word, they, without a word, may be won by the conduct of their wives, when they observe your chaste conduct *accompanied* by fear."[1320]

Second, Jesus said, "You are the salt of the earth; but if the salt loses its flavor, how shall it be seasoned? It is then good for nothing but to be thrown out and trampled underfoot by men."[1321] Salt is an important element in the economy of the Kingdom of God. Jesus said, "Every sacrifice will be seasoned with salt."[1322] The Law of Moses states, "And every offering of your grain offering you shall season with salt; you shall not allow the salt of the covenant of your God to be lacking from your grain offering. With all your offerings you shall offer salt."[1323] Every Levitical offering required the shedding of blood except the grain offering. Each offering was a type or shadow of the redemptive work of Jesus Christ. But all the Levitical offerings were to be seasoned with salt. The most familiar use of salt is for seasoning because it enhances the flavor of food. It is unusual to come to a

---

1319. Matt. 5:16.
1320. 1 Peter 3:1-2.
1321. Matt. 5:13.
1322. Mark 9:49.
1323. Lev. 2:13.

table and no saltshaker available. Salt also serves as a preservative when it permeates the texture of meat. When I was a boy, my family butchered their own meat and always salted a portion of it to preserve it for a few months. When I lived in Russia fish preserved with salt was quite common.

The significance of salt can be found in the words of the Apostle Paul. He said, "I now rejoice in my sufferings for you, and fill up in my flesh what is lacking in the afflictions of Christ, for the sake of His body, which is the church."[1324] There is nothing that can be added to the all sufficient atoning work of Jesus Christ. Paul suffered time and again for the sake of Christ. He testifies:

> Three times I was beaten with rods; once I was stoned; three times I was shipwrecked; a night and a day I have been in the deep; *in* journeys often, *in* perils of waters, *in* perils of robbers, *in* perils of *my own* countrymen, *in* perils of the Gentiles, *in* perils in the city, *in* perils in the wilderness, *in* perils in the sea, *in* perils among false brethren; in weariness and toil, in sleeplessness often, in hunger and thirst, in fastings often, in cold and nakedness--besides the other things, what comes upon me daily: my deep concern for all the churches. Who is weak, and I am not weak? Who is made to stumble, and I do not burn with indignation? If I must boast, I will boast in the things which concern my infirmity. (2 Corinthians 11:25-30)

Paul did not complain about his sufferings. Rather, he said, "I rejoice in my sufferings for you." That is what I consider adding salt to a sacrifice. He was not forced to suffer and could have taken a different approach to those painful experiences, but of his own free will he persevered against the attacks of the enemy. He said to the

1324. Col. 1:24.

Ephesian Church ,"I ask that you do not lose heart at my tribulations for you, which is your glory."[1325] He often found himself face to face with the hostile powers of darkness, but did not yield, give in, or give up. When Paul reported to the Jerusalem Church the many things he had experienced on his mission journeys, the brethern in Jerusalem responded by glorifying the Lord.[1326] It is impossible to improve on the finished work of Jesus, but is necessary to take up our cross daily, and if need be, to suffer for Him. Suffering is not the intended end of the story, even if suffering cost us our life. For to be absent from the body is to be present with the Lord. "If indeed we suffer with Him, that we may be glorified together."[1327] Our ultimate goal is to be well pleasing to the Lord.

"For to you it has been granted on behalf of Christ, not only to believe in Him, but also to suffer for His sake, having the same conflict which you saw in me and now hear *is* in me."[1328] Paul concluded his life the way all of us would like to conclude. Paul told Timothy, "I have fought the good fight, I have finished the race, I have kept the faith. Finally, there is laid up for me the crown of righteousness, which the Lord, the righteous Judge, will give to me on that Day, and not to me only but also to all who have loved His appearing."[1329] The point is that Jesus says to you and me, "You are the salt of the earth, but if the salt loses its flavor, how shall the sacrifice be seasoned."[1330] Salt should season our actions and our words with the nature of Christ. "*Let* your speech always *be* with grace, seasoned with salt, that you may know how you ought to answer each one."[1331] Our words reflect our attitudes and a good attitude in difficult situations has a powerful influence upon the hearers of our words.

1325. Eph. 3:13.
1326. Acts 21:20.
1327. Rom. 6:17.
1328. Phil. 1:29-30.
1329. 2 Tim. 4:6-7.
1330. Matt. 5:13; Mark 9:49; Luke 14:34.
1331. Col. 4:6

Third, the ministry of reconciliation is carried on by the church through the preaching of the gospel of the kingdom. God has put eternity in the heart of every man. The gospel of the kingdom focuses on the birth, ministry, death, resurrection, and Lordship of Jesus Christ. Thus, the gospel has a powerful impact on the hearts of those who hear it. Paul said, "For I am not ashamed of the gospel of Christ, for it is the power of God to salvation for everyone who believes, for the Jew first and also for the Greek."[1332] However, the god of this world will try to hinder the preaching of the gospel. This is why we have prohibitions on prayer and preaching in the public discourse of our country. But the Holy Spirit continues to anoint the preaching of the gospel and open the hearts to receive the message of truth, because "the increase of His government and peace there will be no end."[1333]

The present church age will conclude with the second coming of Jesus Christ. He will not return to earth as a humble servant, but as "the KING OF KINGS and LORD OF LORDS."[1334] Then John's prophetic words will be fulfilled: "The kingdoms of this world have become *the kingdoms* of our Lord and of His Christ, and He shall reign forever and ever!"[1335] Jesus will rule and reign for one thousand years and "the earth will be filled with the knowledge of the glory of the LORD, as the waters cover the sea."[1336] "Blessed and holy *is* he who has part in the first resurrection. Over such the second death has no power, but they shall be priests of God and of Christ, and shall reign with Him a thousand years."[1337] The curse of sin will be reversed as the wolf dwells with the lamb, the lion will eat straw like the ox, and vipers will not hurt children.[1338] This is a beautiful picture of future kingdom of God realities that offers hope to every believer. With con-

---

1332. Rom. 1:16.
1333. Isa. 9:7.
1334. Rev. 19:16.
1335. Rev. 11:15.
1336. Hab. 2:14.
1337. Rev. 20:6.
1338. Isa. 11:6-9.

fident faith we can say, "the sufferings of this present time are not worthy to be compared to the glory which shall be revealed in us."[1339]

Summary:

From the time that Jesus was twelve years old He knew that He had to be about His Father's business. His Father's business was inscribed in The Everlasting Covenant between the members of the Godhead and drafted before the foundation of the world. God as a Father desired to have a family of sons and daughters that would bear His image and nature. It was according to the terms of the Everlasting Covenant that God would express His sovereignty and develop His family. So, God created man in His own image and likeness and related to mankind through a progression of covenants. God started with Adam in the Garden of Eden and the Edenic Covenant, followed by the Adamic, Noahic, Abrahamic, Davidic Covenants, culminating with the New Covenant. In the New Covenant God Himself, Immanuel, became flesh and dwelt among us. His name was called Jesus because He would save us from our sins.[1340] During His earthly ministry He was tempted in all points as we are tempted, yet He never sinned. As He was concluding His earthly ministry and facing execution on the cross He prayed to His Father, "not My will, but Your will be done." And there at the cross God "condemned sin in the flesh,"[1341] and "made Him who knew no sin *to be* sin for us, that we might become the righteousness of God in Him." "He was "holy, harmless, undefiled, separate from sinners, and has become higher that the heavens."[1342]

> Therefore God also has highly exalted Him and given Him the name which is above every name, that at the name of Jesus every knee should bow, of those

---

1339. Rom. 8:18.
1340. Matt. 1:22-23.
1341. Rom. 8:3.
1342. Heb. 7:26.

> in heaven, and of those on earth, and of those under the earth, and *that* every tongue should confess that Jesus Christ *is* Lord, to the glory of God the Father." (Philippians 2:9-11).

Forty days after His resurrection, Jesus ascended to heaven and was seated at the right hand of God.[1343] Ten days later, when the Day of Pentecost had fully come, Jesus poured out the Holy Spirit upon New Covenant believers, empowering them to be His "witnesses in Jerusalem, Judea, Samaria, and to the end of the earth."[1344] Jesus said, "For where two or three are gathered together in My name, I am there in the midst of them." Thus, believers were empowered by personal presence of the Holy Spirit to respond to the call of Jesus by coming out of the world system and become knit together forming the body of Jesus on the earth, the Church. As the body of Jesus Christ gathers together, they established local churches or embassies of the kingdom of God among every tribe and nation of the world.

The members of these local churches or embassies of the kingdom of God bear witness to the presence of the sovereignty of God through: (1) their submission to the Lordship of Jesus Christ, demonstrated by their good works. (2) Their willingness to suffer for their relationship with Jesus, thus being salt and light in the communities. And (3) by preaching the gospel of the kingdom. These ambassadors will continue their witness to the Lordship of Jesus Christ and kingdom of God activities, raising a standard of morality against the powers of darkness until the fulness of times when Jesus will return as the KING OF KINGS and LORD OF LORDS, and establish His kingdom on this earth. At that juncture "the kingdoms of this world will become the kingdoms of our Lord and of His Christ, and He shall reign forever and ever."[1345] And "the earth will be filled with the knowledge

---

1343. Col. 3:1.
1344. Acts 1:8.
1345. Rev. 11:15.

of the glory of the LORD, as the waters cover the sea.[1346] "Therefore, since we are receiving a kingdom that cannot be shaken, let us have grace by which we may serve God acceptably with reverence and godly fear."[1347]

1346. Hab. 2:14.
1347. Heb 12:28.

SELECTED BIBLIOGRAPHY

Barry, John D., *Parables: Portraits of God's Kingdom in Matthew, Mark, and Luke*, Not Your

Average Bible Study. Bellingham, WA: Lexham Press; Bible Study Magazine, 2018.

Bevere, John, *The Bait of Satan: Living Free from the Trap of Offense, rev. ed.,* Lake Mary, FL: Charisma House, 2004.

Bird, Michael F. and Scott Harrow, eds. *Trinity Without Hierarchy: Reclaiming Nicene Orthodoxy in Evangelical Theology.* Grand Rapids, MI: Kregel Academic, 2019.

Blomberg, Craig, *Interpreting the Parables.* Downers Grove, IL: InterVarsity Press, 1990.

Boardman, George Dana, *The Kingdom: The Emerging Rule of Christ Among Men.* 1899. Comp. by Bob Mumford and Jack Taylor. Shippensburg, Pa: Destiny Image Publishers. 2008.

Calderwood, Henry, *The Parables of Our Lord: Interpreted in View of Their Relations to Each Other.* London: Macmillan & Co., 1880.

Capon, Robert Farrar, *Kingdom, Grace, Judgment: Paradox, Outrage, and Vindication in the Parables of Jesus.* Grand Rapids, MI: William B. Eerdmans Publishing Company, 2002.

Carson, D, A., *The Gospel According to John*, The Pillar New Testament Commentary. Leicester, England; Grand Rapids, MI: Inter-Varsity Press; W.B. Eerdmans, 1991.

Conner, Kevin and Ken Malmin. *The Covenants.* Portland, OR: City Publishing Co., 1983.

Erickson, Millard J., *Christian Theology,* 3rd ed., Grand Rapids, MI; Baker Academic, 2013.

Fee, Gordon D., *God's Empowering Presence: The Holy Spirit in the Letters of Paul,* Grand Rapids, MI: Baker Academic, 2011.

France, R. T., *The Gospel of Matthew,* The New International Commentary on the New Testament. Grand Rapids, MI: William B. Eerdmans Publishing Company, 2007.

Geisler, Norman L., *Systematic Theology, Volume Three: Sin, Salvation,* Minneapolis, MN: Bethany House Publishers, 2004.

Gentry, Peter J. and Stephen J. Wellum, *Kingdom through Covenants: A Biblical – Theological Understandings of Covenants.* Wheaton, Il: Crossway, 2018.

Hahn, Roger L., *Matthew: A Commentary for Bible Students.* Indianapolis, IN: Wesleyan Publishing House, 2007.

Hayford, Jack W., *Spirit Filled: The Overflowing Power of the Holy Spirit.* Los Angeles, CA: Foursquare Media, 2007.

_____, Jack W., *The Key to Everything.* Lake Mary, FL: Charisma House, 1993.

Heer, Ken, *Luke: A Commentary for Bible Students.* Indianapolis, IN: Wesleyan Publishing House, 2007.

Heisler, Michael S., *The Unseen Realm: Recovering the Supernatural Worldview of the Bible*, First Edition. Bellingham, WA: Lexham Press, 2015.

Johnson, Bill, *The Power that Changes the World: Creating Eternal Impact in the Here and Now.* Minneapolis, MN: Chosen Books, 2015.

Jones, E. Stanley, *The Unshakable Kingdom and the Unchanging Person.* Bellingham, WA: McNett Press, 1972.

Kendall, R. T., *The Anointing: Yesterday, Today, Tomorrow.* Nashville, TN: Thomas Nelson Publishers, 1999.

Ladd, George Eldon, *The Gospel of the Kingdom.* Grand Rapids, MI: Wm. B. Eerdmans Publishing Co., 1977.

_____, *The Presence of the Future: The Eschatology of Biblical Realism.* Grand Rapids, MI: William B. Eerdmans Publishing, 1974.

Lake, John G., *Your Power in the Holy Spirit,* comp. by Roberts Liardon. New Kensington, PA: Whitaker House, 2010.

Lederle, Henry I., *Theology with Spirit.* Tulsa, OK: Word & Spirit Press, 2010.

Lenski, R. C. H., *The Interpretation of St. Matthew's Gospel.* Minneapolis, MN: Augsburg Publishing House, 1961.

Noll, Mark A., *Jesus Christ and the Life of the Mind.* Grand Rapids, MI: Wm. B. Eerdmans Publishing Co., 2011.

Morphew, Derek. *Breakthrough.* Cape Town, SA: Vineyard International Publishing, 2006.

Mumford, Bob, *The King and You.* Old Tappan, NJ: Fleming H. Revell Company, 1974.

Munroe, Myles, *Understanding Your Place in God's Kingdom.* Shippensburg, PA: Destiny Image, Publishers, Inc. 2011.

Murray, Andrew, *The Holiest of All.* New Kensington, PA: Whitaker House, 1996.

Ogilvie, Lloyd John, *Autobiography of God.* Glendale, CA: Regal Books, 1979.

Ortberg, John, *Eternity Is Now in Session.* Carol Stream, IL: Tyndale Momentum, 2018.

Pink, Arthur Walkington, *The Prophetic Parables of Matthew Thirteen.* Bellingham, WA: Logos Bible Software, 2005.

Ruthven, Jon Mark, *What Is Wrong with Protestant Theology?* Tulsa, OK: Word & Spirit Press, 2013.

Stein, Robert H., *Luke*, vol. 24, The New American Commentary. Nashville, TN: Broadman & Holman Publishers, 1992.

_____, "Kingdom of God," *Evangelical Dictionary of Biblical Theology*. Baker Reference Library. Grand Rapids, MI: Baker Book House, 1996.

_____, *The Method and Message of Jesus' Teachings.* Philadelphia, PA: Westminister Press, 1978.

Synan, Vinson. *The Century of the Holy Spirit: 100 Years of Pentecostal and Charismatic Renewal,* Nashville, TN: Thomas Nelson Publishing, 2001.

_____, Vinson. *The Holiness-Pentecostal Movement in the United States.* Grand Rapids, MI: William B. Eerdmans Publishing Company, 1971.

Taylor, Jack R., *Cosmic Initiative: Restoring the Kingdom, Igniting the Awakening.* New Kensington, PA: Whitaker House, 2017.

Trench, R. C., *Notes on the Parables of Our Lord.* Grand Rapids, MI: Baker Book House, 1981.

Walton, John, *Covenant.* Grand Rapids, MI: Zondervan Publishing House, 1994.

Whitcomb, John C. and Henry M. Morris, *The Genesis Flood: The Biblical Record and Its Scientific Implications.* Grand Rapids, MI: Baker Book House, 1974.

Willard, Dallas, *The Divine Conspiracy: Rediscovering Our Hidden Life in God.* New York, NY: HarperCollins Publishers, 1997.

Williams, J. Rodman, *Renewal Theology: Systematic Theology from a Charismatic Perspective,* three vols. in one. Grand Rapids, MI: Zondervan, 1988.

Worthington Jr. Everett L., *Forgiving and Reconciling: Bridges to Wholeness and Hope.* Downers Grove, IL: InterVarsity Press, 2003.

Yong, Amos, *Who Is the Holy Spirit? A Walk with the Apostles.* Brewster, MS: Paraclete Press, 2011.

Zodhiates, Spiros, *The Complete Word Study Dictionary: New Testament.* Chattanooga, TN: AMG Publishers, 2000.

CPSIA information can be obtained
at www.ICGtesting.com
Printed in the USA
BVHW041933190421
605323BV00025B/453